D0208827

Ecopsychology

Recent Titles in Practical and Applied Psychology

Meta-Physician on Call for Better Health: Metaphysics and Medicine for Mind, Body and Spirit
Steven E. Hodes, M.D.

The Powerful Bond between People and Pets: Our Boundless Connections to Companion Animals
P. Elizabeth Anderson

Sexual Enslavement of Girls and Women Worldwide
Andrea Parrot and Nina Cummings

The Global Muslim Community at a Crossroads: Understanding Religious Beliefs, Practices, and Infighting to End the Conflict
Abdul Basit, Editor

Living in an Environmentally Traumatized World: Healing Ourselves and Our Planet
Darlyne G. Nemeth, Robert B. Hamilton, and Judy Kuriansky, Editors

The Psychology of Black Boys and Adolescents
Kirkland Vaughans and Warren Spielberg, Editors

Lucid Dreaming: New Perspectives on Consciousness in Sleep
Ryan Hurd and Kelly Bulkeley, Editors

The Myth of Black Anti-Intellectualism: A True Psychology of African American Students
Kevin O. Cokley

Borderline Personality Disorder: New Perspectives on a Stigmatizing and Overused Diagnosis
Jacqueline Simon Gunn and Brent Potter

Ecopsychology

Advances from the Intersection of Psychology and Environmental Protection

VOLUME 1: SCIENCE AND THEORY

Darlyne G. Nemeth, Set Editor

Robert B. Hamilton,
Volume Editor

Practical and Applied Psychology
Judy Kuriansky, Series Editor

PRAEGER™

An Imprint of ABC-CLIO, LLC
Santa Barbara, California • Denver, Colorado

Copyright © 2015 by Darlyne G. Nemeth, Robert B. Hamilton, and Judy Kuriansky

All rights reserved. No part of this publication may be reproduced, stored in a retrieval system, or transmitted, in any form or by any means, electronic, mechanical, photocopying, recording, or otherwise, except for the inclusion of brief quotations in a review, without prior permission in writing from the publisher.

Library of Congress Cataloging-in-Publication Data

Ecopsychology : advances from the intersection of psychology and environmental protection / Darlyne G. Nemeth, set editor.
    volumes cm. — (Practical and applied psychology)
  Includes bibliographical references and index.
  Contents: volume 1. Science and theory — volume 2. Intervention and policy.
ISBN 978–1–4408–3172–0 (hard copy : alk. paper) — ISBN 978–1–4408–3173–7 (ebook)
1. Environmental psychology. I. Nemeth, Darlyne Gaynor.
BF353.E29   2015
155.9'1—dc23   2015001807

ISBN: 978–1–4408–3172–0
EISBN: 978–1–4408–3173–7

19 18 17 16 15   1 2 3 4 5

This book is also available on the World Wide Web as an eBook.
Visit www.abc-clio.com for details.

Praeger
An Imprint of ABC-CLIO, LLC

ABC-CLIO, LLC
130 Cremona Drive, P.O. Box 1911
Santa Barbara, California 93116-1911

This book is printed on acid-free paper ∞

Manufactured in the United States of America

Be Gentle My Friends

Be gentle my friends
saddened while we watch
ice to water,
water to drought,
rivers run dry,
eroding shores,
yellow air,
dying fish
and birds soaked in oil.

Be gentle my friends
with Earth's fragile beauty
Be gentle my friends
and
protect it,
treasure it,
save it,
save it.

—Susan Melman

Contents

Prologue

Ecopsychology: The Interaction between Psychology and Environmental Protection is an inspiring concept. When invited to be the lead editor of this two-volume anthology, I enthusiastically embraced the challenge. In retrospect, this title is a mirror image of my 45-plus-year marriage. My husband, Donald F. Nemeth. PhD, is a geologist, and I am a psychologist. Early on in our marriage, my focus was primarily on people; whereas Donald's focus was primarily on the environment. Often, I would not see what he saw. I was one of the many who saw, but did not perceive, the realities of the natural world. On many occasions, I would remark, "he made my world beautiful." Donald would invite me to perceive the breathtaking vistas of nature, perhaps created by the beauty of a field of delicate flowers or the majesty of an amazing rock formation. Being able to perceive nature's delicate majesty has truly made my world beautiful.

Yet nature can also be a destructive, powerful force. It is alive, dynamic, and ever-changing.

As a field of study, ecopsychology combines the science of ecology, which assesses human beings' relationships to their environment, with the field of psychology, which evaluates and seeks to optimize human behavior. This new hybrid field is becoming increasingly popular. It provides a useful framework from which to identify and address important issues. Therefore, ecopsychology consists of two important elements: (1) ecodynamics—how humans affect the environment; and (2) ecokinetics—how the environment affects humans.

In this two-volume anthology, I have focused on one of the most ever-changing ecosystems in the world, the state of Louisiana and its Mississippi River Deltaic Region. Having lived in Louisiana for over 45 years, first as a graduate student at Louisiana State University and subsequently as a practicing psychologist, I have truly seen and experienced the beauty and might of nature and natural forces. I have personally witnessed the power and destruction of hurricanes, such as Katrina, Rita, and Gustav, and I have experienced the suffering that environmental trauma can bring. The loss of days, if not months and/or years, of a functioning regional infrastructure can be debilitating. Furthermore, the psychological costs of posttraumatic distress and the anniversary reactions often caused by these events can linger even long after the natural and/or human-induced destruction has passed and the necessary infrastructure repairs have been completed.

Louisiana has an abundance of natural beauty, natural resources, and an amazing cadre of resilient people from many different cultural backgrounds and heritages. This unique blend of natural beauty and psychological resiliency is what makes Louisiana so special. For me and for many, it represents our oikophilia—our longing for home.

Unfortunately, another unique quality of this region is the politics. Spin and fraud, as you will read in ensuing chapters, is as alive and well in Louisiana as it is in many other places throughout the world. Government officials seem to succumb to and/or invite these experiences on a regular basis. The people are often an afterthought. Money and power typically prevail.

Louisiana's coastline has been and continues to be devastated by this culture of greed. Sadly, cities like New Orleans and Baton Rouge now have far less protection against the raging winds and waters of hurricanes. Many of the coastal barriers are gone and the people and their communities, their oikophilias, are "at risk," as are so many deltaic regions around the world.

Environmental protection initiatives typically fail in Louisiana. Those espousing the need for such comprehensive protection plans are often discredited, derailed, and/or defeated. Louisiana has one of the most fragile ecosystems in the world. It requires protection, not abuse.

This two-volume anthology will address the facts, feelings, needs, and possibilities that must be considered when planning for the future. The psychology of environmental management is just as important as is its ecology. If people do not perceive the need to be good stewards of their environment, then the exploiters will prevail and our "oikophilia"—our need for home—will be lost. What then? The future is up to us.

Darlyne G. Nemeth, PhD, MP, MPAP
Clinical, Medical, and Neuropsychologist
Lead Editor

Preface: Science and Theory

We humans affect the earth environment, and it in turn affects us. Protection of our earth environment must involve both science and psychology. This anthology discusses our relationship with the earth environment and our future. Its Volume 1 explores science and theory, while Volume 2 discusses successful interventions and policy.

We humans have been evolving our cultures, improving our standards of living, and exponentially increasing our population by using the earth's resources. The degree of evolution of culture is proportional to the amount of energy we use, as stated by White's Law. Burning fossil fuels (coal, oil, and natural gas) generates lots of energy, as do nuclear power plants. But the former releases greenhouse CO_2 gas and can spill oil on the environment, as I have observed when I worked on the cleanup of BP's Deepwater Horizon oil spill in the Gulf of Mexico. The latter can have catastrophic nuclear accidents. I have assessed the Chernobyl-affected environment as the U.S. government coordinator of Chernobyl land/aquatic environments, and have been continuously working on remediation of the Fukushima environment contaminated by the 2011 Fukushima nuclear power plant accidents. I have witnessed destruction of the environment throughout my 40+ years of working on environmental remediation caused by radionuclides, toxic chemicals, pesticides, heavy metals, CO_2 disposal, and radioactive and nonradioactive waste disposal.

Human activities are very rapidly changing the earth environment and harming its inhabitants, although much slower changes of the earth have been occurring before human's existence. Many living things are disappearing now from the earth at an unprecedented degree. The mass extinction of earth's living species has occurred five times in our 4.5-billion-year earth history. It is sobering to note that, during each of these five mass extinctions, the dominant species did not survive. Some call the current time the sixth mass extinction period, and we are the current dominant living species on earth. We must protect the environment for ourselves as well as for all life.

The Western civilization founded on Christianity sees humans as masters of the earth and its living things, "Be fruitful and multiply, and fill the Earth and subdue it: and have dominion over the fish of the sea and over the birds of the air and over everything that moves upon the Earth" (Old Testament, Genesis 1:28). This ecopsychology anthology concludes that a basic environmental problem we now have is mainly caused by global overabundance of humans and our unlimited economic growth. We must realize that the earth has finite resources and that the environment destruction by humans in turn devastates us. The chapter authors indicate that we should act as if Nature has intrinsic, primogenital property rights for our own survival and happiness; our present path is unsustainable. Each of us must reflect on this statement. This anthology cites ways to live harmoniously with Nature by presenting successes and failures of the United States, Switzerland, India, Chile, Italy, China, and the United Nations in their attempts to protect the earth environment. Approaches taken by indigenous people in Canada, the United States, and Australia also suggest alternative sustainable lifestyles that we may consider.

This anthology is very insightful, and stimulates our thinking of how we should handle the earth for ourselves, our children, and all living things. I strongly encourage readers to develop concrete actions that save us from ourselves.

Yasuo Onishi, PhD
President, Yasuo Onishi Consulting, LLC
Adjunct Professor, Department of Civil and Environmental Engineering,
Washington State University

Acknowledgments

DARLYNE G. NEMETH

For the second time, I have been so blessed to have Dr. Bob Hamilton and Dr. Judy Kuriansky as coeditors on this amazing anthology. Our first joint endeavor, *Living in an Environmentally Traumatized World: Healing Ourselves and Our Planet*, was published in 2012 by ABC-CLIO/Praeger. To my knowledge, it was the first book of its kind to combine the science and practice of ecopsychology and to offer guidelines for intervention at all levels. Dr. Hamilton, an inveterate scientist and philosopher, addressed the importance of a holistic approach to environmental management. Dr. Kuriansky, an amazing interventionist, championed the need for post-environmental trauma psychological intervention to assist in recovery.

Once again, the team of Nemeth, Hamilton, and Kuriansky has joined forces to produce this current anthology, *Ecopsychology: Advances from the Intersection of Psychology and Environmental Protection*. With the very skilled and supportive guidance of Debbie Carvalko, senior acquisitions editor, we were able to offer an in-depth understanding of the field of ecopsychology. We brought together individuals from many fields to share their very meaningful contributions to this emerging field. Some were scientists. Some were interventionists. Some were activists. Some were lawyers. Others were psychologists. Some represented governments; others represented business entities. All expressed their love and longing for their oikophilia—their home-place. I am very grateful to all our chapter authors for their dedication and final work product. For all of us, it was truly a labor of love.

To Bob Hamilton, I will always remember our many weekend discussions. Listening to his brilliant and free-flowing ideas was truly inspiring. I often found myself documenting Bob's "stream of consciousness." I could hardly keep up. Bob has such an active mind and is able to process information in a very holistic way. His efforts to seek truth and dispel propaganda were deeply appreciated. Bob, the primary editor of Volume 1, kept the scientists, practitioners, and contributors to this volume on track. All deadlines were met. Furthermore, his editorial skills were truly representative of all the many dissertations he guided while a member of the faculty at Louisiana State University.

Now to "Dr. Judy." Words cannot adequately express my appreciation for her robustness, her resilience, and her leadership in her many academic, professional, and nongovernmental activities and for her friendship. Judy is a whirlwind of energy; she appears everywhere she is needed, just when she is needed. As the primary editor of Volume 2, Judy's contributions were inspiring. She was able to invite individuals to share their valuable ideas, work, and experience from many corners of the world, from Azerbaijan to China, and Bolivia. And they did! No one can turn down an invitation from this multitalented woman. Dr. Judy was also a superb editor, picking up large or small problems that had escaped me.

Chelsie Songy, as project contributor coordinator, has been a godsend. I could not have carried out my job as lead editor without her diligent assistance. Chelsie is a very calm, careful manager who is always a part of the solution and never a part of the problem. I know that she will be an amazing doctoral student and future psychologist. She also made many excellent contributions to our chapters on neurocognition and leadership and prepared our anthology for publication.

And then there was the vibrant Traci Wimberly Olivier, whose contributions to our chapters on perception and neurocognition were truly remarkable. Mrs. Olivier, who is a doctoral student in clinical and neuropsychology at Nova Southeastern University, is now serving an elective practicum here at the Neuropsychology Center of Louisiana (NCLA). She is and will be a credit to psychology.

Furthermore, I am deeply grateful to Yasuo Onishi for his thoughtful Prefaces, and to Susan Melman for setting the tone for our anthology with her inspiring poem.

Lastly, without the love and support of my husband, Donald (who authored our chapter on understanding our environment); and my brother, Richard Gaynor, who is an internist; and my former psychology mentor, who is now my sister-in-law, Sue Jensen, this anthology would not have been possible.

ROBERT B. HAMILTON

I want to especially thank Darlyne Nemeth for continuing her efforts to promote ecopsychology as a discipline to combine the physical and biological aspects of ecology with the psychological aspects. She especially understands how our environments affect people and how we should deal with both the positive and negative aspects of this dynamic. She understands how our attitudes and perceptions affect our environmental decisions and the importance of basing them on good science. As a non-psychologist, I have learned how our combined disciplines benefit us all in our responsibility as ultimate controllers of the earth environment. Her guidance, as lead editor, coordinated a rather complicated task, and made my job easier.

Despite her busy schedule, Dr. Judy is always enthusiastic. Her enthusiasm is contagious and has kept all of us inspired. I believe it will inspire our readers as much as it has inspired me.

My interactions with our authors have been overwhelmingly positive; I hope they feel the same.

My wife, Jean, seems to have dedicated herself to the set as much as I have. She has adjusted schedules and plans to accommodate my time needs in preparation for this effort. I do not know what I would do without her.

Lastly, I am grateful to the media that supplies continuous information about what is happening in our confusing and changing world. This information either confirmed or denied many of my ideas in real time. That has been invaluable to me.

JUDY KURIANSKY

My appreciation is on many levels, to many people, and for many influences and collaborations, that have led to my heightened awareness, intense commitment, and rewarding work in the important intersection of ecopsychology and environmental protection addressed in these volumes. I greatly honor and cherish my colleague and friend Darlyne Nemeth, PhD, MP, for her prescience about the importance of integrating the fields of science and psychology and for her vision that led to our previous volume, *Living in an Environmentally Traumatized World: Healing Ourselves and Our Planet,* as well as a special issue of the journal *Ecopsychology,* and these two volumes on this important topic. She is truly a pioneer and a visionary, in the forefront of merging science and psychology, and always on the cusp of what matters in the world. We have shared many wonderful and growth-inspiring times together, personally and also professionally, imprinting wonderful memories, like being together at the World Congress for Psychotherapy in Buenos Aires, when we stayed up all night working at a desk in a hotel lobby drafting a policy statement; presenting so many symposia over so many years at conferences worldwide from Argentina to China; and supporting her in the valuable trainings she organized brilliantly after Hurricane Katrina in her beloved state of Louisiana. Darlyne is creative, caring, devoted, supportive, and loving of her friends, family, interns, and colleagues; her big heart and bright mind are a dynamic and unique combination that I—and all who know her—are blessed to share this life path with.

My appreciation also goes to Bob Hamilton, coeditor of our first book, whose consistently strong voice from his insightful scientific mind always makes me keenly aware of the importance of our biosphere; his combination of sensitivity with a strong ethic of dedication is impressive. Also part of the team for these volumes, production assistants Chelsie Songy and Traci Olivier have been invaluable. As Darlyne's protégés in neuropsychology, it is comforting to know the future is in the hands and minds of young professionals like them, with their dedication, kind hearts, and responsible work ethic.

These volumes are possible because of the vision and brilliance of Debbie Carvalko, our editor at the publishing company, ABC-CLIO/Praeger, who also supervises my series on Practical and Applied Psychology, of which this anthology is a part. Over the many years I have worked with Debbie, I am continually inspired by her and impressed with the breadth of her creativity, incisive thinking and superb judgment. Besides all this, I am proud that she is a good friend, and marveled at how she has balanced being a consummate and hard-working professional with being such a good friend and so devoted to her family. The world is a better place because of people like Debbie being in it.

The hard-working and good-natured efforts of our book's project manager Magendra Varman, of Lumina Datamatics Ltd., are much appreciated, including his impressive attention to detail, with similar recognition of our dutiful copyeditor. Thank you, too, to production editor Nicole Azze of ABC-CLIO in that process, and to Anthony Chiffolo, who in the midst of being an admirable publishing executive at ABC-CLIO—who has always been so supportive of my projects—is a published author of many books himself with multifaceted interests and talents and an appreciation for nature, a subject addressed in these volumes. Another thank you from us goes to the designer of these volume covers, Silvander, for their impressive artistic cover design for these volumes—with the image of a person crossing a bridge in a green environment, out of darkness into light, that captures the essence, intention, and vision of the content and message of the anthology.

I further acknowledge and honor all my colleagues and good friends who are contributors in this volume. They are wonderful human beings who care for others and the environment. They are also all outstanding in their respective fields. Seeing them here as a group representing so many important sectors—including academics, business, environmental activism, government and nongovernment organizations—they truly embody the model of the multi-stakeholder partnership that is essential for a sustainable planet and future. I reflect with great appreciation and pride about how their work covers so many important aspects of programs and policy being explored and advanced in so many parts of the world, from the United States to Haiti, Belize, Bolivia, China, Ecuador, Azerbaijan, and others. They create a very wonderful and touching tapestry of humankind, with their caring for the future of the "world we want," to use a phrase from the vision of the United Nations.

The United Nations plays such a major role in my life, as reflected in my chapters in this book. My perspective in this writing has been greatly influenced by my work there related to so many global issues and to the Post-2015 agenda. Regarding that, I extend intensive appreciation to delegates of member states at the United Nations, colleagues of the Psychology Coalition of NGOs at the UN, and particularly the UN ambassador of Palau and public health physician, Dr. Caleb Otto, who partnered with me in the successful campaign I led with him to include mental health and well-being in the new global goals, as well as to advocate for psychosocial resilience in the face of deleterious climate change. That all came about because of former president of the International Association of Applied Psychology Ray Fowler, PhD—a visionary and kind-hearted soul—to whom I am forever grateful for asking me to be a UN NGO representative so many years ago, out of the blue, as if he knew my childhood dream to make the world a better place. Reflecting about so many years I've spent in countries around the world doing trainings and workshops and providing psychosocial support after disasters, blessings go to my team and all my partners who have been such an important part of those ventures. That includes my dear friend and collaborator Father Wismick Jean-Charles for the strength and love he shows in helping his beloved Haiti heal, and for taking me to his country to share that mission, reflected in a chapter in this book; I smile every time I think of his big heart, bright spirit, quick mind, and deep love of people and God. Endless blessings go to my best friend, Russell Daisey, for his kind heart, wisdom, enthusiasm, caring, sweet soul, creativity, and unending devotion in codesigning and cofacilitating so many projects and presentations with me around the world, and providing brilliant and inspiring original music we have written and performed around the world. The topics, including "Every Woman, Every Child" (the title of the UN Secretary General's initiative), "Towers of Light" about healing from the 9/11 tragedy, "Rebati" about building back better in Haiti (described in Chapter 9 in this volume), and "Hope is Alive" inspiring healing from the West African Ebola epidemic, all make me feel such "Appreciation" (kansha shimasho in Japanese) that is actually another of our song titles.

So much love, encouragement, and appreciation is extended to so many trainees in workshops I've done after many disasters and in dire conditions, as well as to many students and interns who helped, and to many courageous survivors who offered their trust and shared their hearts, thoughts, and feelings.

As a psychologist who believes in how childhood shapes us, I honor my mother Sylvia as a model of unconditional love and support, and my father Abraham as an example of disciplined hard work and unending dedication to always doing the most you can—and your best—for the betterment of humankind. My own appreciation for nature is easily traceable to memories like routine Sunday family trips exploring and enjoying the beauty of parks, caverns, zoos, and all kinds of natural attractions. To see, do, and appreciate everything, was a lesson from my father, along with the encouragement to have multiple perspectives; it wasn't enough to look at Niagara Falls, you had to go through it, under it, behind it, and over it. That multidimensional view has served me in putting together this volume and this team of chapter contributors. I look upon these chapter authors with great appreciation and pride in my colleagues, students, and friends. Working on these volumes has served to intensify my love for people and my interest, awareness, and commitment to the preservation of our planet; I hope it does the same for readers.

1

Introduction

Darlyne G. Nemeth and Robert B. Hamilton

In order to understand the need for environmental protection, we must first understand our ecokinetics, how our changing environments affect us. This is not as easy as it may seem. We come from many cultures that have different perceptions about the ideal environment. Are we an integral and equal part of our environments, as perceived by many indigenous peoples, or are we controllers and manipulators of environments?

Life requires energy and physical resources. Each species has its own survival requirements. The earth has been continually changing since its formation. Eventually, life evolved and differentiated into many forms. Understanding the environment and the resources necessary to sustain life will be discussed in this volume. The relevant physical laws and biological principals will be highlighted. These laws are general and well supported. They will help us to understand the consequences of our actions and plans; however, nature sometimes seems unpredictable and chaotic. According to Gleick (1987, p. 5), "To some physicists, chaos is a science of process rather than state, of becoming rather than being." In other words, nature is changing; it is not static. Changes occur because life requires energy, and some is lost with each use. The sun supplies energy and replaces that which is lost. The importance of energy cannot be overemphasized.

Temporal changes can be either cyclical, which can be anticipated, or sudden, which occur with little to no warning. Annual and daily changes are cyclical and predictable. A tornado is a sudden change; the occurrence is predictable, but the exact site and time of the strike is not. The latter is true of hurricanes as well, wherein the turbulence is expected, yet the site of landfall cannot be precisely determined. These weather patterns have been studied by Edward Lorenz (Gleick, 1987, p. 11) and Keim and Muller (2009). Earthquakes and volcanic eruptions follow the same pattern. Again, nature is both predictable and unpredictable at the same time.

We will explore environmental change in a clear and understandable way from perspectives of a variety of scientists: (1) how human beings have used or misused the environments and their peoples; (2) how species, other than humans, have been affected by environmental change; and (3) how perceptions of reality vary and/or are prone to manipulation. Yet, truth must prevail if we are to succeed in protecting our environment, our people, and all living things.

Before the advent of humans, as environments and their occupants coevolved, most important environmental changes took millions of years. We humans are a social species, possessing unique characteristics that allow us to learn to modify our environments, utilize environmental features in new ways, and communicate this knowledge to one another. As we learn more, our ability to modify our environments increases. With advancing technology, even more modifications become available to us. Time between major changes now has been reduced to decades, and, excluding natural catastrophic phenomena, we are the ultimate agents of change.

Because groups with different histories and environments have developed separate cultures and perceptions, human beings are not homogeneous. With these different cultures have come religions, languages, values, and a sense of "oikophilia," or a longing for home (Scruton, 2012). As cultures are slow to change, they may no longer be suitable for our ever-changing and increasingly globalized world. Until we develop a truly global culture, agreeing on the best path for all will be difficult. Globalization, which has in part been brought about by technology, now must address the ever-increasing human numbers and their needed support systems.

Our current population of about seven billion people is expected to surpass nine billion by 2050. Major environmental changes have occurred in order to support these seven billion people. Future growth will cause even more significant changes, including species extinctions, resource depletion, pollution, and habitat changes. Changes in environments and energy use will be inevitable. There are already more people than can be supported in once traditional ways. As we decide our future, we need to decide what kind of world we want; there are many options. Certainly, with our intelligence and inventiveness, we can find ways to utilize the earth's resources in a more humane and efficient manner. Hopefully, Volume 1 can guide us in this direction.

REFERENCES

Gleick, J. (1987). *Chaos: Making a new science*. New York, NY: Viking.

Keim, B., & Muller, R. (2009). *Hurricanes of the Gulf of Mexico*. Baton Rouge, LA: Louisiana State University Press.

Scruton, R. (2012). *Green philosophy: How to think seriously about the planet*. London: Atlantic Books.

2

Thinking about Our Environment– Gaining Perspective

Robert B. Hamilton

This is the editors' second book in the field of ecopsychology, which is a melding of the fields of ecology and psychology. The purpose of this two-volume anthology is to present sound, scientific information about our environment and our interactions with it.

This first volume emphasizes science and why things are the way they are or perceived to be; the second volume emphasizes how people deal with problems that occur because of their environment and environmental changes as well as models and examples of programs and policy addressing the environment in our new era.

In Volume 1, we discuss principles involved with the earth's formation and evolution. We present the role of energy in causing change and promoting life, and examine how differences in the spatial and temporal availability of energy explain differences in our environments, as well as the availability, advantages, and disadvantages of available and potential energy sources.

We discuss the evolution of life and evolution itself. Because the world is changing, living things need to change along with it to survive. The variation necessary for the selection of better-adapted individuals was made possible by the development of sexual reproduction to produce the variation necessary to provide individuals with the tools necessary for survival in an ever-changing world. The principle of evolution, enunciated by Darwin, one of the greatest holistic thinkers ever, explains how individual variation is key to survival in a changing world.

We also discuss various biological concepts and show how they help us understand our environment. Especially important is the concept of population growth and regulation. Population growth is potentially exponential and supported by energy and resource availability. Resources are finite, thus population level is finite and limited by resource availability. All life competes for the resources; the better competitors survive. Species evolve and become extinct as their resource availability and their competiveness change. Habitats differ because of differences in availability of required resources.

We focus on humans and how our ability to modify environments explains our success in growing our numbers. We discuss how humans have a competitive advantage because of our unique ability to modify environments. Our increased numbers again put a strain on the environment and require us to modify it to increase resource availability. We must continually modify it to survive and support our seemingly ever-growing population. The changes we are making to support our numbers change the environment—often in unanticipated ways. Because of our adaptability, we can flourish physically in the new environments, which are becoming increasingly different from the ones we evolved in. Other species are not as adaptable and are becoming rare or extinct. We have always been dependent on our environments with their characteristic flora and fauna. We evolved in these environments, but we are now changing them from ancestral ones to support more and more humans. We have distanced ourselves from the rules that have regulated population sizes in all species, and affected all of our environments. What are the consequences for the other species? What are the consequences for us?

In these two volumes that build on our previous book (Nemeth, Hamilton, & Kuriansky, 2012), we focus on changes—past, present, and future—and our perceptions of them. When we examine current trends, there are reasons for concern. Resources are being depleted; water is becoming increasingly scarce and polluted; demand is increasing because of our increasing human numbers and their needs. Our air is changing from natural processes and by increasing industrialization with its sometimes accompanying toxic byproducts as well as the insertion into it of gases accumulating from the still-increasing use of fossil and natural fuels to supply necessary energy. Trash in our oceans, our landfills, and elsewhere is increasing at an alarming rate, because we discard material that is no longer useful and we package goods for shipment to remote places, and the packaging is not recycled effectively. Our way of life is changing as we increasingly use fossil energy to industrialize our farming. In rural areas, many people are now abandoning small farms and rural life and moving to urban areas as we become increasingly dependent on large-scale agriculture and resources from distant sources. The changes that are occurring now are not only environmental, but they are also in the psyche of our people, many of whom are facing a new way of life with new challenges.

BACKGROUND

Most governments and people desire an ever-increasing standard of living for everyone and "social justice" for all. That would require even more changes to be made to obtain the necessary resources. Our economies are based on the idea that they should grow forever to support increasing numbers of humans and provide an ever-improving standard of living for them. Growing economies may be justified to provide for the needs of an expanding population, but when will the exponential growth stop? Do we have resources for an ever-expanding economy? We cannot expand forever. Our world will become almost unrecognizable if we keep changing it to support human population growth with its expanding needs at the expense of the environment that has always been our support.

Herman Daly, an American ecological economist and professor at the School of Public Policy of the University of Maryland, has proposed moving toward a steady state economy and has repeatedly argued for sustainability (Victor, 2013). This is a promising approach and is the only feasible one for the long term, unless the economy loses its linkage to resource use. The longer the policy of an ever-growing economy continues, the longer environmental changes inevitably occur and resource availability inevitably decreases. Can humans be as happy and successful in rapidly changing and less-familiar environments than those we evolved in and have occupied since our beginnings?

Because we humans and our environments are not homogeneous, planning for the future is not easy. In addition, as our numbers are increasing, we will need more resources in the future. Human societies have discovered how to provide for previously impossibly high numbers by changing our natural environments to heavily managed, human-controlled ones and increasing production with energy augmentation of various kinds. We are now using energy sources that have not been used previously. In addition, as a result of our actions, there have been many unintended environmental changes. As we encounter and create new or modified environments, how do we perceive the changes? Do we prefer the new or the old environments? Does that answer depend on our particular culture, or on the specific environments we are changing now or will be changing? In other words, what are the psychological implications of the changes we are making and those we must provide in the future for our still-increasing numbers? Are our perceptions influenced by our particular culture? In this volume, we will discuss the characteristics of the habitats we have historically inhabited and the changes we are making to them to obtain and provide for our needs.

Cultural differences among societies are related to their different ancestral environments and evolutionary histories. Can the current cultural differences among societies become reconcilable? Is this necessary in a world that is developing a global economy? In Volume 2, successful interventions, strategies, and policies that can propel us through the inevitable natural and human-facilitated changes are presented and emphasized.

RATES OF CHANGE

Some change, such as earthquakes, tornadoes, and volcanic eruptions, are caused by natural factors that are the result of the earth's makeup and physical laws; they cannot be prevented, but damage from them, physical and psychological, can be reduced with proper planning and warning. Ways of dealing with the effects of these traumatic events were a main theme of our previous book, *Living in an Environmentally Traumatized World: Healing Ourselves and Our Planet* (Nemeth et al., 2012), and is a theme in these two volumes as well. These events are traumatic because quick rates of change affect environments almost instantly, changing them, and making them unsuitable or greatly less suitable for us than the ones they replaced. All components of our environment may be affected by rapid changes. Direct mortality can be caused by the rapid changes that occur. Behaviors that were previously suitable and necessary for survival are no longer feasible. Ways must be found quickly to provide necessary resources for immediate survival and to return the habitat to its previous condition or other suitable ones; or, at least, begin a process that leads to a healthy environment. The sudden changes are physically dangerous to those exposed, and to their psychological well-being as well. Their physical and psychological needs must be supported. Help is often global and is a good example of the globalization that is taking place in our changing world and the altruistic behavior of many. Public and private organizations provide it. Unfortunately, the aid may be slow or hindered because of bureaucratic problems. Some monetary and physical help may be stolen by unscrupulous and opportunistic authorities and others.

After the earth was formed about 4.5 billion years ago, it has changed from an amorphous accumulation of space debris to an inhabited plant with continents, oceans and other water bodies, an atmosphere above the surface, and a complicated structure below (see Hazen [2012] for details). After life developed about 3.8 billion years ago, the rate of change increased, but still was extremely low. Physical changes were continuing and will continue because the fundamental causes are still present. Details of changes vary as physical laws act on current conditions that are constantly changing.

After some humans learned to change their environments, rates of environmental change increased. We communicated the results of our previous actions through the development of language and the ability to communicate with future generations orally and in writing. This facilitates our ability to change our environments at an accelerating rate.

The psychological responses to these rapidly occurring changes must be determined. As our standard of living increases, does our happiness increase accordingly? How are cultures that have been historically belligerent to each other affected by higher population densities and changing conditions? This needs to be determined as well.

Change seems to beget changes, and new ways of living develop very rapidly, both locally and globally. The changes are especially noticeable when tribal societies that live in tune with their environments are overrun by societies that have developed more intrusive methods of environment management. Examples are given in this anthology from Australia, North America, Brazil, Belize, and Africa.

Although it is clear that the development of modern agriculture and other changes can produce more food and support more people, we do not know the psychological effect to both the remnants of tribal societies and the co-occupying, more intrusive colonizing societies. For that matter, we do not even understand completely the psychological effects of crowding as our numbers are increasing. Modern agriculture and other changes allow the environment to support more people, but how do we determine if the changes are positive or negative? Is the answer the same for all societies, or not? How can we assure that our adaptations are benign or positive to all societies that experience these changes? (see Diamond, 2012).

Recent Changes

In my lifetime, I have witnessed many major changes in our physical, social, communication, and psychological environments. The discovery and use of fission as atomic bombs were dropped on Hiroshima and Nagasaki, Japan, in 1945 were significant. The energy released was unprecedented, as were the damage and radiation that followed. Even more energy was produced by a hydrogen bomb that was tested in 1952.

The development of female birth-control pills in the early 1950s has had a profound effect on our cultures. Women now have a way to control fertilization and can control birth rates effectively without resorting to abortions or infanticide, which are ethically and morally more controversial. This has had, and is continuing to have, a profound effect on our cultures. Population growth rates are affected by birthrates and mortality rates (Population growth rate = birthrate − mortality rate) and thus birth control has a strong negative influence on our environmental needs as our population growth rate decreases, but our numbers are still increasing.

Numbers are still increasing because mortality rates are also being greatly reduced through many changes in modern medicine. Infant mortality has been greatly reduced, and longevity is increasing through the development of new drugs, improved imaging, development of artificial limbs and other body parts, genetic testing, use of genetic information in medicine, and new testing procedures. Medical research has facilitated treatment and cures for various diseases and conditions that had formally been almost untreatable. Development of robotic surgery and other improvements have increased the safety of many medical procedures. In addition, the availability of all these medical changes is increasing through increased access to government and private health insurance and charity.

Many of these medical improvements and innovations have differentially affected specific age groups and resulted in important demographic changes in our populations. People are surviving longer now. Many of our older citizens, who are not as able to work as younger ones, need to be provided for longer and are increasing our total resource needs; they have a significant impact on our environment.

Life expectancy is increasing rapidly, especially in wealthy countries. In the United States, it has gone from about 50 years in 1900 to 79.74 years in 2014 (Countryeconomy, n.d.) and is still increasing. Much of the improvement is due to improved infant mortality, but improved nutrition, public health, and medicine have also contributed. All of these changes have facilitated population growth.

The Significance of DNA in Inheritance and Our Biology

I can now get my genes mapped and soon could likely get myself cloned, the ethics of which has not yet been determined. Many of our crops are being genetically modified (GMO) to increase production to support our growing human population. This development is new and is considered dangerous by some.

Some Effects of Recent Electronic Changes

The development of computers and cell phones is changing everyone's life. The recent development of social media is revolutionary, and new changes occur almost daily. Can the changes be occurring too rapidly? Our economic system seems to encourage it, but I doubt it can be sustained without worrisome corresponding changes in our ancestral environments and our cultures.

For much of human history, our environment was relatively static and not greatly affected by us. We needed to know our surroundings so we could obtain food and avoid death. We needed to find a mate and reproduce. We needed shelter. Now, our concern seems centered on social media. Most of us do not directly obtain food in the wild or even through agriculture. Instead, we perform some activity to receive money to acquire our needs, or they are provided to us by others. I do not know how any of this affects our psyche. I personally prefer closer relationships with our historical environments and customs. I would like to be in the wilderness; yet I realize that if everyone could do that, there would be no wilderness. This seems to be almost a tragedy to me. Our success is leading to our unease. I hope my perception is atypical and our changes make life better for everyone, both physically and psychologically.

Climate Change

As we write these volumes, many of our readers are focusing on climate change as a threat to our future. There is no doubt that our climate is changing; it always has, but on a longer time scale (Zalasiewicz & Williams, 2012). It was changing before humans evolved and continues to do so now; perhaps, changes are even accelerating. There have been alternating periods of glaciations and warming. The earth is relatively cold now as demonstrated by the presence of glaciers. We are now in an interglacial period preceding the next period of anticipated glacial advance (Eldredge & Biek, 2010). Ironically, I remember extensive warnings about future ice ages when I was in college in the 1960s.

While climate change is not the focus of the book, our relationship to our environment and our future is. Therefore, many of our authors discuss climate change in their chapters.

To plan our future, we must know the condition of the present and the factors that have brought us to now. We must also know how our environment affects us and our views of it. What makes us happy? What frightens us? What are our responsibilities to the environment and its living and nonliving components? Part of this is natural science; part of it is psychological science. We may never reach consensus on our goals, but we must still act responsibly to protect ourselves, our environment, and other life with which we share our planet. Our actions will affect us all, whether we individually agree or disagree with them. We must, as individual citizens, do all we can (Scruton, 2012) to ensure our actions are as objective as possible and are chosen first and foremost to benefit ourselves and our environments—the decisions should not be made by an elite group of decision makers or any particular special-interest group or groups. Moreover, they should be holistic, altruistic, and not selfish.

ECOPSYCHOLOGY

Ecology is the science that relates humans to the environment. Psychology is the science that studies the behavior of humans and seeks to understand and optimize it. Although humans are unique, we evolved from other animals and share their legacy. What applies to them applies to us. As animals, we require food, water, shelter, oxygen, and opportunity to reproduce. We share the living world with plants and animals that nourish us, compete with us for resources, prey on us, and provide other resources and cause other problems. This is the heritage that is common to us all. But humans have acquired special characteristics during evolution that enable us to control our environment and various elements in them to a much greater extent than other life forms can. Moreover, the changes we have made facilitated other changes, until we now have the ability to modify our environments almost completely. Many of the modifications we have made, are making, or are planning to make affect not only humans, but many other living things as well as the physical aspects of our environment.

The environments in which we evolved are disappearing and changing in ways that may ultimately be destructive to us in the short term or in the long term, in both the physical and the psychological sense. Biologists and ecologists can evaluate these changes with respect to their effects on abundance and survival of affected animal and plant species, as well as the effects on nonliving environmental components. They can also evaluate how landscapes, as defined by the sizes, shapes, and spatial relationships of habitat components, are changing, and the effects of these changes on the distribution and survival of the existing flora and fauna. All of these affect the survival of the living components and the diversity of all living things.

As changes accumulate, our environments become more differentiated from the earlier ones wherein we and the flora and fauna on which we depend evolved and thrived. Species become endangered and extinct, and diversity changes as environments change. Generally, when environments become less diverse, they become less stable and less likely to persist. That is certainly not a good thing for all the plants and animals that share our planet with us. We cannot be sure from either a physical or psychological perspective of our long-term survival in these new habitats because we have no prior experience with them. This is much more difficult to evaluate from the psychological perspective. Each of us has our own views and can decide how we perceive specific changes. Those who do not share our culture and upbringing may have different perceptions of the changes taking place. To all of us, survival is important, but is happiness in the future just about survival? Do we require other species and companion animals in our environments? Do we need green spaces? Many city planners say that we do and incorporate open spaces in their plans. Is an urban existence as satisfying as a rural one? What kind of future is optimal for us all? These are questions ecopsychologists should ask.

We share our world with other life forms with various characteristics. We can study the physical effects of change on them, but what are our responsibilities to them? Do they have rights? Does the amount of their perceived intelligence matter? Does it matter if they feel pain as we grow and harvest them for food or use them for experiments? Tribal cultures accept nature and respect it; more modern cultures control their environment without understanding how energy is necessary and how energy flows from one organism to another. For carnivores and omnivores, killing or harvesting energy from other animals is how they acquire their necessary energy. Is this evil? This is how natural systems work. Can killing and eating meat be immoral for humans?

SEEKING TRUTH

Our anthology is about seeking truth about ourselves and our environments. Our subject is complex, and there are many opinions and theories about many of the relationships we will discuss in this book. Because of the complexity involved in our subject and the ease in finding information, each of us can search and find additional information about the terms and concepts discussed herein. The reference sections in the chapters have valuable sources for essential information and ideas in classic books and scholarly papers that summarize specific ideas very well. But readers can also follow their own path and look up terms and principles to increase their understanding as much as they wish. We are fortunate now to have so many sources available almost instantaneously on the Internet; it is no longer necessary to go to a library in order to find most relevant information. We just need to know how to use a search engine. Now, most of it is available at our fingertips 24/7. Some sources promote an agenda but still contain facts that are useful for all. Focus on the facts. Be skeptical about agendas; evaluate these ideas and contrasting ones holistically in your search for truth.

To find the truth, information needs to be available and can be objectively verified and logically analyzed. This seems relatively simple, but many of our problems are complicated and require holistic analyses. In addition, we differ politically and psychologically, and we may be predisposed to accept certain viewpoints. Because environmental problems are complex, many may benefit from intervention, while others may not. Some people and groups may have specific agendas they are encouraging. These agendas may be thoroughly investigated with a holistic, logical analysis and may be quite objective. Other agendas may be quickly developed and narrowly focused with the intent of the proposer(s) and supporters to benefit personally or as a group from the decisions made. There can also be legitimate differences of opinion. As citizens, we are bombarded by various groups promoting particular agendas and asking for us to sign petitions or to communicate with specific authorities to support their agendas. Groups sometimes propagandize and market their ideas and are not necessarily being holistic in their search for truth. They may go public and attempt to affect our perceptions with propaganda, spin, and marketing campaigns. They may appeal to our emotions rather than to reason. Patrick (2011) claims much public speech now is mostly propaganda; I agree with him.

To make logical decisions, our language must be precise. When all participating in a decision do not interpret the wording in the same way, agreements or disagreements may be hidden. We should always strive to communicate as precisely as possible in our search for truth. We must also learn to discern when others are not speaking precisely or even when they are attempting to deceive. Many politicians parse their language to mislead, but not be accountable for their words. Remember, we should be seeking truth. We must also learn to discern those methods, like parsing, that appeal to emotions and not necessarily to logic.

Sometimes, we seem more concerned with obtaining agreement rather than truth. This is especially true when politics are involved. Making political decisions should not be the same as deciding what product to buy. It seems that many politicians do not necessarily seek truth or encourage it; they seek reelection. Misinformation and spin is acceptable; even propaganda sometimes is utilized to promote agendas. Those utilizing these deceptive practices should be ashamed. Deception helps to derail truth, yet the end does not justify the means.

We should not be attempting to manage perceptions, we should be seeking truth. It is here that psychologists may be able to help us to identify and practice methods to help us find truth. If we identify these methods and techniques, we will be on the path to the best future possible for us and our environments.

Communication and discussion must be encouraged. Instead, many discourage discourse and even seek to prevent discussions of ideas that are not considered to be "politically correct." The concept of political correctness is new and counter to a thorough discussion of problems; instead, we are vilified if we are not politically correct and want to have an open discussion. This approach is sometimes practiced by those who would manipulate us by using emotion rather than logic to influence our perceptions and promote their own agendas. We must identify these methods and reject them.

Ideas are often marketed, like soap. The same principles used to develop brands and influence buyers apply in politics and making environmental decisions. We must learn to be objective in our search for truth and learn to resist the psychological tricks that affect our perceptions.

Our schools should encourage the ability to find truth and determine the logic in arguments. Rote learning of facts encourages future reliance on the statements of authorities, but authorities sometimes deliberately mislead or may simply be mistaken.

Curricula should be objective and not designed to develop a particular world view. We all should be more involved in preparing our children for their future in a complex and ever-changing world.

HOLISTIC APPROACH

Because our environments are so complex and interconnected, many factors affect them and us. To understand these relevant factors and their interactions requires a holistic approach and analysis of all factors, or at least as many as are appropriate. When we go to a physician to evaluate our health, we often first go to a general practitioner, who asks us questions about our subjective impressions of our health and our symptoms. The general practitioner then conducts various tests to determine if our various systems are functioning properly. The results may indicate we should consult a specialist. When we do so, the specialist may also have a holistic approach. He or she may conduct further tests, but ones specialized for the particular system that seems to be of concern. An additional specialist in a more specific medical discipline might then be consulted. Eventually, the diagnosis is made and recommendations are offered. The rise in holistic medicine is an indication of the importance of the whole when dealing with complex systems like the human body.

If our approach to environmental problems is not holistic, an overlooked factor may be a root cause of problems, or several factors may contribute to them.

Often spatial or temporal factors are involved, so they too must be investigated. We must look at our environments—as holistically as possible.

When we instigate change, we have a specific goal in mind. If the evaluation of the plan was not holistic, the goal may or may not be accomplished because of incomplete analysis. Yet, even though the goal may be accomplished, unforeseen difficulties may arise later or at distant places. These are unintended consequences and, if the evaluation did not include all relevant factors originally, are almost inevitable. Factors often omitted are temporal or spatial ones: the action has effects at a different time from when the action occurred or at a different place. These lead to unintended consequences that may be quite severe, and sometimes may not even be attributed to the action that caused them. Actions may also affect additional organizational levels than the intended targets. They affect not only the whole, but also the parts. They often affect a larger whole than the one considered. All affected levels must be evaluated.

Temporal and Spatial Scales

In reviewing issues of a global nature, two scales with accompanying questions should be considered. They are:

The Temporal Scale

The essential question here is: What is the effect in time? Suppose we want to prevent floods and build a levee. As long as the levee is not overtopped, there will be no floods. Because there are no floods, nutrients from flooding will not be provided. To maintain productivity, additional fertilizer must be provided every year, because the effect of the levee occurs after it is built. The monetary and environmental cost of the additional fertilizer must be included in the cost/benefit decision as to whether to build a levee or not.

The Spatial Scale

The essential question here is: What is the effect outside of where the levee is built? Downstream, there will be more flow. This will make flooding worse there than if there were no levee upstream and will increase the apparent need for a levee downstream. Nutrients that would have been in floodwater on a farm will go downstream instead. Levees thus contribute to the rates of movement of silt and nutrients downstream. They can even make flooding downstream worse. When levees border a whole river, silt and nutrients eventually reach open water, where they are deposited and affect conditions there.

Effect at Different Levels of Organization

For example, when the flood water, reaches the gulf, the river water spreads out and deposits the silt and nutrients. This contributes to land deposition and is responsible for deltaic growth. Levees on a stream or river affect larger bodies of water downstream. They not only affect rivers, but they also affect the body of water that the river enters. Levees channelize the river and will affect its plants, animals, and physical characteristics. Some of these initially unanalyzed affects may be quite detrimental; they certainly were not anticipated if prior analyses were not holistic.

Unintended Consequences

In the example above, there were unintended consequences of the original decision to build a levee to protect farmland, because the natural fertilization that occurs with flooding no longer will occur. Chemical fertilizers must be applied instead, or a loss of productivity will occur. Some of the fertilizers run off and eventually find their way back to the river, where they are carried downstream and settle in open water. Because of natural currents, they accumulate in specific places and fertilize them. The growth can be so much that the new biomass from the increased productivity accumulates and is eventually decomposed. The decomposition of the new biomass consumes the available oxygen, and a dead zone can be formed. This occurs every year after fertilizer runoff, and throughout the world where levees prevent overbank flooding. This is a major problem in the Gulf of Mexico and more than 400 other locations worldwide, where the runoffs accumulate (Achenbach, 2008). Similarly, damming of rivers starves deltas of the nutrient-rich silt that is necessary for land building and contributes to land loss and subsidence downstream (Nemeth et al., 2012, pp. 66–69).

Thus, there can be consequences of our actions that were not anticipated originally, even though the original objective may have been met. In the example above, the levee does protect the leveed farmland, but the presence and extent of the downstream "dead zone" was not anticipated; the need for additional levees downstream may have been. If the initial analysis was not holistic, such unintended consequences are all almost always inevitable. Some examples of unintended consequences are discussed below. The reader can probably think of other examples because most decisions are not holistic and unintended consequences are usual.

DDT's Use as an Insecticide

After DDT and its chemical relatives were universally used as an insecticide, some unintended consequences were reported by Rachel Carson (1962) in a book that some say started the environmental movement. The pesticides also affected the reproduction of birds and other animals. Because the effects were subtle, they were not originally noticed; but the pesticides almost caused the extinction of Bald Eagles, Peregrine Falcons (Peregrine Fund, n.d.), Brown Pelicans, and other species. Fortunately, the cause was discovered, and these species recovered slowly after the pesticides were no longer used. Recovery has been slow because pesticide residues persisted in the environment for years.

Venting of S and N Compounds into Atmosphere

Acid rain was caused by the release of acid into the atmosphere with ultimate deposit into the environment through settling and precipitation. In the 1970s, many lakes and streams were becoming acidic with accompanying damage to aquatic life and water quality. The main causes were release of acidic sulfur and nitrogen compounds into the air by upwind power plants, smelters, and other industrial plants as well as the exhausts of motor vehicles. The compounds produced were acidic and precipitated out of the air downwind. The effects were not necessarily at the points of release, and at first the cause was unknown because the sources were distant. When the pollutants entered lakes and other environments, they caused acidification and many associated environmental problems. Most power plants that burn coal to produce their energy had sulfur as a common contaminant. It and other contaminants occur in gas. These caused acidification when they were vented to the atmosphere. The contaminants were eliminated by removing the sulfur from the fuels, as much as possible, and adjusting the process so atmospheric nitrogen was not involved when the fuels were used. Developing sulfur scrubbers for power plants and reducing sulfur and nitrogen in gasoline, as well as installing catalytic converters in vehicles solved the problems (EPA, "Acid Rain," n.d.). When I was an engineering student in Tennessee, my class visited a copper-smelting plant at Ducktown that had been built in a forested area, but then had a desert-like landscape formed mostly downwind of the acid-emitting chimney (Nemeth et al., 2012, pp. 51–53). The plant was built to smelt copper ore, which was mostly copper sulfate. The sulfur and water vapor were vented out of the stack, mostly as sulfurous acid. The problems caused by the acid that was deposited downwind were not anticipated but had to be solved. The plant installed equipment to capture the sulfur and convert it as sulfurous acid, which was very profitable. Removing the sulfur in copper smelters by converting it directly into acids was so profitable at Ducktown that the acid became the prime product of the plant, and copper became the by-product.

Freon Use

Another unanticipated consequence was the breakdown of our protective ozone layer, primarily at the poles, by the use of Freon and other halide compounds for cooling in our refrigerators and freezers as well as a propellant for aerosol products. No one seemed to anticipate a problem with venting Freon into the atmosphere. This was unanticipated, and potentially very harmful. A holistic analysis of the use of Freon (chlorofluorocarbons [CFCs]) implicated in the ozone layer was not initially made. When the effect was discovered, the

Freon was reformulated to replace the chlorine with fluorine, which does not affect the ozone layer nearly as much (Molina & Rowland, 1974).

THE IMPORTANCE OF CONSIDERING THE CONCEPT OF CHANGE

Change happens when energy is used, and life uses energy. We cannot over-emphasize the importance of change. It is inevitable. To maintain stability, energy must be used and more change is caused.

Perspectives of Change

Our approach in these volumes is holistic because change is ubiquitous and inevitable due to the laws of nature, and because the consequences of energy use are essential for the universe and its components to exist. Fragmented analyses of change do not explain its totality, and the results of any analysis reflect only the fragments involved in an analysis. This is why our management of the environment has so many unintended consequences. Climate change, for example, is of interest to us all and is affected by human factors, but the current focus is on only one—atmospheric carbon dioxide. It certainly has an important effect as do other factors. These all need to be examined to understand the problem and develop an optimal solution. Reacting to only one facet or a subset of a multifaceted problem cannot solve the problem completely and could lead to additional problems. The lack of holistic thinking is a major problem in our quest to understand the world and to manage it for our perceived benefit.

It is a mistake to not recognize the universality of change. We humans seek to control our environments and eliminate or reduce undesirable changes, but our knowledge of the causes and effects is incomplete and the results are often not what were intended. We levee our rivers to prevent flooding, but must forego the advantages of nutrient input to our soil during the expected yearly overbank flooding. We attempt to prevent all forest fires, yet allowing small ones or even initiating small fires would remove the buildup of fuel that makes large fires so dangerous (U.S. Forest Service, n.d.). We allowed Freon to be vented into the atmosphere without knowing its effect and discovered later that it interacts with ozone and caused a depletion of the ozone layer that helps protect us from harmful radiation (Molina & Rowland, 1974). We apply chemicals to our crops to eliminate pests of various kinds, and sometimes harm non-targeted species, even ourselves. There are many examples, and our readers can supply many of their own. The lesson is to fully understand all relevant factors and to be holistic before taking any action. Otherwise, unintended consequences are likely.

Although we are well aware of environmental changes and the dangers of sudden ones such as earthquakes, tsunamis, tornadoes, heat waves, cold waves, etc., we often do not notice slower and more subtle changes as they occur. We want to emphasize that we do eventually notice them as the changes accumulate. All living things cause change as they interact with their environments; some of these changes may be scarcely noticeable, while others may be more severe. The degree of change is related to the energy used to cause the change; for example, damage from plagues of locusts is related to number of locusts, or by lemmings is related to their density. Changes accumulate through the years; animals, plants, and the environment evolve. The volume is for us all; thus we have endeavored to explain things in ways that are easy to understand. Besides our holistic approach, we present information in these chapters as documented essays. The many specific ideas and concepts have readily available sources that can be found on the Internet and can be used to augment and explain further the terms and concepts we discuss. We cite major works that clarify important information and ideas.

Past Changes

The earth formed about 4.5 billion years ago from material associated with our sun. It slowly evolved, from a lifeless, featureless blob through a number of steps into the world we know today. During this period, land and oceans formed, and an atmosphere slowly developed. It was originally toxic but eventually changed through a number of processes (Hazen, 2012). After life formed and evolved, it contributed to the accumulating changes. Details of the physical changes are studied in geology. Paleontologists study the living things of the past. They, too, slowly changed.

The geography of the earth is thus dynamic, although the changes were very slow; there has been 4.5 billion years for them to occur. The physical changes occurred naturally through interactions among various materials on earth, and the enormous energy still present in earth's core that cause volcanic eruptions, earthquakes, and movement of tectonic plates to shape our land-masses and other phenomena like geysers and hot springs. Occasional additional materials from comets, meteors, and asteroids slowly accumulate on earth also. Radiant energy from the sun and outer space also contributed. Even after the continents formed, their physical features, shapes, and locations have been constantly changing. Change continues with erosion of uplands and new mountains forming. Rivers formed, changed their course, and eventually disappeared to be replaced by new rivers. Seas were formed and later buried, with their presence indicated now by underground salt deposits. After life formed, its manifestations contributed to the changes. Living things were buried and occasionally uncovered as manifested in the extensive deposits of fossils and fossil fuels—coal, oil, and gas, as well as peat. The energy stored in these fuels is essential to us now, and the locations of their presence, as well as the locations of other fossil material, are evidence of many of the changes that have been occurring.

These past changes were dramatic and inevitable given the initial conditions and natural laws, but it took a very long time. From now forward, changes will continue. Their directions can be somewhat predicted from the past, but the original conditions are not our present conditions. The factors changing our future are not precisely the same as in the past, and humans now affect the direction and amount of change directly through management and indirectly because of their accelerating use of energy, and the consequences of that.

Present and Future Changes

Even if our concerns are not exaggerated and can be dealt with effectively, there are many other factors that are producing changes that are unfavorable to us and to our environment. Most are related to our numbers and the measures that we are taking to supply their needs in an increasingly crowded world.

Much of our understanding of the environment comes from the studies of biology and ecology of plants and other animals. The rules for them apply to us also. When humans discovered how to farm and utilize new energy sources to modify habitats, the old principles no longer applied because the environments were no longer stable. It was a new ball game. Evolution could no longer keep up, and the prior rules were no longer applicable. That makes future decisions problematic and uncertain. Because of our new knowledge and methods, our numbers, no longer limited by past constraints, continued to grow; they are still increasing in frightening ways. We are in a positive feedback loop, which we must escape.

We discuss planning for the future and the factors involved. To manage the future, we must have goals. Do we have universal values? If so, we should seek to achieve them. Here is where the psychological aspects are so important, because we will have to live in the world we make. We may be able to achieve our physical needs, but perhaps not our psychological ones. With the world changing so rapidly because of our physical demands on it and our inventiveness, perhaps a stable world cannot be attained, and our species will be changing constantly as will our world.

OUR RESOURCES

The earth and the sun were formed at about the same time, a little over 4.5 billion years ago. The sun is the source of most of our energy, and the earth supplies most of our physical resources. The plants and animals we share our planet with are our primary biological resources, and our intelligence and inventiveness are our primary psychological ones.

Our brains give us the ability to analyze and evaluate the world around us. We can study our ever-changing world and evaluate how our actions have contributed to its changes and speculate how future actions will affect us.

The changes are complex and results can be unpredictable (see Gleick, 1987). This is the reason why analyses of problems should be as holistic and as logical as possible to reduce unanticipated consequences. Furthermore, we can communicate information by sight and sound to each other in real time, and we can store it for almost instantaneous retrieval now and into the future. We can evaluate information and act to ameliorate present change as well as plan future changes in order to attain our goals.

Energy

Energy is fundamental to understanding all issues of sustainable development and even psychology. All of life requires energy. Energy is responsible for our survival and affects our standard of living. The more people there are, the more energy we require. Our numbers are increasing, and most, if not all of us, want a higher standard of living; both of these factors contribute to our still-growing energy needs. It is a view of many that successful economies depend on and need a growing gross national product. This too will require energy use to be exponentially expanding unless some or all future growth can be delinked, at least partially, from energy use.

There are many energy sources that have contributed to the formation of earth and its evolution. Many of them are still changing the earth without human initiation or intervention. Additional energy from the sun and space is constantly affecting the earth. Often the internal energy release is sudden and large and leads to almost instant modification of our environment. Earthquakes and volcanic eruptions, with occasional associated tsunamis, are examples. These lead to trauma for many humans; how we deal with it is a major subject in Volume 2.

As humans evolved, we have learned to harness energy to accomplish specific goals. As knowledge accumulates, our energy options increase because of our increasing knowledge of potential sources and their advantages and disadvantages.

Solar Energy

The energy that sustains us mostly comes from the sun. Although the amount available varies somewhat, solar energy output from the sun should be as high as or higher than the present level and sufficient for many millennia (Goldsmith & Owen, 2001). The sun will eventually change and burn out, but should last another 14.5 billion years. The percentage of energy received and used by humans is growing faster than our population, and the solar energy available to natural systems is correspondingly decreasing at an alarming rate.

Solar energy heats the earth, allowing water to evaporate into the atmosphere and eventually fall back to earth as snow, sleet, rain, or hail. The sun basically acts to pump water to the atmosphere, from which it eventually returns to earth.

It is thus pumped uphill where it can flow downhill and be used to carry upland material downstream to be deposited elsewhere. The dissolved soil is the source of material for deltaic formation, and also for soil buildup in our reservoirs and along flowing streams. Before extensive levees were built, it supplied an annual nutrient pulse to flooded land.

Differential heating of air, land, and water caused by solar radiation produces winds and currents that function in dispersal and mixing of materials, and influence the weather and climate. Energy can be harvested from the wind by windmills and sailboats (Bockmann & Steen, 2011). Energy from currents can also be harvested. Even energy from tides can be harvested; it is directly responsible for the high energy production of marshes that is continually awash in nutrient-rich water. This is one reason why building levees and canals in marshes is so detrimental. Water currents carry heated or cooled water long distances. These currents, like the Gulf Stream, greatly affect the climate of areas near where the current flows (Open University, 2001). Solar panels directly convert solar radiation to electricity or heat water to provide hot water and heating.

Radiation Variation

The rate that energy is received from the sun depends on solar output and varies somewhat on both a short-term and a very long-term basis. There is an approximate 11-year cycle that is caused by sunspot cycles on the sun and affects solar output. Although the surface area of the earth is a constant, the amount of solar radiation received varies from place to place because of the orientation of the earth with respect to the sun. The orientation changes throughout the year as the earth orbits the sun and daily as the earth spins on its axis. Because the earth's axis is tilted, the amount of solar radiation striking the earth varies in predictable ways to produce the seasons that are different in the Northern and Southern Hemispheres. The differential heating and day lengths between the equator and the poles account for many climatic differences. The sun is thus a major factor affecting our climate, which affects our habitats and us.

Chemical Energy

All our materials consist of atoms and their combinations into molecules through chemical reactions. All atoms and molecules contain energy. As the atoms and molecules change their configurations, energy is added or lost. Release of energy is called oxidation, and addition of energy is called reduction. The energy produced through oxidation can be utilized in many ways but also can be very destructive when not controlled. Forest fires are a prime example of the immense devastation that is possible. Many oxidation reactions, such as rusting, occur naturally; energy input through reduction can return molecules to their original unoxidized condition.

Photosynthesis

All life requires energy, and most energy on earth is produced through a process called photosynthesis. Although it developed rather late in the evolution of plants, its success attests to its value. It enables the incorporation of solar energy into organic chemical compounds that can be converted into useful energy by plants. Almost all life depends on them.

Water and carbon dioxide are the main raw materials for photosynthesis. Plants use these and energy from solar radiation to synthesize energy-rich carbon compounds and release oxygen (O_2). These compounds supply the energy in almost all living things and are the basis for life when the process is reversed through a process called "respiration" that uses O_2 and the stored energy to maintain life and release the raw materials and energy. Chlorophyll, a green pigment, is necessary for photosynthesis. Chlorophyll is green, so green has become symbolic for life because photosynthesis is necessary for most life as we know it. "Green" has also become a symbol for environmental conservation.

Fossil Fuels

Organic material primarily contains hydrogen and carbon. It can be harvested as wood or biofuels and used for energy. Organic material produced long ago and not decomposed is eventually covered by new layers of soil and rock as the earth's surface continually changes through normal geologic processes. It can eventually be harvested as fossil fuels and burned to ultimately produce electricity (energy). Carbon dioxide and water are the main products of the burning along with the energy produced. The proportion of carbon dioxide and water that is released into the atmosphere depends on the organic compounds being burned. Pure coal produces only carbon dioxide, and hydrogen fuel cells produce only water. Carbon dioxide is a greenhouse gas that helps to trap solar radiation and produce the greenhouse effect. Water vapor too is a greenhouse gas but it also produces clouds that reflect sunlight away from earth and its effect on climate is complicated and difficult to evaluate.

Hydroelectric Energy

Electricity can be produced by turbines that are usually turned by flowing water or steam. We build reservoirs to store water and release it through turbines to produce electricity. The dams are also important in storing water for various uses. Water for the reservoirs comes from precipitation upstream that is made possible by the evaporation of water caused by solar radiation. The dams impede the flow of water and convert streams into lakes. This is a major problem when the streams are migratory routes for salmon and other fish to complete their reproductive cycles upstream (Brown, 2010), and river habitats are different from lake ones.

Geothermal

The earth is warmed externally by solar radiation. Hot springs and volcanism are common at some locations. Energy can be tapped from these sources. Some buildings utilize the more constant temperature of the soil to reduce heating and cooling costs.

Wind and Current

Differential heating at the surface produces winds containing energy that can turn turbines and generate electricity. Humans have used the winds and currents to propel boats and facilitate other movement. Even today, new boats are being designed to utilize wind power (Bockmann & Steen, 2011).

Spatial Considerations

Historically, winds and currents move material and modify our environments. Winds have moved soil and other material and can cause major damage when present in tornadoes, hurricanes, and other cyclones. Visibility has been greatly reduced when windblown particles are dense enough. Particle density can be sufficient to interfere with the operation of aircraft engines or even screen sunlight from the earth's surface and cause winter-like conditions. Air-blown soil particles and molecules are deposited downwind and can accumulate as loess soil and bluffs, or cause acid rain. Currents are important in regulating temperatures as water is transferred from warm waters to colder nearby areas (e.g., Gulf Stream) and colder to warmer areas (The North Pacific Current, for example). Migratory birds use the wind to facilitate their migrations, and rising thermals (i.e., heated air that is rising) facilitate soaring and flight of many birds and insects, and even glider aircraft.

The energy in the winds and currents can be harvested and converted into electricity. This does not change the composition of the air much and is being encouraged by many as an alternate energy source. Because wind intensity is variable, wind energy production is variable and not always available, so it must be augmented by other sources (battery or otherwise) where reliable energy production is needed.

Temporal Considerations

Ways to store wind energy must be developed for it to be a reliable sole energy source. Wind energy is produced by large windmills with turbine blades that can be lethal; some wildlife mortality, including endangered and threatened species, is an unfortunate consequence of the large wind farms that are being created to harvest the energy (Mehlman, 2014). Some believe that the current design of wind turbines is unattractive and a visual eyesore.

The wind farms tend to dry the ground. Habitat loss and change is another undesirable effect. Wind farms require space that might be better used for other purposes. A less-obvious problem is that, when energy is removed from the air, it is no longer available on the surface and thus does not do what it would have done otherwise. This changes the environment as well. These changes could be considered positive or negative, but they must be identified to be understood. As always, a holistic analysis and approach is desirable.

Generators can also be placed in moving water to produce energy. Output would be affected by current strength that would be affected by water flow. Because these generators could be hidden, they could be a navigation and safety hazard if carelessly placed. Here, too, harvesting the energy would reduce the current where the turbines are located and there might be beneficial or detrimental effects due to that placement.

Fission

Energy can be obtained from splitting atoms, as was done in the atomic bomb developed during World War II that released unprecedented-for-the-time energy and radiation. In nuclear power plants, nuclear fission is much slower and does not produce an explosion, only heat and radiation. The radiation produced can be lethal once a threshold is exceeded and can persist for many years, depending on the exact fission process being used and its byproducts. Because of this, the radioactive isotopes and radiation must be shielded and stored for many years (Cohen, n.d.). These by-products have been released or have escaped when accidents occur, as in Fukushima, Japan, with dangerous radiation that can persist and cause damage for a very long time. Nuclear power plants are designed to eliminate danger from the associated radiation, but accidents have occurred (e.g., Chernobyl and Fukushima Daiichi) and have caused problems that are very difficult to solve. Environmental disasters, such as earthquakes and tsunamis, can cause serious problems if planning is insufficient.

The main problem seems to be keeping the contaminated wastes contained in a foolproof manner. Nuclear power plants have the advantages of not producing greenhouse gases and a relatively high energy production per plant, but problems with the disposal of radioactive wastes make them difficult to gain approval. Finding a repository for the wastes was attempted in the United States and a deep repository for spent rods and other wastes at Yucca Mountain, Nevada, was approved in 2002, but political opposition continued, and although it was constructed, Yucca Mountain was never used for storage. Funding for operations was withdrawn in 2010, but the need for proper disposal is increasing, and a decision must be made even if it is inconvenient politically. As concerns for climate change and land availability increase, additional attempts to use nuclear power may also increase (IAEA, 2014).

Fusion

Fusion is obtained by fusing elements. In hydrogen bombs, isotopes of hydrogen were fused to produce helium and energy in the form of neutrons. There are theoretical reasons and advantages of fusion power, which would generate steam to be used for generators (Tamarkin, 2014). Radioactive wastes would only be at the plant site, but last for 50 to 100 years. Fission radiation would last thousands of years and need to be transported to a safe site (EUROfusion, n.d.), but the fusion reaction cannot be controlled now and fusion power will not be available until it is. Once developed, it has the potential to supply the earth's energy needs for thousands of years because deuterium (an isotope of hydrogen), the raw material, is readily available in the ocean. There are many obstacles to be overcome before fusion power plants can be operational. Initial plants would not be completed before the 2030s (World Nuclear Association, 2014). The reaction used in fusion power is the same one that powers the sun.

Energy Availability and Transmission

All life requires energy. We humans, like all animals, acquire energy with our food. We use it to power our metabolism to ensure our survival. We originally were hunter-gatherers, so we hunted meat and gathered fruits and vegetation to obtain our food. As we evolved, we discovered ways to be more efficient in food acquisition and thus require less food for our survival because of reduced energy requirements. When humans began to become independent of the environmental restraints of other animals, they found ways to use energy more efficiently through the development of tools, the use of shelter, etc. Eventually, we domesticated animals and plants and retained even more of our energy intake as we used the energy of the domesticated animals and the increased efficiency provided by the tools. We gained more control of our environment by discovering new ways to obtain and utilize energy. Our history has become one of finding ways to be more efficient in the energy we had available, or of developing new ways to make more energy to meet our needs. Ironically, we often needed to expend energy use to acquire even more energy. We discovered we could increase agricultural productivity by inputting energy to cultivate, till, seed, control pests, harvest, and transport the crops to various markets. We supplemented the natural energy with other sources. That has been the key to our success—we have developed new technologies that utilized energy for our benefit and have developed an infrastructure to deliver it. Our success has been due to our ability to utilize energy in innovative ways to increase production.

Most of us now use electricity to supply the energy we need, but few of us produce electricity except with mobile generators or rooftop solar panels. It is usually produced elsewhere and transported to wherever it is needed by a grid of electric power lines. For smaller needs, we use generators and batteries, which we can purchase and take to where they are needed. Battery development is essential to use electric power and not be permanently tied to the grid. The development of electric cars depends on sufficient battery power to power a vehicle far enough for the vehicle to be practical.

As we evaluate our energy needs, we must evaluate all costs. This is another example of being holistic. Included in a holistic analysis should be the costs for obtaining raw materials and transporting them to where they are used. We also need to calculate the costs of transporting the electricity throughout a transmission network to where it is used as well as the cost of constructing, protecting, and maintaining transmission corridors and other infrastructure. We must calculate the costs of environmental damages in every step and the costs of mediating them. We must make a complete accounting.

These calculations are rarely used in public discussions of costs, although they must be made by those designing, approving, and managing our power grids. They are not often promulgated to the public, who do not seem very interested. I never see these results published or discussed (although I have not looked hard). Instead, I see very superficial discussions about energy problems. A typical example is the justification for electric-powered cars by those promoting their development and use. They emphasize that the cars no longer need fossil fuels, so they reduce the quantity of carbon we emit (our carbon footprint). The cars operate on electricity provided by a battery that can be recharged as needed. Most electricity now is produced by power plants that use fossil fuels to produce the electricity. Thus, fossil fuels are being used, but only indirectly to recharge the batteries. Somehow the electric cars are being promoted as not using carbon. If the electricity to charge the batteries comes from a coal-fired power plant, more carbon is probably being burned because there is an additional step in powering the cars. Each step loses energy. Also not discussed is the cost of the production and distribution of the batteries as well as the cost of mining and transporting the material used in them. The cost of constructing recharging stations and maintaining them is not discussed, either. Storage space in electric vehicles is lost because of battery bulk, and the risk of fire is increased. These hidden costs are also not likely to be discussed—certainly not all of them together. This information is necessary to evaluate the real cost of electric cars, or any car. Public perception is important in these decisions, but the public is not currently interested in these details. I am omitting some costs here, but the reader should get the idea. We do not know whether electric cars are a good idea or not. Of course, to make the comparison, we also need to know the costs of the alternatives. How can we make good decisions without knowing the answers to these questions? This is an illustration of the desirability of holistic decision-making.

The same sort of scrutiny should be used in evaluating and comparing energy sources. There are human factors involved that should be taken into consideration. Sometimes it seems that the decisions are made based on cronyism or political connections, or similar practices that benefit some at a cost to others. A careful holistic analysis and discussion might change this outcome. We all should be interested and informed, and we must demand responsible decision-making and management. Propaganda and spin are not good enough.

The Concept of Matter

The earth is a planet that orbits the sun. It contains matter that is fundamentally present as elements, which can be combined into compounds, each having unique properties. There are 98 naturally occurring elements and 16 more that have been synthesized or identified in laboratories. The total quantity available on earth for each is a constant, except for radioactive ones like uranium and thorium that slowly transfer from one form to another or from one element into another while emitting radiation. The emission of radiation is dangerous and can be lethal, depending on its type—alpha, beta, or gamma. Elements emitting radiation are called radioactive and must be handled and treated with care to avoid radiation damage. Some elements like carbon, oxygen, hydrogen, and nitrogen are very common everywhere, and others like iodine are absent or rare in many places. Many of these elements and compounds made from them are used by us to provide resources for our use. The number of uses increases as we learn more about the elements and their characteristics and the attributes of the resources we need to accomplish our goals. As we learn more, we create new compounds as needed and we learn to better use the ones already known. We could develop extreme shortages, especially if alternatives cannot be found to accomplish our goals.

The Earth's Surface

Our main energy source is the sun, which strikes the earth or is reflected back into space. The amount reflected depends on the material on the surface. If the material changes, so does the amount reflected. Albedo is the term for differential reflectance. The amount retained will heat the surface or be utilized by vegetation to synthesize energy-rich organic compounds. These will ultimately supply energy to almost all living things. Climate is affected by the differential heating and cooling at the surface. Humans can affect albedo directly by changing the material at the surface. Deforestation, constructing reservoirs, and building cities, highways, and other infrastructure are a few examples of disruptions that can affect albedo and thus affect climate. Albedo is rarely mentioned when climate change is being addressed.

Land

The earth is approximately sphere-shaped and of constant size. Although the nature of its surface features has been changing since the earth was formed, in terms of the human occupancy of our planet, the surface is essentially constant with slowly rising mountains and slowly eroding landscapes. Occasional volcanic eruptions, earthquakes, and tsunamis make little long-term difference, but do cause short-term perturbations. The amount of solar radiation to reach our surface varies only by as much as solar output changes and its differences are relatively low. This radiation supports almost all of our biota. The precise nature of the environments, which depends primarily on local climates, will be discussed in Chapter 12 (Hamilton, 2015). The point here is that the amount of energy we are receiving is relatively constant.

Another point is that once humans learned to modify the environments, more and more land has been modified by us, and less is available to maintain our original habitats. If we want to conserve our natural habitats, we should minimize our disturbance of them. This is difficult when our population is increasing and needing additional resources, especially energy sources. A good plan would be to minimize surface area disturbance as we increase our energy availability. Instead we are developing plans to create biofuels by growing vegetation on land that could hold natural habitats, and we are setting up wind and solar farms on these lands to produce renewable energy. We encourage ethanol addition to fuel and thus encourage more land diversion. Ethanol used for that purpose is controversial from energy considerations (my car gets better mileage when using non-ethanol fuel) but has political advantages. This is all at the price of disturbing more land. We must learn to value our land surface where availability is essentially a constant. Mining underground sources could be less disruptive, except their distribution is somewhat clumped together in specific places, supplies are finite, and extensive infrastructure is required to acquire and transport mined resources from the point of extraction to where they are processed. Additional infrastructure may be required to transport final products to where they will be used. Our fossil fuel sources are finite and will eventually be unavailable. They will need to be replaced with other ones. As long as our population is increasing, additional energy supplies to feed us and are considered necessary for social justice. Our economy is expected to grow and we will have problems supplying the additional energy without impinging further on the relatively undisturbed land that we are devoting to the conservation of critical habitat. Surface area is a variable that should be strongly valued as we consider our future energy sources. This seems to be largely underappreciated, even among some conservation organizations.

I have not discussed landscape issues here, but the arrangement of habitats and their sizes is critical to the distribution and abundance of plants and animals and thus greatly affect habitat. Landscape features should be evaluated when decisions are made as to land utilization and should be included in any holistic analysis of habitat disturbance or management.

As I have stated, the surface area, both terrestrial and aquatic, is essentially static. As we grow, we will impinge on it more unless we are able to increase use in already disturbed areas or develop more efficient sources like fusion power.

I will defer to psychologists to evaluate the consequences of any action that affects habitats and thus us.

The modification of our environments to support our increasing density and needs has its problems. Do we know an ideal use? Can we be happy in environments with little presence of the habitats in which we evolved? Is it moral to force those tribes who still live in undeveloped or underdeveloped habitats to abandon their lifestyle because we need the resources of their homeland that are the basis for their existence? Is our culture more valuable than theirs? Does "might make right"?

Atmosphere

We are surrounded by an atmosphere that envelops our planet. It protects us from harmful external radiation and provides protection from meteors and other space debris. It contains and provides oxygen, carbon dioxide, water vapor, and other gases necessary for our existence and the existence of our habitats. The water vapor in our clouds helps us recirculate water and recharge our reservoirs, natural and human-made, as well as moderate temperatures. Its ozone layer protects us from dangerous ultraviolet radiation up high, but harms us, on contact, down low (EPA, "Ozone," n.d.). It is the medium that our weather uses to affect our climate and produce our weather. Although it is invisible and seems almost nonexistent, it supports our aircraft and the flight of birds, insects, and other flying species. Our satellites must have special shielding to dissipate the heat produced by friction as they reenter the atmosphere.

Water

Water is essential to life and covers approximately 70% of the earth's surface. It receives about 70% of our incoming solar radiation; more is reflected back into space when the water is white from being frozen. It is essential to life as being one of the compounds used in photosynthesis. It is an important component of living cells as well as being an important solvent.

Many things dissolve in water and can thus flow downhill with the water. Water occurs in all three states at normal earthly temperatures—gas (water vapor), liquid (water), and solid (ice, snow, and sleet). Water is densest at $4°C$, and consequently, ice will float on the surface and thus protect aquatic life from freezing in the winter. Water is inhabited by a variety of species that are specialized for living in it. The salinity of water is variable and influences the species that inhabit it as well as their size. Sunlight does not penetrate into deep water, so most productivity in deep water occurs at the surface; organic material slowly falls to the bottom. As on land, photosynthesis is accomplished in plants that receive sunshine. In aquatic systems, these are primarily very small and collectively are called phytoplankton. Large plants cannot be rooted in deep water to receive sunlight. There are some larger floating plants, but they are not common. Deep-living life receives its energy from organic material falling from above, except for some very rare forms that do not depend on sunlight for energy. Those unique organisms are concentrated near their sources of energy.

Surface and subsurface water is variable in quantity and location. Because humans depend on water, we must often move it in a variety of ways to make it available where it is needed. We often congregate near the water that ameliorates the climate and provides a medium to transport materials to and from our settlements. Human distribution would be greatly different if we could not utilize, move, and manage water in this way. Large cities, such as Los Angeles, could not exist now without a constant input of imported water.

Water varies in its saltiness (salinity), and that affects the organisms that can live in or use it. Freshwater habitats have different species than saltier habitats. Salinity changes can affect species greatly. For example, salt water is saltier than body fluids, and water would flow out of cells without work being done by salt glands or similar specializations. Similarly in freshwater environments, kidneys remove the water that enters the cells through osmosis.

People tend to congregate in areas with abundant water for transportation. Los Angeles is an example of a city that has an abundance of salt water, yet has a water availability problem. Fresh water must be imported from a series of reservoirs to meet population needs. Desalinization of the salt water is expensive and takes much energy. That is done to supply most of the needed fresh water in many places.

Aquifers are underground sources of water that we tap with wells. With our ever-growing population and consequent increased water needs, these aquifers are being depleted. Because of freshwater depletion, saline water is impinging on freshwater supplies in aquifers. In many places the aquifers will be depleted, and alternate sources must be supplied. Desalinization is being used, but energy use is required for desalinization, and it is expensive. As time goes by, water supplies are becoming more tenuous.

Because humans live on dry land, we do not directly change larger aquatic environments as much as terrestrial ones. We do, however, establish and manage them for water retention and potential power sources by harvesting the potential energy of elevated water. The reservoirs provide water-related recreation as well as storage and habitat for aquatic organisms. We can thus harvest aquatic forms without necessarily destroying their habitats. Many aquatic forms are very social and can be caught in very large numbers. They are, however, caught primarily in international or other waters with no ownership, and there is little constraint on their harvest. Basically, the view is that, if a ship or a country shows responsibility or restraint, overharvesting will still occur because others will still overharvest. Therefore, restraint is not prudent. Hardin's 1968 paper, "The Tragedy of the Commons," offers a more in-depth explanation. International Treaties for whaling have not been completely effective either (see "Whaling: A Bloody War," 2003).

Because water is such a good solvent and carrier of small particles, it is easily polluted. Without energy being expended for cleanup, it can eventually become unusable. When human density was low, many people threw their trash in the water, especially moving water that carries the trash elsewhere. This is still happening today. The polluter's philosophy seems to be stated in the saying I have heard: "The solution to pollution is dilution." That philosophy is not workable in an increasingly crowded world. Amount of trash is increasing because of increasing population and changing trash production for packaging and other reasons. Heavy concentrations of plastics are occurring in the oceans and causing much damage (Ryan, Moore, van Franeker, & Moloney, 2009).

Deadly mudslides sometimes occur when soil gets saturated and slides downhill. A loss of vegetation that holds the soil is often the cause. A mudslide effects a change in the environment where it occurs. The damage can be quite severe at the slide area, where soil and vegetation and even loose rock move downhill. Anything in its path can be covered or swept up into the slide.

Because water in rivers and streams can flow for many miles, and aquifers are quite large, our ancestors and forbearers have established practices to equitably provide and distribute needed water. Canals and pipelines have been built to move water from place to place. These practices have been codified and have legal status. Many were established years ago when conditions were different, but they still exist today. In many ways, their existence complicates the notion of equitable solutions under current conditions. New solutions must be found.

Sometimes, several laws conflict, as is illustrated by conflicts over water use in the California Central Valley, a major area of food production, which has suffered from drought. Endangered small fish are there and need a minimum water flow for their survival and that is encoded in the Endangered Species Act. At the same time, farmers, who supply a large percentage of American fruits and vegetables, have formal water rights that entitle them to a certain amount of water (California Aspire Project, n.d.). Therefore, there is severe competition for the available water. At the time of this writing, there is a serious drought, and there is not enough water for both, and there currently is a major dispute as to how the water should be used. Both sides have a case, supported by tradition and law. These types of conflicts will increase as our numbers increase, our environment keeps changing, and more species become endangered.

MY INTRODUCTION TO ECOPSYCHOLOGY

Even though I had never heard the term ecopsychology when my friend, Dr. Darlyne Nemeth, approached me about preparing a paper to be presented at the United Nations about biosphere management and lifestyle change

(Nemeth et al., 2007), I accepted the challenge because it fit in with my belief in the holistic approach to problem solving. I have always been concerned with avian ecology, primarily on habitats and their management. Management is geared toward modifying the environment to accomplish a desired goal or goals; but the focus was always on the environment and not on how the environment affects people. This started me to focus more on how our environment affects people and how people affect the environment. As my interest increased, I used my biologic and brief engineering backgrounds and long-standing holistic approach to contemplate what we really need to know to properly understand and manage our environment. This volume and our previous book were the ultimate result of these and similar meetings sponsored by the United Nations.

Simultaneously with this series of talks at the United Nations, the dangers of global warming were being promoted throughout the world. With time, the original focus concerning global warming decreased and our concern shifted to "climate change." From this debate, I concluded that global warming and climate change were just examples of change and that change itself should be our concern. To deal with change, it is useful to know the cause, if possible; but usually dealing with the result is sufficient. My education came at a time when students concentrated more and more on less and less until they became experts in very specific areas. Somehow I was able to obtain my PhD degree while focusing on a much more holistic problem that involved interactions between the anatomy, behavior, and ecology of two closely related species of birds that I studied to explain how they survived in the environments they shared. Differences in anatomy and behavior allowed the birds to compete with other species and between the sexes for shared resources (Hamilton, 1975). Both species were flexible in their behavior and ecology within the constraints of their anatomy. In other words, the behavior and ecology could not really be understood from studies at one place, because the behavior and ecology changed as conditions change. They were influenced by the specific characteristics of the place where they were observed. To understand, I needed to think holistically. What I found explained many differences in disputes in the literature where different researchers obtained what they thought were contradictory to the results of others. Neither result was necessarily right or wrong. They both may have been right for the situations they studied. Instead of disputing, they should have collaborated to obtain a more general result.

While in graduate school, I spent one summer trapping brown lemmings (*Lemmus trimucronatus*) for a long-term study by Dr. Frank Pitelka and others who were trying to explain the short-term cycles of brown lemming abundance. It seemed to me at that time that almost any scientist who was seeking to understand the causes of the cycles of abundance demonstrated by lemmings found answers that corresponded with their approaches. Predation in summer and winter were important when lemmings were moderately abundant. When lemmings were very abundant, however, they overgrazed the environment and subsequently starved to death, if they had not already been captured and consumed by predators. Their genotypes differed in high and low abundance years, etc. All the scientists found plausible answers, and I believe they were all correct, but incomplete. No one looked at the situation holistically because that was not the way it was done. I noticed that each researcher found answers, but none found the complete story. My dissertation work on the American Avocet, *Recurvirostra Americana*, and the Black-necked Stilt, *Hihumanstopus mexicanus*, further convinced me that I should be holistic in my approach despite its modern-day uniqueness.

Personal Conversion to Holistic Thinking

Holistic approaches are becoming increasingly common in the world as we switch to group efforts in problem solving. I believe analyses would improve if we became even more holistic. In academia, most advanced degrees require research on individual problems so that the student becomes an expert on a very narrow topic. This is a useful way to increase our understanding of what is being studied, but it does not help much in the understanding required by ecopsychologists. Ecopsychologists tie together relevant information from a variety of disciplines and work together in teams to increase their understanding of holistic problems.

Throughout my life and early experiences, I had a holistic approach similar to what had been more common in the past. During my education, I realized that my approach was somewhat unique, but I believe it has led me to a better understanding of our holistic environment. Einstein and Darwin certainly were practitioners of the holistic approach. Most great scientific discoveries have been holistic and have tied many facts together to understand the whole. In a way, that is the nature of science. That, in fact, is the goal. We do not seek contradictions or questions. We seek an answer to everything like Einstein sought with the Unified Field Theory to explain both relativity and electromagnetism.

I started my college career in chemical engineering, where I learned that it was necessary to account for all of the materials and expenses; that is completely holistic. I debated in high school. To be effective, one had to know and understand all of the arguments possible on each side of the debate. The side that could best counter the other side's arguments, no matter what they were, always won. Again, the approach was holistic. Many of the arguments themselves were also holistic.

Finally, I attended a postdoctoral summer institute sponsored by the National Science Foundation during my early faculty career. The subject was linear modeling; in it we learned the techniques used for modeling systems, and we did so with a model of a cove in Lake Texoma (Patten, Egloff, & Richardson, 1975).

Even though this was years ago, I developed an understanding of how the models worked. The effort is designed to be holistic. After the model is developed, it is tested to ascertain its ability to predict correctly the variables of interest. So it is testable with historic databases. I am sure the technology of the CO_2–Hockey Stick model that is used to predict global temperatures from CO_2 levels (Global Warming and the Climate, n.d.) is laudable and much better than when we worked on our cove model. At that time we needed to estimate many of the variables in the model. Less of that is probably required now. The primary problem with it seems to be that it was oversold. No doubt we should minimize as much as possible the amount of greenhouse gases we are using. Right now that may mean a decrease in energy available to support the needs of a growing population. Alternative sources each have their own problems and may not be better alternatives; they all need to be compared in a holistic, objective manner. More discussion needs to be about the energy aspect of burning fossil fuels and the practicality of all approaches. I do not see that in the public discussion. This must become a part of scientific, public, and policy discussions.

REFERENCES

Achenbach, J. (2008, August 15). "Dead zones" appear in waters worldwide: New study estimates more than 400. *The Washington Post*.

Bockmann, E., & Steen, S. (2011). *Wind propulsion of ships*. Retrieved September 25, 2014, from http://www.marinepropulsors.com/smp/files/downloads/smp11/Paper/FA1-2_Bockmann.pdf

Brown, B. (2010). *Mountain in the clouds*. Seattle: University of Washington Press.

California Aspire Project. (n.d.). Food or fish: Political honesty needed in California water wars, part II. Retrieved September 25, 2014, from https://californiaaspireproject.wordpress.com/2014/09/24/food-or-fish-political-honesty-needed-in-ca-water-wars-part-ll/

Carson, R. (1962). *Silent spring*. Boston, MA: Houghton Mifflin.

Cohen, B. L. (n.d.). *Risks of nuclear power*. Retrieved October 13, 2014, from http://physics.isu.edu/radinf/np-risk.htm

Countryeconomy. (n.d.). *United States: Life expectancy at birth*. Retrieved September 21, 2014, from http://countryeconomy.com/demography/life-expectancy/usa

Diamond, J. (2012). *The world until yesterday: What can we learn from traditional societies?* New York: Penguin Books.

Eldredge, S., & Biek, B. (2010). Ice ages—what are they and what causes them? *Utah Geological Survey*. Retrieved March 11, 2015, from http://geology.utah.gov/maps-publications/survey-notes/glad-you-asked/ice-ages-what-are-they-and-what-causes-them/

EUROfusion. (n.d.). *Does fusion give off radiation?* Retrieved September 20, 2014, from http://www.euro-fusion.org/faq/does-fusion-give-off-radiation/

Gleick, J. (1987). *Chaos: Making a new science*. New York: Penguin Books.

Global Warming and the Climate. (n.d.). *The causes of global warming and climate change*. Retrieved October 12, 2014, from http://www.global-warming-and-the-climate.com/index.htm

Goldsmith, D., & Owen, T. (2001). *The search for life in the universe* (p. 96). Hernden, VA: University Science Books.

Hamilton, R. B. (1975). *Comparative behavior of the American Avocet and the Black-necked Stilt (Recurvirostridae)*. Ornithological Monographs, No. 17. Lawrence, KS: American Ornithological Union, Allen Press.

Hamilton, R. B. (2015). Managing the future: Reconciling differences and perceiving truth. In D. G. Nemeth & R. B. Hamilton (Eds.), *Ecopsychology: Advances from the Intersection of psychology and environmental protection*, Volume 1 (pp. 233–274). Santa Barbara, CA: ABC-CLIO.

Hardin, G. (1968). The tragedy of the common. *Science, 162*(3859), 1243–1248.

Hazen, R. M. (2012). *The story of earth: The first 4.5 billion years from stardust to living planet*. London: Penguin Books Ltd.

International Atomic Energy Agency (IAEA). (2014). *International Status and Prospects for Nuclear Power: Report by Director General*. Retrieved September 20, 2014, from http://www.iaea.org/About/Policy/GC/GC58/GC58InfDocuments/English/gc58inf-6_en.pdf

Mehlman, D. (2014). Wind turbines and birds: What's the real story? [Web log post]. The Nature Conservancy, *Cool Green Science*. Retrieved September 25, 2014, from http://blog.nature.org/science/2014/05/28/wind-turbines-bird-mortality-bats-science-impacts/

Molina, M. J., & Rowland, F. S. (1974). Stratospheric sink for chlorofluoromethanes: Chlorine atom-catalysed destruction of ozone. *Nature, 249*, 810–812.

Nemeth, D. G., Albuquerque, J., Garrido, G., Hamilton R., Nemeth, D. F., & Onishi, Y. (2007, September). *Strategies to facilitate biosphere management and lifestyle change. Measures to protect the environment and prevent drastic sequelae of current and future climate changes*. Symposium presented at the 60th Annual United Nations DPI/NGO Conference Midday Workshops, New York.

Nemeth, D. G., Hamilton, R. B., & Kuriansky, J. (2012). *Living in an environmentally traumatized world: Healing ourselves and our planet*. Santa Barbara, CA: Praeger.

Open University. (2001). *Ocean currents*. Oxford: Butterworth-Heinemann.

Patrick, B. A. (2011). *The ten commandments of propaganda*. Palmyra, MI: Goatpower Publishing.

Patten, B. C., Egloff, D. A., & Richardson, T. H. (1975). Total ecosystem model for a cove in Lake Texoma. In B. C. Patten (Ed.), *Systems analysis and simulation in ecology* (pp. 205–421). Salt Lake City, UT: Academic Press.

Peregrine Fund. (n.d.). *Peregrine falcon restoration*. Retrieved September 19, 2014, from http://www.peregrinefund.org/projects/peregrine-falcon

Ryan, P. G., Moore, C. J., van Franeker, J. A., & Moloney, C. L. (2009, July 27). Monitoring the abundance of plastic debris in the marine environment. *Philosophical Transactions of the Royal Society of London, Series B, Biological Sciences, 364*(1526), 1999–2012. doi: 10.1098/rstb.0207. PMCID: PMMC2873010.

Scruton, R. (2012). *How to think seriously about the planet: The case for an environmental conservatism*. New York: Oxford University Press.

Tamarkin, T. (2014). *Fusion, nature's choice for energy (special report)*. Retrieved August 3, 2014, from http://www.inquisitr.com/1369894/

U.S. Environmental Protection Agency (EPA). (n.d.). *Acid rain in New England*. Retrieved September 19, 2014, from http://www.epa.gov/region1/eco/acidrain/history.html

U.S. Environmental Protection Agency (EPA). (n.d.). Ozone—good up high bad nearby. Retrieved September 20, 2014, from http://www.epa.gov/oar/oaqps/gooduphigh/good.html

U.S. Forest Service. (n.d.). *Fire and fuels buildup*. Retrieved September 12, 2014, from http://www.fs.fed.us/publications/policy-analysis/fire-and-fuels-position-paper.pdf

Victor, P. (2013). Herman Daly festschrift: Herman Daly and the steady state economy. Retrieved April 3, 2015, from http://eoearth.org/view/article/153483/

Whaling: A bloody war. (2004, January 3). *The Economist*. Retrieved August 11, 2014, from http://www.economist.com/printedition/2004-01-03

World Nuclear Association. (2014). *Nuclear fusion power*. Retrieved August 3, 2014, from http://www.world-nuclear.org/info/Current-and-Future-Generation/

Zalasiewicz, J., & Williams, M. (2012). *The Goldilocks planet: The four billion year story of earth's climate*. New York: Oxford University Press.

3

Understanding Our Environment

Donald F. Nemeth

We live in a technological age of almost instant global communication—an age where we can travel to distant places in a matter of hours and the far ends of the globe in tens of hours. Our dependence on our physical world for our very existence is often obscured by our apparent ability to master and control our environment. Since its very beginning, the earth has been in a constant state of change, evolving from a lifeless planet to one teeming with living organisms, whose existence was or is sustained by adequate sources of food, water, and proper atmospheric or oceanic and climatic conditions. The alteration of one or more of these factors could lead to catastrophic consequences and the ultimate extinction of a species. Naturally occurring events run the spectrum from slow and progressing through time, to sudden and catastrophic. An understanding of how our physical world operates gives us the means to prepare and possibly minimize the effects of natural events that we do not have the means to control. Natural events can be facilitated by human actions. Events may also occur that are entirely brought about by humans. The actions of humans (e.g., energy consumption, wars, urban development, etc.) on a local and global scale and their consequences on our earth, from the short term to the long term, need to be addressed. It is impossible, however, to touch on every aspect of this subject. Therefore, this topic will be considered selectively. Humans must understand (1) the possible consequences of their actions on our physical world, and (2) why naturally occurring events entirely unrelated to human activity occur. Only in this way can we hope to develop a strategy to minimize human suffering. The ultimate question is, "Will a world altered by human-induced chance be able to sustain life as we know it today?" That is the focus of this chapter.

BACKGROUND

What price are we willing to pay to maintain our standard of living? Is our standard of living sustainable? Are there sufficient natural resources on earth to sustain development in the third world and also allow us to maintain our standard of living? What damage have we already done to our planet? Are the effects already being felt? Will we continue with the status quo without regard to the consequences for future generations? Will we continue to consume natural resources without regard for the consequences on poverty-stricken global regions, where we may be sowing the seeds for future wars, untold human suffering, and degradation of the planet? These and other questions must be addressed if we are to minimizing human suffering on our planet today and for future generations.

The planet we inhabit, earth, is at present our only home. From the earth's beginning some 4.54 billion years ago, it has been in a constant state of change, slowly evolving to its present state. Since the first forms of life appeared some 3.5 billion years ago, living organisms have left their mark and contributed significantly to change. No living beings, however, have had such a profound effect on the earth as have humans. In fact, the time in which we are living is now being referred to as the Anthropocene Epoch of geologic time. The term first proposed by Paul Crutzen (*New York Times*, 2011) in 2000 generally is considered to have begun in the 1800s with the Industrial Revolution. This was the time when humans began to significantly alter the earth's environment and in particular the atmosphere with the production of greenhouse gases. In 1896, Sevante Arrhenis, a Swedish scientist, recognized the potential for increased global average surface temperature from coal burning and the consequential release of carbon dioxide into the atmosphere (Weart, 2011). He proposed that a significant increase in global average temperature would occur over the next 1,000 years (Weart, 2011). Caitlyn Kennedy (2009) reported that, over the last 150 years, the concentration of carbon dioxide in the atmosphere has risen "38 percent higher than the highest value measured for over the previous 800,000 years." LuAnn Dahlman (2014) reported that the earth's global average surface temperature from, 1880 to 2012, has increased by 1.5 degrees F. This may not seem like much for a time span of 132 years. However, the rate of increase is accelerating. Over the last 50 years, the rate increased twice as fast as the previous 50 years (Dahlman, 2014).

How is the average surface temperature determined? Surface temperature measurements are taken all over the globe; "the difference between the observed temperature and the long-term average temperature for each location and date" (Dahlman, 2014) is calculated, and then these values are used to determine an average for the entire globe. What is of significance is that the departure of the average surface temperature from the expected normal is on the increase (Dahlman, 2014).

Planet earth sustains us. Only through an understanding of processes active within the earth, on or near the earth's surface, the oceans and continents, water resources, atmosphere, climate, and biosphere can we hope to manage the earth in a meaningful way. Knowledge of the earth and how it operates is essential in order to make meaningful decisions with acceptable consequences. An understanding of the interconnectivity of all aspects of the earth is essential if we are to succeed in preserving the earth as a livable planet. The consequences of our actions can only be anticipated through knowing the mechanics of natural processes. Without this, we and/or future generations may become nothing more than victims of our actions.

Since the earth's inception, it has undergone constant, unrelenting change. The evolution of planet earth will continue until the end of time, with or without humans. After human beings, some other intelligent being may evolve to find layers of asphalt, plastic, concrete, dispersed metals, and human fossils in the geologic record. The earth has only a finite supply of natural resources. As we use mineable natural resources (i.e., nonrenewable natural resources), what we leave behind and discard will not be concentrated in a recoverable form and will be lost to future generations. With the development of new technology and economic incentives, hopefully, it will become possible to recover and recycle much of what we discard. Our concern, however, should not be with the distant future, but with the present. How do we slow the pace of environmental change?

DISASTERS

Cataclysmic events have occurred on the earth at various geographic locations throughout geologic time. These occurrences, such as earthquakes, tsunamis, floods, volcanic eruptions, meteor impacts, etc., are only disasters when life is involved. Otherwise, they are natural events. In terms of human existence (i.e., life), the causes of disasters may be (1) natural events, (2) human-induced, or (3) a combination of the two. We cannot stop natural events, but we can manage them to minimize their effects. In many cases, a human-generated disaster probably can, with proper precaution, be prevented or minimized. A disaster often sets into motion a chain of events culminating in many localized smaller disastrous events, some due to human oversights and/or miscalculations. Humanity must not only be prepared to deal with sudden catastrophic events, but must also be able to deal with slowly occurring events. The slow, almost imperceptible, contributions of humanity to earth's change in the end, however, may lead to irreversible changes with possible devastating consequences. Sudden catastrophic events may actually be easier to cope with. Their duration in time is limited; whereas, slow, continuous events go on and on over time, obscuring their ultimate effects.

OUR RESTLESS EARTH

Looking at a globe of the world with the continents and oceans, a striking feature is how the bulge of eastern South America appears to fit into the indentation of western Africa. This and other natural occurrences, such as similar rocks of similar age on opposite sides of the Atlantic, appeared to indicate that the continents had split apart. The concept of drifting continents had been proposed by Alfred Wegener in the early twentieth century; but to most people, it was unimaginable for continents to be on the move. With the advances made over the last half century, primarily from geologic oceanographic studies, geophysical studies, and satellite data, the theory of plate tectonics (see USGS, 1999) evolved.

The earth's surface is fractured into gigantic plates that are in motion. Some slide past each other, some collide with each other, while others separate from each other and some descend under neighboring plates. These plates are so vast that they may be composed of both oceanic and continental rocks.

The theory of plate tectonics explains where and why some of the greatest forces released on or near the earth's surface occur—forces that are large enough to build mountains and volcanoes and form deep-ocean trenches. Some forces rupture rocks and form faults along which movement occurs. This results in earthquakes, which send vibrations through the earth. Some forces are great enough to displace rock below the sea to form undersea landslides that sometimes cause tsunamis.

Hawaii

On an August 2013 day, the Hawaiian evening rains were drawing to a close as the sun slowly set over the caldera of Kilauea Volcano (Figure 3.1). As the sky darkened, the orange and red glow of the active summit crater became increasingly intense. Looking over the unobstructed vista, the glowing crater was only a few miles from my hotel window at the Volcano House Hotel. Kilauea Volcano, one of the most active volcanoes in the world, has been considered one of the safest volcanoes in the world; however, there is always danger.

In 1912, the Hawaiian Volcano Observatory (USGS, 2001b), located a short distance from the Volcano House Hotel, was founded as a research facility for the U.S. Geological Survey (USGS) to monitor and study Kilauea and its activity. The volcano has been in continuous activity since January 3, 1983 (USGS, 2009). The two aforementioned facilities are located on the edge of the cliff of Kilauea's caldera and are considered safe. Yet, if these buildings had been located where they now are in 1790 when an explosive eruption occurred, the consequences would have been disastrous. In fact, the eruption occurred as a war party of Hawaiians was crossing the summit. A third of the warriors were killed (Decker, R. & Christiansen, R., 1984) with their foot prints preserved on the summit of the volcano. Unfortunately, the prints are slowly being destroyed by the erosive action of gases (primarily sulfur dioxide) presently being emitted from the summit crater. Most of the time, the prevailing trade winds blow the potentially toxic volcanic gases away from the Volcano House Hotel and the Hawaiian Volcano Observatory. In order to be aware of possible dangerous

Figure 3.1.
The caldera and active summit crater of Kilauea Volcano as seen from the Hawaiian Volcano Observatory, August 2013. (Photo by Donald F. Nemeth, PhD)

condition, the National Park Service does constantly monitor atmospheric conditions and closes sections of the park that they deem as unsafe.

The volcanic activity that built Kilauea Volcano is estimated to have begun some 300,000 to 600,000 years ago with the source of the molten rock (i.e., magma) being some 36 miles below the surface (USGS, 2009). All of the islands comprising the state of Hawaii are volcanic in origin. From the big island of Hawaii northwestward, the age of each island increased, with the oldest at the end of the archipelago. With each succeeding island, the volcanoes progress from active to inactive to extinct. The Pacific Plate under the state of Hawaii is slowly drifting northwest, carrying the islands built on it away from a hot spot deep within the earth. The hot spot has remained relatively stationary through time in its geographic position, whereas the Pacific Plate has been moving at a rate of 2.8–3.5 inches per year (USGS, 2001a). As the Pacific Plate carries it northwest, Kilauea one day will be cut off from its molten source. The newest of all of the Hawaiian volcanoes is actively forming south of Kilauea in the sea out of sight below the Pacific Ocean's surface. The summit is some 3,000 feet below present sea level (USGS, 2001a).

VOLCANOES AND EARTHQUAKES

The Hawaiian Islands, located in the middle of the Pacific Ocean 2,000 miles from the nearest landmass, are a physiographic feature built on the Pacific tectonic plate. The edges of the Pacific Basin are where plates come in contact with neighboring plates. This leads to the formation of active fault systems that follow the entire circuitous edge of the basin with many zones of active volcanism. Volcanic and seismic (i.e., earthquake) activity is so prevalent that the area is referred to as "The Ring of Fire." It extends from Chile along the west coast of South America, along the west coast of North America, through the Aleutian Islands, along the coast of Japan, through Indonesia and all the way to New Zealand. It is within this zone that, "about 90 percent of the world's earthquakes occur" (USGS, 2012a). For example, earthquakes occurred in: Chile, February 2010, magnitude 8.8; Chile, April 2014, magnitude 8.2; Northridge, California, January 1994, magnitude 6.7; Fukushima, Japan, March 2011, magnitude 9.0; and New Zealand, February 2011, magnitude 6.3.

The Pacific Northwest of the United States is within "The Ring of Fire." On a clear day the Cascade Volcanoes can be seen from the large metropolitan cities of Portland and Seattle.

In order to protect life and property, the volcanoes of the northwest are continually being monitored by the USGS as part of the Volcano Hazards Program. Continuous date collection is conducted using instruments permanently located in remote areas near the volcanoes. In some areas, extensive grid systems of instruments are in place, measuring swelling of the volcano's surface, emission of volcanic gases, and earthquakes (USGS, 2013c). The eruption of Mount St. Helens in 1980 is a warning that other Northwest sleeping giants pose a substantial risk (e.g., Mount Shasta in California, Mount Hood in Oregon). Mount Rainier, located in close geographic proximity to the populous Puget Sound, Seattle area in the state of Washington, presents a particularly ominous situation. Mount Rainier (elevation 14,410 feet) is the highest of all the cascade volcanoes. It glows in its picture-perfect white appearance of glacial cover. Such glaciers provide a beneficial steady, source of water during the warm portion of the year for downslope agriculture and domestic use. If a major eruption were to occur, these same glaciers could be the source of extensive mud and debris flows with unbelievably destructive force.

The next most active region extends from the Mediterranean to northern India (USGS, 2012a). Within this belt, repeated earthquakes and volcanic disasters have occurred, with the most famous one occurring in AD 79 at Pompeii, Italy. The eruption of Mount Vesuvius destroyed a thriving city having a population of between 10,000 and 20,000 people (Stewart, 2006). There was forewarning of the potential disaster with approximately 80 percent of the population evacuating; approximately 2,000 people remained and perished from the suffocating gases and ash (Stewart, 2006). The population of Pompeii did not know that a Bronze Age settlement in the same area had been destroyed 2,000 years earlier (Stewart, 2006). Today, some 3.5 million people live in the area surrounding Vesuvius, which continues to be one of the most dangerous volcanoes in the world (Stewart, 2006). Christopher Small and Terry Naumann (2002) reported that in 1990, 9% of the world's population (455 million people) lived within 60 miles of historically active volcanoes. Today, almost a decade and a half later, the percentage is likely to be even greater.

Another active zone is in the Caribbean, where the Caribbean Plate meets with the North American and South American Plates. Along this complex boundary in the Lesser Antilles, Mount Pelee on the island of Martinique exploded on May 8, 1902, with an eruption reminiscent of the fury and devastation of the AD 79 eruption at Pompeii (Reed, 2002). For months prior to the catastrophic eruption, there were signs of eminent danger as exhibited by the development of increasing numbers of fissures on the volcano from which volcanic gases were escaping (i.e., fumarole activity). Two weeks prior to the main eruption, explosive eruptions of ash occurred on the summit (San Diego State University, n.d.) forcing people to flee parts of the island. Most of them relocated to the city of St. Pierre, increasing the population from about 20,000 to an estimated 28,000 (Reed, 2002). Government officials did not heed the forewarnings and declared the city safe. Their decision was based entirely on an ulterior motive. A forthcoming election was planned for May 11, and the government officials knew they could sway the election in their favor if the financially less able were forced to remain in the city and vote (Reed, 2002). On May 8, the volcano exploded, sending a suffocating cloud of gas and ash over the city, killing an estimated 28,000 people with only two survivors. One survivor—a jailed prisoner, subsequently pardoned—spent the rest of his life with the Barnum and Bailey Circus exhibiting his scars (Reed, 2002). This eruption alerted scientists of the need to study volcanoes and spurred the movement to establishing volcanic monitoring facilities, such as the Hawaiian Volcano Observatory at Kilauea Volcano (Reed, 2002).

Global Impact of Volcanic Eruptions

A volcanic eruption can have an impact far beyond the immediate location of the volcano. It can disrupt air transport of both passengers and goods, as occurred in 2010 with the eruption of the Icelandic volcano Eyjafjallajokull that sent a cloud of ash into the atmosphere. This presented a major threat to the safe operation of jet aircraft and disrupted air travel across the North Atlantic for a week (Calder, 2014). As of September 2014, another Icelandic volcano, Bardarbunga, was exhibiting increased earthquake activity that may be a precursor to an eruption and another disruption of jet aircraft (Calder, 2014).

Volcanoes also have the potential to bring about climate change. Two important gases are emitted by volcanoes. One, carbon dioxide, can warm the climate; the other, sulfur dioxide, can cool the climate (USGS, 2012c). The amount of carbon dioxide contributed to the atmosphere by volcanoes when compared to that contributed by humans is considered insignificant (USGS, 2012c) and thus is not a major factor in climate change. The other important gas, sulfur dioxide, is known to have brought about cooling of the earth surface. In 1991, the eruption of Mount Pinatubo in the Philippines cooled the earth surface by about 1 degree F for a period of about 3 years (USGS, 2012c). It is reported that the ash-and-gas cloud caused about $100 million in damages to jet aircraft flying far to the west of the volcano (USGS, 2005).

EARTHQUAKES

The boundaries of the earth's plates are where movement is occurring. This is where the plate edges are being splintered into a series of active faults, forming fault zones that delineate the plate boundaries. Volcanoes may or may not be present. The fault zones, however, extend for tens, hundreds, and/or thousands of miles. Their almost-incomprehensible extent places a large proportion of humanity at risk.

Haiti and Chile

Haiti Earthquake, 2010 Compared with the Chile Earthquake, 2010

The volcanism at Mount Pelee occurs along one small segment of the Caribbean, North American plate boundary. Westward along this boundary, the Caribbean Plate is sliding past the North American Plate. It is along this boundary that the destructive magnitude 7.0 Haiti earthquake of 2010 occurred. The quake left an estimated 230,000–316,000 dead and missing with 1.5 million homeless (CNN, 2013). The *Christian Science Monitor* notes an ironic fact that the fault system in Haiti was little studied (Spotts, 2010). This can be attributed directly to the social and economic conditions in Haiti and the undesirable conditions that researchers must endure there while they conduct geological studies (Spotts, 2010) there. The unforeseen consequences of poverty led to a lack of information that could have assisted in mitigating the deplorable situations brought about by the earthquake.

There were historical records of major earthquakes occurring in this area, e.g., 1860, 1770, and 1751 (USGS, 2010). The USGS (2010) reported that, after the 1751 earthquake, "the authorities required building with wood and forbade building with masonry." Poor construction added significantly to the Haitian disaster. When the past is forgotten, complacency is bound to occur. This is especially true in poverty-stricken areas where immediate needs must come first.

Professor Stephen A. Nelson (2013) of Tulane University in New Orleans, Louisiana, in his outline of earthquake risk said, "Earthquakes don't kill people, buildings do." The 2010 Haitian earthquake resulted in a great loss of life.

Almost five years later, the recovery efforts are still ongoing. The aftermath of the 2010 Chilean earthquake with a magnitude of 8.8 was quite different. The death toll was significantly lower, officially listed as 720 (UN, 2010). Within one year, the Chilean government reported that all infrastructure had been repaired (Long, 2011). Poverty-stricken victims of the quake were, however, still suffering as they lived in inadequate makeshift shelters, with cold showers and no indoor cooking facilities (Long, 2011).

China

Halcheng Earthquake, 1975

In 1975, a magnitude 7.3 earthquake occurred in Halcheng, China, a city of one million people. Many months prior to the big quake, ground elevation changes were noted, water levels in wells fluctuated, some animals behaved strangely, and minor earthquakes (i.e., foreshocks) were occurring in increasing frequency (USGS, 2012b). This led wise officials to order an evacuation of the city, preventing a great loss of life. In urban areas, the devastating effects of a major earthquake and subsequent loss of life is greatly increased. This can be attributed to the large number of people concentrated in a small area and poor or inadequate construction.

Sichuan Earthquake, China, 2008

Today we can move mountains with modern machinery. We sometimes forget that thousands of years ago, humans had devised methods of engineering structures that rival today's technology. In 256 BC, the Chinese constructed a flood control and irrigation system at Du Jiang Yan (Chongneng, 2004, p. 95). The system, which is still operating today, turned the Chengdu plain into a productive, thriving agricultural area. The area surrounding the control structures were so revered by the local residents that many temples were built there. These temples stood for almost 1,000 years, only occasionally suffering some damage from seismic activity. On May 12, 2008, however, most of the temples were damaged, some severely, by the magnitude 7.9 Sichuan earthquake (Figure 3.2). The adjacent city of Du Jiang Yan, located near the epicenter of the earthquake, sustained extensive damage with a great loss of life. I traveled down one of the major avenues of the city in October 2008. At first, it appeared that there had not been much damage. The street was lined with buildings. When I looked into the buildings, it became apparent that only the front of the structures had survived. Beyond the facades, almost complete devastation was visible.

The presence of 1,000-year-old temples would lead one to think that they were not in danger. If you are in an earthquake-prone (i.e., seismically active) area, however, you are always at risk. In human terms, 1,000 years is a long time.

Figure 3.2.
An ancient temple at Du Jiang Yan damaged by the 2008 Sichuan earthquake undergoing repairs. Photo taken October 2008. The temple is part of the Mount Qingcheng and Du Jiang Yan Irrigation System, UNESCO World Heritage Site. (Photo by Donald F. Nemeth, PhD)

In geologic time, it is hardly noticeable. What appears to be stabile now may not be when viewed in respect to geologic time.

For 50 million years, the Indian tectonic plate has been colliding with the Eurasian plate (CIT, 2008), pushing up the Himalayas and the mountain ranges of Tibet and Sichuan. The Sichuan earthquake was particularly severe because the epicenter was located only six miles below the surface (CIT, 2008). This increased the shaking at surface levels. The duration of shaking was also increased by the thick accumulation of sediment underlying the Chengdu plain (CIT, 2008). The devastating quake left 88,000 dead or missing with 400,000 injured and 5 million homeless (UNICEF, 2010).

Japan

One common factor that the previously discussed Chilean earthquake shares with the yet-to-be-discussed Northridge earthquake and now-to-be-considered Japanese earthquake of 2011 is that they all occur in the "Ring of Fire" surrounding the Pacific basin. The seismic event of March 11, 2011, the Tohoku earthquake with a magnitude of 9.0, ranks fourth among the most powerful earthquakes to occur since 1900 (USGS, 2014b). The earthquake's epicenter was located offshore and generated a tsunami 133 feet high (Onishi, 2012). The toll taken by the quake and tsunami is reported to be 15,880 dead, 2,994 missing and 6,135 injured (Harner, 2013). Compounding the consequences of this seismic event was, and still is, the meltdown of the reactors at the Fukushima Daiichi nuclear power plant.

The earthquake and aftershocks were a natural consequence of Japan's location where the Pacific Plate is descending (i.e., subducting) under the Eurasian Plate. The likelihood of an earthquake occurring under these conditions is great; however, the magnitude of the quake was beyond expectations.

The aforementioned meltdown of the nuclear reactors was a human-induced tragedy. After the quake, there was no way to generate the electrical power necessary to cool the reactors at the Fukushima Nuclear Power Plant. This failure ultimately led to the meltdown of the reactors and the release of radioactive material that contaminates the surrounding land and ocean. Even though barriers were constructed to prevent contaminated water from entering the Pacific Ocean, they have not been completely effective. The prevailing oceanic currents ultimately carried the contaminants toward North America. Although this does not pose a significant danger, it does illustrate how the consequences of a disaster in one part of the world can be felt far removed from the initial problem.

United States

In the United States, it is estimated that a significant seismic risk exists for 75 million people in 39 of the 50 states (USGS, 2013a). You do not have to live directly on an active fault to be impacted. The natural physical conditions (i.e., not due to the actions of humans) affecting how severely an area is impacted will depend upon the magnitude of the quake, the distance from the epicenter (i.e., the point on the earth's surface above the point of movement within the earth) the depth at which movement occurs (i.e., focus), and the underlying soil, rock, and other geologic conditions.

In order to protect life and property in a seismically active area such as California, federal, state, public, and private institutions conduct ongoing research to develop the technology to predict earthquakes. The USGS and other organizations use a variety of instruments, such as: (1) seismographs, which measure vibrations of the earth; (2) magnetometers, which measure local magnetic field variations; (3) pore pressure monitors, which measure changes in pressure in deep boreholes near faults; (4) strain meters, which measure crustal strain near active faults; and (5) tilt meters, which measure ground tilt (USGS, 2013b). In addition to the aforementioned instruments, with GPS technology, the precise location of a point on the earth's surface can be determined to within a fraction of an inch, at any given time. Comparing the initial geographic location of a point with its subsequent GPS locations over time, the rate and direction of the point's movement can be determined (USGS, 2014a). Closely monitoring the data collected from these instruments does give us some indication of what is happening along fault zones. At our present state of technology, it is not possible to predict the magnitude and timing of an earthquake. As happened in 1975 at Halcheng, China, there are times when we do have an indication that one may occur.

The San Andreas Fault (a fault zone) runs for more than 800 miles (BLM, 2012) through the state of California, making it one of the longest faults in North America. It cuts through both the Los Angeles and the San Francisco metropolitan areas. Los Angeles County, in the southern part of the state, in 2013 was reported to have reached a population in excess of 10 million (Gazzar, 2013). California is now the most populous state in the United States, with a reported 2010 population in excess of 37 million. In 2013, it was estimated to be near 38.5 million (World Population Review, 2014). It can possibly be said that every person in California is at risk of a seismic event.

Northridge, California, Earthquake, 1994

The most recent major earthquake that occurred in the lower 48 states of the United States was the 1994 Northridge earthquake, with a magnitude of 6.7, a death toll of 57, and losses estimated at $20 billion (Kandel, 2014). A classic example of how modern engineering and proper design can minimize damage during an earthquake is the University of Southern California's Northridge hospital building, an eight-story, steel superstructure. The building design is such that it was not anchored directly to the underlying rock. Instead, its foundation consists of seismic isolators that allow the entire building to move and absorb the seismic vibrations (Celebi, 1996). The building design performed so well that Celebi concluded that the structure would do well in earthquakes of greater magnitude than the Northridge quake.

Possible Human-Induced Earthquakes

There has been debate regarding a possible link between the Sichuan earthquake and the Zipingpu Dam, located less than four miles from the epicenter of the quake (Naik & Oster, 2009). A definitive connection between the two has not been established. After the construction of Hoover Dam, however, several earthquakes occurred that correlated with the seasonal fluctuations in Lake Mead's water levels (Hiltzik, 2010). Increased frequency of earthquake activity has also been reported at the Three Gorges Dam in China (Adams, 2011), commencing with the initial filling of the reservoir. In Colorado, the drilling of a 12,000-foot well at the Rocky Mountain Arsenal and the injection of waste water triggered a series of earthquakes in the 1960s ("Earthquakes triggered by humans in Colorado—a background paper by the Colorado Geological Survey," 2012).

Protecting Life and Property

We may not be able to predict the time, magnitude, and location of a destructive earthquake, but we do know where they are most likely to occur, and we do have lines of defense. One way is to use the ongoing, continually advancing technology of earthquake engineering in the construction and maintenance of buildings, bridges, and other structures. A wealth of information is available from organizations such as: the National Information Service for Earthquake Engineering, University of California, Berkeley and the National Earthquake Hazards Reduction Program (NEHRP) funded by the U.S. government. The implementation of the technology of earthquake engineering into the design and continued maintenance of structures will greatly reduce the impact of major seismic events and the loss of life as seen when comparing the Chile earthquake of 2010 with the Haiti earthquake of the same year. Earthquake engineering technology, if utilized in building construction, would greatly minimize the effects of seismic events and the resulting human suffering and possible death.

People also need to know how to react when a seismic event happens—whether it happens when they are indoors, outdoors, driving, shopping, or whatever they are doing. Currently in the states of California and Hawaii, earthquake drills, called "The Great Shake Out," are periodically conducted. The urgency for people in seismically active areas to participate in such drills cannot be overstated.

THE ATMOSPHERE

The atmosphere is connected in some way with almost everything occurring on the surface of the earth (Muller, 2012). It is the zone of weather. It is where thunderstorms, hurricanes, typhoons, and tornadoes form. It is where precipitation, rain, and snow occur. The severity of these events, or the lack of these events, can have profound effects on humanity.

Without the atmosphere and water in its three states (i.e., gas, liquid, and solid), there would be no weather on earth. On earth, heating and cooling, freezing and thawing, and precipitation in the form of rain and snow are the main means by which rocks are decomposed mechanically and chemically to form sediments, like the sand on a beach, and/or the first stages of soil formation. Without soil and/or the atmosphere, neither plants nor animals could exist on the terrestrial portion of the earth. The atmosphere is also interconnected with the oceans. The atmosphere transmits heat to the oceans. As the chemical composition of the atmosphere changes, so does that of the oceans. A portion of the carbon dioxide, which man has introduced into the atmosphere, is absorbed by the oceans. As this happens, the oceans become more acidic, and this directly impacts the growth of coral and many other marine organisms.

The climate of the western coast of Europe as we know it today is partially dependent upon the warming influence of the Gulf Stream. This current, originating in the Gulf of Mexico, is driven by the wind as a surface current transporting warm water northward. The flow of the current, however, is part of a complex circulation system encompassing flow through the deeper parts of the Atlantic basin. Warming at high latitudes, with increased rainfall and melt water from glacial ice, could change the temperature and density (i.e., weight) of the surrounding water, and possibly change how the Gulf Stream operates. This could have profound negative effects on the climate of western Europe and eastern North America.

We have used the atmosphere as a dumping ground for our wastes. We transport materials and people and run our machines on fossil fuels and release the exhaust into the atmosphere. We burn fossil fuels to produce energy and usually discharge the wastes, greenhouse gases, into the atmosphere. Greenhouse gases trap heat, and potentially warm the earth.

The two most abundant greenhouse gases emitted into the atmosphere by human activity are carbon dioxide and methane (EPA, 2014b). The physical properties of these two gases differ in their overall effect upon the atmosphere and their long-term consequences regarding climate change. Methane is a stronger greenhouse gas than carbon dioxide; however, its life in the atmosphere is shorter, lasting about 12 years (EPA, 2014a). Its impact on global warming is 20 times greater than carbon dioxide (EPA, 2014b). Carbon dioxide, on the other hand, can remain in the atmosphere for an indefinite time. The U.S. Environmental Protection Agency (EPA) (2014a) ranks carbon dioxide as being the number-one gas for 100-year global warming potential.

Muller (2012) notes that over the last 800,000 years, there have been at least five major ice ages. These periods of cold were separated by warm periods, some as warm or warmer than today. These periods of climate change were natural events, not man-induced. Their causes are under investigation. Current theory attributes these changes to astronomical events, such as variations in the earth's orbit (IPCC, 2007). Currently, as stated at the beginning of this chapter, global average surface temperatures are on the rise. Fluctuations in average global surface temperatures are to be expected regionally and with time. However, within the lower contiguous 48 states of the United States, the EPA's graphs show an overall upwards trend from 1998 to 2013 (EPA, 2014b). This is occurring in unison with an increase in carbon dioxide being contributed by the action of man. How do we know what the earth's atmospheric composition was in the past? This can be and is being determined by studying air trapped in ice, and this is how it happened.

Snow falling on the Greenland ice cap accumulates with air trapped between the snowflakes. Over time, the snowflakes are compressed by the overlying snow cover and crystallized into glacial ice. Not all of the trapped air is squeezed out as the flakes are compressed. Some remain as tiny microscopic air bubbles that preserve the enclosed air with the atmospheric composition at the time of formation. Dr. Celia Separt and her colleagues studied 1,600-foot-long ice cores extracted from the Greenland ice cap (Stromberg, 2013). They found that, over a period going back 2,000 years, the methane concentrations increased and decreased with human historical events. At the time when the Roman Empire in Europe and the Han Empire in China were at their height (i.e., both at approximately the same time), methane emissions were high. With the fall of these empires, emissions decreased. Methane concentrations then increased with the increase in population during the Middle Ages.

For more than 2,000 years, human activities have been altering the atmosphere in a detectable way. About 60% of the methane in the atmosphere is human-produced (EPA, 2012). Humans produce methane from (1) industry, (2) agriculture, and (3) domestic waste. Livestock, for food production, accounts for the largest source of human induced methane (EPA, 2012).

SOME CONSEQUENCES OF A WARMER EARTH AND MAN'S EFFORT TO PREVENT CHANGE

Increase in Sea Level

As the atmosphere warms, the oceans warm and expand. A warmer atmosphere causes glaciers and ice caps to melt, releasing water into the oceans. Sea levels rise. Rising sea levels affect inhabited areas at and/or near present sea level. Major cities of the world, mostly ports, are either partly or totally at risk.

Here are some examples of cities at risk:

New Orleans, Louisiana

Even before Hurricane Katrina struck in 2005, the city of New Orleans, was considered as "one of the greatest American natural disasters waiting to happen" (Keim & Muller, 2009). The city, built on the delta of the Mississippi River, was initially founded on the high ground of the river's natural levee. As the city developed, however, it expanded into less desirable swamp and marsh locations. In order to protect it from flooding, manmade levees were constructed. This allowed the soils to dry out and subside, thereby only compounding the problem that the entire region is subsiding, a natural consequence of the compaction of the loose deltaic sediments and the fact that the whole area is slipping toward the Gulf of Mexico (Dokka, Sella, & Dixon, 2006). The only way the area will remain above sea level is by allowing the river to flood and deposit its sediment load, a totally unacceptable solution in an urban area. As of 1994, only 45% of the city of New Orleans was estimated to be above sea level (Keim & Muller, 2009). The vulnerability of New Orleans to hurricanes was further increased with the dredging of navigation channels through the surrounding marsh to facilitate the transport of supplies and personnel for the oil and gas industry.

Also, a major shipping channel, constructed to shorten the distance to the Gulf of Mexico, exposed New Orleans to the direct impact of Hurricane Katrina. Winds, storms, and hurricanes have expanded these channels to the point where, once there was marsh, now open water exists. The buffering effect, provided by the swamp and marsh environment, is continually decreasing, and the city is increasingly exposed to the direct impact of storms.

Hurricane Katrina's lasting effect upon New Orleans and coastal Louisiana is and was the migration of inhabitants northward away from the coast to regions that will be impacted less by future hurricanes. The same scenario happened after the great Galveston Hurricane of 1909 (Nemeth, 2013), with a large proportion of the population relocating to the more protected area of present-day Houston, which is now the fourth-largest city in the United States.

New Orleans is a city that obtains its needed fresh water supply from the Mississippi River. The discharge of the river is usually at its highest in the spring months due to snow melt and rains occurring upstream in the midwestern states. Its lowest discharge is most commonly in the fall. At this time of low discharge, a wedge of heavier salt water intrudes upstream under the lighter fresh water flowing towards the Gulf of Mexico. As sea levels rise, this wedge of salt water can intrude further upstream and persist for a longer period of time, jeopardizing the city water supply. Without adequate fresh water, a city cannot survive. The only solution is to find an alternate source.

Miami, Florida

Miami, Florida, is another city that is at extreme risk of rising seas. The rock underlying the city is an extremely porous limestone. No barrier can be constructed to prevent the sea from invading the city. If any structure is attempted, the sea would flow under it and through the underlying limestone like a sieve (Folger, 2013).

As sea level rises, not only is the site of the city at risk, but also its supply of fresh water. Miami's water supply is surface water that must be protected from salt water intrusion. With increasing sea levels, salt water can intrude further and further inland and displace the city's freshwater supply.

Satisfying Our Energy Needs

Nuclear Energy

A vast source of energy, one greater than ever imagined, became reality on July 16, 1945, when the first atomic bomb was tested over the New Mexico desert (Gale & Hauser, 1988). The fission (i.e., splitting apart) of atoms had been achieved in a device of mass destruction. On November 1, 1952, the United States tested the first hydrogen bomb. A device that uses the fission of atoms to achieve, among other things, the release of the extreme heat necessary for the fusion (i.e., joining) of atoms. These bombs are also referred to as thermonuclear weapons. It is estimated that a hydrogen bomb is possibly as much as 1,000 times stronger than an atomic bomb (Fox News, 2003). The United States, Russia, Britain, France, and China all possess hydrogen bombs (Fox News, 2003). Without doubt, humans now have the means to destroy themselves.

One of the beneficial effects of nuclear reactions is the release of heat that can be used to heat water to produce steam to turn turbines for generating electricity. In the United States as of 2011, there were 104 nuclear reactors generating high-level nuclear waste (NRDC, 2011). High-level nuclear waste is so lethal that if you stood one yard from a 10-year-old spent fuel rod, you would die within a week (USNRC, 2002). At most nuclear power plants, this waste is currently being temporally stored on site. As of yet, no permanent disposal site has been established. Plutonium, one of the components of the waste, must be isolated from humanity for 250,000 years (Martinez, Kupfer, Thoms, Smith, & Kolb, 1975).

Naturally occurring salt deposits have been considered as possible sites for the disposal and storage of nuclear waste. Salt has many physical characteristics that make naturally occurring deposits attractive (Winterle et al., 2012). It is elastic (i.e., it will not fracture if an earthquake occurs). It is not porous (i.e., water will not flow through it). A possible disadvantage is that salt will dissolve in water.

In the 1970s, at Louisiana State University's Institute for Environmental Studies, I was associated with a team of investigators studying Louisiana salt domes as possible sites for nuclear waste disposal. The salt domes of North Louisiana are 3 to 10 miles in diameter and extend downward 15,000 feet (Martinez et al., 1975). At this depth is the feeder salt bed from which salt was pushed upward as a conical mass through a zone of weakness in the enclosing sediments. In order for these salt domes to be considered as a disposal site, it was necessary to establish that the salt was no longer moving and that the salt was not being actively dissolved by groundwater.

Finding sites that have the necessary physical qualities to isolate nuclear waste is only one of the major hurdles that must be surmounted in an effort to dispose of nuclear waste. People do not want nuclear waste stored in or transported across their property, especially in Louisiana. Louisiana has enacted a legal statute (Louisiana Laws, 2009) that severely restrict future use of salt domes as disposal sites. If we are to use nuclear energy, we must find a way to properly dispose of the waste in a manner that will not jeopardize future generations. To date, a politically acceptable solution has yet to be found.

Nuclear plant accidents have occurred. The most serious in the United States was in 1979, when the Three Mile Island reactor near Middletown, Pennsylvania, partially melted down (USNRC, 2014). The containment structure withstood the meltdown and little effect was felt outside of the plant (USNRC, 2014). This, however, was not the case when the accidents occurred at Chernobyl, Ukraine, in 1986, and Fukushima, Japan, in 2011. Human error was a direct cause of the Chernobyl accident (Onishi, Voitsekhovich, & Zheleznyak, 2007) and Three Mile Island. Fukushima was caused by a combination of factors: earthquake, tsunami, design flaws, and human error. The effects of the Chernobyl and Fukushima disasters were severe contamination of air, water, and soil.

If the containment structure fails when a nuclear plant accident occurs, the radioactive contaminants will be released into the atmosphere to be distributed by the winds. Downwind, the contaminants will either settle out or be washed out by precipitation. Once settled, the contaminants can settle in water and be carried downstream. Soil, streams, lakes, and groundwater can become contaminated.

Is the risk of radioactive contamination with its long-term effects on the environment and humanity worth using nuclear energy as an alternative to fossil fuels? The fact that we do not have an acceptable means of disposing of the waste and protecting future generations from its possible effects should be enough to question its use. We have other sources of clean energy, such as wind, solar, tidal, etc., which all can, in some way, negatively impact the environment. None of these, however, have the lasting, long-term impact of nuclear contamination.

Gulf of Mexico BP Oil Spill

On April 20, 2010, one of the greatest human-induced environmental disasters occurred with the blowout of a British Petroleum (BP) exploratory well in the deep waters (i.e., almost 5,000 feet) of the Gulf of Mexico.

Petroleum companies are continually exploring for new sources of oil and gas. As the shallower waters (i.e., 200–500 feet) of the Gulf of Mexico are explored and fields are developed and depleted of hydrocarbons, the next logical locations to explore are in the deeper waters where geophysical data indicate that production is probable. The technology had been developed and, if used wisely, allows drilling in these environments. This, however, cannot be done without some outside regulatory agency (e.g., governmental) monitoring drilling practices to establish that proper safety procedures are maintained.

In the case of BP's Deepwater Horizon rig disaster, proper procedures were not followed. The ultimate goal was to complete the well as quickly as possible to minimize cost and maximize profit. Taking shortcuts to accomplish this resulted in an explosion that caused the loss of 11 lives with a reported 210 million barrels of oil flowing into the Gulf of Mexico (CNN, 2014) over a period of almost three months. As of 2014, the ultimate effect upon the coastline of the Gulf of Mexico from Texas to Florida is still unknown. The consequences on the ecosystem of the coastal area and the marine environments may not be known for decades. In order to remove the oil slick from the surface waters, two techniques were used, one isolating areas of the oil slick and burning, the other scattering a dispersant agent. The dispersant agent removed the oil from the surface and distributed it throughout the water column; thus, removing the oil from sight. The dispersant was also injected at the point on the sea floor where oil was entering the gulf water. This again further distributed the oil through the water column (Onishi, 2012). We, however, do not know what the long-term effects of the chemical agent will be on the ecosystem. CNN (2014) reports that, on September 4, 2014, a federal judge ruled that BP was "grossly negligent" in their handling of procedures prior to the 2010 disaster.

In the summer of 2010, as I stood on the boardwalk leading to the beach at Grand Isle, Louisiana, I felt deeply saddened and deprived. The beach was closed to the public due to cleanup efforts to remove the oil that was being washed ashore. I know this was necessary in order for the operation to proceed safely; however, as I thought about it, I came to the realization that my feelings could hardly compare with that of the people who had lost so much—the people who lost loved ones, the people who lost their livelihoods, the people who became ill from the floating oil near their homes. Can any amount of financial compensation ever be adequate? Can we ever measure the cost of the wildlife lost, both onshore and offshore, and the damage to the ecosystem of the marshes and beaches?

An Episode of Past Climate Change

A major change occurred in the earth's atmosphere 56 million years ago at the boundary between the Paleocene and Eocene epochs of geologic time. At this time, for some unknown reason, the earth's atmosphere received a great influx of carbon followed by a gradual addition. The total addition of carbon is estimated to have been equivalent to the total carbon in all remaining fossil fuels (Kunzig, 2011). This event occurred long before any humans existed and therefore could not be attributed to human activity. It took the earth 150,000 years before this carbon was reabsorbed and a state of equilibrium was again achieved with the climate (Kunzig, 2011).

The addition of the carbon led to an earth warmer than today. From the fossil record we know that this warming led to mass extinction of many Pliocene species (i.e., living organisms) followed by the rise of new species in the Eocene. Can this be what we may expect as the earth warms due to our present addition of greenhouse gases to the atmosphere?

One possible source of the carbon is methane hydrate, an ice-like solid that occurs on or below the sea floor. This substance is only stable under the proper pressure and temperature conditions. The positive aspect of hydrated methane is that it may become a source of energy for the future (Alley, 2011). The negative aspect of hydrated methane is that, if by some natural mechanism it was to be released from the deep ocean depth, it would be a major contributor to further global warming, although the likelihood of this happening is considered remote (Alley, 2011).

HUMANITY'S EARLY ANCESTORS

Possibly the oldest known human-like fossils (i.e., hominid) ever found occurred 25 miles west of Johannesburg, South Africa, at the Sterkfontein quarry and cave. In the surrounding region, 40 known fossil locals have been recognized, with only 13 being investigated (Cosi et al., 2009). These sites have yielded over 550 hominid fossils (i.e., *Australopithecus africanus*), with some having an age of as much as 3.5 million years. The first evidence of the use of fire, some 1.5 million years ago, is also found here.

The scientific evidence gained from the hominid fossils found at Sterkfontein and nearby environs is considered of utmost importance to the evolutionary history of early humankind and ultimately modern humans. The area has thus been designated by UNESCO as a World Heritage Site, "The Cradle of Humankind" (UNESCO, 2011)

In September 2014, on a visit to South Africa, I visited two sites, Maropeng and Sterkfontein cave, at "The Cradle of Humankind." Maropeng has a museum that not only presents information on the fossil finds, but also has an amusement-type boat ride that gives a synopsis of important events occurring during the geologic history of the earth. In addition, the museum presents questions regarding where humankind may be headed in the future.

One of the most exciting aspects of the visit was descending into the Sterkfontein cave and actually experiencing the environment in which some of the hominid fossils are found. The caverns at Sterkfontein, like other limestone caverns around the world, formed over millions of years, with the dolomitic limestone being dissolved away by water producing a multiple of chambers at various levels below the regional surface. As you go through the cavern, in one or two areas you encounter a shaft of daylight penetrating the darkness of the cave. Here, a sinkhole had formed above your present location. The chamber's ceiling has collapsed and, formed an opening to the outside world. Above on the surface, I can imagine a hominid traversing through the forest a few million years ago, not aware that the vegetation concealed the opening he or she was about to step into, falling into the cave, and having no means of escape. The hominid falls on the debris that previously fell when the sinkhole was formed, dies, and the remains are cemented together and preserved as groundwater seeps through the breccia depositing its dissolved calcium carbonate. It is within these breccia (i.e., rock made up of broken fragments) occurring at various locations within the cave that the fossils of hominids and fauna were found.

CONCLUDING THOUGHTS

From a simple African beginning, humankind has multiplied to 7 billion people. The number continues to grow. Humankind has become the master of the environment, altering the atmosphere, the land, and the sea. Can we continue on this path, or will we be headed to a fate like occurred at the Paleocene-Eocene boundary?

The Arctic is warming faster than any other part of the world. Permanently frozen ground (i.e., permafrost) is defrosting. The defrosting ground constitutes a vast storehouse of carbon (Nemeth, 2012). This presents a danger in that greenhouses gases will be and are being released into the atmosphere. This further enhances warming potential.

Alpine glaciers are receding in many parts of the world. Alpine glaciers are a storehouse of water, which is slowly released during the warm summer months as melting occurs and provides a dependable water supply for areas such as the Pacific Northwest (Onishi, 2012) of the United States and parts of China. As the glaciers melt and are not replenished during the winter months, needed summer runoff will become less dependable.

The world as we know it today is facing a multitude of problems. These problems will be exacerbated as the world's population grows. With decrease in land area due to rising sea levels, desertification of some areas, lack of adequate water supply, lack of productive agriculture regions, the spread of disease, etc., the pressures on society will mount with possible resulting conflicts. It is possible that desperate people will do desperate things that will further destroy needed natural resources.

In our efforts to harness greener sources of energy, have we looked at the consequence to our environment of our actions? These unknown consequences must be determined, and we must be willing to retreat if our actions result in further degradation of our environment.

Climate change in the past has occurred over a long period of time. Plants and animals had time to migrate to regions that were conducive to their survival. Today, climate is changing rapidly. There may not be enough time to migrate. Even if there is time, animals and plants at high latitudes (e.g., near the Arctic Ocean) may not have a suitable habitat to move to because that habitat may no longer exist or be inaccessible. Avenues of migration may have been disrupted by human development, especially in heavily populated urban regions (Hamilton, 2012). Even if a species has the time to move to a more favorable environment, the needed corridors may no longer exist or can no longer be provided because of patterns of land use and ownership.

Through conservation methods, we attempt to reestablish wildlife areas. Hamilton (2012) reports that the final stage in forest development (i.e., climax), when achieved under natural conditions, will have some unique habitats with specific plants and animals. Often, we now harvest reforested areas before the climax stage is reached, preventing the unique climax environment from being achieved again (Hamilton, 2012). This could lead to the extinction of the species occupying these habitats. Nature exhibits for us, over and over again, the interconnectivity of all aspects of the environment. When we lose a species, maybe humanity does not lose much. Often we do not realize what we have lost until it is gone.

I am reminded of a visit I made many years ago to a museum dedicated to the indigenous peoples of the South American rain forest. The curator mentioned the shamans, the medicine men of the tribes, and their knowledge of the healing properties of specific native plants growing in the rain forest. Pharmaceutical companies are very interested in these plants and their potential healing qualities for humanity. Unfortunately, shamans have been taken advantage of by entrepreneurs so often that they have become reluctant to willingly pass on their knowledge. As they age and die, their knowledge dies with them. We may never know their secrets and, as the rain forest is destroyed, these plants may become extinct and lost to us forever. The benefits to humanity may never be realized.

In 1971, UNESCO established an international program to create biosphere reserves as areas in which humanity can learn how to coexist with and preserve the natural environment. The reserves are more than just conservation areas. They are areas of research and areas of sustainable development based upon scientific knowledge in conjunction with the indigenous peoples of the region. A major objective of the program is education through the international sharing of research findings from the various reserves.

The Brazilian Atlantic Rain Forest Biosphere Reserve (i.e., Mata Atlantica Biosphere Reserve) is the largest of the 590 designated by the United Nations (Albuquerque, 2012). Because of its size, the Mata Atlantica Biosphere contains a wide diversity of Brazil's many endangered species of flora and fauna. With Brazil's two largest cities, Sao Paulo and Rio de Janeiro, in close proximity to the reserve, a unique opportunity is presented to develop strategies for maintaining biodiversity where the urban, rural, and natural intersect.

As I sat on a British Airways jet preparing to endure an 11-hour flight from London to Johannesburg, South Africa, I flipped through their in-flight magazine, *Highlife*. An article titled "The Horns of a Dilemma" by Johann Hari (2014) immediately got my attention. In it, the author reports that five years ago, a British conservationist, Sarah Brook, in the wilds of Vietnam came across the corpse of the last remaining Vietnamese rhino, its horn cut off. (A comparison of two rhinos, one with its horn and one without, is shown in Figures 3.3 and 3.4.) An entire subspecies of rhino has been driven to extinction due to the belief that its horn possesses magical powers, a belief totally unsubstantiated by fact. If the current trend continues, it is estimated that in 2026 the last remaining rhino will be killed in the wild (Hari, 2014).

Figure 3.3.
Rhino at a private game reserve outside of Durban, South Africa, August 2014. (Photo by Donald F. Nemeth, PhD)

Extinction of plants and animals does have a relevance to humanity. All are interconnected. The interconnectivity of all aspects of our environment is relevant to our very existence. Robert Hamilton (2012) presents three fundamental questions: (1) Will we be able to deal with inevitable change we cannot control? (2) Will we be able to manage our environment to minimize future change? And (3) will we be able to adapt to change?

As the most significant living organism on our planet, will we humans be willing to restructure our goals? Today, there is a vast body of scientific knowledge available to us. We now have computers with the capability of tabulating and analyzing vast quantities of data from scientific research. We also have an understanding of natural processes operating globally and locally. At our disposal, for our use is a wealth of knowledge that is of little or no value if it is not understood by humanity. Education is the key. Sound scientific findings must not be ignored or discounted to achieve personal gain at the expense of future generations and ultimately humanity.

Figure 3.4.
Rhino at a private game reserve outside of Durban, South Africa, August 2014, with its horn removed. Fortunately, the rhino will live and regrow the horn. (Photo by Donald F. Nemeth, PhD)

REFERENCES

Adams, P. (2011). Chinese study reveals Three Gorges Dam triggered 3,000 earthquakes, numerous landslides. *Probe International.* Retrieved April 3, 2015, from http://journal.probeinternational.org/2011/06/01/chinese-study-reveals-three-gorges-dam-triggered-3000-earthquakes-numerous-landslides/

Albuquerque, J. L. R. (2012). Our biosphere reserves: Conservation, sustainable development, and preparation for future changes—emphasizing the Mata Atlantica Biosphere Reserve in Brazil. In D. G. Nemeth, R. B. Hamilton, & J. Kuriansky (Eds.), *Living in an environmentally traumatized world* (Chap. 6, pp. 99–109). Santa Barbara, CA: Praeger.

Alley, R. B. (2011). *Earth—the operators' manual* (pp. 52–53). New York: W. W. Norton & Company.

Bureau of Land Management (BLM). (2012). Geologic features, Carrizo Plain National Monument: San Andreas Fault. Retrieved August 11, 2014, from http://www.blm.gov/ca/st/en/fo/bakersfield/Programs/carrizo/geology.html

Calder, S. (2014, August 29). Air travel disrupted by fresh volcano threats in Iceland. *The Independent.* Retrieved September 23, 2014, from http://www.independent.co.uk/travel/news-and-advice/air-travel-disrupted-by-fresh-volcano-threats-in-iceland-and-papua-new-guinea-9700353.html

California Institute of Technology (CIT). (2008, November 26). *The science behind China's 2008 Sichuan earthquake*. Retrieved April 3, 2015, from http://www.tectonics.caltech.edu/outreach/highlights/2008MayChinaEQ/

Celebi, M. (1996). Successful performance of a base-isolated hospital building during the 17 January 1994 Northridge earthquake. *The Structural Design of Tall Buildings, 5*, 95–109.

Chongneng, F. (2004). *Du Jiang Yan*. Chengdu, China: Sichuan Fine Arts Publishing House.

CNN. (2013). *Haiti earthquake fast facts*. Retrieved April 3, 2015, from http://www.cnn.com/2013/12/12/world/haiti-earthquake-fast-facts/

CNN. (2014). *Oil spills fast facts*. Retrieved September 17, 2014, from http://www.cnn.com/2013/07/13/world/oil-spills-fast-facts/

Cosi, R., Whitaker, R., & Reinders, S. (2009). *South Africa*. National Geographic Traveler (pp. 226–231). Washington, DC: National Geographic.

Dahlman, L. (2014) NOAA, Climate.gov. Retrieved July 1, 2014, from http://www.climate.gov/author/luann-dahlman

Dokka, R., Sella, G., & Dixon, T. (2006) Tectonic control of subsidence and southward displacement of southeast Louisiana with respect to stable North America. *Geophysical Research Letters, 33*, L23308, 1–5. doi:10.1029/2006GL027250,2006

Earthquakes triggered by humans in Colorado—a background paper by the Colorado Geological Survey. (2012, December 14). Retrieved from http://coloradogeologicalsurvey.org/wp-content/uploads/2013/08/Earthquakes-Triggered.pdf

Folger, T. (2013). Rising seas. *National Geographic, 224*(3), 30–59.

Fox News. (2003, January 29). *Hydrogen bomb*. Retrieved April 3, 2015, from http://www.foxnews.com/story/2003/01/29/hydrogen-bomb/

Gale, R. P., & Hauser, T. (1988). *Final warning: The legacy of Chernobyl*. New York, NY: Warner Books.

Gazzar, B. (2014). Los Angeles County first in U.S. to reach 10 million people. *Huffington Post*, Retrieved July 18, 2014, from http://www.huffingtonpost.com/los-angeles-county-10-million_n_4439611.html

Hamilton R. B. (2012). Our providing biosphere: Flora, fauna, and more. In D. G. Nemeth, R. B. Hamilton, & J. Kuriansky (Eds.), *Living in an environmentally traumatized world* (Chap. 5, pp. 77–98). Santa Barbara, CA: Praeger.

Hari, J. (2014). The horns of a dilemma. *Highlife* (pp. 46–48). London, UK: British Airways, Cedar Communications Limited.

Harner, S. (2013, March 11). At a two year anniversary, the Tohoku earthquake/tsunami and Fukushima nuclear disaster continue to exact a toll. *Forbes*. Retrieved April 3, 2015, from http://www.forbes.com/sites/stephenharner/2013/03/11/at-a-two-year-anniversary-the-tohoku-earthquaketsunami-and-fukushima-nuclear-disaster-continue-to-exact-a-toll/

Hiltzik, M. (2010). *Colossus: Hoover Dam and the making of the American century*. New York, NY: Free Press.

IPCC. (2007). *Climate change 2007: The physical science basis*. Contribution of Working Group 1 to the Fourth Assessment Report of the Intergovernmental Panel on Climate Change, S. Solomon, D. Quin, M. Manning, Z. Chen, M. Marquis, K. B. Averyt, M. Tignor, & H. L. Miller (Eds.). Cambridge, UK, & New York, NY: Cambridge University Press. Retrieved April 3, 2015, from http://oceanservice.noaa.gov/

Kandel, J. (2014) Timeline: The 1994 Northridge earthquake. *NBC Los Angeles.* Retrieved June 30, 2014, from http://www.nbclosangeles.com/news/local/Timeline -The-Northridge-Earthquake-240665071.html

Keim, B. D., & Muller, R. A. (2009). *Hurricanes of the Gulf of Mexico.* Baton Rouge, LA: Louisiana State University Press.

Kennedy, C. (2009). NOAA, Climate.gov. Retrieved July 1, 2014, from http://www .climate.gov/author/caitlyn-kennedy

Kunzig, R. (2011, October). World without ice. *National Geographic* (pp. 90–109).

Long, G. (2011). Chile quake recovery: Back to normal or long way to go? *BBC News, Latin America & Caribbean.* Retrieved July 18, 2014, from http://www.bbc.com/news/ world-latin-america-12534552

Louisiana Laws. (2009). *2009 Louisiana Laws Title 30 minerals, oil, and gas and environmental quality: RS 30:2117 radioactive waste disposal; prohibition of disposal of radioactive waste in salt domes; salt dome usage.* Retrieved April 3, 2015, from http://law.justia. com/codes/louisiana/2009/rs/title30/rs30-2117.html

Martinez, J. D., Kupfer, D. H., Thoms, R. L., Smith, C. G., & Kolb, C. R. (1975). *An investigation of the utility of Gulf Coast salt domes for the storage or disposal of radioactive wastes.* Institute for Environmental Studies, Louisiana State University, Baton Rouge, LA.

Muller, R. A. (2012). Our atmosphere: Friend or foe? In D. G. Nemeth, R. B. Hamilton, & J. Kuriansky (Eds.), *Living in an environmentally traumatized world* (pp. 41–55). Santa Barbara, CA: ABC-CLIO/Praeger.

Naik, G. & Oster, S. (2009, February 6) Scientists link China's dam to earthquake, renewing debate. *Wall Street Journal.* Retrieved April 3, 2015, from http://online.wsj .com/articles/SB123391567210056475

Natural Resources Defense Council (NRDC). (2011). *What if Fukushima nuclear fallout crisis had happened here?* Retrieved April 3, 2015, from http://www.nrdc.org/nuclear/ fallout

Nelson, S. A. (2013). Earthquake hazards and risks. Retrieved July 18, 2014, from http:// www.tulane.edu/~sanelson/Natural_Disasters/eqhazards&risks.htm

Nemeth, D. F. (2012). Our planet earth: Understanding the big picture. In D. G. Nemeth, R. B. Hamilton, & J. Kuriansky (Eds.), *Living in an environmentally traumatized world* (pp. 57–75). Santa Barbara, CA: ABC-CLIO/Praeger.

Nemeth, D. F. (2013). Thoughts on Katrina vs. Sandy. *Ecopsychology,* 5(Suppl.), online journal. New Rochelle, NY: Mary Ann Liebert, Inc.

New York Times. (2011). The Anthropocene: Editorial, The Opinion Pages. Retrieved July 1, 2014, from http://www.nytimes.com/2011/02/28/opinion/28mon4.html

Onishi, Y. (2012). Our living waters: Polluting or cleansing? In D. G. Nemeth, R. B. Hamilton, & J. Kuriansky (Eds.), *Living in an environmentally traumatized world* (pp. 23–39). Santa Barbara, CA: ABC-CLIO/Praeger.

Onishi, Y., Voitsekhovich, O. V., & Zheleznyak, M. J. (2007). *Chernobyl—What have we learned?* Dordrecht, Netherlands: Springer.

Reed, C. (2002, May). Mount Pelee, Martinique 1902–2002. *Geotimes.*

San Diego State University. (n.d.). *How volcanoes work: Mt. Pelée eruption (1902).* Retrieved July 31, 2014, from www.geology.sdsu.edu/how_volcanoes_work/Pelee.html

Small, C., & Naumann, T. (2002). The global distribution of human population and recent volcanism. *Environmental Hazards, 3*, 93–109. Retrieved July 10, 2014, from ftp://ftp.ldeo.columbia.edu/pub/small/PUBS/SmallNaumannGEH2002.pdf

Spotts, P. (2010). The geology underlying the devastating Haiti earthquake. *Christian Science Monitor*. Retrieved July 14, 2014, from http://www.csmonitor.com/World/Americas/2010/0113/The-geology-underlying-the-devastating-Haiti-earthquake

Stewart, D. (2006, February). Resurrecting Pompeii. *Smithsonian Magazine*.

Stromberg, J. (2013, February) Air pollution has been a problem since the days of ancient Rome. *Smithsonian Magazine*.

UNESCO. (2011). *World heritage sites: A complete guide to 936 UNESCO world heritage sites* (p. 593). Buffalo, NY: Firefly Books (USA).

UNICEF. (2010, May). *Sichuan earthquake two year report, May 2010*. Retrieved July 20, 2014, from http://www.unicef.cn/en/uploadfile/2012/0119/20120119034621299.pdf

United Nations (UN). (2010). Death toll from massive Chilean earthquake tops 720, reports UN health agency. *UN News Centre*. Retrieved April 3, 2015, from http://www.un.org/apps/news/story.asp?NewsID=33935

U.S. Environmental Protection Agency (EPA). (2012). Climate change, Greenhouse gas emissions. Retrieved April 3, 2015, from http://www.epa.gov/climatechange/ghgemissions/

U.S. Environmental Protection Agency (EPA). (2014a). Climate change, Climate change indicators in the United States: Greenhouse gases. Retrieved April 3, 2015, from http://www.epa.gov/climate/climatechange/science/indicators/ghg/index.html

U.S. Environmental Protection Agency (EPA). (2014b). Climate change: Overview of greenhouse gases, methane emissions. Retrieved April 3, 2015, from http://epa.gov/climatechange/ghgemissions/gases/ch4.html

U.S. Geological Survey (USGS). (1999, May 5). *Understanding plate motions*. Retrieved August 3, 2011, from http://pubs.usgs.gov/gip/dynamic/understanding.html.

U.S. Geological Survey (USGS). (2001a, June). *Hawaiian volcanoes*. Retrieved July 11, 2014, from http://hvo.wr.usgs.gov/volcanoes/

U.S. Geological Survey (USGS). (2001b). *Hawaiian Volcano Observatory*. Retrieved July 3, 2014, from http://hvo.wr.usgs.gov/observatory/

U.S. Geological Survey (USGS). (2005). *The cataclysmic 1991 eruption of Mount Pinatubo*. Retrieved April 3, 2015, from http://pubs.usgs.gov/fs/1997/fs113-97

U.S. Geological Survey (USGS). (2009). *Kilauea—perhaps the world's most active volcano*. Retrieved July 3, 2014, from http://hvo.wr.usgs.gov/kilauea/

U.S. Geological Survey (USGS). (2010). *Earthquake Hazards Program: Magnitude 7.0—Haiti region*. Retrieved July 31, 2014, from http://earthquake.usgs.gov/earthquakes/eqinthenews/2010/us2010rja6/

U.S. Geological Survey (USGS). (2012a). *Earthquake glossary—Ring of Fire*. Retrieved July 11, 2014, from http://earthquakes.usgs.gov/learn/glossary/?term=Ring of Fire

U.S. Geological Survey (USGS). (2012b). *Earthquake Hazards Program: Repeating earthquakes*. Retrieved July 18, 2014, from http://earthquake.usgs.gov/research/parkfield/eq_predict.php

U.S. Geological Survey (USGS). (2012c). *Volcanic gases and climate change overview*. Retrieved April 3, 2015, from http://volcanoes.usgs.gov/hazards/gas/climate.php

U.S. Geological Survey (USGS). (2013a, January 9). *Earthquake facts and earthquake fantasy*. Retrieved July 30, 2014, from http://earthquake.usgs.gov/learn/topics/megaqk_facts_fantasy.php

U.S. Geological Survey (USGS). (2013b). *Earthquake Hazards Program: Monitoring instruments*. Retrieved July 16, 2014, from http://earthquake.usgs.gov/monitoring/deformation/data/instruments.php

U.S. Geological Survey (USGS). (2013c). *Monitoring Cascade volcanoes—Volcano Hazards Program*. Retrieved April 3, 2015, from http://volcanoes.usgs.gov/observatories/cvo/cvo_monitoring.html

U.S. Geological Survey (USGS). (2014a). *Earthquake Hazards Program: GPS data*. Retrieved July 22, 2014, from http://earthquake.usgs.gov/monitoring/gps/

U.S. Geological Survey (USGS). (2014b). *Largest earthquakes in the world since 1900*. Retrieved July 22, 2014, from http://earthquakes.usgs.gov/earthquakes/world/10_largest_world.php

U.S. Nuclear Regulatory Commission (USNRC). (2002). *Radioactive waste: Production, storage, disposal*. Retrieved April 3, 2015, from http://www.nrc.gov/reading-rm/doc-collections/nuregs/brochures/br0216/

U.S. Nuclear Regulatory Commission (USNRC). (2014). *Background on the Three Mile Island accident*. Retrieved April 3, 2015, from http://www.nrc.gov/reading-rm/doc-collections/fact-sheets/3mile-isle.html

Weart, S. (2011). The development of the concept of dangerous anthropogenic climate change. In J. S. Dryzek, R. B. Norgaard, & D. Schlosberg (Eds.), *The Oxford Handbook of climate change and society* (p. 67). New York, NY: Oxford University Press.

Winterle, J., Ofoegbu, G., Pabalan, R., Manepally, C., Mintz, T., Pearcy, E., . . . Pauline, R. (2012). *Geologic disposal of high-level radioactive waste in salt formations*. U.S. Nuclear regulatory Commission contract NRC-02-07-006, Center for nuclear waste regulatory analyses, San Antonio, TX.

World Population Review. (2014). *California population 2014*. Retrieved August 11, 2014, from http://worldpopulationreview.com/states/california-population/

4

Utilization of Our Environment

Scott P. Nesbit and Andrew S. Nesbit

The first time I visited the 24,000-acre Spanish Lake subbasin was in November 1970. It was my 16th birthday, and like most of my friends in south Baton Rouge, Louisiana, it was time to get your driver's license and buy an illegal beer at a rural bar. The preferred destination for this ritual was the Alligator Bayou Bar, 15 miles east of south Baton Rouge, on the Ascension Parish side of Bayou Manchac at Alligator Bayou near the edge of the Spanish Lake subbasin.

Calling the Alligator Bar a "bar" was a bit of a stretch, as the place was nothing more than a trailer attached to a small, wooden shack located off a gravel road. The bar was outfitted with well-worn pool tables and a series of intimidating bartenders who would sell beer to anyone that looked a day older than 14. While the bar's relaxed policies were what initially attracted me as a teenager, its primitive setting as part of the larger swamp is what brought me back to Spanish Lake 18 years later as a wetlands ecologist and consultant.

An adventure on Alligator Bayou through the Spanish Lake subbasin was like time travel to a primitive land. Most visitors would launch aluminum bateaus with small outboards or canoes off Bayou Manchac Road and navigate upstream to Cypress Flats, a 170-acre bald cypress (*Taxodium distichum*) forest with an abundance of large reptiles and birds. The striking aspect of Cypress Flats was that all of the giant bald cypress trees were dead.

At the time, no one really knew why the old-growth bald cypress in Cypress Flats died, leaving only the standing outer shell or structure of the trees. The towering bald cypress resemble ghostly giants as most have suffered lightning strikes, terminating the single-stem, dominant upward growth and promoting thick lateral branches 50 to 60 feet at the top. The experience of paddling through these large, elegant, relic trees, stripped of bark, and exposing the graceful lines of the inner wood, was unique, eerie, and strangely magnetic.

Discovering the Spanish Lake subbasin's ecological processes and assessing the restoration potential of the subbasin became a personal and professional journey that consumed me for over a decade. Whereas identifying the ecological factors influencing the health and habitat quality is essential to any ecological restoration effort, understanding the relationship and impact of the surrounding human community on this wetland ecosystem is much more challenging and significant.

PHYSICAL SETTING

Bayou Manchac and the Spanish Lake subbasin represent the westernmost boundary of the larger Lake Pontchartrain Basin, which includes all or part of 16 South Louisiana parishes, is shown in Figure 4.1. The 1.7 million–acre, tidally influenced Pontchartrain Basin is the specific geographic and ecological area of interest that includes the Spanish Lake subbasin and can be generally identified as the low-lying area between Baton Rouge and New Orleans, Louisiana, outlined by U.S. interstates 10 and 12 (Lake Pontchartrain Basin Foundation, n.d.). The northern boundary of the Pontchartrain Basin consists of the upper terraces from Baton Rouge to the Mississippi state line at the Pearl River, and its southern boundary is the Mississippi River. The Spanish Lake subbasin is located just southeast of Baton Rouge at historic Bayou Manchac, a seasonal distributary of the Mississippi River. From there, the Pontchartrain Basin incorporates the 144,868-acre Maurepas Swamp, the 39,302-acre Lake Maurepas, and the 403,200-acre Lake Pontchartrain, as shown in Figure 4.2. The eastern boundary of the Pontchartrain Basin consists of a natural land-bridge, yet the basin remains hydraulically connected to Lake Borgne, the Chandelier Sound, and the Gulf of Mexico (Effler, Shaffer, Hoeppner, & Goyer, 2007).

REGIONAL ECOLOGICAL SETTING

The ecological setting within Spanish Lake and that of the Pontchartrain Basin is defined by the natural meandering of the lower Mississippi River as it flows south and east to the Gulf of Mexico. Over several thousand years, the larger Pontchartrain Basin was shaped by river-channel shifting and sediment deposition to create a broad landscape of low ridges (Keim et al., 2006; Kniffen, 1935). The riverine process of delta formation and abandonment slowly enclosed Lakes Maurepas and Pontchartrain, which remains hydraulically connected and tidally influenced by the Gulf of Mexico. The basin's low topographic relief, continuous supply of fertile river sediments, mix of fresh- and saline-water regimes, and subtropical climate have created and sustained some of the largest, most diverse coastal wetland ecosystems in North America. The Spanish Lake subbasin is within the western area of the Pontchartrain Basin near Baton Rouge, on the east bank of the Mississippi River. Bayou Manchac, a natural distributary of the Mississippi River, runs through the center of the Spanish Lake subbasin,

Figure 4.1.
The Lake Pontchartrain Basin contains all or part of sixteen Louisiana parishes.

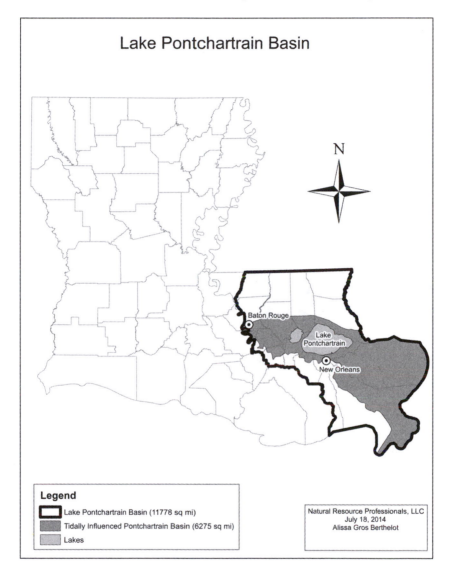

which is entirely a freshwater ecosystem. This circular, forested subbasin was carved out of the adjacent upland silty-clay terraces by the constant channel shifting of the lower Mississippi River. Abandoned deep channels of the

Figure 4.2.
The Lake Pontchartrain Tidal Basin, including Maurepas Swamp, Lake Maurepas, and Lake Pontchartrain.

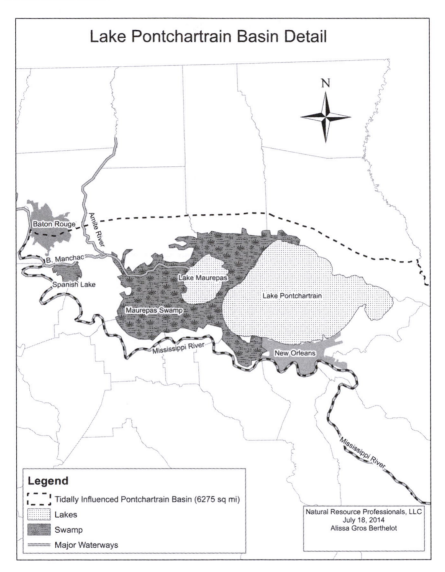

Mississippi River can still be identified within the Spanish Lake subbasin via aerial photography, especially color infrared aerial photography available online through the US Geological Survey (USGS).

Surface Hydrology

All coastal wetland ecosystems and most inland wetlands are created and maintained by surface hydrology. To appreciate the dynamics of surface hydrology within the Spanish Lake subbasin, it may be helpful to visualize the larger Pontchartrain Basin as an elongated, shallow saucer beginning in the west at the Spanish Lake subbasin and extending to the eastern shoreline of Lake Pontchartrain. The western region of this shallow saucer supports a dominant freshwater ecosystem that transitions to a more saline-water regime in the eastern section closer to the Gulf. Surface elevations and salinity gradients shift in response to high winds, storms, and high tides. In the warm months, winds from the Gulf of Mexico dominate and push surface water to the west. During the late fall and winter months, north winds and high rainfall push freshwater from the uplands through the large lakes into the gulf. Essentially, wind and weather events act as if to "tilt" the saucer to the east or west, pushing and mixing the surface waters through various wetland and open-water habitats.

Slowing the movement of surface water between the west and east is an extensive network of slightly elevated forested ridges, small bayous, large swamps, and bottomland hardwood forests. This complex arrangement of forested wetlands, uplands, marsh, and open water naturally buffers and protects inland areas from excessive flooding and direct impacts from hurricanes and tropical storms.

Climate

All of Southeast Louisiana, including the Pontchartrain Basin, has a subtropical climate with an average rainfall of approximately 60 inches per year, with 1 year in 10 having 48.8 inches or less or 69.8 inches or more (Soil Survey of Iberville Parish, Louisiana, 1977). Seasonal storms can generate from 2 to 10 inches of rainfall during a single event and push freshwater into the lower wetlands ecosystem. Large-scale rainfall events often cause bayous to reverse flow and create extensive backwater flooding within the intermediate elevations of the landscape.

Geologic Subsidence and Accretion

Natural subsidence and accretion are two primary geological processes that determine the surface elevation of land within the Pontchartrain Basin and the Spanish Lake subbasin. Natural subsidence is the geologic downward movement of the surface under the weight of its accumulated surface sediments and occurs within the deltaic processes of the lower Mississippi River valley. In contrast, accretion is the accumulation of mineral soils by fluvial processes such as overbank flooding of rivers. In low-lying areas such as the Pontchartrain Basin and the Spanish Lake subbasin, accretion is essential in preventing the wetlands from sinking or converting to permanently flooded and less productive ecosystems as suggested by current estimates of continued sea-level rise within the northern coast of the Gulf of Mexico (Conner, Hackney, Krauss, & Day, 2007).

Anthropogenic Activity

Anthropogenic, or human activity, has adversely impacted riverine ecosystems in temperate, subtropical, and tropical climates throughout the world for thousands of years. River waters and their adjacent fertile floodplains are the lifeblood of many civilizations, not only because all living organisms need water, but because large rivers have tremendous energy that moves mineral sediments and plant nutrients. The Spanish Lake subbasin, with its close proximity to the Mississippi River, an added benefit of Bayou Manchac flowing through its center, has always attracted humans to its abundant forests, fishery resources, and forests. Prior to European colonization in the early 1700s, Bayou Manchac and the Spanish Lake subbasin hosted Native American tribes, including the Choctaw, Bayogoula, Mugulasha, Tunica Biloxi, and Chitimacha Indians (Kniffen, Gregory, & Stokes, 1987). European colonization was initiated in 1541 when the Spanish explorer Hernando de Soto first viewed the Mississippi River. In 1682, Robert Caveller de LaSalle sailed down the Mississippi River to its mouth, claiming all the land for King Louis XIV of France and naming it Louisiana in his honor.

In 1699, two brothers, Pierre LeMoyne Sieur D'Iberville, and Jean Baptiste LeMoyne, Sieur de Bienville, entered the mouth of the Mississippi River. After a six-week journey, D'Iberville arrived in the vicinity of Bayou Manchac and the Spanish Lake subbasin that would later be part of Iberville Parish named by D'Iberville. D'Iberville is said to have spent the night within the Bayou Manchac/Spanish Lake subbasin (Collot, 1826).

Colonization was expensive, and France, unable to financially support the young Louisiana colony, ceded it to Spain following the Seven Years' War in 1763 with the Treaty of Fontainebleau. In 1766, Don Antonio Ulloa arrived in Louisiana to begin the Spanish administration of the territory. Ulloa immediately recognized the need for stabilizing the colonies, and in 1767, he established the settlement of St. Gabriel on the east bank of the Mississippi River near Bayou Manchac and the Spanish Lake subbasin as the destination for 200 Acadians. The Acadians were refugees from the British occupation of Nova Scotia (Acadia). Granting Spanish Land grants to the Acadians proved to be a successful strategy, as this population was resourceful and able to endure South Louisiana's tumultuous beginning.

During the early European colonization, Bayou Manchac became the international boundary between the Spanish and British, since it was an apparent navigable waterway to New Orleans. As such, Bayou Manchac provided a strategic military alternative to access New Orleans without navigating the closely monitored Mississippi River. In 1766, just prior to the American Revolution, the English established Fort Brute as a fortified garrison on Bayou Manchac. In 1779, the Spanish officially entered the American Revolution against the British. In September 1779, the Spanish governor of the Isle of Orleans, Bernardo de Galvez, anticipated a British plan to launch a surprise attack on the Isle of New Orleans from Forte Brute on Manchac Bayou. Galvez led a force of mostly volunteer French, German, and Acadian citizens in a successful preemptive strike (Bayou Manchac, n.d.). The Spanish military not only seized Forte Brute, but also the much larger settlement of New Richmond, the present-day Baton Rouge, Louisiana.

As with the French, Spain could not afford to support the struggling colonies and, in 1800, ceded the Louisiana territory back to France. In turn, France sold Louisiana to the United States in 1803. William Claiborne became the first American governor. He arrived in New Orleans in 1805 and, issued and traded U.S. land grants for most of the existing French and Spanish land grants.

Antebellum Period to 1800–1861

Economic fortunes changed rapidly in South Louisiana along the Mississippi River and Iberville Parish with Etienne de Bore's successful granulation of sugar in 1795. This new process, plus the invention of the cotton gin, brought significant outside investments in land suitable for sugarcane and cotton production. Fertile soils along the Mississippi River in central and South Louisiana became a haven for new planters from throughout Europe and the newly colonized United States of America.

Iberville Parish was one of the South Louisiana parishes that benefited most from the advances in sugar production and the investment in agricultural land. The natural alluvial shoreline of the Mississippi River was regarded as prime sugarcane farmland, and the price of granulated sugar was financially rewarding.

Small farms quickly covered the shorelines of the Mississippi River throughout Louisiana, including those in Iberville Parish, and required abundant cheap labor for land clearing, planting, and cultivation. Flood protection levees were essential as part of sugarcane production, thus each small farm required a significant number of workers and influenced rise in the slave trade. Plantations each had their own sugar mill and a small colony of slaves to do the work needed on these labor-intensive properties.

The Civil War and Evolution of Agribusiness

The Civil War devastated the newly adopted antebellum-based culture and economy in Iberville Parish and throughout the South. In addition to the loss of requisite slave labor, the price of sugar plummeted after the Civil War.

Thus, with low financial return and a scarce labor supply, only 10% of farmers maintained the labor force needed to support sugarcane or cotton production.

The economic reality following the Civil War led to the establishment of large, regional sugar mills and the consolidation of small farms into larger land holdings. Higher production efficiency was essential in the field and at mills in order to make this industry profitable. From 1870 to 1930, the trend toward larger and more consolidated operations plus significant advances in farm equipment reestablished sugar production as a profitable business. Iberville Parish regained its strong sugarcane-based economy and garnered the nickname of "Sweet Iberville."

40-Arpent Canal–Defining Productive Lands and Waste Lands

The industrialization of sugar processing in Southeast Louisiana required large-scale drainage improvements to facilitate reliable, annual crop production. Because the single most important factor influencing crop production in this area was improved drainage and flood protection, farmers dredged large drainage canals parallel to the river within the low elevation where bottomland hardwood forests transitioned into bald cypress swamp. These dredge canals were 20–30 feet wide and 4–6 feet deep and provided significantly improved surface drainage for the adjacent upland agricultural land.

French and Spanish land grants along rivers were issued in French arpents. A French arpent is a unit of measure equal to approximately 192 feet, or 59 meters. A typical land grant was 2–4 arpents along the river shoreline with a length of 40–60 arpents. These parcels were typically rectangular where the shoreline was straight, and pie-shaped along areas where the river meanders, with a narrow access reach on the river shoreline and a wide base at the lower elevations near the backwater swamps. Thus, the 40-arpent canal became a general term used to reference the primary improved-drainage feature of large farms located along the Mississippi River or other large waterways in Southeast Louisiana.

The 40-arpent canal hydraulically connected one farmer to his neighbor, becoming a contiguous drainage feature. The "spoil" from dredging was usually stacked on the backside of the canal and could be as high as 10 feet above natural grade. These canals intercepted and channelized sheet flow from the expansive upland river shoreline into large discharge canals cut deep into the adjacent coastal swamps.

Without a formal declaration, the 40-arpent canal was considered to be a continuous hard line defining "productive land" and "waste land." The general mind-set of the landowners and the parish was that the "waste land" behind the canals had no value at all and represented a physical obstacle to economic prosperity and was the natural location to discharge waste of all types. In general, the vast majority of this land supported cypress tupelo swamp.

Once initially established, the 40-arpent canal with large, elevated spoil banks was improved and fortified by parish governments to become hurricane-protection levees. Communities were built on the elevated natural shorelines of the numerous bayous or the shoreline of the Mississippi River. Thus, these hurricane-protection levees provided protection from Gulf storm surge that pushed water through the interior coastal wetlands. During severe storm surges, the communities would resemble islands, sandwiched between a rising river on one side and storm surges pushing in from the Gulf into the lower wetlands behind the 40-arpent canal. Figure 4.3 is a typical cross section showing the Mississippi River, its elevated shoreline where the plantation home (big house) was built, prime agricultural land for crop production, the 40-arpent canal and spoil bank, and cypress tupelo swamp.

Collectively, the economic need to establish an industrial-based sugar industry and flood protection of its communities required drainage improvements such as the 40-arpent canal to drain hundreds of thousands of contiguous acres in South Louisiana. Unknown at the time, these drainage improvements adversely impacted both the quality and sustainability of the expansive forested wetlands that had been branded "waste lands." Specifically, the canal and spoil bank captured and channelized the overland sheet flow of seasonal floodwater from the Mississippi River, which was sediment- and nutrient-rich. In addition, the large spoil bank facilitated ponding and water stagnation within the bald cypress swamp that inhibited growth and regeneration, and facilitated vegetative species more adaptable to permanently flooded conditions.

Mississippi River Levee Construction—Largest Impact to Coastal Wetlands

After the great flood of the Mississippi River in 1927, flood control became the single most critical issue regarding long term economic growth and development within Southeast Louisiana. The construction of the continuous Mississippi River Levee system from 1927 to 1934 by the U.S. Army Corps of Engineers (USACE) was the largest flood control project in the United States. Since construction, the lower Mississippi River levee system has become the main significant factor influencing ecological degradation in South Louisiana (Barry, 1997). Whereas river communities were largely protected by the levee, the adjacent forested wetlands and marshes became mostly sediment-deprived because of reduced natural accretion as river sediments were no longer dispersed during flooding events by overland sheet flow or distributary channels like Bayou Manchac.

Oil and Gas Exploration/Petrochemical Industry

By 1942, oil and gas exploration and the petrochemical industry had become a booming new industry in South Louisiana. The entry of the United States into

Figure 4.3.
Mississippi River shoreline to the Black Swamp, plan view and cross section.

Natural Resource Professionals, LLC
July 18, 2014
Alissa Gros Berthelot

Typical Plan View/Cross Section of the
Mississippi River Shoreline to the Backswamp

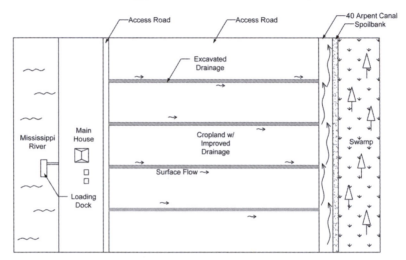

Plan View

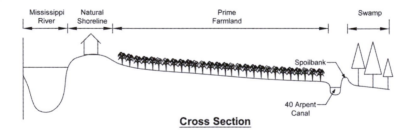

Cross Section

World War II galvanized the public need for fossil fuel as its primary energy source. South Louisiana, including inland wetlands, coastal marshes, and offshore in the Gulf of Mexico, represented a significant oil and gas reserve. Initially, large oil and gas corporations purchased mineral leases on- and offshore to establish the original oil production fields. Subsequently, these larger corporations subleased the drilling and exploration to smaller regional operators.

By the mid-1900s, the result of increased oil and gas exploration led large oil refineries and petrochemical interests to purchase extensive agricultural lands along the Mississippi River for refineries and petrochemical processors, as this location provided ocean access for large container ships via the Mississippi River. To facilitate intrastate commerce, the Gulf Intracoastal Waterway (GIWW) was constructed across South Louisiana to Florida and provided a continuous navigable waterway for oceangoing vessels to transport oil and gas products and commerce without navigating the shallow bays, bayous, and marshes of the coastal shoreline.

Whereas industrial facilities typically required river access, oil and gas exploration was conducted extensively within South Louisiana's wetlands or "waste lands" behind the 40-arpent canal. Landowners were delighted to lease mineral rights to oil and gas exploration companies within this waste land. These leases could often provide revenue that exceeded that of agricultural interests alone.

Within the flooded lands, oil and gas operators constructed elevated access roads for drilling rigs and heavy equipment. Roads were constructed by dredging deep barrow ditches on either side of the proposed road to produce an elevated surface with the physical strength to support the equipment. Within the marshes, equipment access was created by dredging large barge canals through the unconsolidated organic soils, which were structurally weak and frequently flooded. The canals became permanent waterways that altered natural surface hydrologic patterns (Swarzenski, 2003).

Each dredge canal also had a spoil bank created by the placement of the excavated soil. In the organic soils of the marshes, spoil banks quickly sank under their own weight, were oxidized via aerobic microbial degradation, or simply eroded away to leave a permanent canal 30–120 feet wide. Within the mixed mineral/organic mucks of the swamps, the elevated spoil banks remained as permanent hydraulic barriers to sheet flow that altered sediment deposition and caused extensive ponding and conversion to open water (Conner & Brody, 1969). A quick look at South Louisiana's coastal forested wetlands and marshes via Internet-available aerial or satellite images clearly illustrates the long-term adverse impact oil and gas exploration has had on these ecosystems, and contributed to the state's annual coastal land loss rate of 32 square miles a year (SON-RIS—Strategic Online Natural Resources Information System, n.d.).

From 1940 to 1975, oil and gas exploration and the petrochemical industry became the primary economic force and employer in South Louisiana. During this era, very little was known about the potential scale of adverse ecological impacts to wetland ecosystems that resulted from oil and gas exploration and production. Thus, the general public, and certainly the communities dependent on oil and gas employment, simply accepted the fact that the economic benefits of the oil and gas industry generally greatly outweighed the adverse impacts to the flooded wetlands or "waste lands."

The Spanish Lake Subbasin Ecosystem

The 24,000-acre forested wetlands within the Spanish Lake subbasin represent a microcosm of the larger Pontchartrain Basin. As such, the Spanish Lake subbasin has experienced all of the significant anthropogenic impacts and reflects the intimate and shifting relationship between a community and its immediate ecosystem.

Bayou Manchac is the primary waterway through the Spanish Lake subbasin that is internally nourished and drained by Bayou Paul, Bayou Braud, and Alligator Bayou as shown in Figure 4.4. Bayous Paul and Braud channel storm water from the more upland Mississippi River shorelines of Plaquemine Point and Point Claire into the deep, thick, forested wetlands of Spanish Lake, a low-lying 250-acre fresh marsh in the middle of the swamp. During high rainfall, the water level rises in Spanish Lake and eventually pushes water north into Alligator Bayou, which flows and discharges into Bayou Manchac. Figure 4.4

Figure 4.4.
Spanish Lake subbasin.

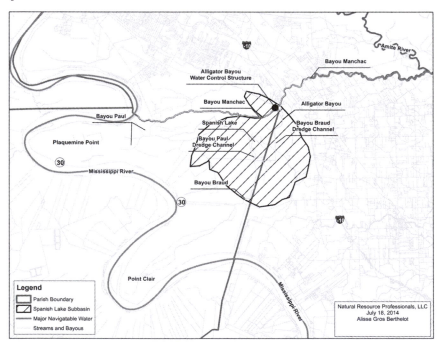

illustrates the network of internal bayous, Bayou Manchac, and the Amite River, which discharges into Lake Maurepas.

Storm events such as heavy seasonal rains, tropical storms, and hurricanes push backwater from the elevated Lakes Pontchartrain and Maurepas, and thus reverses the normal flow of Bayou Manchac and Alligator Bayou, filling the Spanish Lake and the adjacent forested wetlands like a bowl. It is a dynamic ecosystem and a textbook example of a high-functioning, backwater forested ecosystem that provides continuous benefits to its adjacent communities.

From the Native American culture, through European colonists and to the present day, the Spanish Lake subbasin ecosystem has provided its residents with fresh water, timber, fish and wildlife, flood and storm protection, and a center for cultural exchange. Descendants of the Acadians still live near Spanish Lake, which sustained these communities during the Great Depression of 1929 (Harrilson, 1977).

Ascension Parish, which has the most acreage adjacent to the Spanish Lake subbasin, increased population from 18,438 in 1930, prior to the establishment of the petrochemical industry, to 107,215 by 2010 (Historical Census Information: Louisiana State Census Data Center, n.d.). This increase and similar increases in East Baton Rouge and East Iberville Parish during this time span have documented over 300,000 people residing within a 10-mile aerial radius of the Spanish Lake subbasin. This represents both direct and ongoing ecological pressure on the sustainable nature of the forested subbasin.

The Spanish Lake subbasin is 1.75 miles from one of the most industrialized corridors in the United States, situated on the eastern shoreline of the Mississippi River. These industries include over 50 global petrochemical processors and chemical plants, product storage and shipping facilities, product transportation carriers, oil-field suppliers, large-scale construction material yards, and loading/receiving docks for oceangoing vessels. Bayou Braud is the headwater stream that runs through the center of this industrial area. Since the construction of these facilities during the 1960s to 1970, storm-water runoff and other fugitive discharges have migrated into Bayou Braud and through the subbasin.

Current industrial expansion is ongoing, fueled by the low cost of natural gas following the advent of large-scale oil and gas fracking technology beginning in 2007. The unavoidable ecological impacts to air and water resources of the Spanish Lake subbasin due to the continued urban and industrial expansion emphasizes the need to protect the wetland resources within this area.

Spanish Lake Subbasin Ecosystem Degradation

The ecological degradation of the Spanish Lake subbasin paralleled the economic growth of the region from the Civil War to the 1990s. In the early 1950s, a large-scale drainage project was conducted in Iberville and Ascension Parishes to facilitate upland agricultural drainage on farms adjacent to the

Mississippi River. As part of the larger project, a 30-foot-wide, 16,000-linear-foot channel was dredged directly through the forested wetlands of the Spanish Lake subbasin. As part of the project, Bayou Paul was straightened or channelized, and Bayou Braud was deep-dredged. Both bayous were hydraulically cut off from naturally discharging into Spanish Lake and rerouted via a new dredge canal around Spanish Lake, discharged into Alligator Bayou near Bayou Manchac. The five-mile elevated spoil bank created by the dredging of the new channel hydraulically divided the subbasin into two isolated units by preventing natural sheet flow into Spanish Lake. The new dredge channel and spoil bank intercepted natural drainage patterns and increased internal ponding by bisecting ridges.

The single most ecologically damaging feature associated with this large-scale drainage project was the construction and operation of the Bayou Manchac/Alligator Bayou Floodgate (Floodgate). This Floodgate was designed to protect adjacent local communities in Iberville and Ascension Parish from excessive backwater flooding from Bayou Manchac during large storm events such as tropical storms or hurricanes. The operational plan called for closing the Floodgate when Bayou Manchac reversed flow during severe storm events, and reopening it as the surface elevation in the bayou receded. The location of the Floodgate is shown in Figure 4.4.

Instead of operating the Floodgate as designed, it was operated as a dam or fixed weir, to keep water levels elevated in Bayou Braud, Bayou Paul, Spanish Lake, and Alligator Bayou. Spanish Lake was transformed from a seasonally flooded, fresh marsh to a permanently flooded, shallow lake. The elevated water levels in the bayous allowed easier small boat access for the public. The creation of this huge flooded area was very popular, and the gate remained essentially "closed" for over 56 years, from 1953 to 2009.

The adverse ecological impacts associated with operating the Floodgate as a dam were slow to emerge and become evident to the public. Creation of the "green reservoir" within the Spanish Lake subbasin provided the rapidly growing adjacent human population with a recreational opportunity for fishing, canoeing, and partying at the Alligator Bar. Users could paddle or motor down Alligator Bayou to Cypress Flats, where one was sure to see alligators, snakes, and large birds the majority of the year.

During the 56 years that the Floodgate was closed, the numerous adverse ecological impacts were changing the subbasin. These impacts included: excessive and prolonged flooding of adjacent residential areas; annual fish kills from oxygen depletion in Spanish Lake; excessive sedimentation in waterways, especially within Spanish Lake; large-scale hardwood-species tree decline was associated with year-round saturated and reduced soils; and interruption in regeneration of bald cypress.

Impacts to the subbasin were also greatly compounded by continuous timber harvesting by various landowners. Specifically, once the mature forested canopy was removed by clear-cutting, invasive water-tolerant trees and shrub species became established and proliferated and reduced overall habitat quality. Slowly, the once-vibrant, vast 24,000-acre Spanish Lake subbasin was converting to a stagnant low-quality habitat.

Oil and Gas Exploration and Impacts

In 1941, the St. Gabriel Oil and Gas Field was established in the Spanish Lake subbasin by Shell Oil Company. The oil field occurs on an intermediate-depth faulted salt dome structure. Oil and gas operators established approximately 10 miles of elevated access roads throughout the oil field to support heavy drilling rigs and other oil-field equipment. Over 100 wells (productive and non-productive) were drilled by 1959, and generated approximately 26.5 million barrels of condensate (process fluids) and 54 billion cubic feet of natural gas. Several saltwater disposal wells were permitted for the injection of these process fluids. However, the most common practice was to discharge these fluids, which included oil sludge, condensate, and brine, into open earthen pits. These pits had two- to three-foot earthen levees and could be quickly excavated within the land adjacent to the well pad.

The concept of the disposal pits was to provide temporary storage for process fluids until they could be disposed of in a permitted saltwater disposal well. However, because oil-field operations were largely unregulated and not inspected, operators simply left the process fluids in the pits, which were frequently flooded for long durations. The oil field was established within the lowest elevations of the subbasin; thus even with a small levee for containment, these pits were frequently flooded for long periods of time, and process fluids were released into the Spanish Lake subbasin wetland ecosystem.

Collectively, the large drainage projects, improper operation of the Floodgate, and open disposal from oil and gas production greatly compromised the ecology within the Spanish Lake subbasin. Locals also used the elevated oil and gas access roads frequently to dump household wastes. In the 1980s, a dominant landowner in the Spanish Lake subbasin filed a solid waste permit application for a landfill within the lowest elevations of the entire forested wetlands. Even though this landfill initiative failed, by the mid-1980s, the Spanish Lake subbasin was indeed a "waste land."

This takes us back to 1970, when I was having my first underage beer at Alligator Bayou. As we looked at the dead bald cypress in Cypress Flats, we had no appreciation of how this ecosystem had been slowly and continuously degraded over the past 40 years. Cypress Flats, with its majestic ambiance, was just an indicator of how collectively landowners, oil companies, parishes, and recreational users had unintentionally altered the natural ecological processes that sustained this once lively, productive ecosystem. What seemed even more amazing was that there was still an ecosystem worthy of restoring and preserving.

RESTORATION OF THE SPANISH LAKE SUBBASIN

Clean Water Act of 1972

The beginning of direct public involvement and true restoration of the Spanish Lake subbasin occurred in 1972, when Congress passed the Clean Water Act (CWA) along with other key environmental legislation. Even though wetlands were defined nonprecisely as "waters of the United States" in 1972, the CWA was the beginning of an emerging social consciousness that we as a people must be responsible in protecting the very water resources that sustain and nourish our lives and those of our children. The newly formed Environmental Protection Agency (EPA) was responsible for implementation of the CWA.

Wetland Science and Ecology

From 1972 to 1985, an emerging body of research from across the United States identified vegetated wetlands as a vital pollution buffer and an integral functioning component of rivers, streams, lakes, and the coast. The unique, inherent ecological value of wetlands is that they are areas that experience both flooded (reduced) and dry (oxidized) soil conditions. In coastal wetlands, the interface is not only flooded and dry (tidal flux), but also varies in salinity. This oxidation/reduction process within the surface soil profile is unique to wetlands as sediments are deposited and nutrients are delivered to plant roots for adsorption, assimilation, and recycling back into the biosphere.

Approximately 30% of the nation's wetlands are found in South Louisiana, with its river resources and subtropical climate (Chapter 2: State Overview, 2005). These wetlands have been recognized as some of the most productive ecosystems in the world. Thus, the recognition that Louisiana loses 32 square miles of coastal wetlands per year is of national concern.

The Spanish Lake subbasin, with its cypress swamp and bottomland hardwood forests, represents an important wetland landscape position. The forests of the subbasin buffer inland communities such as Baton Rouge from wind and flooding associated with hurricanes and tropical storms. The wetlands support vegetation having dense, shallow root systems that filter pollutants and facilitate soil microbial activity capable of breaking down undesirable pollutants that would otherwise enter streams, rivers, lakes, and coastal estuaries of South Louisiana.

Wetlands Protection-CWA Section 404 Permitting

The growing body of wetland science and ecology prompted perhaps the single most important action affecting the protection of the Spanish Lake subbasin and other wetlands in 1985. Specifically, litigation from national environmental groups forced the EPA and USACE to include wetlands as a "waters of the

United States" and protect them from discharges of pollutants under the CWA. The mechanism to protect wetlands was the CWA, Section 404 permitting process which regulated the discharge of fill in waters of the United States, including wetlands. Implementation and enforcement of the Section 404 regulations was delegated to the USACE. Prior to these regulations, there was no way to bring accountability to private or public interests for adversely impacting wetlands of any type. The implementation of the Section 404 permitting process protecting wetlands has been in itself the most controversial single aspect of the CWA. In order to protect wetlands, they must be officially identified and designated in the field and mapped. In addition, defining what constitutes an "adverse wetland impact" and then developing some methodology to quantify the adverse impact to provide the basis for compensatory mitigation remains a lingering, controversial issue. This is most evident when assessing proposed impacts to previously impacted or altered wetlands, which is typically the case with Section 404 permitting. Further, there are many specific wetland habitat types, such as bottomland hardwood forests, cypress swamps, pine savannahs, prairie pot holes, bogs, fresh marsh-salt marshes, and more, making it difficult to establish consistent methodologies to access impacts.

Collectively, the inclusion of wetlands as "waters of the United States" pushed the USACE into new territory as they were responsible for both defining and protecting wetlands, which included enforcement actions. Effective enforcement by the USACE of the Section 404 regulations (which regulate the discharge of fill within wetlands) was close to impossible in South Louisiana as the business community, land developers, and municipalities (public works) simply could not grasp the idea that wetlands were protected, and that impacting wetlands would require a permit and compensatory mitigation. Wetlands, which are ubiquitous, were still merely regarded as "waste lands" and a hindrance to development. For over a decade, court battles regarding the classification of jurisdictional wetlands had polarized communities.

Several key decisions regarding wetland classification and jurisdiction were decided to some extent by the Supreme Court and include *The Solid Waste Agency of Northern Cook County (SWANCC) v. U.S. Army Corps of Engineers* and *Rapanos v. United States* (Rutkow, 2012). The long-term outcome of the *SWANCC* ruling was that isolated wetlands, those that were not hydraulically connected to "waters of the United States," were not jurisdictional, whereas *Rapanos* specified the need to clearly identify the hydraulic "nexus" in the field prior to assuming regulatory jurisdiction. While most of these legal challenges narrowed the classification of wetlands in some ways, they also further solidified the long-term protection of wetlands as an extension of riverine and coastal fluvial processes.

Wetland Mitigation Banking in the Spanish Lake Subbasin

The third and final important step in the long-term restoration of the Spanish Lake subbasin was the required "compensatory mitigation" of wetlands. Section 404 of the CWA requires avoidance, minimization, and compensation of unavoidable impacts to wetlands through the permit process. Simply put, if you impact wetlands, you have to replace the same functional value of those wetlands. President George H. W. Bush stated it simply in a "no net loss" of wetlands policy during his first term. The question rapidly developed regarding how to accomplish the compensatory mitigation as Section 404 permits were approved.

The need to compensate for wetlands loss or "no net loss" gave rise to the concept of "wetland mitigation banking." The premise is that private or public interests could restore degraded wetlands. This includes lands that were natural, historic wetlands but have been filled or degraded. The mitigation bank owner (Sponsor) had to propose partial restoration of wetland functional processes and assume the legal obligation to maintain the restored wetlands for perpetuity. The proposed restoration actions or "management potential" would create quantifiable "habitat units" (HUs), which can then be used as compensation for the unavoidable impacts to wetlands associated with Section 404 permitting. In some specific cases, wetland habitat credits could be generated by placement of a conservation servitude on specific acreage of high-quality wetlands, preventing any future destruction of this resource.

When compensating for unavoidable impacts to wetlands as part of the CWA Section 404 permitting process, the HUs used must be within the immediate U.S. Geological Survey's Hydrologic Unit Code (HUC) or watershed and be "in kind" regarding habitat type. For example, compensatory mitigation for unavoidable impacts to fresh marsh requires fresh-marsh HUs in the same HUC of the impact, compensatory mitigation for cypress swamp requires cypress swamp HUs in the same HUC, and compensatory mitigation for bottomland hardwood forest requires bottomland hardwood for HUs in the same HUC, and so on.

Mitigation banking has been a controversial program since its conception. Yet, the mitigation banking process satisfied three key objectives regarding wetland protection and policy: (1) develop a regulatory compensation program that facilitated the USACE issuance of Section 404 permits, (2) provide an economic incentive for private and public landowners to restore and protect adversely impacted wetlands, and (3) establish a regulatory market as the basis for the value of HUs.

During the 1990s, two wetlands mitigation banks were approved and opened in the Spanish Lake subbasin. They include the 903-acre Bluff Swamp Refuge and Botanical Garden (Bluff Swamp Bank) and the 4,000-acre Lago Espanol Wetlands Mitigation Bank (Lago Espanol Bank). Both banks were owned by private landowners, referred to as entrepreneurial banks, and approved by the USACE and the Interagency Review Team (IRT) consisting of personnel from the EPA, the U.S. Fish and Wildlife Service, the Louisiana Department of Wildlife and Fisheries, and the Louisiana Department of Environmental Quality. These banks were established and approved to compensate for unavoidable wetland impacts associated with the Section 404 permitting process.

The Bluff Swamp Bank was established by entrepreneurs in coordination with Ascension Parish, the USACE, and EPA to specifically resolve the parish's unauthorized wetlands violations. This entrepreneurial wetland mitigation bank was the preferred compensatory mitigation method at that time. By purchasing the compensatory mitigation credits from a bank approved by the USACE and EPA, the parish's legal issues related to wetland violations were resolved at one time.

The regulatory process required that the entrepreneurs purchase 903 acres in Bluff Swamp and place it under conservation servitude for long-term protection as full compensatory mitigation for Ascension Parish's wetland violations. In turn, Ascension Parish paid Bluff Swamp Bank $265,000 for the HUs created by placing the 903 acres under servitude, and the EPA and the USACE absolved the parish of all legal actions regarding the past wetland violations.

It should be noted that Ascension Parish itself could have purchased the land and established the mitigation bank. However, there are long-term requirements associated with the creation of a wetland mitigation bank that are difficult for public entities to incorporate into their public works operations. These requirements include protecting the bank from any damage such as littering, drainage modifications, clearing vegetation of any amount, and maintaining the conditions of the conservation servitude on the bank for perpetuity. Thus, it was simply easier to pay a mitigation fee to the mitigation bank, and to walk away from maintaining the restored wetlands in the bank.

The second wetland mitigation bank to become operational within the Spanish Lake subdivision was the 4,000-acre Lago Espanol Bank in 1999. The land and bank were owned and established by large timber interests with extensive land holdings in the south. Specifically, the Lago Espanol Bank included 4,000 acres of timberland owned by Denkmann Associates FCA. Denkmann was a German immigrant that ran a grocery store in the same neighborhood as Frederick Weyerhaeuser in the later 1800s. Weyerhaeuser was attracted to Denkmann's machinist skills, and a partnership ensued that established the first large-scale lumber mill in the United States (Rutkow, 2012).

The Lago Espanol Bank was Denkmann timberland. This bank proposed protecting approximately 2,000 acres of cypress swamp and bottomland hardwood forests for preservation credits, and 2,000 acres for enhancement credits. The justification for the 2,000 acres of preservation credits was the eminent demonstrable threat of timber harvest (clear cutting) clearly posed by Denkmann's ownership. Timber management, or silvaculture, is exempt from CWA wetlands regulations, and clear-cutting the cypress would permanently degrade the ecosystem. As such, the Lago Espanol Bank was approved for the compensation of unavoidable wetland impacts associated with section 404 permitting, and offered HU credit sales on a permit by permit basis as approved by the USACE.

The establishment of both banks in the Spanish Lake subbasin created per-acre monetary value that greatly exceeded the appraised value of raw land and timber. These two mitigation banks also provided different financial opportunities. The Bluff Swamp Bank essentially sold all of its HUs during one transaction referred to as a "project specific" bank. The Lago Espanol Bank simply opened as a free-standing, approved mitigation bank. Lago Espanol Bank has continuously sold available credits to compensate for unavoidable impacts to wetlands for over a decade.

Since the banks were opened in the late 1990s, the market value or cost of wetland mitigation credits per acre at the bank in the Spanish Lake subbasin increased from $1,200 to over $7,500 by 2004. Following Hurricane Katrina in 2005, the Lago Espanol Bank was the only mitigation bank with available credits in the immediate watershed and was able to increase its market value to approximately $12,000 per acre. By 2009, there were four mitigation banks in the same hydrologic unit code (HUC) as the Lago Espanol Bank, and prices lowered, to adjust to increased competition and availability of HUs or credits. In contrast, the average appraised value of forested wetlands in the Spanish Lake subbasin was at most $2,500, primarily for recreational use or timber value.

Hydrologic Restoration: The Alligator Bayou/Bayou Manchac Floodgate

In 2001, Tropical Storm Allison ripped through South Texas and ended as a relatively stationary storm hovering directly over the vicinity of the Spanish Lake subbasin. The storm generated record-high rainfall, filling the Spanish Lake subbasin like a bowl. The floodgate remained closed during Allison, and Bayou Manchac's surface elevation rose rapidly, with storm water eventually overtopping Bayou Manchac Road and flowing into the subbasin. Two large vital communities were severely flooded as a result: (1) the Ridge Road community within the southeastern section of the Spanish Lake subbasin, and (2) the Elayn Hunt Correctional Facility in St. Gabriel. The correctional facility required prisoner evacuation. Lingering floodwaters adversely impacted septic tanks, surface drainage, and increased public health concerns for the city of St. Gabriel. It was clear that a real potential of severe flooding threatened the community and its surrounding residential, commercial, and industrial interests.

By 2004, it was also becoming apparent to the large landowners in the Spanish Lake subbasin that their forest was in significant decline. Large sections of bottomland hardwood forests exhibited die-off, a condition in which the upper branches become weak and thin; this allows the large-scale establishment of insect populations and disease. In 2006, two large landowners commissioned a wetlands ecological study to determine the primary cause of the tree death. The study was published in 2007 with the conclusion that closing the floodgate had increased the extent and duration of flooding within the Spanish Lake sub-basin, and was the primary cause of tree decline and ecosystem degradation of the area.

Specifically, the study highlighted the fact that permanent flooding had replaced seasonal inundation within the forested wetlands, especially below the seven-foot elevations, which is over half the acreage of the subbasin. This permanent flooding caused yearlong reduced soil conditions to essentially drown the trees and prevent regeneration. The permanently saturated soil conditions promoted lodging or felling of large hardwoods during large storm events as the soft soils could not support the tree mass under high wind conditions. Over the 40 years and numerous storms, the hardwoods had begun dying or falling over during storms.

The key recommendation of the ecological study was to partially restore the natural hydrologic regime of the Spanish Lake subbasin by opening the Floodgate unless under immediate flood threat. The report and recommendation was presented formally to Ascension and Iberville Parishes, the USACE, and all resource agencies and was publicly available on the Internet. In March 2009, after reviewing the findings, Iberville Parish and Ascension Parish, the owners and operators of the Floodgate, opened the Alligator Bayou Floodgate, restoring the natural flow in Alligator Bayou and the larger Spanish Lake subbasin. Both parish presidents cited their respective parish's obligation to reduce flooding and protect property as the reason to open the Floodgate.

Opening the Floodgate immediately dropped daily surface elevation within Alligator Bayou, Bayou Braud, Spanish Lake, and Bayou Paul over 3.5 feet, from 5.6 feet National Vertical Geodetic Datum (NGVD) to approximately 1.25 feet NGVD. During rainfall events with the gate open, surface elevations within the bayous and lakes would rise appropriately, and then recede within 5–10 days as the storm water naturally drained through Alligator Bayou and the opened Floodgate, and into Bayou Manchac. In essence, the opening of the Floodgate was a major hydrologic and ecological restoration activity, creating the potential to reestablish hardwood forest species that had been declining for over 50 years.

Alligator Bayou Swamp Tours vs. Iberville and Ascension Parishes

The entrepreneurs that had established the Bluff Swamp Mitigation Bank in 1997 also acquired land near the mouth of Alligator Bayou at Bayou Manchac on Bayou Manchac Road, including the infamous Alligator Bayou Bar. Over the following six to eight years, the owners developed and established the for-profit Alligator Bayou Swamp Tours (ABST), catering to the affluent high-density population around the Spanish Lake subbasin. The ABST experience was successful and unique as it focused on up-close encounters with large alligators in a restricted area, followed by a short cruise down Alligator Bayou in a large tour barge to Cypress Flats. The ABST for-profit business attracted school groups, regional patrons, and celebrities.

The partial restoration of Alligator Bayou's natural hydrologic regime was achieved by opening the Floodgate. However, this action essentially lowered the bayou's average water level by over three feet and restricted continuous operation of ABST's 40-foot, twin 200-horsepower tour barge. This barge was much larger than previous watercraft used within the Spanish Lake subbasin and requires a deeper draft than canoes, small fishing boats, or bateaus. Prior to opening the Floodgate, ABST had the benefit of almost continuous use of Alligator Bayou as the surface elevation was artificially maintained at approximately 5–6 feet NGVD, which accommodated the draft of the tour boat. The lower average water level in Alligator Bayou of 1.25 feet NGVD restricted the use of the tour barge to high-water events, which resulted in the closing of the Alligator Bayou Swamp Tour (ABST) business.

In response to the parishes' opening of the Floodgate in 2009, ABST filed a petition for an injunction and damages on July 23, 2009, in 23rd Judicial Court, Parish of Ascension, Louisiana, against Ascension and Iberville Parishes. ABST claimed that their lucrative tour business had been shut down by the parishes' action of opening the Floodgate. They alleged that the parishes' decision completely drained Alligator Bayou, destroying the navigability of the bayou, depriving ABST of their riparian right to access, destroyed fish and wildlife resources, killed cypress trees on their property, and prevented ABST from further use and improvement of their land. ABST pled their case under the legal theory of *inverse condemnation*, which provides a procedural remedy to a property owner seeking compensation for land already taken or damaged against a governmental or private entity having the powers of eminent domain (*Carabell v. U.S. Army Corps of Engineers*, 2004; *United States v. Rapanos*, 2004).

The emotional public appeal and support of ABST's plight was huge, greatly eclipsing that of the parishes' ability to publicize its mandated need to prevent widespread flooding and large-scale forest decline. The ABST owners were skilled and outspoken, calling themselves environmental activists and were very successful in engaging the public and media as to their cause. The ABST successfully portrayed themselves as saviors of the Spanish Lake subbasin and victims of greedy landowners aligned with the parishes to drain the subbasin for development purposes (commercial and residential) and mitigation banking; yet, as stated above, ABST owned the first mitigation bank on the property.

Litigation Summary 2009–2014/Private Need vs. Public Need

ABST filed its original claim against Iberville and Ascension Parishes on July 23, 2009. In May 2011, the trial court granted the parishes' motion to dismiss ABST's claim of inverse condemnation with prejudice. ABST appealed the trial court's ruling for damages on July 6, 2011, and on October 23, 2012, the parishes motioned for summary judgment. The district court upheld the lower court ruling and dismissed ABST's petition with prejudice on December 10, 2012. ABST appealed to the Court of Appeal, First Circuit, State of Louisiana (First Circuit), on March 19, 2014. The First Circuit granted the parishes' motion for summary judgment and, on March 12, dismissed ABST's petition with prejudice. Costs were assessed against ABST.

The unanimous ruling by the courts addressed the heart of the issue, which is the right of a *private interest* versus that of the larger *public interest*. Specifically, ABST, a private business, desired to artificially raise the surface elevation of Alligator Bayou, a public resource and state water-bottom, to maintain the success of its business to the detriment of other landowners who were being flooded and their forest resources diminished.

Regardless of ABST popularity and support from environmental groups, this is no different from an industrial, commercial, or agricultural interest using a public resource such as aquifers, streams, or other "waters of the United States" for their private use and gain, regardless of the adverse impacts to the public. The courts rejected ABST's claim at every level with prejudice, sending a clear message that a *private need* does not supersede the larger *public need*.

Since 2009, the parishes have kept the Floodgate open, only closing it during severe backwater flooding from Bayou Manchac. The Spanish Lake subbasin's hydrologic regime was partially restored overnight, and Spanish Lake once again became a seasonally inundated fresh marsh and swamp. The 56 years of maintaining an artificially high water level by closing the gate caused many changes that may not be restored, such as excessive erosion of the upper shoreline of Bayou Braud and Alligator Bayou, sedimentation of the Spanish Lake, shifts in plant communities that may be permanent, and physical and chemical alterations of soils from oil and gas exploration. However, some ecological processes have already begun as the forest floor experiences seasonal flooding and drying driven primarily by a riverine system. The wildlife appears to be shifting to fewer waterfowl, and there are many acres of dry land for wildlife to browse that were permanently flooded. In summary, there is no doubt that the opening of the Floodgate was the beginning of true and permanent wetland habitat restoration throughout the subbasin.

PATH FORWARD

Complete ecological restoration is a lofty goal that is rarely, if ever, achieved in highly impacted ecosystems. Seemingly small alterations of surface hydrology, the construction of elevated surface roads, and oil and gas exploration on any level have long-lasting impacts. However, wetland ecosystems, especially in subtropical climates, have a remarkable ability to heal themselves if their natural hydrologic regime is restored. This is exactly what is now occurring within the Spanish Lake subbasin.

The key to future successful and sustainable restoration efforts of the Spanish Lake subbasin rests with the public's willingness to remain engaged in a positive dialogue with all stakeholders including affected landowners, parishes, and municipalities. The very nature of this process is controversial as the perception of the Spanish Lake subbasin has evolved from a harsh barrier to colonization, a waste land, an oil and gas field, an artificial reservoir, a federally protected ecosystem, and now a potential restoration area. Simply put, the Spanish Lake subbasin is an endearing wetland ecosystem that has been and will remain a permanent influence and attraction of the region's cultural development, hopefully for generations to come.

REFERENCES

Barry, J. (1997). *Rising tide: The great Mississippi flood of 1927 and how it changed America.* New York: Simon & Schuster.

Bayou Manchac. (n.d.). Retrieved July 14, 2014, from http://www.bayoumanchac.org

Carabell v. U.S. Army Corps of Engineers, 391 F.3d 704 (6th Cir. 2004).

Chapter 2: State overview. (2005, December). Retrieved August 2014, from http://www .wlf.louisiana.gov/sites/default/files/pdf/document/32855-chapter-2-state-overview/ 11_chapter_2_state_overview.pdf

Collot, V. (1826). *A journey in North America containing a survey of the countries watered by the Mississippi, Ohio, Missouri, and other affluing rivers* (Vol. II). Paris: Arthus Bertrand.

Conner, W., & Brody, M. (1969). Rising water levels and the future of southeastern Louisiana swamp forests. *Estuaries, 12*(4), 318–323.

Conner, W., Hackney, C., Krauss, K., & Day, J., Jr. (2007). Future research needs and an overview in ecology of tidal freshwater forested wetlands of the southeastern United States. In W. Conner, T. Doyle, & K. Krauss (Eds.), *Ecology of tidal freshwater forested wetlands of the southeastern United States* (pp. 461–488). Dordrecht, the Netherlands: Springer.

Effler, R., Shaffer, G., Hoeppner, S., & Goyer, R. (2007). Ecology of the Maurepas Swamp effects of salinity, nutrients, and insect defoliation. In W. Conner, T. Doyle, & K. Krauss (Eds.), *Ecology of tidal freshwater forested wetlands of the Southeastern United States* (pp. 349–384). Dordrecht, Netherlands: Springer.

Harrilson, L. (1977). *Memories: A hard road but a pleasant journey growing up in Bayou Paul.* Personal Memoir.

Historical Census Information: Louisiana State Census Data Center. (n.d.). Retrieved August 2014, from http://louisiana.gov/Explore/Historical_Census/

Keim, R., Chambers, J., Hughes, M., Nyman, J., Miller, C., Amos, J., . . . Shaffer, G. (2006). Ecological consequences of changing hydrological conditions in wetland forests of coastal Louisiana. In Y. Xu & V. Singh (Eds.), *Coastal environment and water quality* (pp. 383–396). Highlands Ranch, CO: Water Resources Publications.

Kniffen, F. (1935). Bayou Manchac: A physiographic interpretation. *Geographic Review, 25*, 462–466.

Kniffen, F., Gregory, H., & Stokes, G. (1987). *The historic Indian tribes of Louisiana, from 1542–present.* Baton Rouge: Louisiana State University Press.

Lake Pontchartrain Basin Foundation. (n.d.). Retrieved August 13, 2014, from http://www.saveourlake.org

Rutkow, E. (2012). *American canopy: Trees, forests, and the making of a nation.* New York: Scribner.

Soil survey of Iberville Parish, Louisiana. (1977). Retrieved April 3, 2015, from http://www.nrcs.usda.gov/Internet/FSE_MANUSCRIPTS/louisiana/ibervilleLA1977/

SONRIS—Strategic Online Natural Resources Information System. (n.d.). Retrieved August 1, 2014, from http://sonris.com/

Swarzenski, C. M. (2003). *Surface-water hydrology of the Gulf Intracoastal Waterway in South-Central Louisiana, 1996–1999.* Professional Paper 1672. Denver, CO: U.S. Geological Survey.

United States v. Rapanos, 376 F.3d 629 (6th Cir. 2004).

5

Understanding Other Species' Needs: The Monetization of Nature—Self-Restraint and a Global System of Rationing of Natural Resources as an Antidote

Dominique G. Homberger

Contradictions, denials, and wishful thinking underlie most mainstream discussions concerning the impending ecological catastrophe that will occur unless humanity changes its course of unfettered consumption and procreation. The incongruity of the current trend of trying to save the remnants of Nature[1] by calculating the profits that could be realized by exploiting (monetizing) its natural resources and the ensuing psychological malaise have paralyzed most humans into learned helplessness with respect to environmental issues and into giving in to the current *Zeitgeist*[2] of monetizing everything. A fresh analysis of some of the scientific and cultural issues at the basis of this predicament, however, will generate arguments for replacing the overarching ideology of unlimited economic growth by principles of self-restraint and empathy not only toward our kin, but also toward Nature and our earth's co-inhabitants.

Humans have become the dominant and most widespread terrestrial vertebrate species on earth. As a biological species, humans are extremely flexible and can adapt to almost any environmental conditions, from hot deserts (e.g., the Tuaregs in the Sahara of northern Africa or the San in the Kalahari of southwestern Africa) to cold near-polar regions (e.g., the Inuits in Alaska or the Yaghans south of Tierra del Fuego in southern South America). Human ingenuity in finding and creating physical comfort through the use of fire; tools; building materials for protection from extremes of temperature, wind, and precipitation; and of fibrous materials for clothing and soft bedding has been essential for this unique adaptive capacity of humans among vertebrates. It has also set humanity on a path toward overexploitation of Nature and its resources, as well as toward human overabundance.

Since the 1960s, it has become quite obvious that the relentlessly burgeoning human population and its increasingly consumptive postwar[3] behavior are unsustainable as natural resources are being depleted and destroyed. Nevertheless, warning signs have been disregarded, attempts at corrective measures by some national leaders have been politically undermined, and the ideology of an unrestrained and unlimited economy of growth[4] has been pursued as if our earth and its resources were growing, too. But as wealth and affluence in human societies have increased, albeit to varying degrees, so has a loss of optimism as people experience, witness, or learn of natural disasters, epidemics, and crimes, as well as wars and other disputes over ever-scarcer resources. The additional loss of natural places through urbanization and expanded mining and agricultural production to support an increasing population deprives humans of places where they traditionally have been able to restore their sense of place and rootedness. The resulting loss of cultural and environmental memory not only affects mental well-being, but also our capacity to adapt to changing conditions by diminishing the breadth and depth of knowledge from which to draw.

This chapter will start with my personal journey as an example of how the understanding of the relationship between humans and Nature can change within an individual life span. I will proceed by tracing some recent political and societal developments to illustrate the processes that have led to our current ecological impasse and to our collective confusion about how to deal with it. I will then posit that humans depend on Nature for more than just their physical survival: A focus on monetary gain destroys not only Nature, but also forces humans to make impossible choices, such as between preserving their genealogical, historical, cultural, and evolutionary roots on the one hand, and ensuring their physical and economic survival on the other. I will finally argue that nurturing the capacity for self-restraint and empathy in humans may provide fresh approaches for a conscious preservation of Nature, a better understanding of our ecological role on this earth, and a refocusing on the fundamental problem of how to live in a non-expanding world.

CAPACITY FOR CHANGE: A PERSONAL JOURNEY

Through an aggregate of various experiences as a biologist and human being, I came to understand how economic development imperils Nature, and how a wounded Nature not only affects the physical survival of the humans, but also threatens the mental integrity of humanity.

I was born in postwar Switzerland, which had escaped the ravages of two world wars and benefited from the economic boom that came with the rebuilding of the infrastructure of its devastated neighbors. Nevertheless, I learned about scarcity and rationed necessities through my parents, who were young adults during World War II. At that time, Switzerland's population of about 4.5 million allowed for sufficient green spaces to separate individual villages and towns, and to permit camping vacations in what were considered to be natural places. But the subsequent population increase eventually led to about 8 million inhabitants by 2014, and to villages and towns that have almost coalesced to a single agglomeration. An early inkling of these changes was felt during elementary school when our teacher told us that picking wildflowers (as we had always done) would eventually eradicate them and, therefore, had to stop. The reality of the extinction of wild animals in Europe was also brought into our consciousness with the examples of the last wild aurochs (*Bos primigenius*) and Bald Ibis (*Geronticus eremita*) having been killed only relatively recently in the 1600s. Nevertheless, I still considered the forests and alpine meadows in Switzerland to represent Nature.

However, an internship in Naples, Italy, where I saw for the first time live swallowtail butterflies (*Papilio machaon*), which, according to textbooks, were widespread in the Northern Hemisphere, confronted me with the fact that an economically prosperous Switzerland had an impoverished Nature, while an economically struggling southern Italy seemed to have a richer Nature. This insight regarding the nexus between humans and Nature was reinforced during my fieldwork in the Kanha National Park (India) under India's "Project Tiger" (Panwar, 1987), when I came in direct contact with a much larger number of butterflies and the kind of large mammals—e.g., Bengal tiger (*Panthera tigris tigris*), Indian elephant (*Elephas maximus indicus*), barasingha deer (*Cervus duvaucelii*), gaur (*Bos frontalis*), Hanuman langur monkey (*Semnopithecus entellus*)—which I had previously seen only on television. My stay in India also provided me with my first glimpse of an ancient tribal people (the Baigas[5]) and the shock of seeing starving people.

Subsequent travels and field work in North America, Australia, and Patagonia, where large-scale and intensive exploitation of the natural environment started much later than in Europe, clarified my perception about the differences between virgin old-growth forests and managed second-growth forests, because they could be seen and compared side by side, such as in the Joyce Kilmer Memorial Forest in North Carolina with its 400-year-old giant tulip trees (*Liriodendron tulipifera*) and the Muir Woods National Monument in California with its 1,000-year-old coastal redwoods (*Sequoia sempervirens*), on the one hand; and second-growth forests, such as those in Switzerland, South Louisiana, or the northeastern United States that resulted from various forms of forest management, on the other. My subsequent field work brought me to Australia, where large-scale exploitation of forests started more recently than in North America and, therefore, has left scars that are more readily recognizable. My ecological work on parrots and cockatoos in Australia (e.g., Homberger, 2003) allowed me to gain a deeper understanding of the correlation between the richness of natural environments and their wild inhabitants, which is based on a complex interplay among all components of an ecological system. It was also in Australia where I could observe how human actions diminish and degrade the natural environment through deforestation, burning, mining, and the introduction of exotic animals (e.g., rabbits, feral cats, and cane toads), all with devastating results for the native flora and fauna.

During fieldwork in central Chile (South America) I observed how environmental destruction by humans in turn devastates humans. The ancient temperate rainforests with its majestic monkey puzzle trees (*Araucaria araucana*) and immense coniferous Mañios (*Podocarpus nubigenus*) along the western side of the Andes have changed little in the last 65 million years,[6] but have been replaced to a major extent by plantations of Australian eucalypts and North American pines under a totalitarian regime since the early 1970s. As a biologist, I mourned the loss of natural beauty and evolutionary history; but as a human being, I also fully empathized with the helpless grief that Chileans felt over the loss of their natural environment. Through my own pain, I was struck by the insight that this must have been the kind of mind- and backbone-breaking pain that indigenous people all over the world and over centuries and millennia must have felt when their environments were destroyed by invaders. My experiences in Chile also brought back the memory of a visit to the *Externsteine* near Detmold, Germany, and my empathizing with the overwhelming grief that the ancient Germanic Saxons must have felt when their sacred oaks were felled by Christian missionaries and the victorious Franks under Charlemagne in an orgy of power and destruction more than 1,000 years ago (Cusack, 2011).

History has shown that human societies, such as the Germanic Saxons (Arnold, 1997), can recover from such traumatic destructions of Nature, sometimes to such a degree that their descendants have lost the immediate memory of them together with the memory of how Nature used to be. Swiss children, for example, may feel perfectly happy to play outdoors and feel that they are enjoying Nature—at least until they discover the truth as they grow up and mourn the irretrievable loss of Nature in their country. Hence, the current environmental crisis not only imperils the physical survival of the human species, but also threatens its mental integrity through the loss of its connection to Nature. Nevertheless, through my own experience, I remain convinced that humans do and should have the capacity to change their actions toward Nature by analyzing their own motivations and attitudes with a clear mind, as well as by mobilizing and redirecting their inner resources.

GOVERNMENT RESPONSES TO HUMAN POPULATION INCREASES: EXAMPLES

Human societies differ significantly in their actions toward the natural environment. In general, the needs and demands of people (e.g., for food, fuel, jobs) are given priority over the needs of Nature (i.e., to be protected from human destructions), but there are exceptions, and it is these exceptions that can provide alternative models for how humans can act toward Nature.

Giving Nature Its Due: Switzerland and the United States

In 1914, some prominent Swiss citizens had become increasingly alarmed at the disappearance of natural areas in their country through the destructive effects of a burgeoning human population (Kupper, 2012). They decided to establish a national park in the most remote part of southeastern Switzerland to protect Nature from further encroachments on its integrity by humans. The motion to establish such a protected area was introduced to the Swiss parliament by Walter Bissegger with a quote from Sophocles's *Antigone*: "Many things are powerful, but nothing is more powerful than man" (Kupper, 2012).[7] The implication was that humans, who by that time had established their absolute rule over the earth and its inhabitants, do have the inner strength and resources to restrain themselves and their drive to dominate Nature and, therefore, to set aside places where Nature can thrive by itself without being modified by the intrusive and generally destructive behavior of humans as in the rest of the country. Implicit in the plan for a protected area was also the idea that Nature, if protected from human influence, would revert to, or evolve into, its original natural state. This natural state was an abstract concept without direct utility to humans, but of intense cultural interest at a time when Darwin's theory of evolution (1859) was still fresh and stimulating. Even though smaller than originally conceived, the Swiss National Park has nevertheless survived as an area that has been spared economic and touristic development and has become the home of reintroduced populations of steinbock (*Capra ibex*) and Bartgeier (*Gypaetus barbatus*) and of European brown bears (*Ursus arctos*) that immigrate from Italy.

In contrast, the national park movement in the United States, which had originally motivated the plans for a Swiss counterpart and similar movements in other parts of Europe, had created its first national park, Yellowstone National Park, in 1872 primarily as "public park ... or pleasuring-ground ... for the benefit and enjoyment of the people" (Runte, 1997; Spence, 1999).[8] Despite this originally anthropocentric conceptualization of national parks, the United States (and similarly Canada) has largely been able to manage the human impact on them by retaining federal control over the national park system. In addition, the United States under President Lyndon B. Johnson established the National Wilderness Preservation System in 1964 for the same reasons as the Swiss government had done half a century earlier, as an "area where the earth and community of life are untrammeled by man ... so as to preserve its natural conditions" (Wilderness.net, 2014). More recently, two million acres (8,000 km^2) were added to this wilderness area through the Omnibus Public Land Management Act of 2009 signed by President Barack H. Obama (U.S. Congress, 2009), who also proposed an additional 12 million acre refuge of permanent wilderness in Alaska on January 25, 2015 (Editorial Board, 2015a). The ambitious preservation of wilderness areas in the United States has been possible because of the vastness of its territory and unpopulated areas, in contrast to Switzerland, one of the smallest and most densely populated countries.

The Swiss national park movement and the U.S. wilderness movement (National Park Service, 2014) are, thus, examples of self-confident, wealthy, and politically stable countries being able to consciously decide to desist from following an inclination to pursue economic profit, even though both movements have encountered political hurdles.[9]

An Anthropocentric Focus: The IUCN[10] and UNESCO[11]

The IUCN was originally founded in 1948 to protect and "maintain functioning natural ecosystems, to act as refuges for species" (Dudley, 2008) but has come under pressure to adjust its mission by considering the needs of an increasing population (see Dudley, 2008). Hence, its revised list of protected areas comprises six categories with different degrees of human interference from strict wilderness areas (e.g., the Swiss National Park and the wilderness areas in the United States) to areas that allow the use of natural resources (Dudley, 2008). Hence, the current mission[12] of the IUCN is to "influence, encourage and assist societies ... to conserve the integrity and diversity of nature and to ensure that any use of natural resources is equitable and ecologically sustainable."[13]

Another example of an anthropocentric attitude toward Nature is the establishment of a network of Natural World Heritage sites and biosphere reserves by the United Nations in 1970 under its "Man and the Biosphere Program" (Natural Resources Defense Council, 2014; UNESCO, 2014a). The underlying philosophy in the creation of these reserves is an acceptance of man as a legitimate part of Nature so that the sites are places "of cooperation, education and experimentation, where scientists and managers can share research data to better understand man's impact on nature, and where local communities, environmental groups, and economic interests can work collaboratively on conservation and development issues" (Natural Resources Defense Council, 2014). In such places, therefore, Nature is not protected from human intrusions.

A recent example of the type of abuse that is brought to some of these sites is the dredging of parts of the Australian Great Barrier Reef (a UNESCO World Heritage Site) in Hay Point south of Mackay in Queensland in order to build "one of the largest coal export ports in the world" (Australian Associated Press, 2014; Marks, 2014; North Queensland Bulk Ports Corporation, 2014). This project was recently halted temporarily, though, because of slumping coal prices (Smyth, 2014), and not because of worldwide criticism or the condemnation by UNESCO, which has threatened to place "The Great Barrier Reef" on the "List of World Heritage in Danger" (UNESCO, 2014b).

The well-meant efforts by the IUCN and UNESCO to conserve some of the most beautiful places on earth for future generations exemplify the difficulty in creating and maintaining a global conservation program in the face of an increasing human population with increasing demands on natural resources. Since multinational organizations lack funds for oversight and do not have the power to enforce strict regulations and punitive actions that would hold individual countries responsible for destructive actions, it comes as no surprise that Nature in these reserves is often exploited for economic gain, while a decorum of conservation is maintained (see R. Hughes & Flintan, 2001; Mora & Sale, 2011; Winkler, 2007). Hence, the UNESCO and IUCN programs remain Sisyphean projects with an uncertain future as long as their focus is not the protection of Nature, but includes benefits for humans as an integral part of their mission (see Mora & Sale, 2011; Winkler, 2007), and as long as the fundamental problem of human overabundance and overconsumption is ignored (see also Kitzes et al., 2008).

Dealing with an Overabundance of Humans: India and China

It may not have been an accident that some of the strongest actions on behalf of Nature have been taken by two countries that were experiencing the detrimental effects of a burgeoning human population, although their motivations and approaches differed. All such efforts, however, ultimately failed in their objectives.

In India, for example, the tension between forces dedicated to nature conservation and the needs of an impoverished human population has been intense. When Indira Gandhi became prime minister in 1966, she established several conservation projects, initiated conservation laws, and created a Department of Environment. She understood that top predators, such as the tiger, are indicators of the health of an ecosystem, and she set for herself the goal of ending tiger hunts and the exporting of tiger furs and trophies (Sridhar, 2004). Under the auspices of "Project Tiger" (Panwar, 1987; Project Tiger, 2014; Thapar, 1999), which was established in 1972 with funding from the World Wildlife Fund, international biologists were invited to study the wildlife, while villagers within the designated reserves were relocated elsewhere. In addition, under Gandhi's Emergency Rule (1975–1977), her son, Sanjay Gandhi, led a campaign of family planning with strong incentives given to men and women to get sterilized in an effort to curb the rapidly growing population (from about 340 million in 1950 to about 540 million by 1970 [Trading Economics, 2015]) and to reduce its adverse effects on society and Nature. This unpopular program was soon discontinued due to its coercive approach (Gwatkin, 1979). After Indira Gandhi's assassination in 1984, her other son, Rajiv Gandhi, succeeded her as prime minister until

1989 and continued the conservation policies his mother had established. However, with the opening of India's economy to international interests in 1990 and the prioritizing of economic development, poaching and mining activities within nature reserves resumed (Gadgil, 2011; Ghandi, 2014; Thapar, 1997; Ward & Ward, 1993). Although the number of tiger reserves has increased in India, the estimated number of tigers has decreased from about 1,800 in the 1970s to between 1,400 and 1,600 in 2011 (Wildlife Protection Society of India, 2014), while the human population of India had grown to 1.2 billion by 2011 (Government of India, 2011). Predictably, conflicts between wildlife and humans have increased in frequency, and the poaching of tigers continues to be a problem (Burke, 2015; Lenin, 2014a; Roy, 2013).[14]

A different example of a nation's attempt to slow the growth of its human population is China's one-child policy, which was not so much driven by concerns for Nature, but rather by famines that had claimed the lives of millions. China's leadership, not being dependent on popular elections, was able to embark on a massive education and enforcement campaign of family planning for the majority Han population, which represented about 94% of China's population in the 1960s (Goldstein & Beall, 1991; National Bureau of Statistics of China, 2013). At the same time, the Han were encouraged to migrate and settle in regions that were the traditional homelands of non-Han ethnic groups. Together with an unprecedented economic growth starting in the 1990s, the bane of famines and abject poverty has been checked, but unanticipated problems have tempered this success; China has to contend with a problem of air, water, and soil pollution as well as with unrest among the colonized non-Han populations. With the pressure rising from a still-growing population with increased expectations for a comfortable life, the preservation of Nature is not a matter of priority and is under great threat from various development schemes, such as the flattening of entire mountains to create land for urban housing (Clark, 2014; Li, Qian, & Wu, 2014). Despite its one-child policy, China's population doubled from about 600 million in the 1950s to about 1.3 billion in 2010, but it is estimated that an additional 200–400 million people were not born because of rigorous family planning (Feng & Cai, 2010; FlorCruz, 2011). China's government has recently eased its one-child policy, and it remains to be seen what the effect will be on the rate of population growth in China (Kaiman, 2014). The prospects for China's natural environment to be protected in China are uncertain.

India and China, hence, exemplify large countries that were already struggling with limited natural resources and an impoverished population when their population sizes were less than half of what they are today. Hence, they face extreme challenges in dealing with an ever-growing human population that has begun to expect better living conditions. The ensuing degradation of air, water, living spaces, and natural environments has become an overwhelming problem in both countries. Political pressures, as manifestations of *Sachzwang*,[15] result in the prioritization of human demands with short-term solutions at the cost of Nature.

IDEAL VERSUS REALITY: PREHISTORIC HUMANS AND NONINDUSTRIALIZED COMMUNITIES

Nonindustrialized communities are often idealized by people living in industrialized and postindustrialized countries as living in complete harmony with their environment and using resources only to the extent that it does not disrupt the ecological balance (Hames, 2007). This idealization has a long history as exemplified by the bucolic tales of ancient Greece and some of the narratives by early European explorers of the Age of Enlightenment (e.g., Bougainville, 1771; Chamisso, 1835). It is usually based on preconceived ideas and superficial observations, and it derives from an unease of urbanized people who are critical of their living conditions and rigid social norms. The idea of a more "natural" life with fewer social constraints and a possible harmonious coexistence with Nature may provide some comfort in the belief that it may be possible for humans to live under idyllic conditions without doing any harm to Nature. The imagined Shangri-La,[16] the fictionalized American Indians led by Winnetou,[17] the current search for sustainable uses of natural resources as a panacea for the current environmental crisis, and some television programs that "highlight that humans . . . can live in harmony . . . with an ecosystem" and "prove [that] animals and humans can thrive side by side"[18] can be traced back to this old idea.

A more sober view of the impact of preindustrial human populations on Nature is supported by recent research that reveals that even prehistoric humans thousands of years ago had a significant effect on their environment by being responsible for extinctions of animals (Vignieri, 2014), especially large ones, through overhunting, changing the environment (e.g., through fire), or both (Lyons, Smith, & Brown, 2004). The demise of the megafauna at the end of the ice ages during the Quaternary period around 12,000 years ago in the Americas coincided with the arrival of humans (Lyons et al., 2004; Martin & Klein, 1989; Miller et al., 1999). Hence, even prehistoric humans had a more disastrous effect on prey species than any other mammalian predators, which usually coexist with their prey without exterminating it. This idiosyncratic effect of prehistoric humans on Nature may have its roots in a combination of factors. Prehistoric humans were capable of killing large mammals because of their sophisticated social organization that enabled them to hunt in collaborative groups and because of their capacity for tool- and weapon-making. Also, when prehistoric humans migrated to new places, they encountered a naïve native fauna that had not evolved appropriate defense or flight responses upon seeing humans. And the apparent preference for killing large animals (Dirzo et al.,

2014; Lyons et al., 2004), such as wooly mammoths (*Mammuthus primigenius*) and giant armadillos (glyptodonts) may have been connected to the feeling that killing a large and potentially dangerous animal is more manly and heroic than killing a mouse.[19] Hence, prehistoric man may have started the human trend of killing wild animals for sport and enjoyment, and not just for food and other necessities, thereby initiating a string of global extinctions through overkill. This human characteristic has also been the cause for subsequent waves of destruction of the native fauna and flora in the wake of the precolonial arrival of non-European humans on Pacific islands (Anderson, 2003; Steadman, 2006) and of European invaders on islands around the globe (e.g., Quammen, 1997). More recently, the remorseless killing of wild animals has continued not only for sport and enjoyment, but also for short-term monetary profit from trade with animal products, such as bush, whale, and bird meat; crocodile skin; elephant teeth; rhinoceros horns; tiger penises; bear feet; etc. (e.g., Editorial Board, 2015b; Fears, 2014; Tella & Hiraldo, 2014; Zajtman, 2004). It has even led to the defaunation[20] of protected national parks (e.g., Stokstad, 2014a).

Nevertheless, and remarkably, some nonindustrialized hunter-gatherer peoples, as exemplified by the Jívaros in Ecuador (Dauphiné, Tsamajain-Yagkuag, & Cooper, 2008) and the Sentinelese on North Sentinel Island of the Andaman Archipelago in the Indian Ocean (World Rainforest Movement, 2013), demonstrate that it is possible for humans to be less destructive to their natural environment than the surrounding colonizing dominant populations (see also Hames, 2007). It appears that their success[21] is based on their fierceness and capacity to resist intrusions by dominant populations, on their communal lifestyle, and on their lower population size and density relative to those of surrounding dominant populations. However, most nonindustrialized peoples and communities have been decimated through loss of their land rights and consequent poverty and cultural disorientation. Well-meaning interventions by dominant populations, such as missionaries, NGOs, the International Monetary Fund (IMF), and the Food and Agriculture Organization of the United Nations (FAO), to provide supposedly better living conditions usually led these communities to adopt various aspects of the capitalistic, industrial and postindustrial lifestyle, which, in combination with a concomitant population increase, made them as destructive to their environment as the dominant populations. But even contemporary subsistence-hunting and farming by monetarily poor communities on confined land areas, such as those of the Banggai Archipelago near Sulawesi in Indonesia (Indrawan, Garnett, Masala, & Wirth, 2014), are often forced to overexploit and, thereby, destroy their natural environment in order to survive at least for the immediate future. Ironically, the common well-meaning advice for such communities is to modernize and intensify agricultural practices and to develop ecotourism, both of which inevitably lead to an increase in the human population and land use, and, thus, negatively impact the extent and quality of Nature (see also Winkler, 2007).

GLOBAL OVERABUNDANCE OF HUMANS

The common denominator of the above examples of interactions between humans and Nature is the growing size and density of the human population. In each case, particular actions were taken in response to a burgeoning human population and its effect on the environment, but the actions differed depending on the available resources and established governance system. Of the three countries that decided to set aside land for Nature alone, only Switzerland and the United States have ultimately been successful. At the time of their decision, both countries were relatively prosperous and had a firm legal system to enforce laws. But perhaps more importantly, they did not suffer from an overabundance of humans: Switzerland had been able to regulate its population through emigration, and the United States had cleared space for its growing population by removing the native population. The third country, India, which had the same enlightened attitude toward Nature as Switzerland and the United States, though, has not been successful: It is a relatively poor country, and its legal system is too weak to prevent a huge and still-growing human population from continuously encroaching on the remaining pieces of Nature. The examples of China and the Banggai Islands further support that the size and density of human populations is the critical issue, as neither industrial development nor retaining a preindustrial lifestyle allow a sustained and strict protection of Nature as long as the human population and its needs grow unchecked.

The realization that the burgeoning human population and the increasingly consumptive postwar behavior of humans is unsustainable entered the common consciousness forcefully through articles and popular books in the 1960s and early 1970s, such as *Silent Spring* (Carson, 1962), *The Population Bomb* (Ehrlich, 1968), "The Tragedy of the Commons" (Hardin, 1968), *The Limits of Growth* (Meadows, Meadows, Randers, & Behrens, 1972), *Toward a Steady-State Economy* (Daly, 1973), and *Human Environments and Natural Systems* (Greenwood & Edwards, 1973). It was further reinforced by reports of contemporary famines and food shortages in India, Biafra (Nigeria), Ethiopia, and China, although famines and food shortages have been the bane of human populations probably since the advent of agriculture[22] during the Neolithic Revolution about 12,000 years ago. At the same time, fuel shortages, such as through the oil embargo by OPEC (Organization of the Petroleum Exporting Countries) in 1973 heightened the realization that the earth's resources are limited, which came to most Swiss as a shock. Many people had replaced their coal-burning, central home-heating systems with oil-heating ones in the belief that the oil reserves would be "unlimited" for "hundreds" of years as was generally advertised in the 1960s. Now, for the first time, people, even those in wealthy countries, had to consider the real possibility that humanity will eventually run out of natural resources.

Yet, half a century after the first serious warnings about the dangers inherent in an exploding human population and the accompanying environmental degradation, the situation has only worsened throughout the world. Recent, increasingly urgent warnings have come from Tim Flannery (2002) in Australia, Jared Diamond (2005) and Al Gore (2006) in the United States, David Suzuki and David Taylor (2009) in Canada, and many others, and have had negligible effects on policy decisions by governments. Quite to the contrary, many destructive human activities have increased as a result of the interdependent nexus between affluent and impoverished countries, societies, and individuals. Some examples are the expansion of European and Asian agricultural corporations into traditional landholdings in Africa to offset current and future food shortages in their own countries (Bourne, 2014) and the building booms that transform farmland into urban and suburban areas in China and North America (Flattau, 1985; Mitchell, 2001; Wang, 2010). Current urgent warnings about possible irreversible and unpredictable state shifts in the earth's biosphere (Barnosky, 2012) and about the disappearance of vital services that are provided by Nature (Haig, Martin, van Riper, & Beard, 2013) are likely to be largely disregarded, too.

CONFUSION, DENIAL, WISHFUL THINKING, AND PARALYSIS REGARDING ENVIRONMENTAL CRISES AND OTHER CATASTROPHES

As the warnings about the impending environmental crisis reach an ever-increasing degree of urgency and frequency, many or even most people feel increasingly powerless.[23] They have grown up believing that recycling paper and plastics and purchasing locally grown food was saving the environment, but now realize that eating sushi and fish (even though advised by health experts) is leading to the extinction of some of the most glorious fishes; that washing their hair with shampoo or purchasing a newspaper is contributing to the destruction of tropical forests (to make space for oil palm plantations or eucalypt plantations for wood chipping, respectively); and that taking a flight to visit grandparents is polluting the air and water. They are bombarded with appeals to save the environment and iconic animals, such as the giant panda (Ailuropoda melanoleuca) and the polar bear (Ursus maritimus), in far-flung places, and at the same time they observe how trees and natural places in their own neighborhoods are bulldozed and replaced by new apartment complexes and how wild animals that stray into suburban areas are captured or killed.

As a result of all these contradictory experiences, most people are confused, and they are frightened, numbed, and turned off by the barrage of news with weather-related catastrophes and dire predictions about future climate change, whereas some industries and corporations use this situation to maximize their short-term economic interests.[24] Most people, therefore, tend to resort to wishful thinking by believing that the impending crisis is not real, or at least not as dramatic as portrayed by some, and that it is just another politically charged ploy; that science and technology will eventually solve the problems as they always did in the past; and that it is not in their power to change the state of affairs. With this point of view, it may be understandable that large segments of society are in denial of what has become obvious to farmers, gardeners, and biologists who have been able to witness the changes in the seasons and the weather over the last three decades.[25] Many people, in an apparent effort to hold fear and despair at bay, maintain that climate change is not due to human activity, but is rather just one of the earth's normal occurrences that in the past have been responsible for the demise of dinosaurs, even though such an argument is hardly comforting as it implies that the demise of humans on earth may also become an instance of this normal occurrence. The very complexity of the issue of climate change not only tends to overwhelm most people, but challenges even the scientists who are engaged in trying to understand the causes and long-term effects of climate change.[26] Most scientists have been trained to identify cause and effect by using experiments, but climate change defies such standard approaches because the causes for climate change are multifactored, such as changes in the composition of the atmosphere, in the number of humans on earth, in the technology used by humans to exploit the earth's resources, in the vegetation covering the continents, and in many other factors.

The contradictory emotions and feelings of helplessness vis-à-vis impending environmental crises are only exacerbated by conflicting information provided by the mass media, which are increasingly owned by corporations with their own economic and political agendas. Several issues that have clear implications for an understanding of the impending ecological crisis are instead used to manipulate the population for political gain. For example, the current and projected numbers of humans on this earth are often portrayed as a "God-given" phenomenon that is not open for discussion. Ecological problems created by the overabundance of humans on this earth are not openly discussed in the mass media, and family-planning efforts in most of the world are undermined and even officially prohibited. The drop in the birthrate in some countries is occasionally portrayed as leading to a shortage of workers and a slowdown of the economy, and bonuses are promised to women who agree to bear more children (Bryant, 2008; Hookway, 2014; Wakabayashi & Inada, 2009). At the same time, the issue of overpopulation is used implicitly by politicians who raise the specter of mass immigration by refugees and illegal immigrants who are portrayed as putting pressure on already scarce social services and as taking away jobs that are already in short supply globally as increasing numbers of people of all ages are facing long-term unemployment and concomitant economic hardship (e.g., Foulkes, 2014).[27]

From this vantage point, it is not surprising that the current reaction to the impending environmental crisis is, on the one hand, paralysis or unproductive busy-ness or, on the other hand, continued unrestrained belief in the capitalistic credo of continued economic growth as a solution. Some cynics like to predict that the overabundance of humans on this earth will eventually be cut back by wars and epidemics. This flippant attitude is not only immoral, but is also not supported by history and science. Wars, even wars with cataclysmic slaughters of humans (e.g., the Civil War in the United States, and World Wars I and II), are generally followed by an increased birthrate, and so are pandemics (e.g., the Black Death in the fourteenth century; the Spanish flu after the end of World War I in 1918) (see also Marques, 2014). In considering the current state of affairs, it is difficult to avoid thinking of the analogy between the current behavior of humans on this earth and the allegory of the Ship of Fools so aptly depicted by Hieronymus Bosch in his famous painting (Bosing, 2000), in which mindless and frolicking passengers are drifting without a captain toward an uncertain destination, and by John Alexander (Livingston, 2008) in a contemporary rendition[28] in which the boat is already in a precarious situation.

The lack of initiative and action among political leaders with respect to the current environmental crisis is frustratingly demonstrated by the series of conferences organized by the United Nations and designed to tackle the environmental crisis at a global level (United Nations, 2014a). Each conference was announced with much fanfare, but each ended with little to show for it (see, for example, Vidal, Stratton, & Goldenberg, 2009). A possible reason for the current collective paralysis to have taken hold also of political leaders may lie not only in economic *Sachzwängen*,[29] with each country wanting to take action only if other countries were to take it also,[30] but also in the wishful thinking that humans will be able to manage any environmental problems, as we supposedly always have in the past. This wishful thinking may be encouraged by the experience with other looming dangers, such as nuclear accidents, with potentially cataclysmic effects on earth, but so far with "only" local damages that have not been as bad as originally feared.

Some human-caused terrifying nuclear accidents in the last three decades (Knauer, 2012) have become unintentional experiments that show how humans are capable of rendering the earth uninhabitable for the foreseeable future. These should have served as wake-up calls and propelled humanity to reevaluate its role and actions on this earth. Instead, they have added to the general confusion. One of these catastrophes, in Chernobyl in northern Ukraine, was the worst nuclear accident so far. Since it occurred in 1986, it has been an exclusion zone for people, and it is estimated that it will have to remain so for the next 20,000 years. Chernobyl, thus, stands as an example of a disaster that humans have not been able to manage. Yet, while scientists are trying to understand how living organisms manage to survive in radiation-contaminated places despite deleterious effects on their genome and development (American Genetic Association, 2014; Featherstone, 2015; Mousseau & Møller, 2012; Taira, Nohara, Hiyama, & Otaki, 2014), the World Nuclear Association (2009) confidently announced the results of its review of health effects on humans: "In the centuries to come, the Chernobyl catastrophe will be seen as a proof that nuclear power is a safe means of energy production." Ironically, the next unmanageable nuclear catastrophe occurred only two years later, in 2011, in Fukushima on the western coast of Japan.

Contrary to initial expectations, though, the region around Chernobyl is now teeming with wildlife and is used as a wildlife reserve for rare and endangered animals, such as Pzrewalski's horse (*Equus przewalskii*) and the European bison (*Bison bonasus*) (Chesser & Baker, 2006; Hayden, 2007). There are indications and anecdotal observations that the region around Fukushima is also being reclaimed by wildlife (Nippon Hoso Kyokai, 2013), possibly because radiation-resistant individuals are selectively favored and are able to multiply (American Genetic Association, 2014) without interference by humans. The fact that Nature appears capable of contending with nuclear contamination if humans are removed, but generally loses out in any direct competition with humans, should give us pause for sobering thoughts about the destructive role played by humans on this earth.

It is not surprising that most people are completely confused about nuclear and radiation issues. At the extremes, they believe that all life will be wiped off the earth by nuclear bombs, or they seek shelter in wishful thinking that nuclear accidents and bombs can be survived. The latter, and the receding memory of the atomic bombs thrown on Nagasaki and Hiroshima in 1945, has likely led some politicians to seriously consider the use of nuclear bombs in armed conflicts (see, for example, Borger, 2015; Watt, 2012). Most countries, except Germany through its *Energiewende*[31] (Gillis, 2014), have failed to take decisive future-oriented actions toward nuclear issues and have avoided addressing the central issue of energy and fuel overuse. A comparable kind of confusion, denial, and wishful thinking has probably taken hold of political leaders when they consider the dangers of climate change without addressing the central issue of human overabundance (see also Engelman & Codjoe, 2014; United Nations, 2014b).

CONFUSION, DENIAL, WISHFUL THINKING, AND PARALYSIS ON HOW TO SAVE NATURE

Monetizing Nature in Order to Save It

Despite the challenges, scientists are the only people with the expertise necessary to analyze and clarify the causes and effects of climate change. Even though a full understanding of climate change is still evolving, as all sciences are, it is currently sufficient to realize that the observed warming trend of our climate is driven by the consumptive behavior of a growing human population and that it needs to be stopped in order to maintain the earth as a living planet (United Nations, 2014a, 2014b, 2014c). As scientists struggle to find and develop arguments for saving at least some of the remaining natural environments from the contemporary headlong rush toward economic growth, they find themselves in the grip of $Sachzwängen$.[32] These have grown out of our current $Zeitgeist$,[33] which tends to quantify the economic value not only of products that have monetary value in order to be traded without having to barter for them, but also of all aspects of human life and in general of all living things on earth. Quantification, by itself, is not necessarily a negative force; it increases the confidence of scientists in their data and facilitates the communication between scientists and decision-makers, who are not necessarily scientifically trained and generally function under a perceived mandate of spurring economic growth (see also Cardinale, 2012; Haig et al., 2013). The problem for Nature, though, lies in the easy transformation of quantified data into the ultimate quantifiable economic instrument—monetary value.

Originally and under the currently dominant economic model of capitalism, Nature by itself has no economic value. Marx (1867) described uncultivated land (wilderness) as being "unproductive" and, thus, without value. Value would accrue only through the labor of humans, which would create products from natural resources and use or sell them. Hence, land and natural resources are believed to be free for the taking. Under this precept, even gold and diamonds have no value as long as they rest in the depth of the earth. This belief expressed itself when immigrants to North America and Australia cut down trees and plowed up the prairies and grasslands in order to make the land fertile and productive, and it continues to this day with corporations mining, polluting, and making large stretches of land uninhabitable in their search for minerals and fossil fuels without paying for or mitigating the damage to Nature. This way of thinking has deep roots in human history and even prehistory, when humans hunted large animals to extinction, and has led to the belief that the depletion of and damage to Nature and its resources do not need to be accounted for in calculations of economic costs and benefits (for a discussion, see Daly, 1973, 2008a; J. B. Foster, 2002; Gore, 1993; Max, 2014; Roberts, 2013).

In an apparent attempt to beat the current economic model by its own rules, some scientists have tried to estimate the economic value of natural environments to facilitate comparisons with the economic value they would have if they were exploited for agriculture, forestry, or mining. In doing so, they have pursued two main lines of research (for a review, see Cardinale, 2012) by either estimating the economic value of the services and resources that ecosystems provide for humans (e.g., Banks-Leite et al., 2014; Bateman et al., 2013; for a critical review, see Naeem, 2012), or by trying to explain how biodiversity makes our earth livable (e.g., Cardinale, 2012). In contrast, ecologists and conservation scientists try to understand the interactions among organisms,[34] as well as the interactions among organisms and their environment in natural and transformed[35] environments. The number of these interactions and, hence, the degree of biological diversity, have been shown in numerous studies to correlate positively with the productivity of the earth's land and water and with human well-being in general (Cardinale, 2012), but these intricate and complex interactions are difficult to quantify. Nevertheless, scientists are continuing to try to refine the tools that allow them to quantify the effects of biological diversity on natural and transformed environments in an effort to present their results in a quantifiable manner that has come to be expected in science and political decision-making. However, in doing so, they play into the hands of political and commercial forces that see Nature only in terms of its potential monetary value and as a resource to be exploited.

A focus on generating quantifiable data that can be transformed into monetary value tends to overlook Nature as a provider of intangible benefits to humanity, such as happiness, a sense of balance in life, a sense of place and time, and a sense of ecological and evolutionary rootedness, probably because these benefits evade attempts at quantification and, ultimately, monetization. Similarly, Nature's benefits to nonconsumptive human activities (e.g., recreation, education, and science) are difficult to quantify and are often not included in ecological studies (Cardinale, 2012). Interestingly, emotionally beneficial, nonconsumptive enjoyments of Nature (e.g., hiking, bird watching) are increasingly harnessed for economic profit through gadgets, gear, and infrastructure that are marketed as necessary for the enjoyment of Nature.[36] By putting a price tag on everything, even on one's time and friendships, as well as on Nature, and by demanding that everything, even Nature, pays for itself, greed is finding no limits as everything is for sale and is harnessed to generate and increase profit. This is why the well-meaning attempts of biologists and conservationists to save Nature by placing a monetary value on its resources will ultimately fail: Monetizing Nature is unleashing a storm that biologists will not be able to control (see also Flocken, 2014).

Exploiting Nature in Order to Save It

The trend of placing a market value on the environment in an effort to save Nature from being destroyed by market forces has recently been accelerating because of the belief that humans will be more inclined to protect Nature if they perceive it as being useful in more tangible ways than in just providing a home for polar bears and tigers. However, this line of thinking leads inevitably to a feeling of human entitlement to the bounty of Nature. This claim of human supremacy over Nature and the current interdependent global nexus between, roughly speaking, urban affluence and rural poverty has resulted in some incongruous uses of Nature, which are now ubiquitous and often advertised as part of a good life to be aspired to.

Despite the worldwide decline of wildlife, recreational hunting has been enjoying increasing popularity. Hunting is often justified as being part of our evolutionary heritage and is considered, especially in North America and Australia, to be an activity that is compatible with a love for Nature (see, for example, Gewertz & Errington, 2015). In this context, safaris are organized for wealthy people to shoot, for example, highly endangered elephants and rhinoceroses in Africa for huge fees,[37] while native people are shot or incarcerated as poachers if they do the same. Such trophy hunts are rationalized, even by some conservation-minded groups (Pearce, 2014), as providing funds for the protection of the remaining individuals of the hunted animal species. This argument has been shown to be a fallacy, bordering on irrationality[38] (e.g., Flocken, 2014).

Various other approaches to exploiting natural resources are encroaching on Nature around the world. In Australia, conservative governments have passed laws that promote tourist concessions, recreational hunting, cattle grazing, and commercial logging in national parks with the rationalization that the income from licenses and commercial exploitation serve to preserve Nature (Arup, 2014; Howden, 2014) or that it helps to offset the carbon footprint of energy-intensive industries,[39] such as luxury airliners (carboNZero, 2010). Luxurious lodges in pristine landscapes of economically emerging countries, such as Chile, Brazil, China, and India, are rationalized as part of ecotourism that supposedly helps preserve Nature. This particular land use is especially problematic for islands, with their limited land area and the limited number of plant and animal individuals and populations that are usually distinct from mainland populations, such as the gazelles on the Dahlak Kebir Islands off Eritrea (Chiozzi, Bardelli, Ricci, de Marchi, & Cardini, 2014). Selective logging of valuable timber in old-growth forests in North America, Madagascar, and Southeast Asia, for example, is rationalized as a benign exploitation of Nature in contrast to clear-cutting of forests, even though it has been shown (Asner et al., 2005) that it affects the integrity and health of forests. The nexus between increasing affluence in developed and emerging countries and persistent rural poverty in less-developed countries has also seduced native people into destroying their own environment by poaching wildlife parts, wildlife, and plants, such as elephant ivory, rhinoceros horn, parrots, tortoises, orchids, cacti, and bromeliads, to supply illegal international markets mostly in the Middle East, East Asia, and, increasingly, also local markets (e.g., Editorial Board, 2015b; Fears, 2014; Tella & Hiraldo, 2014; Zajtman, 2004).

Managing Nature in Order to Save It

Because genuinely pristine environments are rapidly vanishing and may not be salvageable given the current *Zeitgeist*,[40] much biological research is directed toward monitoring the status of habitats and species in the hope that such documentation may lead to improved management practices and the restoration of degraded natural environments. The most common causes for dysfunctional ecosystems are a loss of key species, such as natural predators, and the fragmentation of natural habitats that become too small to sustain healthy animal and plant populations. Such habitats are usually marked by an overabundance or underrepresentation of particular species, which becomes apparent when plants are depleted by herbivorous insects or mammals—e.g., white-tailed deer (*Odocoileus virginianus*) in some part of the Eastern United States (Rawinski, 2008)—or when wildlife start to appear in human settlements. Trespassing animals are generally the result of humans having trespassed into and reduced the natural ranges of animals by expanding urbanization and agricultural development. Nevertheless, when wildlife is considered to be trespassing, it is removed or killed, as happened to "Bruno," the hapless European brown bear who ambled through Germany and was killed by hunters even though it had not been a threat to humans (Harding, 2006); to "Echo," the hapless gray wolf (*Canis lupus*) that had been collared in Wyoming and walked 750 miles to Utah, where she was shot by a hunter "by mistake" (Ketcham, 2015), or to gray wolves that move beyond the confines of Yellowstone National Park in Montana (Associated Press, 2014).

Most current biological management practices aim at preserving Nature without considering what would seem to be the obvious option, namely the reduction and halting of the continuing encroachment on natural places by humans, as was done a century ago by Switzerland and half a century ago by the United States, and as was attempted four decades ago by India (see above). Instead, biological management actions concentrate on controlling the number of animals by culling them or by trying to rescue individual species from extinction, respectively. The problems created by invasions of introduced exotic species are legendary: Burmese pythons (*Python molurus bivittatus*) devour almost all animals in the marshes of Florida (Walsh, 2014); fire ants (*Solenopsis* spp.) displace native invertebrates across the southern United States (Tschinkel, 2006); feral cats

(*Felis catus*) decimate songbirds in North America (Loyd, Hernandez, Carroll, Marshall, & Abernathy, 2013) and small native marsupial mammals in Australia (Dickman, 1996; Lewis, 2014; Woinarski, Burbidge, & Harrison, 2015); and North American beavers (*Castor canadensis*) destroy ancient forests in Tierra del Fuego in southern Argentina and Chile (Choi, 2008). In contrast, some heroic efforts costing billions are directed toward efforts at saving iconic species from extinction, such as the Puerto Rican Parrot (*Amazona vittata*) (Snyder, Wiley, & Kepler, 1987) and the California Condor (*Gymnogyps californianus*) (Snyder & Snyder, 2000) in the United States or the Greater bilby (*Perameles lagotis*) in Australia (Moseby & O'Donnell, 2003; Pavey, 2006). Many other endangered species are being bred in zoos and special facilities in the hope of re-leasing them into the wild once their captive populations have reached a sus-tainable number. Such reintroductions, however, have met with mixed success (Kleiman, 1989; Russon, 2008; Seddon, Griffiths, Soorae, & Armstrong, 2014), especially because usually little is known about the ecological needs of the spe-cies by the time they have become endangered, and because the original habitats have often been altered or destroyed and are no longer suitable for the species. Even apparent success stories are not reasons for unadulterated joy. Although the American bison (*Bison bison*) was saved from extinction (Kleiman, 1989), it survives only in carefully controlled reservations in very small numbers (ca. 5,000–15,000) compared to its original population size of 20–30 million (Kleiman, 1989); and the Whooping Crane (*Grus americana*) has encountered serious problems with numerous individuals having been shot in several states from South Dakota to Louisiana despite its protected status (Dave, 2014).

It may ultimately be an illusion to believe that species in danger of extinction can be saved through breeding programs in zoos because most often there are no natural places left for them to return to (see also Kleiman, 1989). Similarly, it is an illusion that Nature can be restored and returned to its original pristine, pre-human natural state, as has been recognized after a century of scientific monitor-ing of the Swiss National Park (see Kupper, 2012). Many of the efforts to restore natural landscapes are unlikely to recreate an original, prehuman Nature, because the restorations are conceptualized by people who have never seen the places in a state uninfluenced by humans (see Bilney, 2014; Pauly, 1995). Fur-thermore, many of our most cherished "natural" landscapes, such as the Lüneburger Heide in northern Germany (Urban, Kunz, & Gehrt, 2011), the alpine pastures in central Europe (Soane, Scolozzi, Gretter, & Hubacek, 2012), or the fenlands in eastern England (Dee, 2013), have actually been fundamentally influenced, often for millennia, by humans and need to be managed to remain in their current state of environmental and cultural importance.

It is presently not known how many years Nature would need to return to its natural state, but it is estimated that it would take thousands of years. For exam-ple, the footprints of the Mayan culture can be discerned even after the roughly

1,000 years since the Mexican rainforests have repossessed the Yucatan. Furthermore, most forests in the developed part of the world are at most century-old second-growth forests and in no way comparable to the few remaining virgin old-growth forests with their often 2,000- to 3,000-year-old giant trees. Finally, habitats are dynamic systems that undergo constant modifications under the influence of environmental changes, irrespective of human influence.

Most shocking, however, is the fact that some ecological systems can never recover from the actions by humans and are irretrievably lost. The history of clear-cutting or burning of forests for shipbuilding, for grazing of cattle, or for establishing monocultures of crops for the world market over millennia has been well documented (Chew, 2001; Jacks & Whyte, 1939; Williams, 2006; M. C. Hansen et al., 2013). Many of these excesses have had irreversible effects not only on the land itself, but also on the climate, for example, by a significant reduction of rainfall in central Chile since the German immigration 150 years ago (Otero, 2006) and the aridification and desertification of the Mediterranean region of Europe (Jacks & Whyte, 1939). Today, most humans are unaware that the iconic deserts of northern Algeria and Libya and the gleamingly white rocks of the Aegean Islands are a result of the hunger for timber and food by the expanding populations of the Romans and Greeks (J. D. Hughes, 1993). The protection of the last few remaining wild places on earth would, therefore, be of greatest urgency, but is generally obstructed by short-term goals of powerful transnational commercial, timber, and mining interests.

Another cause for the irredeemable degradation and loss of parts of our earth is pollution by humans through agriculture, mining, and waste products since ancient times (e.g., Borsos, Makra, Béczi, Vitányi, & Szentpéteri, 2003; Chew, 2001; Hong, Candelone, Patterson, & Boutron, 1996) and more recently also through nuclear accidents and oil spills. Pollution has grown in tandem with increased consumption and is now pervading all parts of our earth, including our water and food sources (Halden, 2010; Yosim, Bailey, & Fry, 2015; Zhang, 2012; Zuber & Newman, 2011). Whereas air and fresh water can be filtered, contaminated oceans are too vast to be cleansed, and contaminated soils can only be removed and stored elsewhere on earth, thereby confirming the adage that cleaning consists of only transferring dirt from one place to another.

THE BIOLOGISTS' DILEMMA

Through their research, most biologists[41] directly or indirectly monitor and describe what happens in Nature and are, thereby, well aware that biological management efforts are ultimately just stopgap operations that only postpone, but do not prevent, the impending environmental catastrophe unless humanity were to change its course of unrestricted procreation and consumption. It is their work that showed that Nature has been changing visibly and measurably, especially in the last four decades, and how this change has affected Nature around the world.

Under the current *Zeitgeist*, though, biologists, and in particular those in academic settings, face a terrible dilemma. Based on their training, knowledge, and research, they are fully aware of the precarious situation that Nature faces. By inclination, they ought to be the most dedicated, strongest, and most vocal defenders of Nature. Biologists have usually decided on their career path because they love animals or plants and feel a strong connection to Nature since childhood. However, Nature finds its strongest advocates among nongovernmental organizations (NGOs), whose staff members are not necessarily trained biologists. One reason for this counterintuitive situation is that scientists have been trained and conditioned to avoid becoming emotionally involved in their research and to aspire to an often unrealistically rigid understanding of objectivity (e.g., Lackey, 2014; Sarewitz, 2014; but see Sabine, 1912, for a discussion), because emotions are considered to distract from the path toward scientific truth.[42] As a consequence, most biologists tend to stay out of politically sensitive issues (see Stokstad, 2014b), which generally demand emotional involvement. Given the increasing corporatization of universities and colleges, and the need for often substantial funding from governmental and private sources to conduct research projects, scientists also feel reluctant to become actively involved in potentially controversial issues and to advocate for policies that they feel may appear too radical or different in the context of the current political climate.

Because of the limited employment options, many biologists often accept positions to prepare environmental impact assessments and make recommendations for government agencies or private corporations (e.g., timber industry, coal and mineral mining, oil extraction, fracking, etc.) on development plans, which are usually a foregone decision. Such studies dare not be too critical of developmental schemes, even though large-scale industrial exploitation or building schemes generally destroy Nature (e.g., Gadgil, 2011; Meijaard et al., 2005). Most such reports are likely to be simply filed away to serve corporations as a protective shield against legal liabilities and are largely disregarded by governments (see, e.g., Gandhi, 2014).

Biologists may also see their work misused for political machinations. Most research papers in biology conclude that more research is needed for the complete clarification of a particular problem, even if they deal with issues that have clear implications for conservation and policy issues (see, for example, Chiozzi et al., 2014). To be sure, in science, each answer and each result spawns more questions; but many recommendations by biologists that more research is needed play into the hands of corporations, such as the tobacco, timber, mining, or energy-producing industries, who have continuously been asking for more research as a maneuver to delay legislative actions that may harm their business. Political decision-makers, in turn, have seized on the calls for more research by biologists and used them as a cover for not taking decisions that may be politically sensitive and could endanger the financial support of corporations and, thus, their position of power.

Even fieldwork to study the behavior and ecology of animals and plants in their natural environments, one of the most cherished and interesting areas of work for biologists, has become problematic in our times. If the locations of rare or endangered species are described and published in scientific papers, this information may be used by collectors and poachers. Through well-meaning efforts in describing and inventorying the fauna and flora of unexplored places, biologists may open up tracks through which predators and hunters may gain access to an intact ecosystem, then disturb, modify, or destroy it. For example, 100–200 large flightless parrots, called Kakapos (*Strigops habroptilus*), were unexpectedly found by biologists in the interior of Stewart Island south of New Zealand's South Island in 1977, after it had been believed that this species was about to become extinct (Powlesland, Merton, & Cockrem, 2006). Soon after their discovery, however, the Kakapos started to be killed by introduced feral cats following the tracks that people had created through the dense heath, and the remaining 62 individuals had to be transferred to mammal-free islands to ensure their survival (Elliott, Merton, & Jansen, 2001).

Hence, many biologists find themselves in a psychologically unsustainable situation in which they feel that they cannot follow their inclination to work on behalf of Nature. They feel that they have to censure themselves in order to ensure their livelihood, or they have to be circumspect about their fieldwork in order to protect Nature. They also realize that no amount of remedial and conservation efforts by humans will reduce the impact by people on Nature as long as the problem of an overabundant and expanding human population persists. Hence, no amount of positive thinking and optimism can prevent biologists from feeling helpless and in no position to prevent the destruction of Nature, the object of their interest and love.

THE PRIMIGENIAL RIGHTS OF NATURE

The efforts to put an economic value on Nature, though originally well intentioned, fail to consider the fact that Nature has intrinsic, primigenial property rights on this earth independent from whether it is of any use to us humans. These rights derive from the fact that humans have joined the earth's inhabitants as late guests and, therefore, do not have the right to usurp all resources of this earth for their own use to the detriment of all other inhabitants of our earth (see also Naeem, 2012).

For most of human history, it was believed in one way or the other that life on earth was created by some extraterrestrial agent or agency for the benefit of humans. By believing this, humans were able to feel innocent about their effects on Nature and to rationalize their domination over the earth's creatures as a sign of being favored by the extraterrestrial agent. This naiveté, however, could no longer be maintained from the moment that Jean-Baptiste Lamarck (1809) and Charles Darwin (1859) showed that life on earth has had a long history and that humans played only a relatively brief, though significant role in it. The so-called Darwinian revolution in the middle of the nineteenth century coincided with several fundamental innovations in the natural and social sciences and the arts (Homberger, 1998) and forced humans to reevaluate their place within Nature. We have seen at the beginning of this chapter that this change of thinking had taken roots a century ago at least in some parts of the educated citizenry (Kupper, 2012), who logically concluded that humans needed to step back and relinquish resources and space to Nature, not because they had to do so, but because they wanted to do so. This conclusion becomes even more persuasive with a better understanding of the evolutionary and cultural roots of the human tendency to overuse natural resources by taking them not only for survival, but also for enjoyment and sport.

A century later, however, this enlightened attitude toward Nature has been all but beaten into retreat by our current *Zeitgeist*. The theory of evolution and the scientific account of the history of evolution on earth are doubted or rejected by an increasing portion of society under the influence of ultraconservative political and religious leaders. In addition, the contemporary discussion concerning the current environmental issues by social scientists, economists, and decision-makers is guided by an anthropocentric focus on the right and feasibility of humans co-inhabiting our earth with Nature (e.g., Brookshire, 2015; Main, 2015; Rozzi, 1999, 2012) and on finding an equitable and sustainable use of the world's resources by humans (United Nations, 2014c). Notable in these kinds of discussions is an absence of reflection, introspection, and sober analysis of the inner motivations of humans and their effects on and actions against Nature. This avoidance precludes an uninhibited discussion of the central problem that lies at the root of our current environmental crisis, namely the fact that the current size of the global human population already has reached a size that cannot be supported by the earth, as the millions of malnourished and undernourished children (ca. 25% of the global population of children under 5 years) demonstrate (United Nations, 2014b; UNICEF, 2014). More and more people can have their needs satisfied only by taking away more land and resources from Nature (United Nations, 2014b). Therefore, unless real actions are taken, all the natural places will eventually have been used to support the needs of dominant populations of humans, with the needs of minority human populations and wildlife completely disregarded.

At this point in time, the fact that the rights of humans to use the earth as a playground to live as we please is questionable, if not unwise, and the fact that Nature has primigenial rights on our earth, are subjected to collective denial.

As a consequence, sensible discussions of ways how to address our current environmental crisis, such as family-planning issues, also need to be repressed[43] with similar neurotic effects that repressed thoughts have on individuals. Many vigorously disagree with these facts and their logical consequences for society and individuals, just like many disagree with the proposition that dominant populations should pay reparations to exploited people and should return land to dispossessed native people. Such reactions are to be expected but do not need to be condoned, because the liberation from psychological defense mechanisms, though often arduous, has immeasurable benefits for the lives of individuals and entire societies.

PSYCHOLOGICAL COSTS OF DISRESPECT FOR NATURE AND FELLOW HUMANS

Since the groundbreaking work of Oskar Heinroth (1971), Konrad Lorenz (Burkhardt, 2005), and Niko Tinbergen (Burkhardt, 2005), science has been making progress in demonstrating that many animals (e.g., elephants, parrots, crows, porpoises and whales, apes, monkeys, wolves, and many others) are sentient and endowed with cognition and emotions that are in principle not different from those of humans (de Waal, 2009, 2010). Humans who have been in close contact with domesticated animals, especially dogs, have been aware of this fact for millennia. And yet, humans have been decimating wild animals, even those that are cognitively most similar to humans, by capturing or killing them for profit, sport, and enjoyment and by destroying their natural habitats, while rationalizing that wild animals do not feel the kind of physical and emotional pain that humans can experience. In the past, analogous colonizations, genocides, and ill treatments of vanquished, captive, or enslaved humans were similarly justified by declaring that the subjugated people do not possess the same psychological makeup as the dominant population. However we may feel that times have changed and that we need to look toward the future and move on, history will never absolve a society that has committed cruelties against fellow humans, whether they are Australian aborigines; Patagonian Mapuches and Yaghans; prisoners in concentration camps in South Africa and Turkey during World War I; prisoners in concentration camps in Germany, Poland, and the Ukraine during World War II; or native Americans and African slaves in the Americas. Similarly, our current and continuing assault on Nature will not be absolved by future generations, especially because they will suffer the consequences of our actions and inactions and will feel with some justification that the current generation should have known better.[44]

The capacity of humans to feel remorse and guilt about past events, even if, individually, they did not participate in them, is part of the general human capacity to remember and be emotionally affected by the past. Such memories ground, root, and shape humans, and their centrality in what makes people human is shown by the predilection of humans to collect and recount personal and family stories, and biographies.[45] Tales of origins in sacred books, legends, chronicles, and histories of nations have been crucial resources for individuals, tribes, societies, and nations to retain a sense of identity and rootedness despite changes in their environment. This human need to position oneself within a grander scenario than one's immediate present revealed itself long before an evolving world and universe was considered and eventually accepted as a scientific fact. Hence, the fact that humans have plumbed the past as far as possible with the tools of physics, astronomy, geology, and evolutionary biology is not simply a by-product of technological and scientific advances, but is part of the human need for rootedness.

As is known from geological and fossil records, the earth has been constantly changing through the eons of its existence. When organisms started to populate the earth, they were able to persist only by being able to change and adapt to constantly changing environmental conditions. This survival process is possible because organisms vary individually in their interactions with their environment; the individuals that are able to interact successfully with their changed environment survive and continue to breed and multiply. The result of this never-ending process is what we call evolutionary history, which has been documented to have continued for the last 2.7 billion–3.5 billion years (Smithsonian Institution, 2014). Humans are part of this process even though they are latecomers to it as their evolutionary history can be traced back only about 4 million years (White et al., 2009). The longest unbroken cultural and historical connection of humans is even shorter; the longest being those of the San people in southern Africa that can be traced back to about 44,000 years ago (Balter, 2012; d'Errico et al., 2012; Smith, 2000), and of the Australian aborigines, which can be traced back to about 60,000 years ago (Vickas, 2013). But the prehistoric[46] roots have been lost for the great majority of contemporary human populations. Many people have lost even their historical and genealogical roots through cataclysmic catastrophes (wars[47] and epidemics), forcible deportations of entire communities, or voluntary emigration. Nevertheless, people generally feel the need to reconnect with their past and roots.

Landscapes[48] and natural environments tie humans to their past and root them at an even more fundamental level than history and genealogies (Otero, 2010). Humans retain emotional ties and are drawn to landscapes where they grew up and even to those places they know only through family stories and legends told to them by their grandparents. Distinct landscapes and their climates, such as forests, steppes, marshes, high-altitude mountains, and deserts, influence their inhabitants in subtle but distinctive ways, giving rise to some proverbial personality traits of societies, such as mountain people with their pronounced desire for independence (see Griffin, 2001). A recent groundbreaking study supports the imprinting effect of landscapes on humans. It revealed that the psychological characteristics of rice-cultivating and wheat-cultivating societies have been molded by their environments and cultivation practices, with rice demanding intensive and collaborative work and wheat requiring less intensive work that can be performed by fewer people (Henrich, 2014; Talhelm et al., 2014). These differences have had long-term effects on characteristics and social organization of the two populations even after most of their members stopped being farmers, presumably because the different behavioral norms had been internalized and imparted to each subsequent generation. Future comparative cross-cultural studies are likely to provide more evidence of how the environment shapes human cultures and to what degree.

At present, however, humans are involved in destroying the last remaining natural landscapes and environments and, thereby, their evolutionary roots, even though pristine Nature cannot be brought back even with the greatest remediation efforts, and even though archaeological and paleontological studies can provide only a partial description of past natural environments. For biologists and cultural anthropologists, this environmental catastrophe is anguishing; but for human populations that are more immediately interacting with and dependent on Nature, it is mind- and backbone-crushing. The destruction of Nature as a means of subjugating people and crushing their resistance has a long and dreadful history, even though it is usually portrayed only as a means of realizing profit for the dominant population. Nevertheless, biologists are in a unique position to empathize with the travails of native peoples, as the two are united by their common love and respect for Nature (see, for example, Majnep, Bulmer, & Healey, 1977; Rozzi, 2010). Although subjugated societies can recover from such traumas, the destruction of natural landscapes anywhere in the world erases our common evolutionary history and, thereby, affects the entire humanity.

However, for billions of humans, Nature is largely an abstract concept. Millions live and grow up in densely populated megacities, such as Beijing, China, or São Paulo, Brazil, and are unlikely to have the opportunity to visit natural places. Even most Europeans have never seen unspoiled Nature unless they have traveled to natural places on other continents. Convincing this increasing part of humanity that its habits of overexploitation of natural resources, overconsumption,[49] and overprocreation[50] need to be reined in to save Nature (as well as the evolutionary history and future generations of humans) will require the harnessing of the human capacity for clear thinking—free of denial and wishful thinking.

SOLUTIONS FOR AN AGE OF SCARCITY

It may come as a surprise to most people in economically prosperous continents, such as Europe, North America, and Australia, that we are living in an age of scarcity, because its starkest manifestations are played out on other continents and are usually explained away as solvable through better resource distribution and economic development (United Nations, 2014c), even though this has never been demonstrated in practice at the global scale. Yet, the various civil wars and popular revolts that are erupting in Africa, Asia, and South America are, in the final analysis, struggles about resources, foremost among them water, food, and energy (United Nations, 2014c). Hence, the current ecological impasse that threatens Nature is also a threat to humanity at the existential level, and it is necessary to conceive genuinely new approaches to save Nature, and thereby humanity, instead of trying to improve old approaches and temporizing by dealing with smaller problems at the margins of the major issues. This will require a return to an analysis of the fundamental issues underlying our understanding of the rights and roles of Nature and humans on this earth.

Until now, humans have considered the proverbial Mother Nature to be like the idealized human mother[51]—forever giving with breasts full of nourishing milk, forever undemanding, forever resilient in the face of deprivations, forever forgiving of insults, and forever providing without demanding payment. The problem, though, is that real Nature, just like a real mother, eventually dies when her physical resources and her capacity for renewal are depleted. Hence, one of the first steps for reform of our interactions with Mother Nature is to step back and to recognize her as a separate entity with primigenial claims on this earth. A logical second step is to requisition our inner resources to restrain our tendency to demand and expect that our every desire and need should and can be satisfied and is free for the taking from Nature. Tempering this tendency is likely to be facilitated by the realization that the ideology of unlimited economic growth is ultimately a futile enterprise (Daly, 2008a, 2008b), because whatever natural resources are still available will soon be depleted anyway (e.g., Anderson, 2012; Kerr, 2014; Post Carbon Institute, 2012; Ruz, 2011; Valero & Valero, 2010), if not in our lifetime, so certainly during the lifetime of our children and grandchildren.

Our current ecological crisis can be understood at a basic level as a result of our innate drive for physical and mental comfort leading to overconsumption and overprocreation. This basic drive is not unique to the human species. Many animals are motivated by the same drive, as is shown, for example, by chimpanzees fashioning every night a platform for sleeping in the trees, by birds lining their nests with soft materials, and by all animals producing and enjoying their offspring. To be sure, the human drive for comfort (warmth during the nights and winters, cooling during sweltering summers, dry shelter, sufficient food and water, hygiene, security from pests and predators, children for security and emotional comfort, etc.) has continuously raised the life span and quality of life of humans over the past centuries and especially over the last 50 years (World Health Organization, 1998). But it is the uniquely evolved mental capacity of the human species that has made this drive uninhibited and excessive and, thus, a destructive force. Under this point of view, the current environmental crisis can be conceptualized in essence as a result of a loss of boundaries and a concomitant crisis of the human psyche. In earlier times, the limits of their pocketbook imposed constraints on people; but with increasing affluence, these constraints have been loosened (Offer, 2006). Boundaries, however, provide a necessary mental framework to guide individuals and societies in their development and their actions. Such boundaries can and need to be established and maintained by humans themselves through laws and personal decisions to follow such laws (e.g., Associated Press, 2015; Cohen, 2009; Green, 2015; Halden, 2010; Kitzes et al., 2008; Offer, 2006).

The currently predominant economic model that drives human societies is capitalism, which is fueled by human greed, which has become accepted as the emotion that can be most successfully mobilized in humans (Cohen, 2009; Marx, 1867; Offer, 2006) and is, thus, responsible to a major extent for the apparent political success of the ideology of unlimited economic growth as well as for the environmental crisis we are currently facing. However, greed is only one of many aspects of our psyche (see also de Waal, 2009, 2010). Cohen (2009) quite correctly pondered whether it might be possible to establish aspects of our psyche that will motivate humans to be less selfish and to act in a manner that is conducive to building a more just and equitable economic system. The best candidate for this objective seems to be the human capacity for self-control and self-restraint.

Among the many human emotions besides greed, the capacity for empathy with and compassion for vulnerable living things is also an innate characteristic attributes of humans. Both emotions are already incipient in various animals (de Waal, 2009, 2010), and evidence of them has been found in our earliest ancestors (Spikins, Rutherford, & Needham, 2010a, 2010b). Given the innate human adaptability and capacity for learning and introspection, a redirecting of the currently cultivated dominant emotion of greed toward a self-imposed focus on the equally innate capacity for empathy and compassion not only toward our kin and fellow humans, but also toward Nature and our co-inhabitants on this earth, should, and actually must, be achievable if we want to avoid the otherwise inevitable collapse of Nature and, thus, the demise of humanity.

History teaches us that in times of real danger, humans can, and are willing to, adapt to new situations. For example, during World War II in Europe, food, clothing, and energy were rationed (Theien, 2009), with specific amounts of calories apportioned to individual needs, so that, for example, nursing mothers, children, and construction workers would receive more and richer food than middle-aged office workers. Humans are also able and willing to discard cherished traditions and adopt new attitudes that are more enlightened and civilized. For example, the burning of witches in Switzerland (until 1782), animal fights in England, and public lynchings in the United States used to serve as entertainment for families with children, but were discontinued as societies realized how barbaric these spectacles were.

Given that we are currently living in an age of scarcity from a global point of view (see above), as well as one of increasing inequality between classes of society and between countries (Picketty & Saez, 2014), the introduction of an international system of rationing food, water, clothing, transportation, and energy around the globe is a sensible and rational proposition to ensure that the current population and future generations have equitable access to basic necessities (see also Offer, 2006; Kitzes et al., 2008; Theien, 2009). A system of global rationing of the basic necessities (water, food, fiber, energy, and construction materials) will require sacrifices by some and alleviate or prevent suffering of others and, therefore, was called a "shrink and share" approach by Kitzes et al. (2008). Such an equitable sharing of the world's natural resources among all people and across generations (including future generations) will also reduce the risk of popular uprisings and wars for economic reasons,[52] which generally further destroy already scarce resources. It is also a rational alternative to some of the current solutions that have been proposed. Simply raising the price of basic necessities, such as water, as Anderson (2012) suggests, would only mean misery, deprivation, and death for millions of already impoverished and marginalized people. And UNESCO's and IUCN's programs to save Nature while at the same time also improving the lives of people is a plan that resembles an attempt at eating the cake and having it, too.[53] Actually, should the proposed global system of rationing be instituted, the United Nations' (2012) motto "The Future We Want," which highlights what people want, will have to be modified to reflect a focus on shared sacrifice in order to provide basic necessities fairly and equitably to all people, as well as to ensure the survival of Nature and its nonhuman inhabitants.

A global rationing system is necessary, but not sufficient to ensure the preservation of Nature and its resources. It needs to be combined with a fundamental change of attitudes of humans. The engrained ideology of unlimited economic growth based on raping Nature and exploiting its resources will have to stop and be replaced by an economic model that takes into account that the earth is not expanding (see, for example, Daly, 2008a, 2008b). Such a new model will require self-restraint in most consumptive behaviors and a self-imposed willingness to follow laws that enshrine such a fundamental change. New laws that prevent trespassing into Nature can be established (e.g., Wood, 2013), just as there are existing laws against trespassing and breaking into private properties. New laws can also prevent the expansion of housing developments with ever-larger buildings at the cost of fertile agricultural lands and Nature, or the expansion of agricultural developments at the cost of Nature (e.g., Kitzes et al., 2008). New laws can also encourage the donation of cultivated land to be returned to protected natural areas and forego personal monetary gain, as was done by Gewertz and Errington (2015). Old practices and laws that reward and promote greed and large families can be replaced by new practices and laws that reward restrained and responsible behaviors toward society and Nature (e.g., Associated Press, 2015; Green, 2015; Guthrie, 2015). Self-analysis and critical analysis of issues can lead to the question of whether traditions that were established more than 12,000 years ago, such as killing animals for enjoyment, really still have a place in a modern and cultivated society. There are hardly any limits to possible changes that we humans can undertake once we reject denial and wishful thinking and instead clear our minds and face the fundamental problems as they are, not as we wish them to be.

Of course, it is to be expected that such ideas and laws would meet the usual resistance on the grounds of that it "will never work" or "cannot be done." But such defeatist answers, generally based on cynicism and learned helplessness, can be challenged by asking the non-rhetorical question, "Why not?" (see also Cohen, 2009), and by letting the skeptics explain why things, in their opinion, cannot be done. The customary objection in a capitalistic society that it "will cost too much" can be countered by inviting fiscal conservatives to reapportion the budget from expenses for destructive wars to investments in constructive projects. Another question that can be asked is, "What are the alternatives given that what has already been attempted has not worked?" And finally, one can confidently point toward recent examples of the acceptance of fundamental behavioral and attitudinal changes by humans, such as the universally accepted recycling of discarded materials, which was first introduced during the World Wars; the ban of plastic bags in California and in India and many other countries (Cemansky, 2014); the *Energiewende*[54] in Germany (Gillis, 2014); the rationing of water in Santa Cruz, California (Gonzalez, 2014); the fossil fuel divestment campaigns by universities in North America, Europe, and Australia (Vaughan, 2014); the decision not to invest in coal-mining industries by Stanford University (Wines, 2014); or the *Cool Biz* campaign in Japan (McKean, 2014), which encourages businessmen to wear short-sleeved shirts without jackets during the hot summer months to reduce the energy needed for air conditioning because all nuclear power plants were shut down in the wake of the Fukushima nuclear accident.

What would the incentives be that would ensure and sustain a change from greed as the driving force in human society toward self-restraint, as well as empathy with and caring for Nature? By necessity, in order not to fall back into the old ideology of the monetization of everything, these rewards will have to be intangible. But most people know from experience the feelings of relief and empowerment that come with the ability to restrain oneself for the benefit of others (e.g., Nature) and the accompanying capacity to stand up to and resist forces with which one disagrees. That emotional rewards for such a change in attitude exist and have been reaped is evidenced by people who have made this transition, such as the Bishnoi[55] community (Thapar, 1997) and Valmik Thapar himself in India (Sridhar, 2004), Walter Bissegger[56] in Switzerland (Kupper, 2012), the

American legislators voting for the Wilderness Act (U.S. Congress, 2009), Deborah Gewertz and Frederick Errington in South Dakota (Gewertz & Errington, 2015), and the increasing number of people around the globe who have already embraced this change.

CONCLUSIONS

Faced for the first time in history with the real prospect of a global shortage of natural resources, humanity appears incapable of facing reality and instead seeks refuge in denial and wishful thinking. The complexity of the current ecological impasse requires an integrated solution based on underlying issues. Most humans, however, try to deal with individual, less controversial issues separately and sidestep fundamental ones. This chapter has illustrated this state of affairs with evidence from a variety of sources encompassing science, conservation, economics, politics, evolutionary and cultural history, and psychology. Although humanity's inherent search for comfort lies at the root of the current human overabundance, overconsumption, and overpollution, and, thus, of the current environmental crisis, humans are capable of changing course if they renounce denial and wishful thinking. Nature has primigenial rights on this earth—as evolutionary newcomers, humans do not have a God-given right to plunder Nature's riches and defraud the rest of the earth's inhabitants. Furthermore, and most importantly, the loss of our evolutionary history through the destruction of Nature would be as tragic as any loss of our cultural and social history. Because the current human population, consumption and pollution have already reached the limits of the carrying capacity of our earth, self-restraint and a system of global rationing of water, food, energy, clothing, and building materials will be necessary to secure a fair access to life's necessities by all humans, including future generations, while also giving Nature its due by confining humanity to the areas it has already appropriated from Nature. Such a fundamental societal and philosophical readjustment will require sacrifices by some and at the same time provide for the needs of others. It will also liberate Nature and humans from a path that is unsustainable within the limits of our earth. If now is not the moment for such a change of course, when will it be?

ACKNOWLEDGMENTS

I thank Darlyne G. Nemeth for inviting and encouraging me to write this chapter, as well as Robert Hamilton, A. Ravi P. Rau, Juan Masello, Urs Glutz von Blotzheim, Megan Cotterell, Mochamad Indrawan, and Bradley M. Wood for their comments questions that improved early drafts of the manuscript. Over the years, many friends and colleagues have knowingly or unknowingly provided me with materials that have inspired many of the ideas presented in this chapter.

NOTES

1. The term "Nature," as used in this chapter, is a conceptualization of the natural environment and all its organismal and physical components (e.g., air, water, soil, animals, plants), excluding humans, in contrast to the places that are used and exploited by humans. Natural environments free of human interference are also called "wilderness."

2. *Zeitgeist*, an anglicized German word, is the "trend of thought and feeling in a period [of time]" (Guralnik, 1970).

3. "Postwar" in this chapter refers to the time immediately following World War II, from 1945 until the 1960s.

4. On the dogma of the economy of growth, see, for example, Commission on Growth and Development (2008), Daly (2008a; 2008b), and Roberts (2013).

5. I thank Hashim Tyabji and Aasheesh Pittie for the identification. See also http://www.peoplesoftheworld.org/hosted/baiga/

6. The supercontinent Gondwana broke up into the southern continents of South America, Africa, and Australia about 65 million years ago.

7. Translated from the German translation of Πολλὰ τὰ δεινὰ κ' οὐδὲν ἀνθρώπου δεινότερον πέλει (as cited by Kupper, 2012). Johnston (2014) translates this passage as "There are many strange and wonderful things, but nothing more strangely wonderful than man."

8. Native American tribes were dispossessed and removed as was the general policy of the United States at that time.

9. A second Swiss National Park on the Lake of Neuchâtel could not be realized (Urs Glutz von Blotzheim, in litt. 30 December 2014). For the United States, see Howe (2010). For a general discussion, see Wuerthner, Crist, and Butler (2014).

10. International Union for Conservation of Nature

11. United Nations Educational, Scientific and Cultural Organization

12. Retrieved April 3, 2015, from http://www.iucn.org/about/

13. A similar *volte-face* can be observed in other NGOs, such as the Nature Conservancy (http://www.nature.org/) and the National Geographic Society (http://www.national geographic.com/) which produced a documentary championing this new anthropocentric approach (Brookshire, 2015; Main, 2015). See also Tercek (2013) and Max (2014).

14. According to the National Tiger Conservation Authority, India's tiger population has grown by more than 30% to 2,226 individuals in the last four years (Burke, 2015; Kumar, 2015), ". . . but concerns remain" (Balachandran & Ghoshal, 2015).

15. *Sachzwang* is often translated as "inherent necessity" or "factual constraint" (http://en.bab.la/dictionary/german-english/sachzwang). However, the true meaning in German (literally "coercion by an impersonal thing or matter") is a pressure on human decision-making, which seems imperative and inevitable even though, upon closer analysis, it is not.

16. Originally described as a fictional place of complete harmony in James Hilton's 1933 novel *Lost Horizons*.

17. Winnetou the Apache chief and his friend Old Shatterhand are the quintessential good guys fighting against bad outsiders in the highly successful and iconic series of novels by Karl May (1842–1912), who had not visited North America before writing them. http://www.nytimes.com/video/world/europe/100000003056479/native-fantasy-germanys -indian-heroes.html

18. *Earth: A New Wild* (Brookshire, 2015; Main, 2015).

19. Dr. Herculano Alvarenga (Taubaté, Brazil), personal communication. Fifth-century Buddhist commentary also differentiates between killing a large animal (e.g., elephant) and killing a small animal (e.g., mouse) with the former creating a greater karmic burden because it takes more energy and intention (Barash, 2014). See also Chapman (1987) regarding the catching of large fishes by men and of small fishes by women and children.

20. Defaunation is a term for the extermination of animals on earth. In particular areas, it has led to so-called empty forests.

21. The degree of biodiversity of their homeland before their arrival cannot be assessed; hence, their effect on Nature in comparison to that of modern humans may be a matter of degree.

22. Agriculturists are sedentary and dependent on favorable weather conditions to produce food. Famines and food shortages have repeatedly been the result of bad weather conditions and political turmoil in the past (see also Diamond, 2005; Ó Gráda, 2010).

23. See also Norgaard (2011) and Kolbert (2014).

24. The available literature is too large to cite, but good starting points on the controversial topic are Lever-Tracy (2010) and Klein (2011).

25. Changes in the timing of the first plants to flower in the spring, migratory birds to arrive or leave, lakes to ice over or defrost, or the length of the growing season of vegetables and crops have been documented extensively. For a review, see, for example, Cotton (2003), Tooke & Battey (2010), Primack and Miller-Rushing (2012), and Primack (2014).

26. I thank Robert Hamilton for this insight.

27. For a more differentiated view supported by research, see, e.g., Winegarden and Khor (1991) and Withers and Pope (2007).

28. http://ggreentechnology.files.wordpress.com/2014/03/john-alexander-ship-of-fools.jpg (painting).

29. Plural of *Sachzwang*; see footnote 15.

30. See, however, the recent U.S.-China agreement on climate change (S. Hansen, 2014; Lenin, 2014b; Nuccitelli, 2014).

31. *Energiewende* has become an anglicized word for "energy transition" to describe the transition from traditional coal and nuclear energy to renewable solar and wind energy.

32. See footnote 29.

33. See footnote 2.

34. Organisms comprise all living entities, such as terrestrial and aquatic plants, vertebrates, invertebrates, bacteria, and fungi.

35. Transformed environments have been changed by human activities to serve economic needs, such as agriculture, mining, and urbanization. Some of these environments are considered "degraded" if they serve neither their economic nor their natural purpose any longer.

36. Similarly, direct personal interactions are replaced by electronic interactions through cell phones, which need to be paid for (personal communication by Richard Robbins, Department of Anthropology, SUNY-Plattsburgh).

37. For example, Safari Club International (http://www.scifirstforhunters.org/); Dallas Safari Club (http://biggame.org/).

38. See also the biting satire by *The Colbert Report*, "The Word—Philanthrophy," http://thecolbertreport.cc.com/videos/6zcsyl/the-word—-philantrophy

39. Australia's carbon pricing scheme, under which carbon offset schemes would fall, was repealed in 2014 (Taylor & Hoyle, 2014).

40. See footnote 2.

41. The term "biologist" in this chapter is meant in a very broad sense and stands for a scientist who deals with living things at all levels of organization, from cells to ecosystems.

42. Although most scientists see themselves as "truth" seekers, it would be more accurate to say that scientists are "reality" seekers who try to understand the mechanisms and processes of the material-physical aspects of the world.

43. This can be illustrated by a true incident. During a panel discussion on conservation issues with six prominent ecologists and conservation scientists at an international scientific congress in Hamburg in 2006, I asked why the topic of family planning had not been brought up. The large audience clapped in support and apparent relief that the elephant in the room was at last acknowledged. Five of the panelists declined to answer, and the sixth admitted that the conservation community had decided to avoid this politically sensitive issue.

44. The 1968 rebellions in Europe are often interpreted as a rebellion against the parent generation involved in World War II (see Cornils & Waters, 2010).

45. "Hold those things that tell your history and protect them." Maya Angelou as quoted by Lee (2010).

46. Prehistory refers to history before written records were generated.

47. For example, most genealogies in central Europe cannot be reconstructed beyond the Thirty Years' War (1618–1648), during which Germany's population was reduced from 20 million to 4 million, because of the devastation it wreaked on buildings and written records stored in them.

48. The term "landscape" is used here in its general meaning, such as in "landscape paintings."

49. As shown by He et al. (2014), overconsumption has a measurable negative impact on Nature and is distinct from and additive to the negative impact of human population growth.

50. See also Associated Press (2015) and Green (2015).

51. Mother Nature and human mothers are celebrated only on one day out of 365 days (i.e., Earth Day and Mother's Day, respectively).

52. For a discussion of the nexus between diminishing wildlife and social exploitation, see Brashares et al. (2014).

53. For a discussion of the problems related to "sustainable development", see J. M. Foster (2008).

54. See footnote 31.

55. The Bishnoi are desert people in northwestern India, who protect anything that lives.

56. Walter Bissegger chaired the commission that proposed the creation of the Swiss National Park in 1914.

REFERENCES

American Genetic Association. (2014, August 14). Fukushima's legacy: Biological effects of Fukushima radiation on plants, insects, and animals. *ScienceDaily*. Retrieved April 3, 2015, from http://www.sciencedaily.com/releases/2014/08/140814124535.htm

Anderson, A. (2003). *Prodigious birds: Moas and moa-hunting in New Zealand.* Cambridge, UK: Cambridge University Press.

Anderson, R. (2012, June 11). Resource depletion: Opportunity or looming catastrophe? *BBC News: Business.* Retrieved April 3, 2015, from http://www.bbc.com/news/business-16391040

Arnold, B. (1997). *Medieval Germany: 500–1300: A political interpretation.* Basingstoke, Hampshire, UK: Palgrave Macmillan Limited.

Arup, T. (2014, March 6). Greg Hunt approves Victorian Alpine National Park cattle grazing trial. *Sydney Morning Herald.* Retrieved April 3, 2015, from http://www.smh.com.au/environment/conservation/greg-hunt-approves-victorian-alpine-national-park-cattle-grazing-trial-20140306-348do.html

Asner, G. P., Knapp, D. E., Broadbent, E. N., Oliveira, P. J. C., Keller, M., & Silva, J. N. (2005, October 21). Selective logging in the Brazilian Amazon. *Science, 310* (5747), 480–482.

Associated Press. (2014, May 22). Montana FWP approves killing of 100 wolves per year by landowners. *Billings Gazette.* Retrieved April 3, 2015, from http://billingsgazette.com/news/state-and-regional/montana/montana-fwp-approves-killing-of-wolves-per-year-by-landowners/article_42187512-67ab-5600-9579-735424a404ed.html

Associated Press. (2015, January 20). Catholics don't have to breed "like rabbits," says Pope Francis. *The Guardian.* Retrieved April 3, 2015, from http://www.theguardian.com/world/2015/jan/20/catholics-dont-have-to-breed-like-rabbits-says-pope-francis

Australian Associated Press. (2014, July 23). Great Barrier Reef contaminated by toxic coal dust, inquiry told: Coral reef expert says "damning" report found coal dust had spread hundreds of kilometres from dredging sites. *The Guardian.* Retrieved April 3, 2015, from http://www.theguardian.com/environment/2014/jul/23/great-barrier-reef-contaminated-by-toxic-coal-dust-inquiry-told

Balachandran, M., & Ghoshal, D. (2015, January 21). Future of the feline: How India rescued its tiger populaion from the brink—but Modi is risking it all. *Quartz India.* Retrieved June 8, 2015, from http://qz.com/330023/how-india-rescued-its-tiger-population-from-the-brink-but-now-risks-losing-it-all/

Balter, M. (2012, August 2). Ice age tools hint at 40,000 years of bushman culture. *Science, 337*, 512.

Banks-Leite, C., Pardini, R., Tambosi, L. R., Pearse, W. D., Bueno, A. A., Bruscagin, R. T., ... Metzger, J. P. (2014). Using ecological thresholds to evaluate the costs and benefits of set-asides in a biodiversity hotspot. *Science, 345* (6200), 1041–1045.

Barash, D. P. (2014, November 24). Life is good, but that's just the start of the argument. *Chronicle of Higher Education.* Retrieved April 3, 2015, from http://chronicle.com/article/Life-Is-Good/150129/?cid=at&utm_source=at&utm_medium=en

Barnosky, A. D. (2012, June 7). Approaching a state shift in Earth's biosphere. *Nature*, 486, 52–58.

Bateman, I. J., Harwood, A. R., Mace, G. M., Watson, R. T., Abson, D. J., Andrews, B., . . . Termansen, M. (2013, July 5). Bringing ecosystem services into economic decision-making: Land use in the United Kingdom. *Science, 341*, 45–50.

Bilney, R. J. (2014). Poor historical data drive conservation complacency: The case of mammal decline in south-eastern Australian forests. *Austral Ecology, 39*(8), 875–886.

Borger, J. (2015, January 4). US and Russia in danger of returning to era of nuclear rivalry. *The Guardian*. Retrieved April 3, 2015, from http://www.theguardian.com/world/2015/jan/04/us-russia-era-nuclear-rivalry

Borsos, E., Makra, L., Béczi, R., Vitányi, B., & Szentpéteri, M. (2003). Anthropogenic air pollution in the ancient times. *Acta Climatologica et Chorologica (Universitatis Szegediensis), 36–37*, 5–15.

Bosing, W. (2000). *Hieronymus Bosch, c. 1450–1516: Between heaven and hell*. Berlin, Germany: Taschen.

Bougainville, L. A. (1771). *Voyage autour du monde, par la frégate du roi la Boudeuse et la flûte l'Étoile en 1766, 1767, 1768 & 1769*. Paris: Saillant et Nyon. Retrieved April 3, 2015, from http://gallica.bnf.fr/ark:/12148/btv1b8602974k

Bourne, J. K. (2014, July 1). The next breadbasket. *National Geographic, 226*, 47–77.

Brashares, J. S., Abrahms, B., Fiorella, K. J., Golden, C. D., Hojnowski, C. E., Marsh, R. A., . . . Withey, L. (2014). Wildlife decline and social conflict: Policies aimed at reducing wildlife-related conflict muss address the underlying causes. *Science, 345* (6195), 376–378.

Brookshire, B. (2015). "Earth: A New Wild" puts people in the picture. *Science News, 187* (3), 28.

Bryant, E. (2008, August 10). European nations offer incentives to have kids. *SFGate (The San Francisco Chronicle)*. Retrieved April 3, 2015, from http://www.sfgate.com/news/article/European-nations-offer-incentives-to-have-kids-3201278.php

Burke, J. (2015, January 20). India's tiger population increases by almost a third. *The Guardian*. Retrieved April 3, 2015, from http://www.theguardian.com/environment/2015/jan/20/india-tiger-population-increases-endangered-species

Burkhardt, R. W. (2005). *Patterns of behavior: Konrad Lorenz, Niko Tinbergen, and the founding of ethology*. Chicago, IL: University of Chicago Press.

carboNZero (2010). Summary of carboNZero certification: Emirates Wolgan Valley Resort and Spa. Retrieved April 3, 2015, from http://www.carbonzero.co.nz/documents/disclosure_wolgan_0910.pdf

Cardinale, B. J. (2012, June 7). Biodiversity loss and its impact on humanity. *Nature, 486*, 59–67.

Carson, R. (1962). *Silent spring*. Cambridge, MA: Houghton Mifflin.

Cemansky, R. (2014). How many cities have a ban on plastic bags? *HowStuffWorks*. Retrieved April 3, 2015, from http://people.howstuffworks.com/how-many-cities-have-a-ban-on-plastic-bags.htm

Chamisso, A. von. (1836). *Reise um die Welt mit der Romanzoffischen Entdeckungs-Expedition in den Jahren 1815–1818*. Stuttgart, Germany: J. G. Cotta'sche Buchhandlung. (Re-published in 2012, Berlin, Germany: Die Andere Bibliothek.)

Chapman, M. D. (1987). Women's fishing in Oceania. *Human Ecology, 15*(3), 267–288.

Chesser, R. K., & Baker, R. J. (2006). Growing up with Chernobyl: Working in a radioactive zone, two scientists learn tough lessons about politics, bias and the challenges of doing good science. *American Scientist, 94*(6), 542–549.

Chew, S. C. (2001). *World ecological degradation: Accumulation, urbanization, and deforestation, 3000 BC–AD 2000* (p. 232). Lanham, MD: AltaMira Press.

Chiozzi, G., Bardelli, G. Ricci, M., de Marchi, G., & Cardini, A. (2014). Just another island dwarf? Phenotypic distinctiveness in the poorly known Soemmering's Gazelle, *Nanger soemmeringii* (Cetartiodactyla: Bovidae), of Dahlak Kebir Island. *Biological Journal of the Linnean Society, 111*, 603–620.

Choi, C. (2008). Tierra del Fuego: The beavers must die. *Nature, 453*(7198), 968.

Clark, S. (2014, June 4). Scientists warn against China's plan to flatten over 700 mountains. *The Guardian.* Retrieved April 3, 2015, from http://www.theguardian.com/environment/2014/jun/04/scientists-warn-against-chinas-plan-to-flatten-over-700-mountains

Cohen, G. A. (2009). *Why not socialism?* Princeton, NJ: Princeton University Press.

Commission on Growth and Development. (2008). *The growth report: Strategies for sustained growth and inclusive development.* Washington, DC: The World Bank. Retrieved April 3, 2015, from http://www.growthcommission.org/index.php?option=com_content&task=view&id=96&Itemid=169

Cornils, I., & Waters, S. (2010). Memories of 1968: International perspectives. Bern, Switzerland: Peter Lang AG, Internationaler Verlag der Wissenschaften.

Cotton, A. P. (2003, October 14). Avian migration phenology and global climate change. *Proceedings of the National Academy of Sciences, 100*(21), 12219–12222.

Cusack, C. (2011). Pagan Saxon resistance to Charlemagne's mission: "Indigenous" religion and "world" religion in the Early Middle Ages. *The Pomegranate, 13*(1), 33–51.

Daly, H. E. (1973). *Toward a steady-state economy.* San Francisco, CA: W. H. Freeman.

Daly, H. E. (2008a). Growth and development: Critique of a credo. *Population and Development Review, 34*(3), 511–518.

Daly, H. E. (2008b). *A steady-state economy: A failed growth economy and a steady-state economy are not the same thing; they are the very different alternatives we face.* London, UK: Sustainable Development Commission, UK. Retrieved April 3, 2015, from http://steadystaterevolution.org/files/pdf/Daly_UK_Paper.pdf

Darwin, C. (1859). *On the origin of species by means of natural selection, or the preservation of favoured races in the struggle for life.* London, UK: Penguin Classics. (Edited and republished in 2009)

Dauphiné, N., Tsamajain-Yagkuag, S., & Cooper, R. J. (2008). Bird conservation in Aguaruna-Jívaro communities in the Cordillera de Colan, Peru. *Ornitologia Neotropical, 19*(Suppl.), 587–594.

Dave, P. (2014, February 8). Struggling whooping crane population loses three to gunfire. *Los Angeles Times.* Retrieved April 3, 2015, from http://articles.latimes.com/2014/feb/08/nation/la-na-whooping-cranes-20140209

Dee, T. (2013). *Four fields.* London, UK: Jonathan Cape.

d'Errico, F., Backwell, L., Villa. P., Degano, I., Lucejko, J. J., Bamford, M. K., . . . Beaumonti, P. B. (2012, August 14). Early evidence of San material culture represented by organic artifacts from Border Cave, South Africa. *Proceedings of the National Academy of Sciences, 109*, 13214–13219.

de Waal, F. (2009). *Primates and philosophers: How morality evolved.* Princeton, NJ: Princeton University Press.

de Waal, F. (2010). *The age of empathy: Nature's lessons for a kinder society*. New York, NY: Broadway Books.

Diamond, J. (2005). *Collapse: How societies choose to fail or succeed*. New York, NY: Viking Press.

Dickman, C. R. (1996). *Overview of the impacts of feral cats on Australian native fauna*. Canberra, ACT: Australian Nature Conservation Agency; Sydney, NSW: Institute of Wildlife Research.

Dirzo, R., Young, H. S., Galetti, M., Ceballos, G., Isaac, N. J. B., & Collen, B. (2014, July 25). Defaunation in the Anthropocene. *Science, 345*(6195), 401–406.

Dudley, N. (2008). *Guidelines for applying protected area management categories*. Gland, Switzerland: IUCN.

Editorial Board. (2015a, January 27). President Obama protects a valued wilderness. *The New York Times*. Retrieved April 3, 2015, from http://www.nytimes.com/2015/01/27/opinion/president-obama-protects-a-valued-wilderness.html?emc=eta1

Editorial Board. (2015b, February 14). Wildlife slaughter goes unabated. *The New York Times*. Retrieved April 3, 2015, from http://www.nytimes.com/2015/02/15/opinion/sunday/wildlife-slaughter-goes-unabated.html?emc=eta1

Ehrlich, P. R. (1968). *The population bomb*. New York, NY: Ballantine Books.

Elliott, G. P., Merton, D. V. & Jansen, P. W. (2001). Intensive management of a critically endangered species: The Kakapo. *Biological Conservation, 99*(1), 121–133.

Engelman, R. & Codjoe, S. (2014, September 18). Hey, U.N.: Climate change and population are related. *Grist*. Retrieved April 3, 2015, from http://grist.org/climate-energy/hey-u-n-climate-change-and-population-are-related/

Fears, D. (2014, October 17). Overwhelmed U.S. port inspectors unable to keep up with illegal wildlife trade. *The Washington Post*. Retrieved April 3, 2015, from http://www.washingtonpost.com/national/health-science/overwhelmed-us-port-inspectors-unable-to-keep-up-with-illegal-wildlife-trade/2014/10/17/2fc72086-fe42-11e3-b1f4-8e77c632c07b_story.html

Featherstone, S. (2015). The swallows of Fukushima. *Scientific American, 312*(2), 74–81.

Feng, W., & Cai, Y. (2010). Did China's one-child policy prevent 400 million births in the last 30 years? *China Reform, 7*, 85–88.

Flannery, T. (2002). *The future eaters: An ecological history of the Australasian lands and people*. New York, NY: Grove Press.

Flattau, E. (1985, November 25). The loss of farmland in China. *Chicago Tribune*. Retrieved April 3, 2015, from http://articles.chicagotribune.com/1985-11-25/news/8503210456_1_chengdu-farmland-loss-arable-land

Flocken, J. (2014, January 9). Black rhino hunt auction won't help conservation. *National Geographic News Watch*. Retrieved April 3, 2015, from http://newswatch.nationalgeographic.com/2014/01/09/black-rhino-hunt-auction-wont-help-conservation/

FlorCruz, J. (2011, October 28). China copes with promise and perils of one-child policy. *CNN World*. Retrieved April 3, 2015, from http://www.cnn.com/2011/10/28/world/asia/china-one-child/

Foster, J. B. (2002). *Ecology against capitalism*. New York, NY: Monthly Review Press.

Foster, J. M. (2008). *The sustainability mirage: Illusion and realty in the coming war on climate change*. London, UK: Earthscan.

Foulkes, I. (2014, February 9). Swiss immigration: 50.3% back quotas, final results show. *BBC News Europe*. Retrieved April 3, 2015, from http://www.bbc.com/news/world-europe-26108597

Gadgil, M. (2011). Report of the Western Ghats Ecology Expert panel. Delhi: Government of India, Ministry of the Environment and Forests. Retrieved April 3, 2015, from http://www.moef.nic.in/downloads/public-information/wg-23052012.pdf

Gandhi, D. (2014, May 7). State agrees to ban mining in the Western Ghats. *The Hindu*. Retrieved April 3, 2015, from http://www.thehindu.com/todays-paper/tp-national/tp-karnataka/state-agrees-to-ban-mining-in-the-western-ghats/article5984220.ece

Gewertz, D., & Errington, F. (2015). Doing good and doing well: Prairie wetlands, private property, and the public trust. *American Anthropologist, 117*(1), 17–31.

Gillis, J. (2014, September 13). Sun and wind alter global landscape, leaving utilities behind. *The New York Times*. Retrieved April 3, 2015, from http://www.nytimes.com/2014/09/14/science/earth/sun-and-wind-alter-german-landscape-leaving-utilities-behind.html?emc=eta1

Goldstein, M. C., & Beall, C. M. (1991). China's birth control policy in the Tibet Autonomous Region: Myths and realities. *Asian Survey, 31*(3), 285–303.

Gonzalez, R. (2014, October 15). Santa Cruz enforces California's toughest drought restrictions. *National Public Radio Morning Edition*. Retrieved April 3, 2015, from http://www.npr.org/2014/10/15/356302486/santa-cruz-responds-to-california-s-drought-with-stringent-restrictions

Gore, A. (1993). *Earth in the balance: Ecology and the human spirit*. New York, NY: Plume Books.

Gore, A. (2006). *An inconvenient truth*. Hollywood, CA: Paramount Classics.

Government of India (Ministry of Home Affairs). (2011). *Population enumeration data: A-2 decadal variation in population since 1901*. Retrieved April 3, 2015, from http://www.censusindia.gov.in/2011census/PCA/A-2_Data_Tables/00%20A%202-India.pdf

Green, E. (2015, January 20). The pope, official global spokesman against rabbit sex? *The Atlantic*. Retrieved April 3, 2015, from http://www.theatlantic.com/international/archive/2015/01/the-pope-official-global-spokesman-against-rabbit-sex/384667/

Greenwood, N. H., & Edwards, J. M. B. (1973). *Human environments and natural systems: A conflict of dominion*. North Scituate, MA: Duxbury Press.

Griffin, N. (2001). *Caucasus: Mountain men and holy wars*. London, UK: Macmillan.

Guralnik, D. B. (1970). Zeitgeist, def. 1. *Webster's new world dictionary of the American language* (2nd ed.). New York, NY: Houghton Mifflin Harcourt.

Guthrie, A. (2015, January 23). Mexico announces plan to stem rising rate of teen pregnancies. *The Wall Street Journal*. Retrieved April 3, 2015, from http://www.wsj.com/articles/mexico-announces-plan-to-stem-rising-rate-of-teen-pregnancies-1422056520

Gwatkin, D. R. (1979). Political will and family planning: The implications of India's emergency experience. *Population and Development Review, 5*(1), 29–59.

Haig, S. M., Martin, T. E., van Riper, C., & Beard, T. D. (2013, July 19). Pathways for conservation. *Science, 341*, 215.

Halden, R. U. (2010). Plastics and health risks. *Annual Review of Public Health, 31*, 179–194.

Hames, R. (2007). The ecologically noble savage debate. *Annual Review of Anthropology, 36*, 177–190.

Hansen, M. C., Potapov, P. V., Moore, R., Hancher, M., Turubanova, S. A., Tyukavina, A., . . . Townshend. J. R. G. (2013). High-resolution global maps of 21st-century forest cover change. *Science, 342*(6160), 850–853. Data available online from http:// earthenginepartners.appspot.com/science-2013-global-forest

Hansen, S. (2014, November 14). The China-US climate change agreement is a step forward for green power relations. *The Guardian.* Retrieved April 3, 2015, from http:// www.theguardian.com/commentisfree/2014/nov/14/the-china-us-climate-change -agreement-is-a-step-forward-for-green-power-relations

Hardin, G. (1968). The tragedy of the commons. *Science, 162,* 1243–1248.

Harding, L. (2006, June 26). Bavarian hunters kill Bruno the bear. *The Guardian.* Retrieved April 3, 2015, from http://www.theguardian.com/world/2006/jun/26/ animalwelfare.germany

Hayden, P. (2007). *Chernobyl reclaimed: An animal takeover.* Documentary for TV. Germany/Netherlands; released in the USA in 2007. Retrieved April 3, 2015, from http://www.imdb.com/title/tt1832311/

He, Q., Bertness, M. D., Bruno, J. F., Li, B., Chen, G., Coverdale, T.C., . . . Cui, B. (2014). Economic development and coastal ecosystem change in China. *Scientific Reports, 4,* 5995. doi:10.1038/srep05995

Heinroth, K. (1971). *Oskar Heinroth: Vater der Verhaltensforschung, 1871–1945 [Oskar Heinroth: Father of behavioral sciences].* Stuttgart, Germany: Wissenschaftliche Verlagsgesellschaft.

Henrich, J. (2014, May 9). Rice, psychology, and innovation. *Science, 344*(6148): 593–594.

Homberger, D. G. (1998). Was ist biologie? *[What is biology?].* In A. Dally (Ed.), *Was wissen Biologen schon vom Leben? Die biologische Wissenschaft nach der molekular-genetischen Revolution [What do biologists really know about life? The biological sciences after the molecular-genetic revolution].* Loccumer Protokolle 14/97 (pp. 11–28). Rehburg-Loccum, Germany: Evangelische Akademie Loccum.

Homberger, D. G. (2003). The comparative biomechanics of a prey-predator relationship: The adaptive morphologies of the feeding apparatus of Australian Black-Cockatoos and their foods as a basis for the reconstruction of the evolutionary history of the Psittaciformes. In V. L. Bels, J.-P. Gasc, & A. Casinos (Eds.), *Vertebrate biomechanics and evolution* (pp. 203–228). Oxford, UK: BIOS Scientific Publishers.

Hong, S., Candelone, J.-P., Patterson, C. C., & Boutron, C. F. (1996). History of ancient copper smelting pollution during Roman and medieval times recorded in Greenland ice. *Science, 272*(5259), 246–249.

Hookway, J. (2014, March 19). Slumping fertility rates in developing countries spark labor worries. *The Wall Street Journal.* Retrieved April 3, 2015, from http://www.wsj .com/articles/SB10001424052702304773104579265520447488200

Howden, S. (2014, February 15). NSW national parks open to amateur shooters. *Sydney Morning Herald.* Retrieved April 3, 2015, from http://www.smh.com.au/nsw/ nsw-national-parks-open-to-amateur-shooters-20140214-32rb5.html

Howe, J. (2010). *Wilderness—the Great Debate* [Video; 57 minutes]. Salt Lake City, UT: KUED at the University of Utah.

Hughes, J. D. (1993). *Pan's travail: Environmental problems of the ancient Greeks and Romans.* Baltimore, MD: Johns Hopkins University Press.

Hughes, R., & Flintan, F. (2001). *Integrating conservation and development experience: A review and bibliography of the ICDP literature.* London, UK: International Institute for Environment and Development.

Indrawan, M., Garnett, S., Masala, Y., & Wirth, R. (2014). Compromising for conservation: A protocol for developing sustainable conservation plans in biologically rich and monetarily impoverished communities. *Pacific Conservation Biology, 20*(1), 3–7.

Jacks, G. V., & Whyte, R. O. (1939). *The rape of the earth: A world survey of soil erosion.* London, UK: Faber & Faber; Ithaca, NY: Cornell University Press.

Johnston, I. C. (2014). *Antigone by Sophocles.* Nanaimo, BC: Vancouver Island University. Retrieved April 3, 2015, from https://records.viu.ca/~johnstoi/sophocles/antigone.htm

Kaiman, J. (2014, January 31). Time running out for China's one-child policy after three decades: As list of exemptions grows, experts predict scrapping of rule said to have prevented 400m births. *The Guardian.* http://www.theguardian.com/world/2014/jan/31/time-running-out-china-one-child-policy-exemptions

Kerr, R. A. (2014). The coming copper peak. *Science, 343*(6172), 722–724.

Ketcham, C. (2015, February 12). Grand Canyon wolf that made epic journey shot dead in Utah. *National Geographic News.* Retrieved April 3, 2015, from http://news.nationalgeographic.com/news/2015/02/150212-gray-wolves-grand-canyon-animals-science-rockies-dead/

Kitzes, J., Wackernagel, M., Loh, J., Peller, A., Goldfinger, S., Cheng, D., & Tea, K. (2008). Shrink and share: Humanity's present and future ecological footprint. *Philosophical Transactions of the Royal Society of London B, 363*(1491), 467–475.

Kleiman, D. G. (1989). Reintroduction of captive mammals for conservation. *BioScience, 39*(3), 152–161.

Klein, N. (2011, 9 November). Capitalism vs. the climate. *The Nation.* Retrieved April 3, 2015, from http://www.thenation.com/print/article/164497/capitalism-vs-climate

Knauer, K. (2012). *Disasters that shook the world: History's greatest man-made catastrophes.* New York, NY: Time Home Entertainment.

Kolbert, E. (2014). Rethinking how we think about climate change. *Audubon, 116*(5), 46–48.

Kumar, H. (2015, January 20): India's rebounding tiger population grows 30 percent in 4 years. *The New York Times.* Retrieved April 3, 2015, from http://www.nytimes.com/2015/01/21/world/asia/indias-rebounding-tiger-population-grows-30-percent-in-4-years.html?emc=eta1

Kupper, P. (2012). *Wildnis schaffen: Eine transnationale Geschichte des Schweizerischen Nationalparks.* [*Creating wilderness: A transnational history of the Swiss National Park*]. *Nationalpark-Forschung in der Schweiz, 97,* 380. Bern, Switzerland: Haupt Verlag.

Lackey, R. T. (2014). *Is science biased toward natural?* Keynote Lecture, 35th Annual North American Meeting of the Society of Environmental Toxicology and Chemistry, November 9–13, Vancouver, BC. Retrieved April 3, 2015, from http://aquadoc.typepad.com/files/2014x-is-science-biased-setac-keynote-lackey-nov-12-2014.pdf

Lamarck, J.-B. (1809). *Philosophie zoologique: Ou exposition des considérations relative à l'histoire naturelle des animaux.* Paris, France: Dentu et l'Auteur. [(1984). *Zoological philosophy: An exposition with regard to the natural history of animals.* Chicago, IL: University of Chicago Press.]

Lee, F. R. (2010, October 28). Schomburg Center in Harlem acquires Maya Angelou archive. *The New York Times,* p. C1. Retrieved April 3, 2015, from http://www.nytimes.com/2010/10/27/arts/design/27archive.html

Lenin, J. (2014a, October 14). Tiger survival: Mapping poaching and trafficking hotspots. *The Guardian.* Retrieved April 3, 2015, from http://www.theguardian.com/

environment/india-untamed/2014/oct/14/mapping-areas-most-vulnerable-poaching -trafficking-tigers

Lenin, J. (2014b, November 18). US-China climate deal's ambition fails to impress India. *The Guardian*. Retrieved April 3, 2015, from http://www.theguardian.com/ environment/india-untamed/2014/nov/18/indians-not-impressed-with-us-china -climate-deal

Lever-Tracy, C. (2010). *Routledge handbook of climate change and society*. London, UK: Routledge.

Lewis, D. (2014, September 5). Small mammals vanish in northern Australia. *Science, 345* (6201), 1109–1110.

Li, P., Qian, H., & Wu, J. (2014, June 4). Accelerate research on land creation. *Nature, 510*(7503), 29–31.

Livingston, J. (2008). *John Alexander: A retrospective*. Houston, TX: Museum of Fine Arts.

Loyd, K. T., Hernandez, S. M., Carroll, J. P., Marshall, G. J., & Abernathy, K. J. (2013). Quantifying free-roaming domestic cat predation using animal-borne cameras. *Biological Conservation, 160*, 183–189.

Lyons, S. K., Smith, F. A., & Brown, J. H. (2004). Of mice, mastodons and men: Human-mediated extinctions on four continents. *Evolutionary Ecology Research, 6*, 339–358.

Main, D. (2015, February 3). Behind the scenes of "Earth a New Wild," PBS's new nature show. *Newsweek*. Retrieved June 8, 2015, from http://www.newsweek.com/behind -scenes-earth-new-wild-pbss-new-nature-show-304206

Majnep, I. S., Bulmer, R., & Healey, C. (1977). *Birds of my Kalam country = Mnmon Yad Kalam Yakt*. Oxford, UK: Oxford University Press.

Marks, K. (2014, June 15). Plans for five "megaports" along Queensland coast threatens Great Barrier Reef. *The Independent*. Retrieved April 3, 2015, from http://www .independent.co.uk/environment/nature/plans-for-five-megaports-along-queensland -coast-threatens-great-barrier-reef-9537733.html

Marques, N. (2014, September 12). Ebola: The post-conflict fever. *OpEdNews*. Retrieved April 3, 2015, from http://www.opednews.com/articles/Ebola-the-post-conflict-f-by -Nadejda-Marques-Conflict_Ebola_Poverty-140912-593.html

Martin, P. S., & Klein, R. G. (1989). *Quaternary extinctions: A prehistoric revolution*. Tucson, AZ: University of Arizona Press.

Marx, K. (1867). *Capital: A critique of political economy* (Vol. 1). London, UK: Penguin Classics. (Edited 1990)

Max, D. T. (2014, May 12). Green is good: The Nature Conservancy wants to persuade big business to save the environment. *The New Yorker*. Retrieved April 3, 2015, from http://www.newyorker.com/magazine/2014/05/12/green-is-good

McKean, C. A. (2014, May 19). Japan eliminates millions of tons of CO_2 by ditching the business suit. *Resilient Cities*. Retrieved April 3, 2015, from http://nextcity.org/daily/ entry/japan-eliminates-millions-of-tons-of-co2-by-ditching-the-business-suit

Meadows, D. H., Meadows, D. L., Randers, J., & Behrens, W. W. (1972). *The limits of growth: A report for the Club of Rome's project on the predicament of mankind*. New York, NY: Universe Books.

Meijaard, E., Sheil, D., Nasi, R., Augeri, D., Rosenbaum, B., Iskandar, D., . . . O'Brien, T. (2005). *Life after logging: Reconciling wildlife conservation and production forestry in Indonesian Borneo*. Jakarta, Indonesia: Center for International Forestry Research.

Miller, G. H., Magee, J. W., Johnson, B. J., Fogel, M. L., Spooner, N. A., McCulloch, M. T., & Ayliffe, L. K. (1999, January 8). Pleistocene extinction of *Genyornis newtoni*: Human impact on Australian megafauna. *Science, 283*(5399), 205–208.

Mitchell, J. G. (2001, July). Urban sprawl. *National Geographic.* Retrieved April 3, 2015, from http://ngm.nationalgeographic.com/ngm/data/2001/07/01/html/fulltext3.html

Mora, C., & Sale, P. F. (2011). Ongoing global biodiversity loss and the need to move beyond protected areas: A review of the technical and practical shortcomings of protected areas on land and sea. *Marine Ecology Progress Series, 434,* 251–266.

Moseby, K. E., & O'Donnell, E. O. (2003). Reintroduction of the Greater Bilby, *Macrotis lagotis* (Reid) (Marsupialia: Thylacomyidae), to northern South Australia: Survival, ecology and notes on reintroduction protocols. *Wildlife Research, 30,* 15–27.

Mousseau, T. A., & Møller, A. P. (2012, November 11–15). Chernobyl and Fukushima: Differences and similarities, a biological perspective. *Transactions of the American Nuclear Society, 107,* 200–203.

Naeem, S. (2012). Ecosystem services: Is a planet servicing one species likely to function? In R. Rozzi, S. T. A. Pickett, C. Palmer, J. J. Armesto, & B. Callicott (Eds.), *Linking ecology and ethics for a changing world: Values, philosophy, and action* (pp. 303–321). New York, NY: Springer.

National Bureau of Statistics of China. (2013). *China statistical yearbook.* Beijing, China: China Statistics Press.

National Park Service. (2014). *Wilderness timeline.* Retrieved April 3, 2015, from http://www.nature.nps.gov/views/KCs/Wilderness/HTML/ET_04_Why.htm

Natural Resources Defense Council. (2014). *What is a biosphere reserve?* Retrieved April 3, 2015, from http://www.nrdc.org/land/wilderness/fbios.asp

Nippon Hoso Kyokai. (2013, July 11). Wildlife reclaims Fukushima. *NHK's Today's Close-Up* (Japan Broadcasting Corporation). Retrieved April 3, 2015, from http://www.nhk.or.jp/japan311/kuro-wild.html

Norgaard, K. M. (2011). *Living in denial: Climate change, emotions, and everyday life.* Cambridge, MA: MIT Press.

North Queensland Bulk Ports Corporation. (2014). *Hay Point Port.* Retrieved April 3, 2015, from http://www.nqbp.com.au/hay-point/

Nuccitelli, D. (2014, November 14). Fact check: China pledged bigger climate action than the USA; Republican leaders wrong. *The Guardian.* Retrieved April 3, 2015, from http://www.theguardian.com/environment/climate-consensus-97-per-cent/2014/nov/14/fact-check-china-pledged-bigger-climate-action-republican-leaders-wrong

Offer, A. (2006). *The challenge of affluence: Self-control and well-being in the United States and Britain since 1950.* Oxford, UK: Oxford University Press.

Ó Gráda, C. (2009). *Famine: A short history.* Princeton, NJ: Princeton University Press.

Otero, L. (2006). *La huella del fuego: Historia de los bosques nativos—Poblamiento y cambios en el paisaje del sur del Chile.* Santiago, Chile: Pehuén Editores.

Otero, L. (2010). *De la naturaleza al paisaje: Ecología y arquitectura del paisaje del sur de Chile.* Valdivia, Chile: Ediciones Kultrún.

Panwar, H. S. (1987). Project Tiger: The reserves, the tigers, and their future. In R. L. Tilson & U. S. Sel (Eds.), *Tigers of the world: the biology, biopolitics, management, and conservation of an endangered species* (pp. 110–117). Park Ridge, NJ: Noyes Publications.

Pauly, D. (1995). Anecdotes and the shifting baseline syndrome of fisheries. *Trends in Ecology and Evolution, 10*(10), 430.

Pavey, C. (2006). *National recovery plan for the Greater Bilby Macrotis lagotis*. Northern Territory, Australia: Department of Natural Resources, Environment and the Arts. Retrieved April 3, 2015, from http://www.environment.gov.au/system/files/resources/37646d5b-a355-45d6-9c78-604833626a37/files/m-lagotis.pdf

Pearce, F. (2014, January 14). Conservation group backs killing rare rhino for cash. *New Scientist*. Retrieved April 3, 2015, from http://www.newscientist.com/article/dn24869 -conservation-group-backs-killing-rare-rhino-for-cash.html#.U8s_VuNdXng

Picketty, T., & Saez, E. (2014, May 23). Inequality in the long run. *Science, 344*(6186), 838–842.

Post Carbon Institute. (2012, January 19). Natural resource depletion and the changing geopolitical landscape. *Oilprice.com*. Retrieved April 3, 2015, from http://oilprice .com/Geopolitics/International/Natural-Resource-Depletion-and-the-Changing -Geopolitical-Landscape.html

Powlesland, R. G., Merton, D. V., & Cockrem, J. F. (2006). A parrot apart: The natural history of the Kakapo (*Strigops habroptilus*), and the context of its conservation management. *Notornis, 53*(1), 3–26.

Primack, R. B. (2014). *Walden warming climate change comes to Thoreau's woods*. Chicago, IL: University of Chicago Press.

Primack, R. B., & Miller-Rushing, A. J. (2012). Uncovering, collecting, and analyzing records to investigate the ecological impacts of climate change: A template from Thoreau's Concord. *BioScience, 62*(2), 170–181.

Project Tiger. (2014). *National Tiger Conservation Authority/Project Tiger*. Retrieved April 3, 2015, from http://projecttiger.nic.in

Quammen, D. (1997). *The song of the Dodo: Island biogeography in an age of extinctions*. New York, NY: Scribner.

Rawinski, T. J. (2008). *Impacts of white-tailed deer overabundance in forest ecosystems: An overview*. Newtown Square, PA: U.S. Department of Agriculture.

Roberts, P. C. (2013). *The failure of laissez faire capitalism and economic dissolution of the West: Towards a new economics for a full world*. Atlanta, GA: Clarity Press.

Roy, S. (2013, December 26). The worst year ever for tigers in India. *Huffington Post*. Retrieved April 3, 2015, from http://www.huffingtonpost.com/sourav-roy/2013-the -worst-year-ever-_b_4494230.html

Rozzi, R. (1999). The reciprocal links between evolutionary-ecological sciences and environmental ethics. *BioScience, 49*, 911–921.

Rozzi, R. (2010). *Multi-ethnic bird guide of the subantarctic forests of South America*. Denton, TX: University of North Texas Press.

Rozzi, R. (2012). Biocultural ethics: From biocultural homogenization toward biocultural conservation. In R. Rozzi, S. T. A. Pickett, C. Palmer, J. J. Armesto, & B. Callicott (Eds.), *Linking ecology and ethics for a changing world: Values, philosophy, and action* (pp. 9–32). New York, NY: Springer.

Runte, A. (1997). *National parks: The American experience*. Lincoln, NE: University of Nebraska Press.

Russon, A. E. (2010). Orangutan rehabilitation and reintroduction: Successes, failures, and role in conservation. In S. A. Wich, S. S. U. Atmoko, T. M. Setia, & C. P. van

Schaik (Eds.), *Orangutans: Geographic variation in behavioral ecology and conservation* (pp. 327–350). London, UK: Oxford University Press.

Ruz, C. (2011, October 31). The six natural resources most drained by our 7 billion people. *The Guardian*. Retrieved April 3, 2015, from http://www.theguardian.com/environment/blog/2011/oct/31/six-natural-resources-population

Sabine, G. H. (1912). Descriptive and normative sciences. *Philosophical Review, 21*(4), 433–450.

Sarewitz, D. (2014). Science should keep out of partisan politics. *Nature, 516,* 9.

Seddon, P. J., Griffiths, C. J., Soorae, P. S., & Armstrong, D. P. (2014). Reversing defaunation: Restoring species in a changing world. *Science, 345*(6195), 406–412.

Smith, A. B. (2000). *The bushmen of southern Africa: A foraging society in transition.* Athens, OH: Ohio University Press; Cape Town, South Africa: David Philip Publishers.

Smithsonian Institution. (2014). *The first life on earth.* Department of Paleobiology, National Museum of Natural History, Smithsonian Institution. Retrieved April 3, 2015, from http://paleobiology.si.edu/geotime/main/htmlversion/archean3.html

Smyth, J. (2014, June 20). Queensland shelves a $10bn Great Barrier Reef coal port. *Financial Times*. Retrieved April 3, 2015, from http://www.ft.com/intl/cms/s/0/75251f0c-f86b-11e3-a333-00144feabdc0.html#axzz3E6lrs4cS

Snyder, N., & Snyder, H. (2000). *The California Condor: A saga of natural history and conservation.* Princeton, NJ: Princeton University Press.

Snyder, N. F. R., Wiley, J. W., & Kepler, C. B. (1987). *The parrots of Luquillo: Natural history and conservation of the Puerto Rican Parrot.* Los Angeles, CA: Western Foundation of Vertebrate Zoology.

Soane, I. D., Scolozzi, R., Gretter, A., & Hubacek, K. (2012). Exploring panarchy in alpine grasslands: An application of adaptive cycle concepts to the conservation of a cultural landscape. *Ecology and Society, 17*(3), 18–29. Retrieved April 3, 2015, from http://dx.doi.org/10.5751/ES-05085-170318

Spence, M. D. (1999). *Dispossessing the wilderness: Indian removal and the making of the national parks.* New York, NY: Oxford University Press.

Spikins, P., Rutherford, H., & Needham, A. (2010a). From homininity to humanity: Compassion from the earliest archaics to modern humans. *Time and Mind: The Journal of Archaeology, Consciousness and Culture, 3*(3), 303–325.

Spikins, P., Rutherford, H., & Needham, A. (2010b). *The prehistory of compassion.* San Francisco, CA: Blurb.

Sridhar, L. (2004, January). "If only Indira Gandhi was sitting there, asking, is that tiger safe?" Interview with Valmik Thapar. *InfoChange News & Features*. Retrieved April 3, 2015, from http://infochangeindia.org/environment/changemakers/if-only-indira-gandhi-was-sitting-there-asking-is-that-tiger-safe.html

Steadman, D. W. (2006). *Extinction and biogeography of tropical Pacific birds.* Chicago, IL: University of Chicago Press.

Stokstad, E. (2014a). The empty forest. *Science, 345*(6195), 397–399.

Stokstad, E. (2014b). The mountaintop witness. *Science, 343*(6171), 592–595.

Suzuki, D., & Taylor, D. (2009). *The big picture: Reflection on science, humanity, and a quickly changing planet.* Vancouver, BC: Greystone Books; Toronto, ON: David Suzuki Foundation.

Taira, W., Nohara, C., Hiyama, A., & Otaki, J. M. (2014). Fukushima's biological impacts: The case of the pale grass blue butterfly. *Journal of Heredity, 105*(5), 710–722.

Talhelm, T., Zhang, X., Oishi, S., Shimin, C., Duan, D., Lan, X., & Kitayama, S. (2014, May 9). Large-scale psychological differences within China explained by rice versus wheat agriculture. *Science, 244*(6148), 603–608.

Taylor, R., & Hoyle, R. (2014, July 17). Australia becomes first developed nation to repeal carbon tax. *The Wall Street Journal.* Retrieved April 3, 2015, from http://www.wsj.com/articles/australia-repeals-carbon-tax-1405560964

Tella, J. L., & Hiraldo, F. (2014). Illegal and legal parrot trade shows a long-term, cross-cultural preference for the most attractive species increasing their risk of extinction. *PloS ONE, 9*(9): e107546. doi:10.1371/journal.pone.0107546

Tercek, M. R. (2013). *Nature's fortune: How business and society thrive by investing in nature.* New York, NY: Basic Books.

Thapar, V. (1997). *Land of the tiger: A natural history of the Indian subcontinent.* Berkeley, CA: University of California Press.

Thapar, V. (1999). The tragedy of the Indian tiger: Starting from scratch. In J. Seidensticker, S. Christie & P. Jackson (Eds.), *Riding the tiger: Tiger conservation in human-dominated landscapes* (pp. 296–306). Cambridge, UK: Cambridge University Press.

Theien, I. (2009). Food rationing during World War Two: A special case of sustainable consumption? *Anthropology of Food* [Online], S5. Retrieved April 3, 2015, from http://aof.revues.org/6383

Tooke, F., & Battey, N. H. (2010). Temperate flowering phenology. *Journal of Experimental Botany, 61*(11), 2853–2862. doi:10.1093/jxb/erq165

Trading Economics. (2015). *India Population 1950–2015.* Retrieved April 3, 2015, from http://www.tradingeconomics.com/india/population

Tschinkel, W. R. (2006). *The fire ants.* Cambridge, MA: Belknap Press of Harvard University Press.

UNESCO (United Nations Educational, Scientific and Cultural Organization). (2014a). *FAQ—Biosphere Reserves?* Retrieved April 3, 2015, from http://www.unesco.org/mab/doc/faq/brs.pdf

UNESCO (United Nations Educational, Scientific and Cultural Organization). (2014b). *List of World Heritage in Danger.* Retrieved April 3, 2015, from http://whc.unesco.org/en/danger/

UNICEF (United Nations Children's Fund). (2014). *Nutrition.* Retrieved April 3, 2015, from http://www.unicef.org/nutrition/

United Nations. (2012). *RIO + 20: United Nations Conference on Sustainable Development.* Retrieved April 3, 2015, from http://www.uncsd2012.org/

United Nations. (2014a). *Global issues: Climate change.* Retrieved April 3, 2015, from http://www.un.org/en/globalissues/climatechange/

United Nations. (2014b). *Global issues: Population.* Retrieved April 3, 2015, from http://www.un.org/en/globalissues/population/

United Nations. (2014c). *Sustainable development.* Retrieved April 3, 2015, from http://sustainabledevelopment.un.org/

Urban, B., Kunz, A., & Gehrt, E. (2011). Genesis and dating of Late Pleistocene-Holocene soil sediment sequences from the Lüneburg Heath, northern Germany. *Quaternary Science Journal (Eiszeitalter und Gegenwart), 60,* 164–184.

U.S. Congress. (2009). *Omnibus Public Land Management Act of 2009.* Washington, DC: U.S. Government Printing Office. Retrieved July 27, 2014, from http://www.gpo.gov/fdsys/pkg/PLAW-111publ11/html/PLAW-111publ11.htm

Valero, A., & Valero, A. (2010). Physical geonomics: Combining the exergy and Hubbert peak analysis for predicting mineral resources depletion. *Resources, Conservation and Recycling, 54*(12), 1074–1083.

Vaughan, A. (2014, October 8). Fossil fuel divestment: A brief history. *The Guardian.* Retrieved April 3, 2015, from http://www.theguardian.com/environment/2014/oct/08/fossil-fuel-divestment-a-brief-history

Vickas, M. (2013, February 26). On this day: Mungo Man fossil found: The 1974 discovery of Mungo Man doubled the known length of Aboriginal history in Australia. *Australian Geographic.* Retrieved April 3, 2015, from http://www.australiangeographic.com.au/blogs/on-this-day/2013/02/on-this-day-mungo-man-fossil-found/

Vidal, J., Stratton, A., & Goldenberg, S. (2009, December 18). Low targets, goals dropped: Copenhagen ends in failure. *The Guardian.* Retrieved April 3, 2015, from http://www.theguardian.com/environment/2009/dec/18/copenhagen-deal

Vignieri, S. (2014). Vanishing fauna. *Science, 345* (6195), 392–395.

Wakabayashi, D., & Inada, M. (2009, October). Baby bundle: Japan's cash incentive for parenthood. *The Wall Street Journal.* Retrieved April 3, 2015, from http://www.wsj.com/articles/SB125495746062571927

Walsh, B. (2014, July 28). Invasive species, coming soon to a habitat near you. *Time.* Retrieved April 3, 2015, from http://time.com/3000963/invasive-species-coming-soon-to-a-habitat-near-you/

Wang, G. (2010). *Shrinking arable land adds concern on China's grain security.* Retrieved April 3, 2015, from http://news.xinhuanet.com/english2010/china/2010-10/18/c_13562418.htm

Ward, G. C., & Ward, D. R. (1993). *Tiger-wallahs: Encounters with the men who tried to save the greatest of the great cats.* New York, NY: HarperCollins Publishers.

Watt, N. (2012, June 15). Pakistan boasted of nuclear strike on India within eight seconds. *The Guardian.* Retrieved April 3, 2015, from http://www.theguardian.com/world/2012/jun/15/pakistan-boasted-nuclear-strike-pakistan

White, T. D., Asfaw, B., Beyene, Y., Haile-Selassie, Y., Lovejoy, C. O., Suwa, G., & WoldeGabriel, G. (2009). *Ardipithecus ramidus* and the paleobiology of early hominids. *Science, 326*(5949), 75–86.

Wildlife Protection Society of India. (2014). *Current status of tiger in India.* Retrieved April 3, 2015, from http://www.wpsi-india.org/tiger/tiger_status.php

Wilderness.net. (2014). *The Wilderness Act of 1964.* Missoula, MT: University of Montana. Retrieved April 3, 2015, from http://www.wilderness.net/index.cfm?fuse=NWPS&sec=legisAct

Williams, M. (2006). *Deforesting the Earth from Prehistory to Global Crisis: An Abridgment.* Chicago, IL: University of Chicago Press.

Winegarden, C. R., & Khor, L. B. (1991). Undocumented immigration and unemployment of U.S. youth and minority workers: Econometric evidence. *The Review of Economics and Statistics, 73*(1), 105–112.

Wines, M. (2014, May 6). Stanford to purge $18 billion endowment of coal stock. *The New York Times.* Retrieved April 3, 2015, from http://www.nytimes.com/2014/05/07/education/stanford-to-purge-18-billion-endowment-of-coal-stock.html?_r=0

Winkler, R. (2007). *Why do ICDPs fail? The relationship between subsistence farming, poaching and ecotourism in wildlife and habitat conservation.* Working Paper 07/76, Swiss

Federal Institute of Technology. Zurich, Switzerland: Economics Working Paper Series. Retrieved April 3, 2015, from http://www.cer.ethz.ch/research/wp_07_76.pdf

Withers, G., & Pope, D. (2007). Immigration and unemployment. *Economic Record*, *61*(2), 554–564.

Woinarski, J. C. Z., Burbidge, A. A., & Harrison, P. L. (2015). Ongoing unraveling of a continental fauna: Decline and extinction of Australian mammals since European settlement. *PNAS Early Edition*. Retrieved April 3, 2015, from http://www.pnas.org/cgi/doi/10.1073/pnas.1417301112

Wood, M. C. (2013). *Nature's trust: Environmental law for a new ecological age*. New York, NY: Cambridge University Press.

World Health Organization. (1998). *50 Facts: Global health situation and trends 1955–2025*. Retrieved April 3, 2015, from http://www.who.int/whr/1998/media_centre/50facts/en/

World Nuclear Association. (2009). *Health impacts: Chernobyl accident appendix 2*. Retrieved April 3, 2015, from http://www.world-nuclear.org/info/Safety-and-Security/Safety-of-Plants/Appendices/Chernobyl-Accident—Appendix-2—Health-Impacts/

World Rainforest Movement. (2013, September). The Sentinelese—the world's most isolated tribe? *WRM Monthly Bulletin, 194*. Retrieved April 3, 2015, from http://wrm.org.uy/bulletins/issue-194

Wuerthner, G., Crist, E., & Butler, T. (2014). *Keeping the wild: Against the domestication of earth*. Washington, DC: Island Press.

Yosim, A., Bailey, K., & Fry, R. C. (2015). Arsenic, the "king of poisons," in food and water. *American Scientist, 103*(1), 34–41.

Zajtman, A. (2004, September 17). The battle for DR Congo's wildlife. *BBC News*. Retrieved April 3, 2015, from http://news.bbc.co.uk/2/hi/africa/3667560.stm

Zhang, S. (2012, July 16). Charts: What your trash reveals about the world economy. *Mother Jones*. Retrieved April 3, 2015, from http://www.motherjones.com/environment/2012/07/trash-charts-world-bank-report-economy

Zuber, S. L., & Newman, M. C. (2011). *Mercury pollution: A transdisciplinary treatment*. London, UK: CRC Press.

6

The Changing Needs of the African Elephant

Darlyne G. Nemeth and Donald F. Nemeth

Before going to southern Africa in August 2014, our only knowledge of elephants was gained by watching videos or visiting zoos. The videos focused on elephants in the wild; whereas, the zoos presented elephants in captivity. They always looked so unhappy, walking back and forth with little room to roam. In Africa, due to the efforts of governments such as South Africa and their various Natural Parks, as well as private conservancies, such as André and Collen Kotzé's The Elephant Whispers, elephants are both free and protected at the same time. This chapter focuses on our trip to Africa and our experiences with those "Silent Giants." For reference information, we relied on Bob Preller's 2013 book, *The Silent Giants of Southern Africa*.

BACKGROUND

Elephants have long been a symbol of strength and good fortune. The first author's mother, Marie Gaynor, collected little statues of elephants, always with their trunks up, for good luck. Such collections are wonderful; yet collecting actual elephant tusks is horrible. Elephants must be killed, usually by poachers, to obtain these coveted ivory tusks. The rest of their body is typically just left to rot (Hammer, 2014, p. 45). But elephants live in groups, often referred to as herds, or families, and their deaths are mourned. They are very humanlike.

After attending the World Congress for Psychotherapy in Durban, South Africa, Donald and I set out on a grand adventure—to visit Kruger National Park and experience elephants, up close and personal, at the Elephant Whispers conservancy. In Kruger, the elephants walk freely in groups. The park is designed to hold approximately 15,000 elephants, and yet there are currently over 17,000 elephants there (personal communication). Just like humans in protected environments, elephants are overpopulated in Kruger. Yet, somehow, the poachers still have found ways to get to them.

As stated earlier, elephants live in groups referred to as either herds or families. They are very similar to humans in so many ways, both "socially and developmentally," states Caitlin O'Connell-Rodwell (quoted in Hammer, 2014, p. 48). They express feelings, communicate with one another, and live a very long time. Some live into their 80s. Besides being poached by human predators, elephants' life spans often depend on the condition of their teeth. In their lifetime, elephants may have as many as six pairs of molars; each pair is automatically replaced when they are worn down, until the sixth pair emerges. When this pair is worn away, the elephant, now old and unable to chew, usually dies from lack of nutrition (Preller, 2013, p. 54).

ELEPHANTS HAVE FEELINGS

Male elephants have a temporal gland halfway between their eyes and ears. Via this gland, when experiencing negative feelings, they secrete dark streaks down their faces (Preller, 2013, p. 52). Female elephants have glands or "mammae" just behind their forelegs. Thus, their feelings are not so readily discernable.

THE TRUNK: A MULTIPURPOSE ORGAN

An elephant trunk is equivalent to a hand. Similar, yet different. It is called a proboscis (Preller, 2013, p. 58). It can hold water, lift weights, breathe, and gently, or not so gently, grab things. We were amazed to experience how gently an elephant, even a very large elephant, was able to remove treats from our hands. Yet right afterwards, the elephant picked up a huge branch, stuck it in its mouth, chewed it, and swallowed it. Elephants, like pandas, eat constantly. Whereas pandas' diets are restricted to only a certain type of bamboo, elephants eat everything in sight.

When on an elephant ride, we noticed that it was not uncommon for this animal to stop and help herself to a tree branch or bush. It is easy to tell where elephants have been. The vegetation is usually devastated. Just like humans, elephants are typically into overconsumption at the cost of the environment.

Also, like humans, elephants have a dominant side. This can be discerned by looking at the muscle patterns on the lower side of the trunk. The one that is more slightly worn (right or left) represents the elephant's dominant side.

REPRODUCTION AND BIRTH

Here, the female elephant is clearly in charge. Between the ages of 25 and 45, male elephants experience "musth" periods when their testosterone levels are raging. Their temporal glands secrete a sticky solution, and they begin to secrete dark green odorous urine (i.e., green penis syndrome) (Preller, 2013, p. 62). They become very aggressive and begin looking for a mate. If she is ready, the female's urine odor will have changed as well. Basically, cows are in oestrus for only three to six days, whereas bulls are in musth much longer. After mating, the cow will carry a calf for 22 months (Preller, 2013, p. 63). When it is time to give birth, it is not uncommon for two or three "midwife" elephants to protect her and help her through the process. When threatened, however, elephants will stop breeding. According to Rian Lanbuschagne, "the constant shooting at them, the stress, like humans in a war situation" is just too much for them (Hammer, 2014, p. 53).

COMMUNICATION

Elephants are able to communicate over large distances by means of infrasonic calls (Preller, 2013, p. 64). Their feet are both shock absorbers and communication devices. Elephants live in a matriarchal society. The senior cow is in charge, and the bulls merely show up for breeding (Preller, 2013, p. 69).

Elephants have vocal chords and can produce either subsonic rumbles or powerful screams; some are inaudible to the human ear (Preller, 2013, p. 70). At night, calls can be detected as far as 10 kilometers away (Preller, 2013, pp. 71–72). Elephants can detect low-frequency sounds through the ground via their sensitive feet. So they are never really out of touch with one another. They do not need cell phones. They can sense the deep rumbles of the earth, severe weather, and even ocean waves (Preller, 2013, p. 74). They have an extensive network that can even span an entire country. Therefore, culling (i.e., killing for population control) elephants, as Preller (2013) points out, "becomes a nonsense affair" (p. 74). Once again, human's non-holistic attempts to manage their environment did not take into account the intrasound effect and how upset all the elephants would become after such an event.

ELEPHANT SYMBOLS

In myth and religion, elephants have come to symbolize erudition, wisdom, levelheadedness, and restrained strength, as well as such positive virtues as intelligence, honesty, justice, respect, and reverence, heretofore usually attributed only to human beings (Preller, 2013, p. 75).

Current scientific research is exploring elephants' cognitive and affective abilities. Elephants think, plan, and display basic emotions, such as empathy and grief. They are capable of executive functions. Births and deaths are announced with the strong behavioral and vocal reactions of either excitement or grief, respectively (Poole, 1996). Both sounds call other elephants to stay by the side of the birthing or grieving cow. Current research by Soltis et al.

(2011) suggests that it is the intensity of the emotion, rather than the quality (i.e., positive or negative) that is communicated. Preller believes that an elephant's "subjective experiences may match that of us humans" (2013, p. 77). It is clear that animals/elephants have feelings. Charles Darwin and Konrad Lorenz wrote about this many years ago. According to Preller (2013), "the feelings of anger, love, terror, and the pleasure of relief ... provide evidence of a world of deep emotional experience on the part of animals" (p. 79).

Feelings require freedom of expression, of being, of living. So, how can we cull such feeling beings? Is it for their good, our good, and/or the good of the environment? These questions need to be addressed in a holistic manner.

Elephants can be traumatized. When culling or poaching begins, neighboring elephants experience fear and huddle together. The young of those culled are so traumatized that they have nightmares and often do not survive (Hammer, 2014, p. 45). Likewise, when elephants are lucky enough to find each other again, they experience great joy, which, according to Cynthia Moss, "plays a very important part in their whole social system" (as cited in Preller, 2013, p. 84).

ELEPHANT POACHING

According to Preller (2013), "many years of persecution almost led to the demise and extinction of the African Elephant" (p. 91). This process still continues in the African countries north of South Africa. But even in Kruger National Park, "over two thousand elephants were slaughtered during 2011," merely for their ivory tusks (Preller, 2013, p. 91). In Zimbabwe, more than 15,000 elephants were killed between 2009 and 2011. If this level of hunting and poaching continues, Preller (2013) predicts that elephant populations will be lost in these countries in the near future.

Reportedly, according to Preller (2013), each elephant killed is worth 40,000 pounds to the poacher. This global crime conspiracy links "African political turmoil and organized Asian racketeering through the soaring value of illegal ivory" (Preller, 2013, p. 91). It is reportedly as lucrative as cocaine or heroin smuggling.

According to Preller (2013), before hunters and poachers, Africa's elephant population was once estimated at 5–10 million. Now, a mere 600,000 remain. Clearly, the African elephant is "at risk"; this is despite the efforts of conservationists, ecologists, and environmentalists. There is just too much money to be made off of their destruction. Basically, humans are the only predators of elephants! What gives them/us (the ones who mainly control this poaching process) the right to do so? In China, if a panda is killed, the poacher is executed. But, what happens to the poachers in Africa? Fines? Prison? One such poacher, Hassan Idress Gargaf, has been the mastermind of "some of the biggest elephant slaughters in Chad's history" and was actually "very proud of his killings" (Hammer, 2014, p. 49)—for example, "26 elephants in a single day at Zakouma in 2010" (Hammer, 2014, p. 52). Another poacher was booked in Am Timan prison in Chad only to escape along with 26 other prisoners and disappear (Hammer, 2014, p. 53). Likewise, Gargaf escaped and disappeared only to return and murder another 86 elephants a few months later (Hammer, 2014, p. 53). According to Hammer, Gargaf was arrested three times, imprisoned, and escaped twice, and his current whereabouts, either in prison or hiding, are undetermined.

According to Preller (2013), elephants possess a magnificent ability to survive. He calls this the "spirit of the elephant." But, will this spirit prevail, or will it be doomed by the more sociopathic individuals in our midst? Those who perceive themselves as conquerors, rather than caretakers, of our Earth Environment and its living beings are the greatest problem the elephants face today.

Elephants, like horses and dogs, have the ability to bond to humans and to work alongside us. They are understanding and sensitive animals who can work with us and even protect us. Mutual trust can develop. Thus, according to Henry Beston, "we need another and wiser and perhaps a more mystical concept of animals ... they are not brethren, they are not underlings; they are other nations, caught with ourselves in the net of life and time" (as cited in Preller, 2013, p. 99).

THE CONFLICT OVER LAND USE

Human Elephant Conflict (HEC) is a major concern in countries where elephants roam. Crop raiding, property destruction, and deaths "are becoming more frequent as human population increases and encroaches on elephant habitat" (Preller, 2013, p. 109). As opposed to culling, birth control and translocation have been discussed as possible solutions. Creating wildlife corridors and trans-frontier parks have also been suggested. All involve political and logistical challenges (Preller, 2013, p. 109). These all require holistic management strategies.

As Preller concludes, "Animals that have been symbolically embedded into our culture for centuries are now disappearing at an alarming rate. The importance of these animals in our lives is often overlooked, but animals are truly symbols that not only inspire us, but are essential for a healthy future. Elephants are religious deities and majestic icons. They have provided companionship, carried us on their shoulders and ploughed our fields. Few are as inspiring as the elephants" (Preller, 2013, p. 112).

OUR EXPERIENCES

We encountered elephants in three different locations—Kruger National Park in South Africa, the Elephant Whispers conservancy in Hazyview, South Africa (Figure 6.1), and the Elephant Back Safaris in Victoria Falls, Zimbabwe.

Figure 6.1.
The authors at the Elephant Whispers Conservancy in Hazyview, South Africa. (Photo by Donald F. Nemeth, PhD)

In Kruger, we rode in a jeep and spent our entire time observing and photographing these gentle giants as they freely roamed over the landscape. In Hazyview, we were able to speak to the owners of the Elephant Whispers conservancy and had a hands-on learning experience. We touched their ears, trunks, and feet. We saw their temporal glands, through which they expressed their feelings; we learned how to discern whether or not an elephant was right- or left-side dominant; and we saw the tremendous affection they displayed for the people who cared for them. In fact, to avoid overattachment and grief of loss, human caretakers, are switched every few years. André Kotze introduced us to Preller's (2013) *The Silent Giants of Southern Africa*, on whose research this chapter was based. We were amazed at how well cared for these elephants were at this conservancy. All had been wounded, abused, or orphaned previously. Now, they were safe. Knowing what we know now, it is hard for us to imagine how any human, either through culling or poaching, could kill these gentle giants. There is something seriously wrong with

Figure 6.2.
Elephant encounter at Victoria Falls, Zimbabwe. (Photo by Donald F. Nemeth, PhD)

a society that, either intentionally or unintentionally, allows such practices. Yet, they happen with very few consequences. Some even call it "sport."

In the United States, this practice was allowed in the West in the late 1800s. Whole killing fields of buffalo (i.e., bison) were shot for sport. As a result, the indigenous people of the area had nothing to eat. Their food supply and ecological balance was lost for "sport." American Indians killed for food, warmth, etc. All parts of the buffalo were used. There was no "sport," only appropriate need.

Now, in Africa, the same scenario is being replayed. Whether for sport or for profit, there are no good reasons to kill an elephant. Although elephant meat or skin may be used for food or ceremonial purposes, this usually is not a villager's first choice for food or ceremony. So, what is the purpose of this violent behavior? Ivory tusks for collectors is not a sufficient reason for such cruelty!

Our third adventure with elephants was in Victoria Falls, Zimbabwe. Our guide, Tambo, explained that oftentimes, at night, elephants would walk down the main street of town because it is in their migratory route. Unfortunately, Zimbabwe has one of the worst records for elephant poaching in southern Africa. Problems within the various governmental structures abound. In fact, one shop where we were brought to buy native crafts was filled with ivory carvings for sale. It was very disconcerting.

On to brighter events. Early one morning, we went to the Elephant Back Safari where we had an amazing breakfast, were told stories about elephant lore around a campfire, and rode these amazing animals. Our guide, Tom, told us that we would experience muscles we never knew we had. He was right! It was like doing the splits for 45 minutes. When dismounting, we could hardly walk. During this elephant walk, although well-tempered, our elephant, Tatu, would stop randomly to feed—a bush here, a twig there. It was easy to see where the elephants had passed: down the hill, across the stream, up the hill. We were so high up. It was unlike riding a horse. It was truly amazing (Figure 6.2).

We were so fortunate to have had this adventure. We rode atop elephants; we stood underneath them; we touched their feet; we cradled their trunks in our hands; we fed them. It was one of the most wonderful and yet humbling experience of our lifetime—one to be treasured and preserved, as we should all elephants! As Caitlin O'Connell-Rodwell stated, "If we value human rights, we should keep those beings with us here on earth" (Hammer, 2014, p. 48). Perhaps China's 2014 destruction of the more than six tons of black-market ivory will decrease poacher motivation and slow down the slaughter of these gentle giants (Hammer, 2014, p. 54).

REFERENCES

Hammer, J. (2014, July–August). Elephant killer. *Smithsonian, 45*(4), 45–54.

Poole, J. (1996). *Coming of age with elephants: A memoir.* New York, NY: Hyperion.

Preller, B. (2013). *The silent giants of southern Africa: Including the desert giants of the Kaokoveld* (3rd ed.). South Africa: (n.p.).

Soltis, J., Blowers, T. E., & Savage, A. (2011). Measuring positive and negative affect in the voiced sounds of African elephants (*Loxodanta africana*). *Journal of the Acoustical Society of America, 129*(2), 1059–1066.

7

Changing Our Goals from Ownership to Stewardship: Lessons from America's Indigenous People

Gloria Alvernaz Mulcahy

Indigenous peoples of the world understand that words are sacred and that their original language represents the accumulated knowledge, cultural values, and vision of an entire people. As such, language is seen to arise out of place, that is, out of Mother Earth. Moreover, Nettle and Romaine (2000) point to a fundamental connection between the number of indigenous languages in a particular geographical area and the diversity of its animal and plant life. It is tempting to surmise that the complexity of human-environment relations is linked to a diversity of language and culture, and reflects nonhuman species as well as the earth's ecosystems. According to Nettle and Romaine, however, such assertions require more evidence of validation.

It is noteworthy that at an international level, United Nations (UN) documents report that "language is not only a communication tool, it is often linked to the land or region traditionally occupied by indigenous peoples; it is an essential component of one's collective and individual identity and provides a sense of belonging and community. When the language dies, that sense of community is damaged" (United Nations, Department of Economics and Social Affairs, 2009, p. 58). This understanding of our relationship to Mother Earth, as being embedded in the languages we speak, gives us pause to reflect on how place speaks through language in "all our relations." It includes our connections with each other as well as the natural world of plants, trees, and grasses.

Our relationship with what North Americans have come to describe as the environment links us to the surface of earth and the sky. It connects us to our roots in Mother Earth and to our unique indigenous languages that arise out of particular landscapes. In our book *Living in an Environmentally Traumatized World: Healing Ourselves and Our Planet* (Nemeth, Hamilton, & Kuriansky, 2012), my chapter explored traditional indigenous cultural practices of people primarily from southwestern Ontario. This is Haudenosaunee country and includes the People of Six Nations (Onyoto: aka, Cayuga, Mohawks, Onondaga,

Tuscarora, and Seneca) who dwell along with the Annishinaabe and Leenape in surrounding areas. It is important, however, to acknowledge the diversity of nations represented in our urban context. For example, approximately 20,000 indigenous people from various nations reside in the southwestern Ontario region in Canada. In sum, cultural practices vary locally, regionally, nationally and internationally. Nonetheless, indigenous ways of being in the world are related in spite of divergent languages and cultural practices.

Typically, in our local communities encompassing Six Nations, introductions of individuals and groups include disclosure of a person's indigenous name, nation or territory, and location—urban, rural, reserve, or international. Such information locates who we are in terms of "all my relations." It includes our place on earth in relationship with all our relations—people, animals, trees, plants, the land and so forth.

In southwestern Ontario, a person's indigenous name typically is given by an Elder or Traditional Healer who has this community responsibility. Also, being given a name may be followed by a special community ceremony that honors the occasion. Communities have someone who carries this responsibility for naming and has the requisite cultural knowledge to undertake such an important community service. For example, one of our local Onyoto: aka grandmothers has given spirit names to our sons' children and we have had a naming ceremony for our first grandchild. Indigenous naming practices are one of the elements that shape identity within family networks and the larger community. It offers direction regarding the oral tradition of who we are and where we are situated in our network of relations. For example, my Onyoto: aka name is *Ya Ko ni Ku? Li: yo*, which means "she is of a good mind," and it locates me at the present time in southwestern Ontario (London urban context) and within my mother's Tsalagi, Aniyunwiya (Cherokee) family. As a result of uprooting and displacement, naming has been provided for my immediate family by an Onyoto: aka grandmothers, who carries this responsibility in our local indigenous community.

Cultural disjunctions sometimes occur as a part of a larger story about ongoing uprooting and displacement of indigenous peoples. My mother's family moved from the east (Missouri) to the West Coast of California, followed by my move to the University of Maryland on the East Coast for graduate school and then briefly to Philadelphia, Pennsylvania, to teach at the university. This was followed by a move to Canada in Montreal, Quebec, before permission was granted to remain in Canada. Once permission was given for Landed Immigrant Status, we moved to London, Ontario, where I accepted a position at the university.

Indigenous people recognize who they are in response to their place on Mother Earth and in relationship to clans (e.g., bird or eagle) and to one's indigenous nation (e.g., Tsalagi/Aniyunwiya). The Cherokee Nation or the Principal People reside in the Smoky Mountain region of the Carolinas in the United States. Also, there are the Tsalagi from Oklahoma, who were part of the forced removal by the U.S. government under the leadership of Andrew Jackson, their seventh president. The removal of the Tsalagi (by gunpoint) resulted in the death of thousands of Tsalagi along what became known as the Trail of Tears. Casualties were caused by exposure, illness, and starvation when the Cherokee suddenly were forced to leave their territory. This historical atrocity is a derivative of the brutality aimed at First People in North America. The Trail of Tears was a means used by the United States to erase original people in an effort to own our First People's territory.

It is important to remember that similar atrocities were experienced by First Peoples in Australia, New Zealand, and the Saami people in Russia. The Tsalagi (Aniyunwiya) were the focus of the government's displacement of indigenous people westward. Historical accounts of this uprooting have highlighted the journey of the Tsalagi to the west along with its impact on the Chickasaw and Choctaw. The Tsalagi were moved by gunpoint from the East Coast to Oklahoma. They walked along what is now called the Cherokee Highway or "Tsalagi Trail of Tears." The name reflects the pain embedded in the forced uprooting and displacement of a Nation of People who had lived on the land well before the so-called discovery of North America by Columbus. It was in the winter of 1856 when over 2,000 Cherokee died along the Trail—men, women, and children. They died from starvation, exposure, disease, exhaustion, and multiple and interrelated traumas both physical and psychological. It is a well-documented tragic history of indigenous peoples of North America often not included as an important feature of the formal record (http://www .cherokee.org, 2014).

Uprooting and displacement was part of an overarching plan to remove the "Indigenous problem" through the residential school system, i.e., "to take the Indian out of the child." This was to be accomplished through governmental actions, which included removing indigenous children from their families and placing them in boarding schools. The removal of children from families was coupled with both physical and sexual abuse of indigenous children in Canada, the United States, and Australia. These psychosocial disjunctions regarding loss of one's family and culture were coupled with physical and/or sexual abuse of indigenous children and undermined indigenous peoples across all nations and at all levels of social structure—family, school, community.

Internationally, our First People are recognized as indigenous or original people, and identity is inherent in our relationship with Mother Earth. An understanding of who we are is embedded in community and our place geographically, as in region, or a particular area. Also, it includes the plant life, trees, sky, lakes and rivers, birds, sun, moon, and stars—all that supports us as human beings on earth. Identity for indigenous people in North America is embedded in place of origin—one identity nested within another. Each of these relations is located in time and place in the context of community. For example, the Haudenosaunee People of Six Nations are comprised of six separate but related groups with different languages—Mohawk, Onyoto: aka, Cayuga, Onondaga, Seneca, and Tuscarora of upstate New York and Canada. They too have a history of uprooting and displacement.

Today, what territory remains for the Tsalagi includes the Eastern shore group located in the Smoky Mountain region along with those who survived the removal to Oklahoma. It is part of a larger tragic story of uprooting, displacement, and death of Indigenous Peoples on Mother Earth. This disturbing feature of American history is often not part of the stories we spin in institutions of higher learning regarding relations with our First Peoples.

Keeping this historical context in mind contextualizes how indigenous people remember "who they are and where they come from." Indigenous birth names and ceremonies are embedded both in one's place on Mother Earth and in a set of relations with both our environment and with each other in our communities. Also, there are interdependent environmental interactions and cultural connections that link indigenous people with family, immediate community, our nations, and the world. We move from local communities, nested one within the other, to regional, national, and international relational spheres.

In southwestern Ontario and specifically the London area, there are some 90,000 indigenous people—Onyoto: aka, Anninshaabe, and Leenape. There are those who have migrated, or who have been uprooted and displaced due to psychosocial factors—political, historical, and economic. My mother's family provides a useful example of such forces of disconnection arising from political maneuvers that entailed the removal of indigenous children from their families. We were situated on the east coast and migrated west. There is documentation that substantiates the journey from the East Coast to Missouri and later a move west to the San Joaquin Valley and then the coast of California. My grandmother resided in the San Joaquin Valley and was transient between the valley and the coast. This remains an area where Tsalagi are presently living (Four Corners, Cherokee Highway, San Joaquin Valley, Stockton, California).

One of our local Onyoto: aka Elders, who holds the responsibility for naming, gave our first grandchild her indigenous name in the original language. We had a community feast and a ceremony that celebrated her entry into the world through the traditional practice of the Grandmother's coming together to talk with the parents and the grandparents about the newcomer. Also, the grandmothers had an opportunity to connect with the baby—holding and carrying her and engaging with the family. It was out of these community conversations that the grandmothers offered the baby a name. Also, the community ceremony acknowledged the grandchild's Tsalagi (Cherokee) grandmother (Totha). It is through such practices, interactions, and conversations that traditional ways of being in the world shape identity. They provide an earth-centered pathway of understanding that honors the important cultural concept of "all my/our relations" with Mother Earth.

Traditional practices underscore the interconnections among all life forces that "hold us up." Human beings are supported by what indigenous people in Haudenosaunne territory often refer to in ceremonies as "all my relations." One of our Onyoto: aka Elders, in her teachings, noted that we are responsible for listening and remembering that the stones, too, are alive. They are sometimes referred to as our "Grandfathers."

Community ceremonies support indigenous ways of being in the world and include attention to spirit, body, and mind. They represent how indigenous people are intimately interconnected with Mother Earth, or what nonindigenous researchers refer to as the "environment." From an Indigenous perspective *even the stones are listening.*" Although I have been uprooted and displaced in terms of my place of origin, special attention through examples in this chapter have been given to southwestern Ontario where I am now residing. Local communities (urban, reserves, settlements) provided unique opportunities to articulate cultural responsibilities and explore and discuss indigenous practices in our world of ongoing human and earth trauma and to strive to live in harmony and balance with Mother Earth. For example, locally we have monthly moon ceremonies for our indigenous women that offer traditional teachings regarding our relationship with Grandmother Moon. Each month of the year provides a focal point for teachings and ensures that our ways of being in the world are affirmed. This practice provides a connection to Mother Earth and recognizes our relationship as women with Grandmother Moon. We know that the ocean tides are linked to the moon cycle as are the cycles of women. Traditional teachings are provided by Elders and Healers with knowledge in a particular area who communicate understandings to the next generation in their community contexts—urban, rural, or reserve.

Traditions shape communities and include naming ceremonies when a child is born, and seasonal ceremonies such as those in the fall and spring, condolence ceremonies, and sunrise and moon ceremonies. These examples articulate an indigenous "relational perspective" and how ceremonies acknowledge and affirm our connections as humans with Mother Earth (our environment). Ceremonies serve to shape our "ways of being in the world" in an effort to live in harmony and balance with the cycles of the earth (winter and fall ceremonies, and moon ceremonies). These practices connect us with the cycles of life fundamental to living in relationship with Mother Earth. Moreover, being caretakers, we have responsibilities associated with these ceremonies.

In sum, it is generally assumed that indigenous knowledge lives in our communities locally and regionally; however, it moves beyond these boundaries to embrace many nations across North America and across Mother Earth.

Although our cultural understandings formally arise in ceremonies, they are embedded in our daily practices and gatherings. For example, when we use the phrase "all my relations," it becomes an acknowledgment of our connection with each other and all living things including plants, the water, wind, stones, and all facets of life on Mother Earth. Moreover, indigenous ceremonies serve as reminders of our duties and responsibilities as indigenous people to live in harmony and balance with the energy forces that sustain life.

A wide range of cultural observances such as sunrise ceremonies, and seasonal ceremonies, provide cultural practices that keep communities in balance and harmony with the cycles of life and with their relationship to Mother Earth. The focus on "living in relation" to Mother Earth becomes a guiding principle of culture. Communities then, have the responsibility to embody a respectful, spiritual, and protective relationship with Mother Earth—she is alive, and we know that the stones are our relatives as well as the trees and the earth. In our ceremonies such as the sweat lodge, the heated stones are called our grandfathers, and they are speaking to us. This relational view of the earth is in contrast to some academic/scientific perspectives, which prescribe an objective view— that is, a way of standing outside of existing sets of relations being examined.

These points of discussion highlight indigenous ways of being in the world with a focus on how community ceremonies and practices shape our relationship with Mother Earth. In addition, they reveal how communities experience Mother Earth and articulate their connections with her as caretakers. Indigenous people have cultural duties and responsibilities with regard to their relationship with Mother Earth. Their approaches do offer parallel versions of relations in the development of our understanding of the world around us, which we call the physical environment. These groupings are not separate. There is a considerable range of differences regarding our understanding of the "natural world" or Mother Earth.

This brief discussion outlines how an earth-centered indigenous view differs from more traditional "scientific" perspectives, where often there has been a tendency to be less holistic. Trends in psychology and the social sciences, however, do reflect developments in philosophy and the natural sciences. These various ways of experiencing and thinking about the world around us mirror our knowledge bases through philosophy, psychology, social sciences, and the natural sciences. Academic disciplines, although embedded in a cultural context, tend to both reflect and shape our way of seeing the world around us.

The sciences and social sciences both reflect and determine our way of being in the world and how we think about and understand the world around us. They influence our many ways of seeing the world along with philosophy and religion. Psychosocial forces impact on how we live in the world in relationship to both our social lives, psychologically as well as the economic. These areas of knowledge and experience provide an overlapping field of experience that is connected to how we see and understand Mother Earth.

The Thanksgiving Address ceremony, discussed in our book (Nemeth, Hamilton, & Kuriansky, 2012), is a greeting on behalf of the Haudenosaunee to Mother Earth. It is a practice that originated over 1,000 years ago and is connected historically to the formation of what the Haudenosaunee of Six Nations call the Great Law of Peace. The words from the address are heard at ceremonies today and are expressed in an understanding that our Mother Earth, the world around us, cannot be taken for granted. This connection is renewed through our acknowledgment of all living things and serves both as a reminder of our respectful relationship with the earth and also as a guiding principle of culture embodied in our ceremonies and realized in our ways of being in the world.

This chapter explores the cultural meanings embedded in our original languages and cultural practices and how they are reflected in an indigenous relationship with the earth—"Iethinisténha Ohóntsia." It is implicit from this viewpoint that words arise out of our ancestral land, the earth, and are connected to all of her creatures (Nelson, 2002). For example, moving inside an indigenous worldview, humpback whales may emerge in our stories as "singers of the sea." They have a language and songs.

OUR PURPOSE

In our recent book (Nemeth, Hamilton, & Kuriansky, 2012), particular attention was centered on the Haudenosaunee People of Six Nations in southwestern Ontario—the Mohawk, Onyoto: aka, Cayuga, Onondaga, Seneca and Tuscarora people. The present discussion amplifies this earlier perspective and reaffirms the importance of acknowledging our ancestral roots as indigenous people. It is important, however, to acknowledge the connection between my people, the Tsalagi/Aniyunwiya (Cherokee) of the eastern sector of what is now the United States to the Haudenosaunee of Six Nations. These two nations are of the same language group (Iroquia) and share similar traditions and practices. Elders and healers at the Onyoto: aka settlement outside of London, Ontario, report longstanding communications with Tsalagi healers to the south. This substantiates the ongoing oral history in our communities. Moreover, these cultural links have been further confirmed in discussions about, and participation in them, by both groups.

Metis researcher and environmentalist Melissa Nelson (2002) discusses the importance of developing and maintaining a connection with the plant life that nourishes us, and of embodying our ways of being in the world in all relations with Mother Earth. This viewpoint promotes a way of living that establishes harmony on earth and is envisioned in the Haudenosaunee Thanksgiving Address of upstate New York and Canada (Stokes & Benedict, 1993). The address dates back to practices existing over 1,000 years ago. It is a greeting to the "Natural World or Words before All Else: Ohén:ton Karihwatéhkwen." These words that precede all others continue to be acknowledged in our ceremonies today. They form the core of our traditional practices and serve as a guide to "help us to rediscover our balance, respect, and oneness with Nature" (Stokes & Benedict, 1993).

Traditionally, the Haudenosaunee designate a speaker who offers the Thanksgiving Address at the opening and closing of ceremonies. The address recognizes the animals, the four winds, our forests, the water in our rivers, streams, lakes, and oceans, the fish, food plants and medicine herbs, trees, birds, as well as, the thunderers, the sun, moon and stars, our enlightened teachers, and the creator.

Implicit in this ceremony is an affirmation of a way of being "in relations" that incorporates the natural world as we bring our minds together as a people through ceremonies. The Address recognizes all living things and is based on the belief "that the world cannot be taken for granted, that a spiritual communication of thankfulness and acknowledgment of all living things must be given to align the minds and hearts of the people with Nature" (Stokes & Benedict, 1993). Such a perspective provides a core understanding in a belief system and a way of being in the world that is represented in the Haudenosaunee phrase "all my relations." This term serves as an acknowledgment of our Mother Earth.

AN ECO-VISION OF MOTHER EARTH

The focus of my discussion is to explore an eco-vision of Mother Earth that is embedded in a relational perspective with Mother Earth. It acknowledges the sacred relationship we have with Mother Earth as caretakers. Beck, Walters, and Francisco (1992) reveal how in Western civilization, "the trend has been to separate knowledge from the sacred" (p. 47). Moreover, discussion draws on the work of indigenous women writers from North America and includes Jeannette Armstrong (Nsyilxcen), Linda Hogan (Chickasaw), Leslie Marmon Silko (Acoma), and Lee Maracle (Sto:lo Nation of British Columbia).

The writing of Armstrong is central to the discussion in that she has made the unequivocal statement that Nsyilxcen constitutes the most significant influence on her writing. Moreover, she says that her experience of the land "sources and arises in (her) poetry" (quoted in Ortiz, 1998) and that the Okanagan language molds the connection between the two. Nelson reminds us of the diverse sounds that arise out of varied earthscapes, including bird songs, ocean waves, wolf howls, coyote yips, and the whisper of leaves on the wind. Such soundscapes offer an ecocultural context for our Indigenous languages (Nelson, 2002).

In her book entitled *Dwellings*, Chickasaw historian, environmentalist, and Pulitzer Prize nominee Linda Hogan (1995) speaks to the need for a language that arises out of our Mother Earth. She says: "We are looking for a tongue that speaks with reverence for life, searching for an ecology of mind. Without it, we have no home, have no place of our own within the creation. It is not only the vocabulary of science we desire. We want a language of that different yield.

A yield rich as the harvests of earth, a yield that returns us to our sacredness, to a self-love and respect that will carry out to others" (p. 60).

The intent of my eco-vision discussion of our relations with Mother Earth is to explore the writing of indigenous women authors who have been engaged in an animated discourse about reinventing the language to decolonize their writing. Such a perspective creates a pathway through liminal space that explores a syntax of experience that subverts the English language and generates an eco-wordscape that speaks out of and to our Mother Earth—Iethi'nist'enha Oh'ontsia. Moreover, it reflects a worldview that envisions Iethi'nist'enha Oh'ontsia as being alive. It invokes the responsibility to examine and explore the meaning of this relational way of being in the world. An investigation of what this might mean includes exploring a framework of reciprocity or mutuality as well as a caretaking role. Such relations are contrary to the notion of ownership of the land. An indigenous perspective envisions the earth as our Mother—she is alive. Stewardship becomes central in our development of human-environment relations.

In harmony with an eco-vision or relational context, indigenous women writers are "re-inventing the . . . language" and using their mother tongue to decolonize the literature (Harjo & Bird, 1997, pp. 23–25). This creates a pathway through liminal space where Aboriginal authors create a syntax of experience that subverts the dominant language. This perspective is of particular significance in the writing of Okanagan writer Jeannette Armstrong (1998). She explores marginalized zones of intersecting spaces where language and metaphor offer a "rich yield" that is responsiveness to the urgent need to nurture the spiritual seed within us that releases the power to create a life sustaining syntax in relation to Iethi'nist'enha Oh'ontsia/Mother Earth.

The centrality of the notion of "taking care of our seeds" is found in the teachings of many Original Peoples. For example, in Haudenosaunee territory near an Onyoto: aka settlement some 20 kilometers outside of London, Ontario, one of the Ceremonial Leaders and Traditional Healers, Lo^ut Honyust, reminds us that the name Atlohsa, which is used by our urban indigenous family healing center, is derived from the word Atunhetsla in the Onyoto: aka (Oneida) language. Thus, it refers to the spiritual seed within each of us (Atlohsa, 2005). In addition, this way of seeing the world is reflected by my Tsalagi/Aniyunwiya (Cherokee or Principal People) ancestors who have a twin meaning for their word "selu," denoting both woman and corn.

The conceptual links explored here arise out of the knowledge that in the nineteenth century, it was the Tsalagi women who planted corn, tended the stalks, cared for the yield, and sifted the best seeds for the next generation.

It was understood that women both created and sustained life. This way of seeing and being in the world is maintained in our traditional ceremonies that mirror a worldview that recognizes Mother Earth as providing for us. We have a responsibility as First People to continue to recognize, respect, and embrace our Mother Earth who supports and nourishes us.

In sharp contrast to this perspective, at the global or world level, there has been a contemporary debate at the United Nations over corporate development of terminator technologies on genetically engineered sterile seeds that could destroy our capacity to sustain life and maintain our connection to the land. Indigenous peoples in Brazil recently used their collective voices to quash efforts to undermine the global moratorium on terminator seeds. The creation of sterile seeds would impact on our four billion people worldwide who depend on "saving their seeds" (Todhunter, 2013).

Linda Hogan recounts in her book *Dwellings* (1995) the experience of Papago planters of corn in the Southwest. She reports a phrase used by anthropologist Ruth Underhill that highlights our relational perspective as indigenous people and embodies a connection with Mother Earth, i.e., "night after night the planter of corn walks around his field, singing up the corn" (p. 60). Moreover, this reflects a way of being in the world that offers insight into the seamless connection experienced by indigenous people in their relationship with Mother Earth. It reveals how this vision of the world creates a liminal space where writing in the margins features a discourse that breaks through surface of earth and women use their voices—going about singing up the corn.

In her book *The Turquoise Ledge: A Memoir* (2010), Leslie Marmon Silko reminds us of the importance of listening to the voices of the stones. She reports that the "grinding stones" used by the women for hard seeds were left behind in places where the pounding was done because the stones were so heavy. After dark, she notes that on the wind, she sometimes hears the women singing the grinding songs. Marmon Silko (1996) links together her experience and that of her indigenous peoples' language as arising out of the land and as having been birthed by a specific geography. For example, she joins together her experience and that of her indigenous ancestors indicating that identity, imagination and storytelling are "inextricably linked to the land" (Marmon Silko, 1996). She reports that the spoken word in storytelling serves as a connection to the written word and to our visual images. Armstrong understands that, through a deep connection with the earth and specific places, over time there is a distinctive interplay between geography and language, where indigenous words, thoughts, and knowledge are created and indigenous speakers shift-shape a worldview.

Critical narrative theory has been used to frame a psychosocial picture of identity in Jeannette Armstrong's writing. It reveals the unfolding of her struggle, among other indigenous scholars, to compose in English. The paradox is to adopt the colonizer's language to reinvent the enemy's language. Armstrong, a writer from the northwest of Canada, uses both English and her original language, Nsyilxcen. Discussion of her work involves a crossing of borders and bloodlines—disciplinary, cultural, historical, and personal.

Reliance on the early research of developmental researcher and psychoanalyst Daniel Stern (1985) and Mohawk sociologist Taiaiake Alfred (1995), reveals intersecting points in my academic work as well as my Tsalagi ancestry. Alfred's perspective challenges notions of "clearly-delineated identity by postulating the concept of nested identities" (p. 18) and challenges Stern's concept of the four senses of self. Critical to Stern's theory is the identification of a shift in the notion of the self with the onset of language—i.e., there is a move to experience the self as "object" as opposed to "subject." That is, the onset of language creates the distancing of the "self" from the "embodied experience of being in the world (subjectivity)." In addition, Jung's (1954/1966) discussion of archetypes provides another angle from which to see the world and an interpretive frame from which to understand it. The psychosocial view of identity highlighted in this environmental perspective pays particular attention to the impact of colonization and genocide on indigenous people. The intent is to un-map the idea of neutrality or innocence embedded in notions of cultural assimilation maintained by mainstream society and to uncover and challenge ideologies of dominance. In so doing, we explore the paradoxes of adopting English to communicate. Indigenous women writers, including Armstrong, Harjo, Bird, and Maracle, have coined a powerful term to describe this colonial process, thus illuminating and exploring its historical roots. Paradoxically, they use English, the *enemy's tongue*, to subvert the colonial agenda.

Armstrong's roots are planted firmly in the storytelling tradition of her Okanagan people, and it has shaped her significant role in the emergence and establishment of indigenous writing and writers. Indigenous knowledge is embedded in a tradition of storytelling as a way of knowing our world and to establish a sense of identity. What is particularly significant in this discussion is our understanding of Mother Earth—our environment, *or all our relations*.

Navajo writer Simon Ortiz (1998) asserts that Armstrong has situated herself among indigenous writers through the creation of an important body of contemporary literature. Most important historically, however, is that Armstrong is the author of *Slash* (1985), which established her as the author of the first published novel by an indigenous writer in Canada. This was followed by *Whispering in Shadows* in 2000. In addition, Armstrong has a book of poems, entitled *Breath Tracks* (1991), and numerous writings located in various anthologies. She comes to these distinguished achievements from a line of storytellers. Armstrong is the grandniece of Hum-Ishu-Ma (Donovan, 1998, p. 115), who is recognized as the first Native American woman novelist.

Armstrong's capacity to publish on a consistent basis as well as her role as director of her *En'wokin* Centre in British Columbia and the International School for Writing establishes her voice as that of an important knowledge holder. The *En'wokin* Centre is organized by and for indigenous people, granting degrees through University of Victoria, and publishing a literary journal. Furthermore, Armstrong is both an established educator and community activist.

LANGUAGE AND THE LAND: JEANNETTE ARMSTRONG

The literature of the First Peoples, as Harjo and Bird (1997) suggest, reads "as a process of decolonization. To that end Native women in particular, who are the caregivers of the next generation, play an important role as mothers, leaders, and writers" (p. 25). Armstrong makes an unequivocal statement that Nsyilxcen, her original language and the language of her people, constitutes the most significant influence on her writing. She points out that her Okanagan ancestors have taught her that the "language was given to us by the land we live within" (1998, p. 175). Most important is her statement that her experience of the land "both sources and arises" in her language and her writing. According to Armstrong, her Okanagan language molds the connection between the land as a source of language and that the "earth speaks."

Armstrong (1998) asserts that the land births her Native language and it is a small step to the understanding that for indigenous peoples, language arises out of Mother Earth. Moreover, it is assumed that words are situated in particular places. For example, the land that births Armstrong's language is the Okanagan section of the Great Columbia River Basin on the interior plateau of British Columbia and Washington State. Her Elders reveal that although Nsyilxcen is of the Salishan languages and it has been altered over time through migration, it has preserved simultaneously the old words in the Okanagan origin stories. Armstrong's father said that "it was the land that changed the language because there is special knowledge in each different place" (pp. 175–176).

Armstrong's community elders say that the land is our constant teacher and it holds "all knowledge of life and death." (Armstrong, 1998, p. 176). Armstrong notes that: "We survived and thrived by listening intently to its teachings—to it. It is the land that speaks N'silxchn through the generations of our ancestors . . . N'silxchn, the old land/mother spirit of the Okanagan People, which surrounds me in its primal wordless state" (p. 176).

As she slips elegantly and seamlessly between her experience of her language and the land, Armstrong reveals the following:

It is this N'silxchn which embraces me and permeates my experience of the Okanagan land and is a constant voice within me that yearns for human speech.

I am claimed and owned by this land, this Okanagan. Voices move within as the colors, patterns, and movements of a beautiful, kind Okanagan landscape.

They are the Grandmother voices which speak. (p. 176)

Out of this deep experience of the Okanagan land, Armstrong has written her grandmother's poem, however it arrived, in English. The word grandmother comes from the Nsyilxcen word "tmixw" in Okanagan, meaning something like loving-ancestor-land-spirit. This sense of connection with the earth is antithetical to a Euro-Western experience where feelings of disconnection predominate; emphasis is placed on claiming and owning the land, and there is the historical reality of conquering and controlling both the land and her indigenous people. By contrast, Armstrong (1998, p. 176) says: "I am claimed and owned by this land." Moreover, the poem was written in Nsyilxcen and interpreted into English. It is not so much a translation into English, but a transformation of English that becomes an act of reinventing the enemy's tongue. Armstrong (1998) says: "the land as language surrounds us completely, just like the physical reality of it surrounds us. Within that vast speaking, both externally and internally, we as human beings are an inextricable part—though a minute part—of the land language" (p. 178). Armstrong's "Grandmother" poem is a good example of how the "language spoken by the land, which is interpreted by the Okanagan into words, carries part of its ongoing reality. The land as language surrounds us completely" (1998, p. 178). The poem begins with the idea that "In the part of me that was always there / grandmothers / are speaking to me / the grandmothers in whose voices / I nestle / and draw nourishment from." Armstrong says that these voices speak to her in the "early morning light/glinting off water," the grandmothers becoming at one with the earth. She speaks to them "fragile green pushing upward" seeking the sun's warmth "pulling earth's breath down and in" to join with stone (pp. 176–177).

THE PARADOX OF LANGUAGE AND THE SPIRIT POWER OF WORDS

The role of language in the development of a sense of self reveals how symbolic thinking links us to others through sharing experiences in the present and past and notions about the future. Language opens a window to the social world of connections with others. This emergent sense of who we are, or the self, is viewed as a universal phenomenon that shapes our social experience. We, the indigenous, recognize the interdependence of the land, language, and the oral narratives of peoples. Ortiz (1998), a Navajo writer from the southwestern United States, insists that the land, people, and language are *absolutely* connected to the concept of self that emerges for indigenous persons. Similar reverberations are found in the writing of Leslie Marmon Silko (Acoma) and Mestiza writers such as Gloria Anzaldua and Ana Castillo.

Indigenous peoples' languages are understood to arise out of the land, having been birthed by a specific geography. Marmon Silko (1996), for example, links together her experience and that of her indigenous ancestors to indicate that identity, imagination and storytelling are "inextricably linked to the land" (p. 21). She reports that the spoken word in storytelling serves as a connection to the written word and to our visual images. Armstrong understands that, through a deep connection with the earth and specific places, over time there is a distinctive interplay between geography and language where indigenous words, thoughts and knowledge are created and Indigenous speakers shift shape a worldview.

Armstrong (1998, p. 180) says she experiences the "land as a fluent speaker of Okanagan (and that) N'silxchn emulates the land and the sky in its unique flow around me." It is as if there are voices inside the words that harken back to the ancestors. Hogan says it seems that the old traditions hold true, that is, the name of something and the object are one and the same. There is no division or separation between the word and the object. Thus, both the language and the story become reality or lived experience. Armstrong (1998) says that "the land as a fluent speaker of Okanagan" reflects her deep connection with the earth that belies the "as if" quality that predominates the thinking of anthropologists and psychologists when discussing the stories of indigenous peoples.

Mohawk sociologist Alfred (1995, pp. 18–19) explores the idea of nested identity and how it reflects the multilayered nature of our experience while incorporating each one of the communities a person inherits. This idea illuminates the crosscutting of allegiances that occur over the course of a people's history. Alfred indicates how each of these communities we live in provides indigenous people with formative identity experiences. The question of identity from a psychosocial perspective becomes personal (self), sociocultural (national), communal (world), and metaphysical (universal or archetypal). At the local level, Armstrong refers to herself as Okanagan, and her language connects her to a larger group called the Salishan, which is further divided to include the South Interior Salsh (Miller, 2001, p. 466). Her language is seen to be given to her and her people out of the land (earth) that shapes her identity.

Original people understand that they are part of all of the elements of creation, as they also are a part of them. This relationship with the earth is a reciprocal one expressed in ceremonies and the oral tradition. Our traditions speak out in the margins where indigenous writers have created a discourse that returns all of us who read their works to future intermingling, and it reminds us of the creative seed (Atunhetsla) within each of us. It is a sign that after we plant the corn we must go out, night after night, walking around the fields "singing up the corn" (Hogan, 1995, p. 60).

CLOSING THOUGHTS ABOUT MOTHER EARTH

In bringing these words to a close, it is noteworthy that it was not until September 13, 2007, that the United Nations General Assembly adopted the

UN Declaration on the Rights of Indigenous Peoples. This action required 20 years of discussion within the UN system. Moreover, it was not until Bolivia, under the direction of Evo Morales, the world's first indigenous president who emerged in 2008, that the Law of Mother Earth was established, providing equal rights to the earth and the people of Bolivia, thus recognizing a spiritual connection with Pachamama (the Center of all life). Also, Ecuador has established constitutional rights for Pachamama—Mother Earth. These important events followed the 1992 Earth Summit and helped to move forward discussion at the international/world level.

Although progress at the international level is recognized as uneven, there are two items that are encouraging. At the June 2012 Rio de Janeiro Summit, culminating in the development of a document that recognizes and establishes Mother Earth rights (United Nations, 2012a), recognition was given to the importance of promoting harmony with nature and to encourage the achievements of a just balance among economic, social, and environmental needs of present and future generations (United Nations, 2012a). The second item was a call for "holistic integrated approaches to sustainable development, which will guide humanity to live in harmony with nature and lead to efforts to restore health and integrity of Earth's ecosystems" (United Nations, 2012b, p. 8).

Indigenous peoples have vigorously pursued status in the international community in an effort to address colonization and exploitation. In 1923, Haudenosaunee chief Deskaheh addressed the League of Nations, affirming and defending the rights of indigenous people on their own land and to do so in a way that placed them in harmony with their own laws, land, values, and beliefs. This was the beginning of a global focus on the equality and freedom of indigenous peoples.

It is noteworthy that it was not until 1982 that space was created for the voices of Original People to be heard and their identity honored at the global level. Furthermore, Canada, the United States, Australia, and New Zealand voted against the Declaration on the Rights of Indigenous Peoples. This declaration arrived "at the tail end of human rights standard-setting" and may be one of the last significant standards on human rights established by the United Nations. The link here regarding the Rights of Indigenous Peoples and the environment (Mother Earth) is significant in terms of the destructive forces that have harmed Mother Earth. It reflects a way of understanding the world that is embedded in a relational perspective that protects the earth as well as the people who live on her surface. It is a way of being that establishes the importance of living in harmony with Mother Earth. She is more than a resource to be used. Moreover, she is our Mother, and our languages emerge out of the earth.

Indigenous people have a responsibility to be caretakers of the earth. We acknowledge her in our ceremonies and see the trees, plants, animals, the sky, wind, and the water as sacred. Moreover, the earth is alive. Ehtho niioht'onha'k ne onkwa'nikon:ra; that is, now our minds are one.

REFERENCES

Alfred, G. R. (1995). *Heeding the voices of our ancestors: Kahnawake Mohawk politics and the rise of native nationalism*. Toronto: Oxford University Press.

Armstrong, J. (1985). *Slash*. Penticton, BC: Theytus Books.

Armstrong, J. (1991). *Breath tracks*. Penticton, BC: Theytus Books.

Armstrong, J. (1998). Land speaking. In S. Ortiz (Ed.), *Speaking for the generations: Native writers on writing*. Tucson: University of Arizona Press.

Armstrong, J. (2000). *Whispering in shadows*. Penticton, BC: Theytus Books.

Atlohsa. (2005). *Information brochure*. London, ON: Atlohsa Native Family Healing Services.

Beck, P., Walters, A. & Francisco, N. (1992). *The sacred: Ways of knowledge, sources of life*. Tsaile, AZ: Navajo Community College Press.

Donovan, K. (1998). *Feminist readings of Native American literature: Coming to voice*. Tucson, AZ: University of Arizona Press.

Harjo, J., & Bird, G. (1997). *Reinventing the enemy's language*. New York, NY: W. W. Norton & Company.

Hogan, L. (1995). *Dwellings: A spiritual history of the world*. New York, NY: W. W. Norton & Company.

Jung, C. G. (1954/1966). *The psychology of the transference*. New York, NY: Bollingen Foundation.

Marmon Silko, L. M. (1996). *Yellow woman and a beauty of the spirit*. New York, NY: Simon and Schuster.

Marmon Silko, L. M. (2010). *The turquoise ledge: A memoir*. New York, NY: Penguin Books.

Miller, B. G. (2001). *The problem of justice: Tradition and law in the Coast Salish Law*. Lincoln, NE: University of Nebraska Press.

Nelson, M. (2002). Introduction. *Revision: A Journal of Consciousness and Transformation*, *25*(2).

Nemeth, D., Hamilton, R., & Kuriansky, J. (2012). *Living in an environmentally traumatized world*. Santa Barbara, CA: ABC-CLIO/Praeger.

Nettle, D., & Romaine, S. (2000). *Vanishing voices: The extinction of the world's languages*. Oxford, UK: Oxford University Press.

Ortiz, S. (Ed.). (1998). *Speaking for the generations: Native writers on writing*. Tucson, AZ: University of Arizona Press.

Stern, D. N. (1985). *The interpersonal world of the infant: A view from psychoanalysis and developmental psychology*. New York, NY: Basic Books.

Stokes, J., & Benedict, D. (1993). *Thanksgiving address: Greetings to the natural world*. Corrales, NM: Six Nations Museum and the Tracking Project.

Todhunter, C. (2013). Genetically engineered "terminator seeds": Death and destruction of agriculture. Centre for Research on Globalization. Retrieved April 3, 2015, from http://www.globalresearch.ca/genetically-engineered-terminator-seeds-death-and-destruction-of-agriculture/5319797

United Nations. (2012a). *Report of the United Nations conference on sustainable development*. New York, NY: Author.

United Nations. (2012b). *Resolution adopted by the General Assembly: The future we want*. New York, NY: Author.

United Nations, Department of Economics and Social Affairs. (2009). *State of the world's indigenous peoples*. New York, NY: Author.

8

Transforming Our Intentions from Extermination to Integration: Lessons from Australia's Aboriginal People

Leslie William (Les) Bursill

AUSTRALIAN CHARACTERISTICS

Australia is a very old land mass and has had almost no contact with the rest of the world for many millions of years. Australia's land mass is almost three million square miles, about 5% of the earth's land area. It is the smallest continent. It is also the lowest, the flattest, and the second driest. Only Antarctica is drier (Australian Government, *The Australian Continent*, n.d.).

Our animals are of an older and more primitive lineage (marsupial and monotreme mammals rather than placental mammals) because Australia had already separated and became isolated before placental mammals evolved elsewhere (University of California Museum of Palaeontology, n.d.). There are comparatively few native placental mammals in Australia now because they had to migrate a great distance after their evolution elsewhere to reach the now-isolated Australia. The flora and fauna are distinctive because they evolved separately from the flora and fauna of other continents.

THE ABORIGINAL PEOPLE OF AUSTRALIA

The Aboriginal people of Australia make up the longest-surviving continuous culture in the world. Various excavations and discoveries of human remains and art work (rock paintings and engravings) indicate human residency in Australia for about 55,000 years. Aboriginal people may have modified the flora and fauna of Australia by their practice of burning off and clearing away underbrush and dead grasses. There is some evidence that ancient Australian forests were mostly acacia, whereas today Australian forests are mostly eucalypt. Whilst the evidence is not conclusive that Aboriginal people were solely responsible for the floral changes, the evidence is compelling. Similarly, the evidence for the extinction of megafauna in Australia is sometimes attributed to Aboriginal hunting practices. As megafauna became extinct throughout most of the world at about the same time, the evidence is less compelling that Aboriginal hunting practices were unique or the only cause of the extinction.

Pickup (1998) has argued that fires and a general drying out of Australia occurred about 100,000 years ago, and natural bushfires caused by lightning strikes may have had a significant role in both floral and faunal changes. Other workers have described practices whereby Aboriginal people increased the economic yield of their "country" by periodic burning. By burning off, grasses were renewed and plant life invigorated. The major proponent of this theory was Australian ecologist Rhys Jones, Jones theorized that the burning off of "country" was a large factor in the reduction of woodlands to savannah in Australia, and Jones has further argued that fire stick farming was a contributor to the extinction of megafauna in Australia (Bird, Bird, Codding, Parker, & Jones, 2008; Jones, 1969). Miller (2005) has also postulated the relationship between burning practices and megafauna extinction.

While Aboriginal people did not indicate specific areas of land as "owned" by any one group of people, there were nevertheless areas controlled by groups whose ceremonies and rituals made that place their "Country." These "Countries" were often distinguished and differentiated by features of land or vegetation like mountains, rivers, or large bodies of water that were natural boundaries. In some instances, areas were marked by the carving of local clan-symbols onto a tree, thus informing strangers of changes in dreaming stories and ceremonies.

Land—or as Aboriginal Australian prefer, "Country"—is the basis upon which is built the whole concepts of Law and Dreaming. Aboriginal people believe that they are a contiguous element of the "Country," as are all plants, animal life, and earthly features of hills, valleys, and even the earth itself. For Aboriginal people of Australia, land is at the core of their belief.

The Dreaming

The Dreaming is a continuous and continuing set of laws and religious instruction that underlies Aboriginal cultural behavior. In precolonial Australia, Aboriginal people had managed the resources of this land for upward of 55,000 years. In his 2012 book, *The Biggest Estate on Earth*, Professor Bill Gammage states that the Aboriginal people of Australia's attitude as expressed in their Dreaming Law is: (1) obey the Law, and (2) leave the world as you found it.

There is a very imprecise estimate of the number of Aboriginal communities in Australia at first European contact. It seems reasonable to assume that there were about 250 distinct cultural groups. Each of these groups is distinguished in the main part by a uniqueness in language. The 250 can then be extrapolated out to somewhere between 600 and 700 groups that had a significant dialectic difference. There are many cultural similarities in the Aboriginal communities within the Australian mainland and in Tasmania.

The majority of differences in language and culture are reflected in ecological zones within Australia. Australia has a very lush and rich source of vegetation and marine life in the northeastern coast, and a very rich and diverse range of food resources in the northwestern areas. In the middle of the continent, there are vast areas of a very dry dessert environment. In the South, Aboriginal people occupied a water-rich and cooler climate with many resources, and in some areas, they developed simple farming practices.

The distinguishing factor in all Aboriginal cultures throughout Australia is kinship relations. To be accepted into another area of country outside of your country, you must be able to demonstrate a kin relationship. These relationships may come from totemic affiliations, or through physical connections. Kinship directly influences all daily behavior and marital relationships and decisions. Kinship informs you of your place in the world and in the Dreaming.

In the Aboriginal Australia of pre 1788, the population density was 1 person per 3.96 square miles. Aboriginal people acted to minimize their impact on the land, and their low population density was a product of this management. Admittedly, modern Australians have a denser population with a longer and resource-richer life than the original people, but with costs to the original environment. The ability to sustain such a lifestyle and a growing population will require further utilization of resources and energy and change the environment even further. The modern system is not self-perpetuating like the old one, and people will need to continuously adapt to the ever-increasing changes. The changes depend on energy supplements, and energy use itself may cause additional problems that reduce the ability of the country to sustain such a wealthy and lush lifestyle without even more energy input.

Aboriginal women in many parts of Australia had access to bush medicines that gave them a limited ability to control their fecundity. Aboriginal women practiced methods of breast feeding and child management, so new births were separated by periods of three to four years. Child mortality and the usual fertility practices meant that population growth was generally well controlled. Marriage practices ensured that children, who survived for about eight years, were well cared for and did well. Aboriginal Australia was a conservative place. Population growth was very slow and dependent on resource availability. There is some evidence of an expansion after the Holocene (about 10,000 years ago), when Australia became wetter and hotter and the carrying capacity increased.

Aboriginal people did not plant gardens or crops or herd animals and relied for the most part on seasonally abundant natural resources for their food and material needs. They accepted the environment as it was, and did not modify it much.

Geoffrey Blainey (1996) made the observation that Aboriginal technology was relatively simple, basically because Aborigines knew and understood their environment so well that they had little need to develop a higher level of technology to maintain their numbers. Blainey indicates that the knowledge of the movements of animals, their habits, and knowledge of their likely location meant that Aboriginal hunters rarely went without. Alternately, Aboriginal women knew the locations of food plants and their seasonal availabilities and had a significant knowledge of fish and their habits. They understood the oceans, rivers, and lake-like environments and were adept fisherwomen and clever gatherers of both plant and marine foods (shellfish, crabs). Women were also very adept at collecting small mammals, birds (ducks, etc.), and reptiles. The women around the Sydney region used a jig and fishing line to catch fish. The jig was made of mother of pearl and the reflections off the shell hook induced the fish to strike the hook.

Care of Country is a primary responsibility of every adult Aboriginal Australian. Not only are individuals expected to care for country, and the area of their clan by virtue of "song Lines" and "Dreaming Tracks," they are also charged with the responsibility to maintain all plant and animal life through a system of totemic responsibilities. They did this with "songlines." Chatwin (1987) described songlines as "the labyrinth of invisible pathways which meander all over Australia and are known to Europeans as 'Dreaming-tracks' or 'Songlines'; to the Aboriginals as the 'Footprints of the Ancestors' or the 'Way of the Lore.'"

A man or woman, once they have reached maturity and have completed ceremonies to induct them into their roles, take up the totem of their clan country and assume particular responsibility for individual species of flora and fauna. Thus, the totem for an area becomes the whole community's responsibility, and the songs and rituals for that totem must be appropriately renewed and revived at each seasonal change and upon moving from place to place.

By the renewal of the Dreaming rituals, the country is revived and the animal species are renewed. Men and women would clear leaves and weeds from around water holes. Individuals charged with the responsibility would burn off old campsites to keep them clear and clean. In doing so, they create a suitable area where new grass would grow and thus make the area they vacated enticing for the grass-eating animals of the area (Gammage, 2012, pp. 130–131). The relationship to country can be summarized by the three "C's": (1) connection, (2) conserve, and (3) clean up.

An Aboriginal man or woman once endowed with a totemic responsibility would be required to deeply study that animal, plant, or other element of their country and to know and understand completely the habits and availability of that item. They would be expected to not only know, with a high degree of certainty, the likely whereabouts of the item, but also its general condition; and then be able to advise those seeking to use the item as a food or drink resource whether it was appropriate at the time, or even which of a number of possible items may be taken without damaging the resource.

A particular wallaby, fish, bird, or reptile may be mating or rearing young and would be unavailable for hunting or use as a food, tool, or weapon. A plant, fruit, or tuber may be out of season or have suffered a poor growing period and would be unavailable on advice of the totem holder. The food collection cycle was very much tied to the seasons, and only those foods in season would be sought after. Movement between campsites was tied to the seasonal availability of plant foods and animal or fishing cycles. An ill Aboriginal man or woman might be advised to seek certain animals or to avoid certain food, or be advised as to what to eat to get well again. Children would be forbidden by law to eat certain foods as they lacked the nourishment required for healthy development.

Anthropologists have estimated that Australia had an indigenous population of between 600,000 and 1 million just prior to the arrival of the first fleet of immigrants. The general consensus is that the Australian ecology could not have supported a population of hunter-fisher-gatherers larger than 750,000 (Thompson, 2001).

EUROPEAN COLONIZATION

In the 1700s, Britain lost their American colonies and needed a place to send their convicted criminals. With the discovery of the Australian land mass by James Cook in 1770, Australia (a.k.a. Botany Bay) was chosen as a convict settlement location.

Early Settlement History

In January 1788, a fleet of 11 ships arrived in Australia. Of the 11 ships, 6 carried 753 convicts and their families (Gillen, 1989); the other 5 carried Marines, their wives, children, and stores. The ships arrived generally together, but some arrived on January 18, others arrived on January 19 and 20. Their initial point of arrival was in a bay that Lieutenant James Cook and botanist Joseph Banks originally named "Stingray Bay" due to the large number and exceptional size of the stingrays they observed there. The bay was later renamed Botany Bay on account of the variety of unique plant specimens collected there. When Cook and Joseph Banks arrived in Stingray Bay, he found the country to be reminiscent of an English country gentleman's contrived park, with grasses and widely spaced trees. By digging in the sand, he found enough water for use by his ship.

On May 1, after the burial of seaman Forby Sutherland who had died of consumption near the watering place, Cook, Banks, and Daniel Solander, a naturalist who accompanied Banks (Gilbert, 1967), made an excursion into the country, which:

we found diversified with woods, Lawns and Marshes; the woods are free from under wood of every kind and the trees are at such a distance from one another that the whole Country or at least great part of it might be cultivated without being oblig'd [sic] to cut down a single tree; we found the soil every where except in the Marshes to be a light white sand and produceth [sic] a quant[it]y of good grass which grows in little tufts about as big as one can hold in one[']s hand and pretty close to one another, in this manner the surface of the ground is coated in the woods between the trees. (From Cook's Journal [The Royal Botanic Gardens & Domain Trust, n.d.)])

Banks's version of this trip is similar:

walkd [sic] till we completely tird [sic] ourselves, which was in the evening, seeing by the way only one Indian who ran from us as soon as he saw us. The soil wherever we saw it consisted of either swamps or light sandy soil on which grew very few species of trees, one which was large yielding a gum much like *sanguis draconis*, but every place coverd [sic] with vast quantities of grass. The gum tree was probably the Red Bloodwood *Corymbia gummifera*, of which they collected a specimen at Botany Bay. (The Royal Botanic Gardens & Domain Trust, n.d.).

Arthur Phillip, the commander of the fleet and proposed governor of the new colony, was dissatisfied with Botany Bay. After staying eight days in the bay, the fleet was moved to a new location that had been discovered 12 miles north. This new location was named "Port Jackson" and the town established there was named "Sydney" by Phillip. He chose this name in respect for Thomas Townshend, first Viscount Sydney. Viscount Sydney was a supporter and friend to Philip.

Contact and the Beginnings of Conflict

Contact with the local people was, at first, relatively friendly, but quickly degenerated once it became obvious that the visitors had come to stay. Arthur Phillip, governor of the colony, was under explicit orders to bring the local "Indians" into the colony and to give them equal rights as citizens.

Unfortunately for the governor, the locals would not participate and refused to support the colonists. This situation continued for some months, and out of frustration, the governor ordered that a number of natives be captured and brought into the colony to be interrogated. At the outset, two children, an old man, and a young man were brought in. Within a few months of their capture, an outbreak of a virulent "Pox like" disease started to spread amongst the local Aboriginal people; the children and old man died of this disease. The younger man lived on for a time.

Phillip then ordered more natives be captured and brought into the colony. Two males were captured and brought in. Those two were Colby and Bennelong. They were young and fit and survived the infection that was prevalent; they were chained and held for some time. Eventually they did escape, but after a series of contacts, Bennelong was persuaded to offer support and advice as to obtaining plant foods, animals, and water sources for the colony. Colby also proved to be a great help.

After some months, Bennelong began to accept the new foods and clothing offered by the colony and even took to consuming alcohol. Eventually he was sent to England to meet King George and spent some time there. Bennelong returned to the Colony and was granted a parcel of land suitable for farming. That place is now known as Bennelong Point. This is where the world-famous Sydney Opera House now stands.

The antipathy felt by the locals for their new neighbors was further exacerbated by a disease that first appeared in the colony in 1789. Deaths in the Sydney Basin and surrounding areas from this pox-like disease exceeded 50% of the Aboriginal population. The disease primarily impacted children and people over 40 years of age. Over the next two years, further outbreaks brought the death toll to 70% of the Sydney Basin Aboriginal population.

Some historical evidence and my own research suggest that the spread of disease was most like that of "contact diseases"; it was probably a form of cowpox, a relative of smallpox. Most of the colonists would have had prior contact with this less virulent form of infection. For the Aboriginal people, who had no immunity to European diseases, even a common cold or measles would have been devastating.

Why the disease spread so rapidly has been a point of conjecture by many historians. It seems certain that the shortage of women in the fleet would have encouraged convicts to trade iron nails and axes for access to Aboriginal women. This is a well-reported activity, and close contact would have facilitated the spread of disease and would account for the time lag between arrival and the first epidemic. Contact diseases are a very common cause of death when native peoples have been separated from outside human contact and have not been exposed to common illnesses and therefore developed resistance (Survival International, n.d.).

As seen in the preceding material, the Aboriginal peoples of Australia have a unique connection to their land. They have a belief system that takes into account the connectedness of all elements of their environment. They see the trees, rocks, earth, sky, water, and animals as having an interconnectedness that is unbreakable. They conformed to the land. On the other hand, the colonizers came from a society that actively managed their land. They were farmers and herders. They made the land conform to them. These philosophical differences cannot be reconciled easily, if at all. The fundamental philosophical differences are the cause of disagreements and probably exist even today in Australia and elsewhere where there are indigenous people. It may be this strong connection to "Country" that was an ongoing cause for conflict between the local people and the colonists. Many believe, as I do, that the cutting down of trees and the clearing of land by the colonists was the very first cause for conflict. Introduction of sheep and other domesticated animals as well as replacement of native forests with pine and other forms exotic in Australia led to competition and ultimate scarcity of native species as well as unfamiliarity to the Aborigines, who hitherto depended on their familiarity with the native flora and fauna.

Certainly there are records from the early contact period about the disgust felt by Aboriginal people upon seeing the use of nets for fishing and the resultant "bycatch" and waste. It is a fundamental belief of Aboriginal people that you take from the country only that which is necessary for survival and only that which is "given" by the country. The concept of surpluses was alien to Aboriginal thinking, and the taking away of surpluses, even the carrying away of water from a water hole, was against customary law as was communicated orally by Aboriginal people. Their law was passed from generation to generation through song and dance. These "Dreamings" were a crucial part of Aboriginal life.

Conflict between the indigenous people and the English continued as the colonizers took over more and more land for farming and settlements and changed the environment more and more. The indigenous people's strong connection with the land was being disrespected and ignored as the English used the land in their own way to obtain their needs. Many indigenous people were killed by the new settlers, and many more were forced off their ancestral land and became displaced (Skwirk Interactive Schooling, n.d.).

Land Use and Abuse—a Philosophical Difference

With the arrival of the First Fleet into Sydney Harbor in January 1788, it seems almost inevitable that conflict would arise over contrasting attitudes about land use and plant, animal, and fish stocks. There are reports of disputation over the removal of trees to make way for housing. There was conflict over the wanton shooting of animals and the netting of large quantities of fish.

What the settlers failed to appreciate was that, taken with care and with a deep and fundamental knowledge of the environment, life, even a rich life, could be obtained from Australia. But Aborigine numbers were near carrying capacity, and additional numbers could not be supported without the introduction of farming and grazing or other new techniques. Cultural differences would inevitably lead to conflicts. Environmental destruction, overhunting, and overfishing would quickly deplete the resources at hand, and indeed, the first colony almost starved. Even then, when food was rationed and children were flogged for stealing food just to survive, the local Aboriginal people looked on in horror. When asked what they would do, the locals responded by saying they would feed the offending child, not punish it.

Many of the first colonists saw the Aboriginal people as ignorant savages. The European attitude about farming prevailed and, in many cases, eventually failed as the land and seasons reacted completely differently to what was the norm for Europe (Britain mainly). The trees were of little value for furnishings, and the native fruits, tubers, roots, and berries bore little similarity to their English counterparts. It was many years, even decades, before the knowledge of the Aboriginal people was finally seen for its value. Even today, we are still discovering methods that enhance production and treat the land with some grudging respect.

The most important major difference in flora found by the colonists was the type of grass present in Australia. The native grasses of Australia grow in clumps, and prior to English occupation and the introduction of European grasses, native grasses were very sparse. With the introduction of grazing sheep and cattle, the competition for food by grazers often led to the extermination of native grazing animals. Once the native grass species had been eradicated, with the native fauna dependent on them, the local Aboriginal peoples had only the European livestock for sustenance. The spearing of sheep and cattle by the hungry Aboriginal people, who had lost an important food source, led to reprisals from the colonists and the further decimation of the Aboriginal population.

In our southernmost state, Tasmania, the problem of dealing with "the Blacks" by the British was a simple one. Settlers and soldiers organized hunts and hunted Aboriginal people for sport. By 1860, only two full-blood Aboriginals were left in Tasmania. Blainey (1996) wrote that by 1830 in Tasmania, "[d]isease had killed most of them but warfare and private violence had also been devastating." Other historians regard the Black War as one of the earliest recorded modern genocides. Benjamin Madley (2008) wrote: "Despite over 170 years of debate over who or what was responsible for this near-extinction, no consensus exists on its origins, process, or whether or not it was genocide." However, using the "U.N. definition, sufficient evidence exists to designate the Tasmanian catastrophe as genocide."

The deliberate destruction of Aboriginal peoples was not limited to Tasmania. There were many dozens of murders and massacres of Aboriginal people. There are a minimum of 51 recorded massacres from 1789 through 1928. The numbers killed ranged from half a dozen to as many as 60 people, with records showing that women and children were very often the victims. There were a number of massacres of Aboriginal people beginning in 1790 and increasing throughout the next century. One of the better-documented massacres was the Myall Creek Massacre, which occurred on June 10, 1838, at the Myall Creek near Bingara in New South Wales, Australia:

The massacre of approximately 30 Wirrayaraay people at Myall Creek, the subsequent court cases and the hanging of the seven settlers for their role in the massacre was a pivotal moment in the development of the relationship between settlers and Aboriginal people. It was the first and last attempt by the colonial administration to use the law to control frontier conflict between settlers and Aboriginal people.

The Myall Creek massacre is outstanding in the course of Australia's cultural history as it is the last time the Colonial Administration intervened to ensure the laws of the colony were applied equally to Aboriginal people and settlers involved in frontier killings. (Australian Government, Department of Environment, n.d.)

Another, the Coniston Massacre, occurred in Western Australia on August 7, 1928. The interesting factor in this massacre was that it was apparently perpetrated by a police officer who kept diary notes of his activities, though there is a substantial dispute over the veracity of those notes.

On 7 August 1928 a white dingo trapper, Fred Brooks, was found murdered on Coniston station in central Australia. Brooks had been killed with traditional weapons and the body hastily buried. Two Aboriginal men—Padygar and Arkikra— were arrested for the murder of Brooks. They stood trial in Darwin in the Northern Territory and were acquitted. ...

Soon after the discovery of Brooks's body, a series of reprisals were undertaken by groups of men on horseback led by Mounted Constable George Murray. The parties were made up of civilians and police, and included Aboriginal as well as non-Aboriginal men. Jack Saxby was one of the civilians who joined the reprisal party led by Murray. (National Museum of Australia, n.d.)

By the mid-nineteenth century, the Aboriginal population of Australia was plummeting downward. By 1853, some state governments were making attempts to mitigate the destruction of the Aboriginal population. But these attempts are seen by many as simply a way to integrate half-caste children into white society as a type of domestic servant class. Children, who were obviously lighter skinned, were taken from their parents and fostered out to middle-class families as live-in domestics.

Aboriginal Welfare Act (The Aboriginal Board)

By the end of the nineteenth century, the Aboriginal population had decreased from about 750,000 to about 90,000. Most of the few remaining were in the more remote parts of Australia in larger groups in the Northern Territory, Western Australia, and South Australia. The survival of larger groups of full-blood people is directly related to their distance from and reduced contact with European population groups. In 1910, the Australian federal government passed an act of Parliament, "The Aboriginal Welfare Act," and any obviously Aboriginal people were rounded up and placed in either mission stations, which were church-run, or into "settlements" run and controlled by white overseers.

Control of Aboriginal people by government-appointed panels and committees led to many extreme examples of racial discrimination. Any half-caste children were taken away as they reached a suitable age—12 to 14, say—and put into service. Young women went into service, and most young boys were sent off to become apprentices and were scattered across the country. This scattering was ostensibly to break up family connections and was clearly aimed at reducing cultural effects (Read, 1981). Speaking in a native tongue was a punishable offense. Any continued contact with Aboriginal customs or ideas were seen to be detrimental to the children, and every effort was made to destroy any cultural connections whatsoever.

When the constitution of Australia came into force on January 1, 1901, the colonies collectively became states of the Commonwealth of Australia. The Australian constitution has two elements that exemplify the attitude of the Australian people toward Aboriginal people: (1) the White Australia Policy, and 2) land rights. These exclusionary elements discussed below were maintained throughout Australia's history until 1967, when a referendum was held and changes to the constitution were put in place.

One of the proud claims was that 90% of the population voted to change our constitution. I find it interesting that 10% of the voters declined the opportunity. I found that when I was training officers in both Corrective Services and NSW Police, there were about 10–15% who made it very clear that they found Aboriginal people "a problem," "trouble makers," and "drunkards."

Aboriginal people could gain a release from being held in missions or settlements if they were able to convince the local police and magistrates that they were of good character and were willing to subscribe to some stringent rules and conditions. If they were able to meet these conditions, they were then issued a license, often referred to as a "Dog Tag" that described them as being "non-Aboriginal" for the purposes of the Aboriginal Welfare Act. They, in effect, became honorary whites. After the referendum of 1967, Aboriginal people were generally allowed to leave their places of residence and seek work outside. It is shocking that until this time, Aboriginal culture and lifestyle was held, and continues to this day to be held, as part of the National Parks and Wildlife Service. Many Aboriginal people, to this day, say that they were considered to be part of the natural flora and fauna of Australia. In January 2014, all Aboriginal cultural items and campsites remain the exclusive property of the National Parks and Wildlife Service, even to the point where Aboriginal people are often prohibited from visiting sacred sites and campsites of ceremonial grounds on fear of financial penalty, while others are allowed to do so.

The White Australia Policy

The White Australia Policy (WAP) came into fruition with confederation in 1901 and comprises various historical policies that intentionally encouraged immigration to Australia from certain European countries, and especially from Britain. It and other discriminatory policies were progressively dismantled between 1949 and 1973.

The White Australia Policy came into being through the concerns of gold miners and laborers in the cane fields. Chinese gold miners were prepared to apply themselves enthusiastically to their work, and the miners saw that they could be a threat. In the cane fields of Queensland, South Seas Islanders (known as "Kanakas") were imported as virtual slave labor and posed, what the white population saw as, a threat to their ability to get work. The extension of this policy came to include any dark-skinned person or person of Asian descent or appearance.

Some influential Queenslanders felt that the colony would be excluded from the forthcoming federation if the Kanaka trade did not cease. Leading NSW and Victorian politicians warned there would be no place for "Asiatics" or "coloureds" in the Australia of the future (Australian Government Department of Immigration and Border Protection, n.d.). Possibly the most notorious element of the policy was that if, upon arrival in an Australian port, a prospective immigrant was seen to be "non-white," then a dictation test to ascertain literacy was immediately applied (often in a language not familiar to the applicant).

World War II put the WAP under some strain as many refugees who had come to Australia during the war were forcibly returned to their home. However, more than 800 had married Australians and wished to stay. The Australian immigration minister, Harold Holt, relented and allowed them to stay and also allowed a number of Japanese war brides to enter the country.

In 1973, the Whitlam Labor government took three further steps in the gradual process to remove race as a factor in Australia's immigration policies: (1) to legislate that all migrants, of whatever origin, be eligible to obtain citizenship after three years of permanent residence; (2) to issue policy instructions to overseas jurisdictions to totally disregard race as a factor in the selection of migrants; and (3) to ratify all international agreements relating to immigration and race.

Land Rights

Since colonization in 1788, there has been a strong sense of loss and resentment by Aboriginal peoples in Australia. Their land and mode of living were usurped by a powerful and technologically superior group of people. There was a struggle and strong resistance to European occupation, but the resources and technology of those interlopers overcame a small population of lightly armed people. Pockets of resistance continued until the early 1900s, but in the end, to no avail.

In the early 1960s, a Land Rights movement commenced and increased in strength with the establishment of a Tent Embassy on the lawns of Parliament House in Canberra in 1972.

In a case brought before Mr. Justice Blackburn on 27 April 27, 1971, the Yirr-kala people argued that they had been unlawfully dispossessed from their traditional lands. Justice Blackburn ruled that under Australian law, there was no provable connection between those peoples and the land they claimed as theirs (*Milirrpum v Nabalco Pty Ltd.*, 1971). Under Australian law, Aboriginal land was considered *Terra Nullius* (no one owns it). In his initial survey of the East Coast of Australia, James Cook stated that he saw no buildings, boundary fences, crops, or controlled herds of animals. The Privy Council of England therefore ruled that Australia had no land that was clearly owned by any person or group. The land was free for the taking. In 1975, the Labor Prime Minister, Gough Whitlam, made a symbolic handover of land to the Gurinji people.

In 1992, a Torres-Strait Islander, Ediie Mabo, contested the law of *Terra Nullius*. *Mabo v. Queensland* (No. 2) ("Mabo case") [1992] HCA 23, (1992) (commonly known as *Mabo*) was a landmark High Court of Australia decision that recognized native title in Australia for the first time. The High Court rejected the doctrine of terra nullius, in favor of the common law doctrine of aboriginal title, and overruled *Milirrpum v. Nabalco Pty Ltd.* (1971)—contrary decision of the Supreme Court of the Northern Territory. The basis for Eddie Mabo's success was that he was able to demonstrate that not only was Aboriginal land (in the Murray Islands) marked out, but also had boundaries, buildings, and means by which food crops were grown and harvested. Fish were also farmed in such a way as to provide a regular food source (ABC, n.d.). The land rights issue continues with the federal governments of Australia regularly changing or refuting various aspects of Aboriginal land claims. The fight goes on to this very day.

FROM 1900 TO THE PRESENT DAY

Missions and Settlements Today

Many of the missions and settlements established under the Aboriginal Welfare Act still exist. They are no longer managed by government or church agencies but are most often overseen by Aboriginal Land Councils. Aboriginal Land Councils (Local Aboriginal Land Councils, or LALC) are bodies established by the federal government and were initially seed-funded. These LALCs are controlled by Aboriginal people, who are encouraged to develop models that allow fiscal growth and responsibility. Most Land Councils do receive small government grants and many receive rental from the houses once owned by the missions and now controlled by the Land Council (Australian Government, *Land Councils*, n.d.).

Unfortunately, many of these LALCs are highly politicized, and many are dysfunctional. Some function well, but most are beset by particular political agenda and petty family jealousies. There are central Land Council bodies that have overall control; these bodies appear better managed and more functional.

It is unfortunate that a large number of Aboriginal people still view all government contact or intervention as unwelcome, and there is a strong element of distrust and disillusionment with state education. Many Aboriginal children are not encouraged by their parents to attend school. Consequently, there is a high degree of unemployment among Aboriginal people. When questioned about their attitudes to "white schooling," some Aboriginal people believe that their children will be drawn away from their culture and lose contact with their past history. The mission and settlement schools quite often severely punished children who spoke their indigenous languages or mentioned or practiced Aboriginal cultural beliefs or ceremonies. It would be impossible for Aboriginal people to resume traditional lifestyles today. Hunter-fisher-gatherer lifestyles require a very low population level and unpolluted resource-rich environments. None of these factors are present today. White Australia completely consumed Aboriginal culture and made great efforts to completely remove Aboriginal belief systems and land management from the minds of the populace. It is only recently that respects for the land and for Aboriginal belief systems have become acceptable and laudable.

The federal government sees the Aboriginal education problem as an underlying cause of much present-day Aboriginal discontent (see Education Dreams [n.d.] for their latest attempts to encourage Aboriginal parents to send their children to school.) In some states of Australia, welfare payments and other government benefit payments are linked to child attendance at school. This problem of "fear of Government contact" also impacts Aboriginal attendance at medical facilities, and many Aboriginal people do not seek medical advice and ignore health warnings issued by health departments. Australian Aboriginal people have a shortened life expectancy, especially males who commonly die 10 years earlier than their white counterparts. Some believe that the introduction of European foods with high caloric content, high sugars and carbohydrates, and meats with high fat content have been a major contributing role (National Health Priority Action Council [NHPAC], 2006).

While about 30% of Aboriginal people are alcohol abstainers, another 32% abuse alcohol and illicit drugs. Aboriginal people have also not acted on warnings about the dangers of smoking. Smoking rates in Aboriginal communities are as much as 30% higher than in commensurate white communities. Many believe that high levels of disenfranchisement and depression are causal factors in overuse of drugs and alcohol. In traditional culture, very little drug use was evident. Most people spent the time not required for food procurement in dancing and traditional forms of song and dance development. Many took great pride in reproducing art work that depicted traditional dreaming stories. There were some instances of drug use in the chewing of nicotine-based plants. This activity was centered on elders and senior medicine men and "Doctors" (Crikey, n.d.).

Some families, who were able to avoid the net of Government collection and were not forced onto missions or settlements, have melded into the mainstream and now many do well. Many of these families have taken up government-funded support for university training and career development, and many of these Aboriginal families now have graduate and postgraduate children.

My Family History

I have been very fortunate in many ways; one of those ways was that I knew my grandparents on both sides of my family, and I also knew my great grand-mothers on both sides of my family. My father's family descended from a well-connected series of shopkeepers and tradespeople, who, for the most part, came to Australia in the early 1800s. My mother's family was less notable. My great-great-great grandfather was William Rollan, a violent drunken thief who had been transported to Australia on the sailing ship *Strathfieldsaye* in 1836. He was sentenced to 15 years and sent to a remote part of New South Wales called Mar-shall Mount, near Kangaroo Valley.

Kangaroo Valley today is a quiet, prosperous village at the foot of the NSW Southern Highlands. It is a very expensive place to purchase a house and to live; it is a great tourist attraction. My ancestor, William Rollan, was sent to work on a farm in the valley. The farm was owned by Henry Osborne; Henry came to Australia as a free settler in 1829 and established his farm at Marshall Mount.

My ancestors' job was as *bushman*, and ostensibly he was to care for the cattle and sheep of the Osbornes and live in a hut in the bush. I suppose he was some type of "shepherd," but to be successful in his position, William Rollan associ-ated with the local Aboriginal people. These Aboriginal people were led by a very well-known and highly respected "Clever Man" (read witchdoctor) called Dr. Ellis. Dr. Ellis had a daughter, Susan, who became the partner of William and they had some children together. My family descended from that union.

All of this information was withheld from me and the family by my great grandmother, Philadelphia Field/Bell (nee Rollan), for a number of reasons: (1) Aboriginal ancestry was considered shameful until very late in the twentieth century; (2) having a convict ancestor was also very shameful until quite recently, when it became fashionable to claim such a heritage; and (3) the ille-gitimacy of my grandmother.

My grandmother, Olive Victoria Smith (Rollan/Cuskelly) was born of a union between brother and sister, another reason for shame and the obfuscation of family history. Our history only fully came to light after Philadelphia's demise in the late 1970s. The family generally knew of our Aboriginal background, but it was not to be talked about. Australia still had laws in place that allowed Aboriginal children to be removed and brought up in a white environment.

The law had been used to take Olive Victoria Rollan (my grandmother) away as a child and have her placed in a convent on the edge of Sydney in a suburb called Arncliffe. My grandmother spent a number of years in that convent, where she was given the task of boiling hospital sheets and washing bedclothes and other linen for the local hospitals, but she was taught to read and write, and she developed a fairly healthy work ethic.

My father's family was well-to-do, middle-class tradespeople at this time, and my father was introduced to my mother through a wartime associate, William Smith, who also became my grandfather. Interestingly, my father's sister Valda Bursill also met and married an Aboriginal man, George Holten. George was a very dark-skinned man, whereas my mother Lorna Bursill was olive-complexioned. Uncle George, when questioned about his dark complexion, always told me he was very susceptible to suntan.

My first clear recollections of my childhood are when I was 2 years old and I remember the very noisy and crowded conditions in our home. My father, having been away in the war, was very poor; my mother and he lived with me in the home of my grandparents, William and Olive. They also shared their home with three other daughters and a son. Later, the husbands of those daughters also lived there. It was only a small weatherboard cottage, with an outside veranda. The house was very crowded. After the war, my father worked very diligently and taught himself the trade of telephone technician, and over a period of 45 years, he worked his way up the ladder to become the area manager for what was then called the Post Master Generals Department (PMG).

In my generation, our family prospered, and all the children completed high school. My brother went on to become a very wealthy businessman, and I was the first person in my family to enter and complete university and postgraduate studies. Until my late 30s, I worked in the newspaper industry, but left and entered public service in 1989. My first position was as probation and parole officer. Later, I became a court officer specializing in dealing with people affected by drugs and alcohol.

From 1993 until 2004, I worked as the Aboriginal drug and alcohol programs coordinator for Correctional Services in New South Wales (NSW), Australia. In 1993, when I began to operate as the state coordinator, there were no Aboriginal counselors in NSW prisons. In 1993, New South Wales had a population of about 5 million people, 180,000 of whom were Aboriginal (about 3.3%). The NSW prison population was about 9,000 (daily count); of those inmates, 2,000 (22%) were Aboriginal. This is a 7 times overrepresentation. In Western Australia, the Aboriginal incarceration rate is about 23% of the daily count. These figures appear startling, but they are a little misrepresentative. Forty percent of all female inmates are Aboriginal in NSW and as many as 70% of juvenile inmates are either aboriginal or of Islander descent.

When I started in my position of state coordinator in 1993, I was told that "I really had nothing to do; Aboriginal people were no different than the general population. I should just settle down and enjoy my job." Over the following two years, I managed to employ and train seven Aboriginal counselors and spread them throughout the state. Many officers of the prison service were reluctant to allow Aboriginal designated counselors to deal with white inmates. So once the counsellors had reached a high enough level of training and expertise, I encouraged them to apply for generalist counselor positions. In that way I was able to expand the number of Aboriginal staff to 14. They proved to be very effective and successful.

When I worked in prisons and with police services, and later when I worked for a number of universities—the University of New South Wales, the University of Sydney, Charles Sturt University—I was confronted with a surprising level of overt racism, especially among prison officers. It is hard to judge the level of racism in the police because they are trained not to make racist comments. They quite often do not reveal their innermost thoughts for fear of retribution.

A very illuminating time of my life was when I was employed part time at two universities. At one of these universities, I was employed as an "Aboriginal Lecturer," and at the other university, I was just a "lecturer." In both positions, my lecturing specialty was "Mental Health/Drugs and alcohol." It was very clear to me that as an Aboriginal Lecturer, I was micromanaged and had to justify each expenditure for even the most mundane office items and had to obtain approval for lecture content and teaching materials output. As a non-Aboriginal lecturer, I was expected to manage these day-to-day items myself and would have had a vastly more accessible source for petty-cash items and production of lecture content and teaching resources output. In the Aboriginal position, the controls on me became so onerous that I resigned from that department. At the other university, I continued to work for 11 more years, and retired at 65.

I witnessed another experience of micromanagement, but in this instance as an observer. Toward the end of the 1990s, a government department, where I was a senior officer, decided to recruit some Aboriginal officers. Twenty-five were chosen: 70% had university degrees, and the rest had other qualifications. These Aboriginal officers had the same qualifications as "normal" government officers, but they were employed at a lower salary and had an extended trial period as "Cadet Officers." Obviously, such discriminatory practices quickly impacted these "Cadets," and within 12 months, half had moved on to other jobs, and by 2 years, the remaining few left with the exception of one who stayed on.

Harassment

In writing this section, I have made contact with a number of Aboriginal people who hold senior positions in both industry and in the government sector. Invariably, they all tell stories of harassment, discrimination, and distrust. Some reported constant challenges or questioning by their peers whenever they were brought before the public, either through legal action or other forms of attention. When the exposure is for legal reasons, it is always pointed out that the accused's behavior is an example of the typical behaviors of Aboriginal people. The author has experienced many such examples. When notice is about some success or other positive activity, it is reported as an example of how Aboriginal people are given advantages and succeed only through the largesse of government support or handouts. Even though Aborigine general health and life spans are markedly lower that the white population, it is seen as somehow unreasonable that Aboriginal health services should receive more government support than they do (Australian Government Department of Social Services, n.d.).

HOPES FOR THE FUTURE

To this point the history of Aboriginal life in Australia and the general underlying racism of Australia has been the main theme. There are however some real attempts to raise public awareness of Aboriginal Culture, Health and Education. Some of these attempts are misguided, perhaps even illegal. Others have been a little more honest and sincere, though these also can be misguided.

I will start this section by looking at a range of attempts of both state and federal governments to deal with fundamental problems facing Aboriginal communities.

The NSW Government

In New South Wales, the state government has a Department of Child Welfare (NSW Government, n.d.). This department has received much criticism over its handling of child welfare. The department's reputation is so poor that any children, raised by the department, are automatically presumed to be at risk and are monitored closely by the department until they are of legal age (18).

The department is notoriously underfunded and under-resourced. The department has often allowed charitable institutions to foster their charges, and there are myriad accounts of child abuse, physical, mental, and sexual, now coming to light. The department funds a number of adults to foster children. This has become a sole occupation for some foster parents who receive substantial amounts for each child, and many foster parents take on multiple children. It would be unfair to say that these foster arrangements are often poorly managed, but there are significant numbers of these "professional carers" who have proven to be opportunistic in their approaches to their parenting duties. There is now a policy to foster Aboriginal children in the department's care, to Aboriginal families; this practice has proven successful. Over the last 10 years, the department has endeavored to employ Aboriginal workers to care for Aboriginal children and has taken some responsibility in ensuring that these Aboriginal workers are supported in obtaining tertiary qualifications. I have had many of these Aboriginal child welfare officers in my university classes.

The NSW courts have also been proactive in seeking to deal with Aboriginal offenders in a unique way. After an Aboriginal offender is found to be guilty as charged, and if the offense was nonviolent with no weapons of any type used, or when the offense carries a maximum of 2-year incarceration or less, the Aboriginal offender is brought before a group of elders from the community who then talk to the offender and offer a sentence option to the magistrate. These Elders Courts are called "Circle Sentencing Courts" (Tumeth, 2011) as the offender is placed within a circle of elders: a magistrate, the police prosecutor, and his defense counsel. As long as all are satisfied with the judgment, then the sentence is agreed upon. The Circle Sentencing Courts are only established in communities where there is a large Aboriginal population and the elders are well known and respected in the community. While the program has been very effective in reducing reoffending, it has proven to be less effective in some areas where community dysfunction is high (Potas, Smart, Brignell, Thomas, & Lawrie, 2003).

The NSW government now has a range of Aboriginal services and agencies. These agencies include specialist Aboriginal community liaison officers for probation and parole services, the NSW Police, and the NSW court system. There are educational services specifically staffed and aimed at Aboriginal content in all curriculums in state schools. Most high schools in New South Wales have elements of Aboriginal culture in many components of the subjects taught. Child care centers now generally make an effort to embrace Aboriginal culture in early childhood teaching. There are specialist Aboriginal health counselors at most state hospitals and programs established to reduce the gap between Aboriginal health and longevity (Australian Human Rights Commission, n.d.) NSW Police and NSW Corrective Services both train their new recruits in Aboriginal culture, and attempts are made to ensure that racial stereotyping is eliminated at the training stages for these people.

One can only hope that these measures are maintained and promoted to the general public, and that the apathy and negativity of the wider population toward Aboriginal people can be overcome. The way(s) forward that appear most likely to be successful are:

- *Sports*: Australia loves its sporting heroes, and many Aboriginal people are successful sports personalities. We have Aboriginal tennis players, golfers, cricketers, and football players. These people are wonderful representatives of Australia.
- *Child care*: In Australia, most couples must work. Home prices and the costs of living in cities are very high. The cost of an average suburban home in Sydney ranges from A$400,000 to A$700,000. Most people in Australia live in a house in the suburbs on a quarter acre of land. Some (a growing number) live on smaller land

blocks and there is a slow movement to townhouses and units (apartments); these properties still cost between A$300,000 and A$500,000. Consequently, one income from a couple is usually consumed in repaying the mortgage. This may continue for as much as 20 years. Child care is therefore an essential part of early married life here. Instilling in children a sense of wonder and acceptance of Aboriginal culture and stories is proving to be effective in changing the perspective of many parents, and the children grow up with a greater level of understanding of Aboriginal culture and practices.

- *Training of Aboriginal peoples and the inclusion of these people into mainstream government positions*: The NSW government has specialist recruiting procedures that limit applicants for some cultural positions to Aboriginal applicants only.

The Australian Federal Government

The Australian federal government is under some political pressure to resolve a number of issues relating to Aboriginal health, alcohol consumption, child protection, and financial management of government payments. As a response to that political pressure, the Northern Territory government established the Northern Territory Emergency Response (NTER). That response is now referred to as the "Intervention" (Amnesty International, 2010). Many Australians believe that the intervention is discriminatory as it applies only to Aboriginal people. Others remark that there does not appear to be any evaluative framework for the NTER program. Others have commented that changes to the racial discrimination laws in Australia demonstrate that the "Intervention" is racially discriminatory. Amnesty International's secretary general, Irene Khan, found that the intervention clearly infringes on human rights and is in direct violation of racial discrimination laws in Australia. Yet the federal government rewrote the laws to allow this program to be undertaken. Was there a need for such laws? (Altman, 2012).

Over the last five years (2008 to 2012), I have traveled around Australia in my motor home. In early 2005, I noted the poor conditions and aggressive nature of many of the Aboriginal people I met in remote locations. Alcohol appeared to play a large part in the behaviors I saw. At this time, the media were reporting that long-distance truckers were going into Aboriginal settlements and sexually abusing young Aboriginal children, both male and female. The money these children received was being used to buy alcohol and drugs. The children I saw were not physically well, poorly clothed, ill nourished, and not attending school. The problems were widespread. The issue really came down to the fact that there were no resources in these towns except alcohol and drugs, there was little of no policing and family, and community structures were absent.

On my last trip through the center of Australia, to Darwin and then across the Gulf of Carpentaria and down through central Queensland, I saw remarkable differences in a whole range of issues. Many resources were still not in most towns—no paving, no government offices, no recreational areas, and very few food stores; but the people were better fed and dressed, and the children looked cared for. I believe that the changes are a reflection of the "intervention" by the federal government.

The population of Australia seems to be, at best, divided over the trampling of human and racial rights and laws or, at worst, too lethargic to respond. There are voices crying out for change, but those voices do not offer alternatives that would deal with the underlying problems. I don't think that this problem is unique to Australia, as I saw the same issues of poverty, ill-health, and lack of community infrastructure in the southern states of the United States. In early 2000, I spent time in the pueblos of New Mexico and saw poverty and disease there. But, across Australia, there are a number of groups who are actively promoting Aboriginal culture and espousing Aboriginal causes. One that I am very familiar with is ANTaR (Australian Native Title and Reconciliation). This group is very active and is completely voluntary (see http://antar.org.au/). "ANTaR listens to and supports the aspirations of First Peoples and works to educate the wider community, shape public opinion, speak up against injustice and influence public policy to advance our vision" (NSW Government: Environment and Heritage, n.d.).

Finally, there is presently a move to add words to Australia's constitution that acknowledges and supports the concept that Aboriginal Australians were the first people of this land and that they were unjustly and illegally evicted from their land by the act of European colonization in 1788. The danger we face as those first peoples is that the wording must at once recognize us as the original people, but, at the same instant, must not make us a separate people lest we once again have special laws written for us.

HEAVEN ON EARTH?

Today, Australian people look around and see the country as a heaven on earth. We are a wealthy and resource-rich country, with a very high living standard for the majority compared to the rest of the world's inhabitants. Our environment appears generally clean and unpolluted. Our air outside the major cities is clean and seemingly without airborne pollutants. The large majority of our island continent is sparsely populated, with the major populations spread around the relatively moist coastline.

However, we are witnessing the decline in our manufacturing sector, and a rise in precarious low-paying jobs. At the same time, we are witnessing an unprecedented plunder of natural resources like that practiced by wood-chip-hungry foresters. Our reliance on fossil fuels makes us one of the highest per capita producers of atmospheric carbon. Our streets and highways struggle with seemingly daylong traffic congestion. We average slightly higher car ownership than two cars per family. Our population is about 23.5 million, and our vehicle registrations were about 17.2 million in 2013.

Some negative impacts on our environment go unnoticed by the general population because our population is low and our country is large. Europeans have occupied this island continent for a mere 124 years. In that time, these newcomers have made significant changes to the environment. Millions of acres of trees have been felled for pastureland and crops. Millions more acres have been logged and turned from pristine forests into fast-growing, pine-tree plantations that are used for furniture. Even today, with climate change becoming more noticed, we continue to clear land for farming.

We are the driest inhabited continent on earth, yet we destroy the very habitat that supports rainfall production and clean air, our forests. In Queensland, we continue to deforest land to make way for large-scale farming that will require additional water and other resources to support production. The Murray-Darling Basin Authority apparently struggles to find even a paltry 6.2-million-acre foot of water in its increasingly difficult attempt to restore the nation's most vital and productive river system. Douglas (2011) reveals Australia to be the world's largest net exporter of virtual water in crop, livestock, and industrial products; "exported virtual water" is that consumed to create items for export.

In a land beset by droughts and fires, we have vast areas of our northern states devoted to the production of cotton and rice. We maintain vast numbers of sheep, 99.3 million of them. This is second only to mainland China in numbers and 33% more sheep than India. Our beef cattle herd totals about 25 million; 60% is exported live to Asian markets.

Australia's mining income represents 55.5% of a GDP of US$1.51 trillion. Australia survives by brutally exploiting its reserves of land, water, and mineral resources. It is clear from a review of past rainfall patterns and temperature changes that Australia is experiencing changes that are not part of any natural cycle of weather or solar activity. As climate change takes hold, our reserves of water decrease. Our largest city, Sydney, came very close to running out of water just four years ago (2010) (Government of Western Australia, Department of Water, n.d.); the city of some 4.3 million people had severe water restrictions put in place, and our largest reservoirs fell to 40% capacity. Perth, our most remote city, has a population of 1.7 million people and is situated at the edge of our driest areas, 2,045 miles from the East Coast of Australia. Its rainfall averages 29 inches annually. Our driest cities in the west of Australia use underground aquifers as their main water supply. These million-year-old aquifers are at critical depletion levels. Many of the larger cities have installed seawater extraction facilities or are in the process of developing seawater extraction plants to supplement natural supplies. Population density is high in our desert areas. But this was not always the case, as witnessed by my people's stewardship of the land before colonial settlement (Government of Western Australia, Department of Water, n.d.).

Clearly Australia must reevaluate its approach to population management. The government must note that continued growth of the population and increasing pressure on resources may soon make habitation of this island more and more difficult to sustain. Australia is also highly dependent on oil as fuel, and coal as an important export earner. Yet our government is moving away from renewable energy and more and more sells off our infrastructure to private owners who have no interest in assisting in reducing dependence on coal, oil, and other fossil fuels. Perhaps it is time for the Australian public to take note of the more sustainable attitudes of those first people of Australia.

REFERENCES

ABC (Australian Broadcasting Corporation). (n.d.). *Mabo: A study of love, passion, and justice.* Retrieved August 29, 2014, from http://www.abc.net.au/tv/mabo/

Altman, J. (2012). *NT intervention: What happened to outcomes?* Retrieved August 30, 2014, from http://www.crikey.com.au/topic/nt-intervention/

Amnesty International. (2010). *Looking back at the Northern Territory Intervention.* Retrieved August 30, 2014, from http://www.amnesty.org.au/indigenous-rights/comments/26430/

Australian Government. (n.d.). *The Australian Continent.* Retrieved August 29, 2014, from http://australia.gov.au/about-australia/our-country/the-australian-continent

Australian Government. (n.d.) *Australian indigenous cultural heritage.* Retrieved August 29, 2014, from http://australia.gov.au/about-australia/australian-story/austn-indigenous-cultural-heritage

Australian Government. (n.d.). *Land Councils.* Retrieved August 29, 2014, from http://australia.gov.au/people/indigenous-peoples/land-councils

Australian Government, Department of the Environment. (n.d.). *Natural Heritage Places —Myall Creek Massacre and Memorial Site.* Retrieved November 18, 2014, from http://www.environment.gov.au/heritage/places/national/myall-creek

Australian Government, Department of Social Services. (n.d.). *FaHCSIA's Aboriginal and Torres Strait Islander Workforce Strategy 2010–2012.* Retrieved September 2, 2014, from http://www.dss.gov.au/about-the-department/policies-legislation/departments-corporate-policies/fahcsias-aboriginal-and-torres-strait-islander-workforce-strategy-2010-2012

Australian Human Rights Commission. (n.d.). *Close the Gap: Indigenous Health Campaign.* Retrieved August 30, 2014, from http://www.humanrights.gov.au/close-gap-indigenous-health-campaign.

Bird, R. B., Bird, D. W., Codding, B. F., Parker, C. H., & Jones, J. H. (2008). The "fire stick farming" hypothesis: Australian Aboriginal foraging strategies, biodiversity and anthropogenic fire mosaics. *Proceedings of the National Academy of Sciences, 105,* 14796–14801.

Blainey, Geoffrey. (1996). *Triumph of the nomads: a history of ancient Australia* (2nd ed.). New York, NY: Overlook Press.

Chatwin, B. (1987). *The songlines*. Toronto, ON: Penguin Books Canada.

Crikey. (n.d.). *Not closing the gap: Indigenous lifespans remain too short*. Retrieved August 29, 2014, from http://www.crikey.com.au/2013/02/08/not-closing-the-gap-indigenous-lifespans-remain-too-short/

Douglas, I. (2011). *The driest inhabited continent on earth is also the world's biggest water exporter!* The Permaculture Research Institute. Retrieved August 30, 2012, from http://permaculturenews.org/2011/06/10/the-driest-inhabited-continent-on-earth-is-also-the-world%E2%80%99s-biggest-water-exporter/

Education Dreams. (n.d.). *An open letter from Cherbourg Aboriginal Shire Council*. Retrieved August 29, 2014, from http://www.educationdreams.com.au/

Gammage, B. (2012). *The biggest estate on earth: How Aborigines made Australia*. Sydney, NSW: Allen and Unwin Books.

Gilbert, L. A. (1967). Solander, Daniel (1733–1782). In *Australian Dictionary of Biography* (Vol. 2). Retrieved September 1, 2014, from http://adb.anu.edu.au/biography/solander-daniel-2677

Gillen, M. (1989). *The founders of Australia: A biographical dictionary of the First Fleet*. Sydney, NSW: Library of Australian History.

Government of Western Australia, Department of Water. (n.d.). *Future Water*. Retrieved August 28, 2014, from http://www.water.wa.gov.au/Future+water./Future+demand/default.aspx

Jones, R. (1969). Fire-stick farming. *Australian Natural History, 16*, 224–228.

Madley, B. (2008). From terror to genocide: Britain's Tasmanian penal colony and Australia's history wars. *Journal of British Studies, 47*(1), 77–106.

Milirrpum v Nabalco Pty Ltd. (1971). 17 FLR 141.

Miller, G. H. (2005). Ecosystem collapse in Pleistocene Australia and a human role in megafaunal extinction. *Science, 309*, 287–290.

National Health Priority Action Council (NHPAC). (2006). *National chronic disease strategy*. Canberra, ACT: Australian Government Department of Health and Aging.

National Museum of Australia. (n.d.). *First Australians*. Retrieved November 18, 2014, from http://www.nma.gov.au/exhibitions/first_australians/resistance/coniston_massacre

NSW Government. (n.d.). *Child protection services*. Retrieved August 30, 2014, from http://www.community.nsw.gov.au/docs_menu/for_agencies_that_work_with_us/child_protection_services.html

NSW Government: Environment and Heritage. (n.d.). *Aboriginal people and cultural life*. Retrieved August 30, 2014, from http://www.environment.nsw.gov.au/nswculture heritage/aboriginalpeopleandculturallife.htm

Pickup, G. (1998). Desertification and climate change—the Australian perspective. *Climate Research, 11*, 51–63.

Potas, I., Smart, J., Brignell, G., Thomas, B., & Lawrie, R. (2003). *Circle sentencing in New South Wales: A review and evaluation*. Sydney, NSW: Judicial Commission of New South Wales, Monograph #22.

Read, P. (1981). *The stolen generations: The removal of Aboriginal children in New South Wales 1883 to 1969*. New South Wales: Department of Aboriginal Affairs, New South Wales Government.

The Royal Botanic Gardens & Domain Trust. (n.d.). *Captain James Cook and the visit of the Endeavour.* Retrieved August 30, 2014, from http://www.rbgsyd.nsw.gov.au/science/Evolutionary_Ecology_Research/Botany_of_Botany_Bay/people/captain_james_cook

Skwirk Interactive Schooling. (n.d.). *First contact with Europeans.* Retrieved August 29, 2014, from http://www.skwirk.com/p-c_s-17_u-455_t-1228_c-4698/first-contact-with-europeans/wa/first-contact-with-europeans/aboriginal-people-and-torres-strait-islanders/contact-with-europeans-the-effects

Survival International. (n.d.). *The uncontacted Indians of Brazil.* Retrieved August 29, 2014, from http://www.survivalinternational.org/tribes/uncontacted-brazil

Thompson, N. (2001). Indigenous Australia: Indigenous health. In J. Jupp (Ed.), *The Australian people: An encyclopedia of the nation, its people and their origins.* Cambridge, UK: Cambridge University Press.

Tumeth, R. (2011, June 7). *Is circle sentencing in the NSW criminal justice system a failure?* Retrieved August 30, 2014, from http://www.alsnswact.org.au/media/BAhbBlsHOgZmSSIgMjAxMy8wNy8xNS8yMl8wMl8xN183NV9maWxlBjoGRVQ/22_02_17_75_file

University of California Museum of Palaeontology. (n.d.). *Monotremes: Egg-laying mammals.* Retrieved August 29, 2014, from http://www.ucmp.berkeley.edu/mammal/monotreme.html

9

Perceptions of the Environment

Darlyne G. Nemeth and Traci W. Olivier

Seeing is one thing. Perceiving is another. For those of us who have the benefit of sight, that does not mean we have the gift of perception. Perception is *insight*. Can we see beyond that which is merely obvious, or do we only wish to see what is obvious? When we look at an area of dead trees, do we ask, "Why?" or do we merely capture the moment and move on? Perception, a biopsychosocial phenomenon, influences the way in which individuals view themselves, others, and the world around them. Perceptions are secondarily developed as a result of sensory input, such as visual and auditory information, and they reveal underlying notions of reality (Myers, 2007). Similarly, insight is "the faculty involved in grasping the inner character or underlying truth" and, in some cases, is a prerequisite for change (Wolman, 1989, p. 179).

With perception comes responsibility, the responsibility to seek out information and to act upon it. For many, remaining in denial is far easier. According to Dunlap and McCright (2011), concerted efforts are being made to promote this denial. Dunlap and McCright have characterized these efforts as "The Climate Change Denial Machine" (p. 147). Is there really such an organized effort from the fossil fuels industry, corporate America, and conservative foundations to undermine the future of our planet and our people? Likewise, is there a similar effort being conducted by those who espouse different views? For example, is there a Climate Change Promotion Machine, like the idea espoused by the Garrison Institute's 2012 Climate, Mind and Behavior Initiative? And why was the concept "Global Warming" renamed "Climate Change"? Can our beliefs be carefully crafted by marketing strategies, or will truth prevail? We do not market truth; we market beliefs. Perhaps, this is the problem.

This chapter will explore the development and marketing of perceptions and offer hypotheses as to how and why the presentation of scientific facts has had such little effect on the current attitudes toward environmental protection and human actions. We will also explore the influence of culture and religion on our perceptions and actions.

THE INFLUENCE OF FEELINGS AND NEEDS

Comfort and distress are the first and foremost feelings one experiences. During the birthing process, a baby moves from a position of comfort in the mother's womb to a position of distress when entering the world. The sound of a baby's cry tells the world that it has arrived; yet the infant continues to long for the security of his mother's womb (Bowlby, 1958). When fed, changed, and swaddled, the baby once again experiences comfort. When this state is interrupted, either naturally or abruptly, the baby experiences distress. As the infant cries in distress, a natural process ensues in the mother—she attempts to reestablish a state of comfort. The infant therefore, gravitates toward states of comfort and attempts to avoid states of distress (Bowlby, 1958, 1988).

All other feelings are learned. Researchers on emotion perception (Cosmides & Tooby, 2000; Ekman, 1992; Hamilton, 2012) outline how children learn to recognize, label, and share such feelings as happiness, sadness, anger, disgust, embarrassment, anxiety, fear, etc. Understanding and perceiving these emotions allow a child to locomote through the world (Nemeth, Ray, & Schexnayder, 2003).

On a more fundamental level, however, people seek comfort and attempt to avoid distress. In a world of chaos, via natural and/or human-induced disasters, such as hurricanes, oil spills, wars, and genocide, this is very hard to do. Disaster reigns. Comfort becomes merely a dream or an aspiration. Instead, survival is the goal. This is an evolutionary imperative.

A review of Maslow's Hierarchy of Needs (Maslow, 1943) points to a hierarchy with the primary level being physiological needs, followed by safety and security. If individuals' physiological needs (e.g., food, water, clothing, shelter) and safety and security needs (e.g., occupation, family, social) are not met, it is impossible for higher needs to be met. Furthermore, when individuals are finally able to reach the highest level of being (i.e., self-actualization), it is not uncommon for disaster to strike. Consider, for example, the ancient Roman city of Pompeii, which was completely destroyed by an eruption of Mount Vesuvius in AD 79. Pompeii was known for its beautiful villas, lovely weather, public bathhouses, thriving trade, and wealthy inhabitants (Gruen, 2014).

People seek comfort. This may require a change of locations. In the last few hundred years, many have attempted to immigrate to places like the United States in search of a better life, in search of comfort. For example, many Hungarians immigrated to the United States prior to World War I in order to avoid the turmoil that was brewing (Frank Nemeth, personal communication, 2000). More recently, many abandon their homeland, as has been happening in Syria, in order to survive (Rudoren, 2013). Abandonment is a very reasonable option in Syria, given that "a third of the [Syrian] population [has been] displaced, over a million homes have been destroyed, and over 100,000 people are dead" (Attar, 2014, para. 3). People cannot live in a state of distress for too long. Distress results in poverty, physical and/or mental illness, and often death. According to Wallie (2005), as cited in Nemeth and Whittington (2012), "For example, one well-known French Quarter artist, Harold 'Napoleon' King, was riding his bicycle to dialysis treatment when he found himself up to his neck in water. He was eventually rescued by a Coast Guard truck and taken to the Superdome. He was then bussed throughout the state to three different medical facilities," for dialysis and died along the way (p. 120). Basically, he lost hope. Hope not only helps individuals to set goals, but to then develop an effective strategy to reach those goals. Although all individuals possess an inherent capacity for hope, some lose it (Lopez et al., 2004; Snyder, et al., 2000) and are unable to seek solutions to their problems.

SEEKING SOLUTIONS

Seeking solutions is a fundamental way of coping with distress. For example, when people face environmental trauma with resilience, they survive (Nemeth & Whittington, 2012). Without resilience, they perish. Walker and Heffner (2010) define resilience as "the positive capacity of people to withstand stressors and to cope with trauma" (para. 1). Resilient people have the ability to learn from yesterday, while being grounded in today, so that they can see themselves in the future—so that they can see themselves returning to a state of comfort.

It is not uncommon for people to immigrate to a new country with the hope of seeking comfort (i.e., a better, safer, secure life), only to find themselves once again confronted by disaster. Those who sought comfort in the Gulf Coast areas of the United States, for example, are now confronted with new forms of disasters, hurricanes, and oil spills. After the Deepwater Horizon oil spill, Vietnamese Americans, like many others, were forced to sit and wait out the disaster until they could resume making a living again (Nguyen, 2010). Following Hurricane Katrina, the United States, for the first time in history, accepted aid from their southern neighbors in Mexico (Pace, 2005). This is particularly ironic considering recent estimates, which suggest that approximately 11.5 million individuals, who were born in Mexico, now reside in the United States (Batalova & Terrazas, 2010). Cuban Americans have had to contend not only with devastating hurricanes in the United States, but also with destructive hurricanes in their homeland. Hurricane Gustav, for example, impacted both countries significantly, but for Cuba, it was the most severe hurricane the country had experienced in 50 years (Sosa, 2008). Such individuals, who left their homelands in search of a better life in the United States, found themselves in distress once again.

No area in the world is impervious to disaster. Yet, people long for Shangri-La— a place of safety and comfort. All too often, however, they end up facing another form of disaster. Nemeth and Whittington (2012) outline a six-stage recovery process from environmental disaster: Shock, Survival Mode, Assessment of Basic Needs, Awareness of Loss, Susceptibility to Spin and Fraud, and Resolution. This process takes years, not days or weeks or months, from which to recover. As can be seen from the aftermaths of Hurricane Katrina and the Deepwater Horizon (i.e., BP) oil spill on the U.S. Gulf Coast, or the Haiti and Philippines earthquakes, or the Chernobyl and Fukushima nuclear disasters, it takes years for people and their environments to recover. Often, it takes years for resolution of such disasters to take place. Regarding the BP Deepwater Horizon incident, authorities were continuing to decide on a punishment as late as September 2014. Due to a court ruling indicating "gross negligence," BP could owe nearly $18 billion in fines (Kunzelman & McConnaughey, 2014, p. 1A). Only after resolution can a state of comfort be rekindled.

RESILIENCE AND PREPARATION

This process requires resilience on multiple levels. Adger, Brown, and Waters (2013) define resilience as "the capacity of a system to absorb disturbances and reorganize while undergoing change so as to still retain essentially the same function, structure, identity and feedbacks" (p. 698). They cite the importance of addressing resilience on many levels (e.g., people, communities, cities, nations, and climates). In regard to the latter, they cite the World Bank's African Development plan, which includes adaptation, knowledge and development, mitigation opportunities, and investment financing. This is a preparation plan, rather than a recovery plan. Preparation is the key. Consider, once again, the inhabitants of Pompeii. These individuals were well aware of the danger lurking within Mount Vesuvius. As Wallace-Hadrill (2011) pointed out, however, "The long inactivity of the volcano naturally lulled the people of the region into a false sense of security, though they were well aware of the signs of burning at the peak of the mountain" (para. 8), resulting in absolute unpreparedness. Scholars believe that the residents of Pompeii carried on with their daily lives until the final moments (Gruen, 2014; Wallace-Hadrill, 2011).

How prepared is the world for the inevitable changes that must and will be made? How accepting are people of the need to recognize, label, and prepare for climate change? In his 2013 State of the Union Address, President Barack Obama said, "The shift to a cleaner energy economy won't happen overnight, and it will require tough choices along the way. But the debate is settled. Climate change is a fact. And when our children's children look us in the eye and ask if we did all we could to leave them a safer, more stable world, with new sources of energy, I want us to be able to say yes, we did" (Obama, 2014, para. 28). Yet, will Americans, who are very invested in seeking comfort, heed President Obama's call, or will they merely assume that this is just another one of his many political agendas? We human beings are so fortunate in that we are capable of perceiving the future (Searle, 2001, as cited in Gowdy, 2007). With the capacity of perception, however, comes responsibility. According to Searle, "The ability to perceive the future consequences of present actions and behave accordingly may be the only hope of preventing catastrophic climate change" (Gowdy, 2007, p. 14).

IS THIS A NONEVENT?

Dunlap and McCright (2011) suggest that denial is at work, perhaps on an individual level, perhaps on a societal level, or even perhaps on an organized level. These researchers suggest a conspiracy involving industry and corporate America, conservative philanthropic organizations, foundations, scientists, conservative medicine and politicians, and Astroturf groups and campaigns, all designed to diffuse the reality of climate change for selfish reasons. Perhaps this is the case. Perhaps this is indeed occurring. But, could there be a simpler, more fundamental explanation?

Years ago, when the Y2K phenomena were occurring, Peter de Jager (1993) and his colleagues were trying to apprise the world of the danger of major systems, that were dependent on Common Business Oriented Language (COBOL) programming, failing as the turn of the century approached. Reportedly, these computer systems were not designed to last forever. Yet, rather than replace these COBOL programs, many business and governmental organizations chose to "upgrade" them instead. Even with upgrades, these systems were not designed to roll over to the next century (i.e., from the year 1999 to the year 2000). Businesses such as Prudential Financial proactively spent millions of dollars on new programs; however, governments were late to the table. By the time this threat was taken seriously, most COBOL programmers had retired. A crisis management program at West Virginia University was instituted to train new COBOL programmers to manage the problem, and manage the problem they did. Most rollovers occurred without incident. There were a few glitches (e.g., U.S. Social Security Checks did not arrive on time, train track programming had glitches, etc.), but, for the most part, the entire world celebrated this "nonevent" on internationally televised programming. Even though millions of dollars were spent throughout the world to avoid this "nonevent," in the end, most people considered Y2K to be a hoax ("Y2K: Social Implications," 1998).

Climate change seems to fall in the same category—a hoax, a nonevent. In general, people are not taking it seriously. Just as with Y2K, they expect someone else to "fix it" without being bothered by it. Talks about global warming (i.e., climate change), whether from scientists or from politicians (e.g., former U.S. Vice President Al Gore), are perceived as self-serving, money-making scare tactics. In general, people did not perceive their efforts as prosocial.

Furthermore, the belief was that it is being pushed to promote "social justice" and other practices, in addition to a means to promote growth through changing our energy sources. The alternatives do not seem feasible, and all had their own problems. Lastly, people did not want to be bothered. Basically, this emphasis on the "gloom and doom" message of climate change began only 15 or so years after the Y2K scare. With the latter "nonevent" fresh in their minds, most people do not want to be bothered. Also, there were predictions of another forthcoming ice age. In general, some scientists actually believed that merely providing information would motivate behavioral change (Garrison Institute, 2012), but there is just too much information for people to absorb. Specifically, "large portions of the population continue to reject ever-growing scientific consensus on climate change and its causes" (Garrison Institute, 2012, p. 13). Perhaps people simply engaged in "information avoidance" (Howell, Crosier, & Shepperd, 2014).

Perhaps it is a matter of personality types. In fact, according to Dan Kahan, Yale Law School professor, too much information tends to drive people "farther toward previously held views that may be culturally determined." Professor Kahan refers to this concept as "motivated reasoning," in that "people tend to tune into information and arguments tailored to conforming, not challenging, their prior attitudes" (Garrison Institute, 2012 p. 14). Basically, if the new scientific information about climate change does not fit into our belief system, we will reject it. A 2013 study conducted by the Yale Project on Climate Change Communication and George Mason University divides Americans into six audiences situated on a continuum regarding the strength of their belief in global warming/ climate change. The six groups, ranging from highest belief to lowest belief, are as follows: Alarmed (16%), Concerned (29%), Cautious (25%), Disengaged (9%), Doubtful (13%), and Dismissive (8%). Those with the highest belief represent those who are most concerned and motivated, while those with the least belief are consequently the least concerned and the least motivated regarding climate change issues (Leiserowitz, Maibach, Roser-Renouf, Feinberg, & Howe, 2013).

Remember, it is fundamental for people to seek comfort and avoid distress. Are we really in denial, as Norgaard (2011) and Dunlap and McCright (2011) would have us believe? Or are we merely avoiding facts that cause distress? As Norgaard (2011) points out, "people actually work to *avoid acknowledging disturbing information* in order to avoid emotions of fear, guilt, and helplessness," especially fear (p. 400). Yet, is it possible that this is a more fundamental process? Rather than active avoidance, it is likely that people are merely passively moving from insightful awareness to homeostatic perception—i.e., they are naturally moving away from psychological distress toward psychological comfort. People do not want to engage in thoughts, feelings, or actions that create distress. People only become concerned when issues of climate change affect them immediately and personally.

WHEN IT BECOMES PERSONAL

The Eskimos who live in Newtok, Alaska (Nemeth, D. F., 2012), a community that is slowly falling into the Arctic Ocean, are experiencing the direct effects of climate change. They are concerned. They are distressed. They must develop a plan to relocate their community before it is too late. Basically, "the more immediate the threat the more likely people will respond" (Gowdy, 2007, p. 23). However, the people in the northeastern region of the United States, who, in early 2014, experienced one of the most severe winters in recent times, became concerned, but not distressed. They experienced the 2014 winter as an inconvenience, with unintended consequences (e.g., mass interstate pileups [Rubinkam & Todt, 2014]); but, even with increased population shifts and infrastructure changes over the last many years, none of these communities have planned to relocate.

Even Atlanta, Georgia, a city caught off guard by the severe 2014 winter weather, had no plans to relocate. Rather, city officials began planning better preparedness strategies for the future. Indeed, there was no "public silence" (Norgaard, 2011, p. 404); rather, there was a public outcry about the lack of preparedness. This may be an example of the perception of climate change. Even though weather reports clearly predicted the massive winter weather systems, both in the northeastern and southeastern parts of the United States, people did not take the information seriously—basically, they were not prepared. Governments failed the people, and the people did not heed the information that was provided to them on every available newscast. Information did not translate into action. Why? Was it the need for cultural comfort (i.e., oikophilia—"the love and feeling for home" [Scruton, 2012, p. 3])? Or the difficulty of relocating? Or just simply denial? According to Gowdy, Bell, Krall, and Walton (2011), "Human behavior is a result of complex interactions between biological inheritance, social conditioning, and random events" (p. 2).

Perhaps it is a matter of priorities. Most people in advanced societies live on a schedule. In the United States, this schedule typically revolves around work, family responsibilities, and community activities. An average adult, who is a member of a family, works at least 40 hours a week. He or she must get the children to school, help them with homework, feed them, and put them to bed. Family time is usually reserved for the evenings (Nemeth, Ray, & Schexnayder, 2003), if at all. Community activities, often religiously focused, absorb several hours a week as well. Leisure activities, although important, are usually last on the list. So, when is there time to contemplate issues of climate change, process feelings, and develop action plans or, for that matter, take action? Most Americans barely have the time to contemplate buying fuel-efficient vehicles, let alone deal with corporate America's Denial Machine (Dunlap & McCright, 2011). Many have livelihoods that depend on the very industries that are reportedly causing the problem. Perhaps trusting leaders to solve the problem may be the problem. Politicians face elections every two to four years, and improbable events probably will not happen within that time frame. In addition, many are not truly representative of their constituents and do not relate to their own problems. Leaders are sometimes reluctant to act because their actions may have perceived and immediate negative effects. They also do not know how many will be affected if they fail to take action. Furthermore, leaders often depend on the very businesses in question for campaign funds and support.

Oftentimes, individuals must make a choice between feeding the family and taking on corporate America. Few have the courage, like Erin Brockovich (DeVito & Soderbergh, 2000), to stand up and take on such a challenge. Are these people in denial, or are they merely focusing on different priorities? Let's remember Maslow's Hierarchy of Needs. Prosocial thoughts and behaviors are not first-level concerns. It is certainly true that these problems need to be addressed. They are most easily seen with a holistic analysis that considers all relevant and spatial scales. Businesses should be required to act responsibly with respect to the environments they affect. Societal inertia and the political connectedness of these industries make responsible management changes difficult to accomplish. We citizens need to insist on them; otherwise, changes will not be made. These changes, however, will not be accomplished without effective communication.

EFFECTIVE COMMUNICATION FOR SURVIVAL

Earlier, we referenced the World Bank's plan for the development of African societies. Although quite a noble plan, many African nations, such as Sudan (Gumuchian, 2013) are still experiencing tribal warfare, genocide, and an unfathomable number of deaths. They have no time to think about climate change. Their effects are focused on survival. Many of their problems are related to overpopulation and resource scarcity. They are immediate and must be addressed. They have a higher priority. In order to survive, people must communicate. Several media sources have reported on the cell phone craze that is currently sweeping over parts of Africa. It is allowing people to survive and, even better, to earn a living (Jidenma, 2014; Romig, 2011) by finding out where work opportunities lie. Researchers in Kenya found that people would be willing to skip meals and walk instead of paying for bus fare, in order to pay for their cell phones ("Kenya's Mobile Telephones," 2012). That shows how important cell phones are perceived to be for employment, growth, protection, and survival. Our world and our societies are ever-changing. Communication is especially important in a changing world so the changes can be perceived. Information obtained can be vital for our survival. Oftentimes, communication is necessary for survival.

Not knowing what surrounding villages were experiencing in the World War II era of Nazi Germany did not allow communities to prepare optimally. Such was the case in Poland, for example, when German forces damaged communication lines (Zabecki, 2014). As a result, many suffered and died. Now, in several African countries, cell phone communication is leading to better outcomes.

We have many tools necessary for effective communication. We are using them in a variety of new ways; in fact, that is the primary change that is occurring in our society now. When we are communicating "gloom and doom" climate change scenarios, people either do not want to hear them because they interfere with their comfort levels, or cannot hear them because they are too busy dealing with distress.

Moser and Dilling (2011) focus on four assumptions that climate change communicators are making: (1) Inspiration with Information, (2) Mobilization by Fear, (3) One-Size-Fits-All Academic Jargon, and (4) Mobilization through Mass Media. These assumptions purport that individuals will not become engaged (i.e., inspired) until they are properly informed. Sometimes, this requires more information and clarification of issues before people are willing to act. Moreover, some become motivated and mobilized by the fears of what would happen should they choose not to act. These assumptions also suggest that discussing the issues in terms of scientific evidence is complicated by academic jargon and that using mass media outlets would be the most effective way to reach and persuade individuals to rally behind climate change efforts. Yet, "climate scientists are naïve about the extent to which their science undermines the established order" (Gowdy et al., 2011, p. 15). According to Hamilton (2010), as cited in Gowdy et al. (2011), "denial is due to a surplus of culture rather than a deficit of information" (p. 15). Thus, Moser and Dilling point out that effective communication must be a two-way engagement, not a one-way series of scientific pronouncements. People must be met "where they are: culturally, emotionally and intellectually" (Garrison Institute, 2013a, p. 12). Whether it is due to a Climate Change Denial Machine (Dunlap & McCright, 2011), or to top-down versus bottom-up leadership, or to the people's fundamental mistrust of science (e.g., visions of Frankenstein's monster and/or genetic engineering), people do not want to be "told" about climate change and "told" what they should think about it and/or do about it. Resistance to authority is a natural phenomenon. Any teenager can speak to this. Even if the authority figure is 100% correct, no teen wants to hear this, let alone follow the advice that is being given.

RESISTANCE VERSUS CREDIBILITY

Even though the psychology of human development is clear in this regard, most scientists espousing the perils of climate change are still using this very authoritative approach to attempt to change behavior. People do not want to be "told the truth." This does not work! There are no immediate rewards and/or consequences. Rather, there is perpetual resistance. No one, especially not rebellious Americans, want to be told how to think, how to feel, and what to do. People need to have the freedom to seek truth. Scare tactics did not work with Y2K, and they certainly will not work now. Yet, scientists and environmentalists persist in sending these top-down, "gloom and doom" messages. Most scientists sent down the message that their model indicated that as carbon dioxide increased, air temperature increased. Others used this model to further their agendas. Some scientists then used "gloom and doom" to seek research funding and were successful because that pleased bureaucrats. They were so successful that many found it necessary to emphasize "gloom and doom" for funding of scientific studies. For example, people were being scolded for being in denial or for not accepting *An Inconvenient Truth* (Bender, Burns, & Gugenheim, 2006). Former U.S. Vice President Al Gore was perceived by many as a self-serving aristocrat who was merely lining his own pockets. His efforts were eventually dismissed by the American public. This was not due to a denial machine as much as to a credibility gap. When Gore did not exhaustively challenge George W. Bush in regard to the outcome of the year 2000 presidential election, many people lost respect for him. According to the Senate Historical Office (n.d.), " 'Somewhere along the line,' commented ABC News' political director Mark Halperin, reporters had turned negative toward Gore. 'Within the subculture of political reporting, there was almost peer pressure not to say something neutral, let alone nice, about his ideas, his political skills, his motivations.' If Gore intended to run again, he would need to overcome negative preconceptions" (p. 15). Nothing that he said afterward mattered. But that probably affected very few people's opinions. The evidence was not convincing for many who listened. Gore did profit. Many people were and are suspicious of the motives of politicians. Furthermore he "talked the talk" but did not "walk the walk." For example, Gore had an extremely high carbon footprint in spite of his espoused concern for our planet. He was hailed as "the world's first 'carbon billionaire' " due to his investments in several "green" companies and initiatives (Broder, 2009). Yet, if the men of the wildly popular American A&E television series, *Duck Dynasty* (A&E Home Video, 2012), stood up to espouse climate change issues, people would listen. Phil Robertson and his family have credibility with the American public, even though they are wealthy. The Robertsons represent home and family and comfort—a simpler way of life (i.e., oikophilia).

This is the fundamental issue. People who are espousing climate change are not believable; they are not "one of us," so to speak. If they were "front line," rather than "ivory tower," people doing this for the common good, they would have credibility. Neighbor communicating to neighbor on an equal/peer level brings about change. Grassroots communication (even on a cell phone) is the most powerful of all. It is fundamental; it is believable; yet, it is not happening.

Americans would rather watch the Super Bowl than a *20/20* special on climate change. One evokes great emotion; the second, mere bewilderment. Bottom-up approaches propagated by regular, everyday people may be more effective at enacting meaningful change. As Scruton stated, "The fact is that, when problems pass to governments, they pass out of our hands," and "it is only at this local level that it is realistic to hope for improvement" (2012, pp. 2, 23).

Perhaps another reason why the climate change campaign has not progressed effectively is because it has been framed by leaders as *a moral issue*. As with many other moral issues, individuals take sides and rally efforts against opposing sides without stopping to objectively analyze the given situation. For example, in an excerpt from his book, *Our Choice*, Gore labeled climate change as a moral issue and wrote the following:

> Not too many years from now, a new generation will look back at us in this hour of choosing and ask one of two questions. Either they will ask, "What were you thinking? Didn't you see the entire North Polar ice cap melting before your eyes? Did you not care?" Or they will ask instead, "How did you find the moral courage to rise up and solve a crisis so many said was impossible to solve?" ("Excerpt," para. 4–5)

Gore continued by saying that he hopes we will be able to answer with, "Although leadership came from many countries, once the United States finally awakened to its responsibilities, it reestablished the moral authority the world had come to expect from the U.S." ("Excerpt," para. 16). It is such pretentious attitudes that add to the unwillingness of Americans (and others) to support climate change efforts. These attitudes create chasms between the everyday American and the "holier-than-thou" experts. A similar scenario was observed during a speech delivered by U.S. Secretary of State John Kerry to a group of Indonesian students in early 2014. Kerry belittled individuals who denied or even questioned climate change, comparing them to people who previously insisted that the earth was flat. " 'We don't have time for a meeting anywhere of the Flat Earth Society' " (Lee, 2014, p. 3A). Kerry labeled nonsupporters as a " 'tiny minority of shoddy scientists and science and extreme ideologues to compete with scientific facts' " (p. 3A). This form of ridicule will merely interfere with problem-solving and invite others to resist even further. For example, Republican presidential candidate, Rick Santorum, in a 2011 interview with Glenn Beck, called global warming a hoax. Santorum went on to state, "There is no such thing as global warming," earlier referring to it as "junk science" (Johnson, 2011, para. 1, 4).

COMMUNICATION THAT BEGETS RESOLUTION

We must stop these failed top-down efforts to either deny or communicate the perils of climate change/global warming and instead bring this discussion to the streets, so to speak. Many motorists stuck on the Pennsylvania and/or Atlanta roadways would perhaps have a lot to say about the effects of climate change on the weather patterns and the failed efforts on their parts or on their governments' parts to prepare for and deal with severe wintry conditions adequately. Such discussions on a basic human level at a time of acute distress may get people's attention. After all, they are captive audiences in distress with one common goal—resolution.

As with any disaster, whether due to climate change, environmental trauma, or human-induced trauma, resolution is the goal. Yet resolution requires planning/forethought/effort. Furthermore, according to Professor Kahan, we must frame our communications "in a way that doesn't antagonize or come across as an assault on one side" or the other (Garrison Institute, 2012, p. 14). It is extremely difficult to achieve resolution in the midst of disaster. Although not all disasters can be ameliorated by preparedness, most can be. Having plans of action on all levels (e.g., national, community, individual) can greatly reduce the expected or unexpected consequences of a disaster. This is what the Dutch have done and continue to do to greatly reduce the effects of storm surges. In response to the Dutch flood in 1953 that killed 1,835 people, the Netherlands reinforced the dikes in the 1960s, yet research in 1985 suggested that these reinforcements still did not provide the needed protection. The Dutch promptly responded by beginning to design a storm surge barrier in 1987; in 1997, the Maeslant Barrier was operational (Bol, 2005). After Hurricane Katrina, representatives from Louisiana went to the Netherlands to study the Dutch efforts. They have, however, yet to develop and/or implement this holistic management approach for the state of Louisiana or the city of New Orleans. Why? Politics.

THE PRICE OF ILLUSIONS

In 1852, Charles Ellet, a civil engineer, developed a holistic plan to protect the city of New Orleans from flooding (Kelman, 2007). It was a visionary approach involving improvements made to the levees, spillways, reservoirs, and wetlands. As Kelman explained, Ellet "suggested that human endeavors— upstream development and levees that climbed ever skyward—exacerbated the flood menace. Ellet offered a multitier alternative: more levee improvements; building outlets or spillways to shunt floodwater from the river; and constructing massive reservoirs, artificial wetlands, to soak up excess rain before it ran off into the Mississippi" (para. 9). Nearly a decade later, in 1861, Andrew Atkinson Humphreys, a U.S. Army engineer, offered an alternative solution that, despite appearing to be brilliant due to the research and details that were included, was fundamentally flawed. Furthermore, Humphreys's approach was reportedly fueled by his anger at Ellet for suggesting an approach that did not include the involvement of military engineers. Kelman continued, stating that Humphreys "consequently undermines nearly all of Ellet's insights, summarily dismissing outlets and reservoirs before arguing that only 'an organized levee system [can] be depended upon for the protection against floods in the Mississippi Valley.' When Humphreys became chief of the U.S. Army Corps of Engineers, he ascended to a position of authority where he could help craft an enduring policy known as 'levees only' " (para. 9). Basically, due to politics and the selfish undermining of one man, the "for profit" rather than the "for people" approach reigned. Instead of protecting the city, these carefully designed levees actually made matters worse, which Ellet had previously predicted. In the end, wisdom was ignored due to "misplaced faith in technology and willful forgetting" (para. 9), and politics prevailed. Rather, the illusion of safety was created.

Under such an illusion, residents of New Orleans went about their daily lives; that is, until Hurricane Katrina struck in 2005. Before Katrina, even though the knowledge of wetlands devastation (some caused by oil companies dredging through the marshes to the Gulf of Mexico) was clearly present (it could actually be seen), few New Orleans' residents had the insight to pay attention. Besides the massive environmental devastation of Katrina, the human toll was immense. Displacement, physical illness, emotional suffering, and even death occurred because people were merely trying to survive, going about their daily lives, and trying to seek some measure of comfort; they were seeing, but not perceiving reality. The fact that they were living in their oikophilia, a community that was below sea level, was not a part of their holistic awareness. As history now tells, the cost for their lack of awareness was immense.

This sense of diminished awareness is likely to only increase, especially given the rapid advances in technology that many are currently experiencing. Today's children and young adults are in danger of losing, or perhaps never even acquiring, the art of survival. Instead, our super-smart devices have created an illusion of safety. Many are so busy burying their faces in digital screens that they would not know how to "survive" even if a situation required them to do so. Moreover, modern societies have developed into "risk-denying and risk-averting" cultures that "have the same effect—to increase the cost of risk to the point where risks really do become irrational" (Scruton, 2012, p. 120). The author explains, "Rational beings, who are risk-takers by nature, no longer take the risks that they ought to be taking, since the cost has been artificially elevated by litigation and law. The result does not damage adults only; it damages their children far more, threatening the very possibility of what was once considered a normal childhood" (pp. 120–121). The results of such a mind-set are potentially disastrous. On the one hand, we do not even realize that there is a problem because our awareness has been diminished by the bright lights of our iPhones. On the other hand, society has taught us that risk is bad and should be avoided! Scruton concludes, "Young people brought up to think their way through practical difficulties acquire the art of survival. The risk-averse and timorous have no capacity to confront, still less to survive, a real emergency, nor are they likely to do well in ordinary competitive business" (p. 121). This mind-set is described as the "Precautionary Principle," which suggests that "if you think there may be a risk, then there is a risk; and if there is a risk, forbid it" (p. 108). Although the Precautionary Principle may prevail, there is no evidence that it is based upon sound research.

And there will be costs. They may not be immediate. Just like Humphreys prevailed over Ellet, it perhaps may take more another 100 years (e.g., 1882 to 2005), but it will happen. And when it does, the costs will be enormous. Politicians, who initially made the decisions, were no longer present to be held accountable. They most likely lived, literally and figuratively, on higher ground and were not truly representative of those affected. So may be the case with the political devastation of the Louisiana Levee Board's lawsuit against 97 oil companies for their destruction of the coastal marshes (Ballard, 2014). Only time and future hurricanes will tell the story.

Understanding our past, while living in the present, will prepare us for the future. Just like the past, it will be a future filled with joy and sorrow, good times and bad times, great discoveries and great setbacks. It is all about the yin and yang, the positive and negative, complementary forces or principles (Guralnik, 1984). We must not be so afraid of risk-taking that we avoid developing an awareness of the problem and dismiss opportunities to formulate solutions.

THE POWER OF TRUTH

In order to move forward in a positive, hopeful manner, we must carry with us three abiding principles—Respect, Resilience, and Resolution. We must also recognize the difference between *sustainability* and *resiliency*. As *New York Times* reporter Andrew Zolli (2012) stated:

> For decades, people who concern themselves with the world's "wicked problems"—interconnected issues like environmental degradation, poverty, food security and climate change—have marched together under the banner of "sustainability": the idea that with the right mix of incentives, technology substitutions and social change, humanity might finally achieve a lasting equilibrium with our planet, and with one another ... Yet today, precisely because the world is so increasingly out of balance, the sustainability regime is being quietly challenged, not from without, but from within ... Where sustainability aims to put the world back into balance, resilience looks for ways to manage in an imbalanced world ... The resilience frame speaks not just to how buildings weather storms but to how people weather them, too. (para. 1, 3, 10)

In order to weather these storms, we must maintain respect for ourselves, our neighbors, and our environment. We must communicate in a way that "affirms, rather than threatens, prior belief and values" (Garrison Institute, 2012, p. 16). We must live in harmony with one another and with our earth. We "must bridge the gap between objective facts and subjective values," (James Hoggan, as cited in Garrison Institute, 2012, p. 17) which "are the lenses through which we view the world" (Brophy, as cited in Garrison Institute, 2012, p. 17), despite the fact that "the scientific method leads us to truths that are less than self-evident, often mind-blowing, and sometimes hard to swallow" (Achenbach, 2015, p. 40). We must maintain and foster resilience at all levels (e.g., self, community, and climate). We must be resolute in our commitment to plan for the future (both the unexpected and the expected). And we must cope with whatever awaits us with hope and dignity, remembering that we are stewards, not owners of our planet (Tucker, as cited in Garrison Institute, 2012, p. 18).

THE POWER OF GREED

There will always be selfish, greedy people in the world and in our lives. Whether they are corporate sociopaths, psychoid leaders (Nemeth & Whittington, 2012, pp. 118–120), character disorders, or just plain bad people, we must not allow their leadership to prevail. At times of crisis, these leaders—e.g., Mayor Roy Nagin of New Orleans during Hurricane Katrina—seem to relish the opportunity to engage in spin and fraud. Although it took nine years, in 2014, Nagin was eventually convicted of 20 counts of crimes against the most vulnerable people in his trust. Nagin was said to have had an "uncanny ability to see the truth as something flexible, rather than fixed" and was known to hold his constituents to standards that he did not uphold himself (Russell, 2014, p. 6A). Furthermore, evidence suggested that Nagin was using city funds for personal expenses, while his own personal resources were being used to fund a family granite business that had secured a contract with a national home improvement retailer around the time that many New Orleans residents were rebuilding homes after the damage from Katrina. On July 9, 2014, in what a local newspaper called a "lenient sentence," Nagin was ordered to serve 10 years in federal prison (Russell & Simmerman, 2014, p. 1A). Due to his selfish opportunism and lack of prosocial empathy, it can be concluded that Nagin was one of many responsible for impeding the recovery of New Orleans.

In addition to local examples, the power of greed and corruption is also quite evident in well-known historical leaders. Adolf Hitler may well be the most infamous, notorious example of a psychoid leader. Hitler's insatiable desire for power was ultimately responsible for sparking World War II ("Adolf Hitler," 2002), promulgating discriminatory views, and executing millions of individuals. Moreover, Napoleon Bonaparte's greedy conquests of Europe led to countless casualties ("Napoleon Biography," n.d.). Or consider Genghis Khan, who stated,

"I am the flail of God. If you had not committed great sins, God would not have sent a punishment like me upon you" ("Genghis Khan Biography," n.d.).

How do these people rise to leadership roles? Most likely, this occurs due to complacency. Most mainstream people are very busy tending to their own lives. When they have a moment, they seek comfort and enjoyment. Either they do not want to be bothered with, or they do not take the time for, meaningful engagement in the politics of life. Thus, they allow those who seek power to have it, often with disastrous results.

THE SOCIAL BRAIN, LOGIC, EMOTIONS, AND PERCEPTION

Social Darwinism, or "survival of the fittest," is often used as a way of describing the idea that the most intelligent ways of thinking and doing will win out. Yet, there are several examples in this chapter demonstrating that this is often not true. Humphreys's plan for protecting New Orleans appeared to be the most intelligent, logical, and well-researched choice, yet it ultimately failed. In reality, Ellet, many years previously, had crafted the most intelligent plan, but it was ignored. Regarding the Y2K events, wise predictions, by de Jager and others, of turn-of-the-century computer and systems failures, were rendered years in advance, but they also were ignored. Instead, rapid and cheap system upgrades were hailed to be the solution. These solutions ultimately failed. Governments and businesses had to hastily work to patch up the problem at the last minute. Why do we allow such things to happen? For example, on the popular television show *Castle*, the lead character, Richard Castle, stated, "This is politics. Perception is reality. The truth won't matter" (Marlow, Boylan, & Woods, 2012). Gowdy et al. (2011) offered a different explanation; he stated that perhaps Darwin's original theory of natural selection has been misused. In their paper, titled *The Social Brain and the Diffusion of Pro-Social Behavior*, Gowdy et al. opined:

> The most egregious abuses of Darwin's theory of natural selection (so-called Social Darwinism) are found not in biology but in political scientists like Herbert Spencer who coined the term "survival of the fittest." The term seemed to be a good metaphor to describe the world of the emerging industrial economy of the 1800s and it paved the way for social Darwinism and a reactionary defense of the existing social order. This school of thought continued in the late 19th century economics, where the survival of the fittest metaphor was used to justify the privilege of the well-to-do and to argue against public policies helping the less fortunate. In this view, who is rich and who is poor is a natural outcome of the struggle for survival. Helping those who are less fit is a violation of the laws of nature. (p. 1)

Such were the views of many individuals post–Hurricane Katrina. Some viewed Katrina victims as deserving of disaster due to their not having evacuated New Orleans well enough in advance. Upon closer examination, however, one would notice that the "privilege of the well-to-do" was that they were able to get out on time. Many of the poor were not so fortunate. Even if they had chosen to evacuate, they were forced to rely on public transportation, which ultimately failed, leaving them stranded in the flooded city. In quoting Yale economist William Graham Sumner, Gowdy explained that "almost all legislative effort to prevent vice is really protective of vice" (p. 1). When the common good is rejected in favor of political vices (e.g., Humphreys's plan, Y2K efforts), suffering is inevitable. As Gowdy (2007) stated, "the effect of money is to make people more individualistic and less social" (p. 13).

PROSOCIAL BEHAVIOR AND INSPIRED LEADERSHIP

Despite the numerous examples of greed, corruption, and mismanaged resources that are present in our world, there are still others who provide inspiring examples of prosocial behavior and leadership. Agnes Gonxha Bojaxhiu, commonly referred to as Mother Teresa, is an excellent example. As a teacher at St. Mary's High School in Calcutta, India, Mother Teresa had a personal view of the anguish and poverty faced by the poor in her city. Mother Teresa left her quiet, stable life as a teacher to meet a need and provide a solution to the problem of poverty around her. By the 1990s, Mother Teresa's efforts had been so successful that her charity, the Missionaries of Charity, contained over one million coworkers spanning 40 countries. Mother Teresa was awarded the Pope John XXIII Peace Prize in 1971, the Nehru Prize in 1972, and the Nobel Peace Prize in 1979. Her example is living proof that the actions of a single, selfless person can make a world of difference ("Mother Teresa—Biographical," 2013). More recently, in 2003, Mother Teresa was beatified by Pope John Paul II (Feister & Zimmerman, n.d.).

Remaining positive and working to create a "vision of the bright future that we are already working for" (Garrison Institute, 2013b, p. 4) is fundamentally crucial to effecting meaningful change. According to Gowdy et al. (2011), we must "frame the climate change debate in terms of core American values of self-sufficiency, leadership and progress, economic security and job creation" (p. 18). We must blend our scientific facts with our conservative values. We must exhibit positive leadership and focus on the "co-benefits of action" (Garrison Institute, 2013b, p. 10).

Many spiritual leaders, regardless of religious background or ethnicity, understand the "deep connection between concern for the environment and spirituality" (Garrison Institute, 2012, p. 18). Stewardship of the poor and stewardship of the environment are inextricably linked. As Fred Taylor (Garrison Institute, 2012, p. 19) points out, "religious groups have been at the forefront of most social change movements." As the Reverend Fletcher Harper states, perhaps the concept of climate change needs to be perceived as a social change movement, in that it speaks "to people's deepest values, deepest beliefs, deepest concerns, and deepest experiences" (Garrison Institute, 2012, p. 19). One can only achieve this change in perception by speaking the truth without punishment (Garrison Institute, 2012). Thus, denial and doomsday strategies must be abandoned in favor of collaborative efforts on both the progressives who espouse the facts and conservatives who espouse cultural values. A reconciliation of the mind and the heart must be achieved in order to prepare for the future. More recently, Foster Campbell, a guest on the June 2, 2014, Jim Engster radio show on Louisiana Public Broadcasting, stated, "There are no wrong ways to do what is right and there are no right ways to do what is wrong" (Engster & Campbell, 2014).

CHALLENGES AND CONCLUSIONS

People seek comfort and, whenever possible, attempt to avoid distress. Unscrupulous, selfish leaders prey upon people's need for comfort by creating distress so that people's natural tendency toward avoidance will be activated. When these leaders go too far and create too much distress, a natural pattern of resistance kicks in instead. Avoidance leads to inaction. Resistance leads to action.

For People

If Dunlap and McCright are correct, manipulating people to inaction via a Corporate Denial Machine can be a very effective method of achieving complacency. Likewise, if the 2012 Climate, Mind and Behavior Initiative approach is correct, bridging natural sciences and social sciences will be the key to resolution. As Gowdy (2007) stated, in the natural sciences, "the theory of natural selection does not contradict the laws of thermodynamics" (p. 11). But in the social sciences, the theories of individual human behavior are often "contradictory and incompatible" (p. 11). Perhaps the laws of thermodynamics could apply to the social sciences, if "entropy [could] be countered indefinitely at the local level by injecting energy and exporting randomness" (Scruton, 2012, p. 10). The problem appears to be that our natural scientists, although typically in sync, are not in sync with our social scientists, who are apparently not in sync with one another. If the many social environmentalists continue to ring the death knell with their doomsday climate change messages, people will become even more resistant. They will dig in their heels and refuse to see, let alone perceive, acknowledge, or accept, the scientific realities before them. The old saying, "You can lead a horse to water, but you cannot make him drink," seems to prevail. Leading Americans to water, so to speak, has never really worked. It is time to stop this top-down method of communicating information and instead invite people to become a part of the process of discovery.

When people experience the climate changing, like the Eskimos in Newtok, Alaska (Nemeth, D. F., 2012), and those involved in the 2014 winter pileups, they will—out of frustration, out of distress, out of being inconvenienced—begin a dialogue. They will begin to make choices. Thus, we must focus more on "how and why people make choices" (Gowdy, 2007, p. 12). Peer-to-peer communication is the best defense against a Corporate Denial Machine, the Doomsday Environmentalists, or any other entity. Until scientific facts become household words, they can be easily discounted. Until scientists are perceived as our neighbors and friends. Until the glitz of corporate America is dispelled. Until people awake from their dream of creating comfort and prosperity for themselves and themselves alone, we will remain in limbo, with no forethought, no feeling, and no plan of action.

For Communities

Communication and connectedness are key elements of effective change. In the introduction to the Garrison Institute's 2013 Climate, Mind and Behavior Symposium Synthesis Report (Garrison Institute, 2013a), the following was stated:

> Adequate change requires the connection of multiple scales and modes of action, including individual mindfulness, local community action, and global activism, in a way that creates community (in the broadest sense), empowers all, and respects diversity. Many forms of civic engagement are needed and many forms of organizational change are needed. So, rather than being crippled by the megalith of climate change, there is great hope to be found by addressing the multiple, specific issues that touch people's lives. (p. 4)

A proposed model for effecting meaningful change was included in the Garrison Institute's 2012 Climate, Mind and Behavior Symposium report (Garrison Institute, 2012). This model succinctly outlines initiatives for Climate, Mind and Behavior, but the concepts could also be applied to climate change efforts. At the heart of this model are the mapping, translation, promotion, and communication of scientific insights (including those from social and cognitive research) from the scientific realm to the community. The premise is that the development of scientific insights (e.g., in social and cognitive research) can result in the implementation of sustainability initiatives through the building, promoting, and maintenance of networks and learning environments. As such, scientific insights and sustainability initiatives work in tandem to contribute to information and growth.

Holistic thinking will be necessary to address the inevitable changes that are occurring and will continue to occur in the future. Furthermore, the concept of sustainability will need to be replaced by the concept of resilience. Because our numbers are still increasing and our world is changing rapidly, man-induced problems are likely to increase. We need to evaluate the consequences of the changes that are occurring as holistically as possible. Information about change has been gathering since humans evolved, and we need to perceive it in order to plan our future. Plans should be as prosocial as possible at all levels in order to benefit as many as possible. Our leaders should be affected by their decisions in the same way as we are. Levels of organization should be minimized, and holistic, prosocial thinking should be practiced at all levels. As much as possible, communication and decisions should be as logical as possible. We must seek truth, not extra gain for select individuals or particular groups.

For Business Entities

In a *Harvard Business Review* article originally published in 1997 and reprinted in 2001, Heifetz and Laurie outline changes faced in today's marketplace. Contemporary leaders who seek to effect meaningful change, regardless of the issue or topic at hand, will find themselves faced with similar challenges. These challenges are adaptive, and not technical, in nature. In an adaptation of Heifetz and Laurie's work, Rowson (2011) compared and contrasted technical versus adaptive challenges. Technical problems are often simple to recognize, are easy to fix, and require small changes in relatively few places. The solutions to technical problems are often able to be solved by the "experts," can be implemented quickly, and are generally well received by people. Environmental issues such as climate change, however, cannot be considered technical problems. They must be considered adaptive challenges. Such challenges are hard to recognize but very easy to deny, and they require changes in several different domains simultaneously. Furthermore, the solutions must be developed by the individuals faced with the problems! And these solutions, which require critical thinking and new ways of doing things, are difficult to implement. Implementing adaptive solutions takes time—lots of time! And how can adaptive solutions be readily accepted by people when many individuals do not even realize there is a problem? As Heifetz and Laurie (2001) point out, adaptive challenges "are forcing organizations to clarify their values, develop new strategies, and learn new ways of operating. Often the toughest task for leaders in effecting change is mobilizing people throughout the organization to do *adaptive work*" (pp. 131–132, emphasis added). The authors continued by explaining:

> Adaptive work is required when our deeply held beliefs are challenged, when the values that made us successful become less relevant, and when legitimate yet competing perspectives emerge. We see adaptive challenges every day at every level ... Adaptive problems are often systemic problems with no ready answers ... Indeed, getting people to do adaptive work is the mark of leadership

in a competitive world. Yet for most senior executives, providing leadership and not just authoritative expertise is extremely difficult.
(pp. 131–132)

For Us All

In conclusion, perception requires insight. Insight involves correctly seeing what is before us. We have the facts. But do we wish to perceive them? Perhaps we merely wish to see, but not see, what is before us. Perception requires responsibility. Responsibility requires action. Action takes time. Do we really want to devote the intellectual, emotional, and behavioral effort required to join with our neighbors to address the issues involved in climate change? Or do we merely wish to seek comfort and remain in the isolation of the present? Remember, it took over 100 years after Ellet's 1882 holistic plans were ignored for New Orleans to be devastated by Hurricane Katrina in 2005. Perhaps we have another 100 years of comfort ahead, or perhaps not! The following quote, featured in a June 2014 article in the American Psychological Association's *Monitor on Psychology*, seems to accurately summarize the issue at hand. "The facts of climate change can cause people to feel anxiety, guilt, anger, and hopelessness. So, as with many things that cause those emotions, people tend to turn away and ignore the cause rather than figuring out how to address it" (Winerman, 2014, p. 33). Nevertheless, as *National Geographic* author Joel Achenbach succinctly stated, "We need to get a lot better at finding answers, because it's certain the questions won't be getting any simpler" (2015, p. 47).

REFERENCES

A&E Home Video (Producer). (2012). *Duck dynasty: Season 1* [DVD]. Available from http://www.shophistory.com

Achenbach, J. (2015). The age of disbelief. *National Geographic, 227*(3), 30–47.

Adger, W. N., Brown, K., & Waters, J. (2011). Resilience. In J. S. Dryzek, R. B. Norgaard, & D. Schlosberg (Eds.), *The Oxford handbook of climate change and society* (pp. 696–710). New York, NY: Oxford University Press.

Adolf Hitler. (2002). In *World of Criminal Justice*. Gale. Retrieved April 3, 2015, from http://ic.galegroup.com.ezproxylocal.library.nova.edu

Attar, L. S. (2014, March 10). Counting Syria's dead. *The New York Times*. Retrieved April 3, 2015, from http://www.nytimes.com

Ballard, M. (2014, April 20). Honoré wants public involved on environment. *The Advocate* (p. 9B).

Batalova, J., & Terrazas, A. (2010, December 9). Frequently requested statistics on immigrants and immigration in the United States. Retrieved April 3, 2015, from http://www.migrationpolicy.org

Bender, L. (Producer), Burns, S. Z. (Producer), & Gugenheim, D. (Director). (2006). *An inconvenient truth* [Motion picture]. USA: Lawrence Bender Productions.

Bol, R. (2005). Operation of the 'Maeslant Barrier': Storm surge barrier in the Rotterdam New Waterway. In C. A. Fletcher & T. Spencer (Eds.), *Flooding and environmental challenges for Venice and its lagoon: State of knowledge* (pp. 311–316). New York, NY: Cambridge University Press.

Bowlby, J. (1958). The nature of the child's tie to his mother. *International Journal of Psycho-Analysis, 39,* 350–373.

Bowlby, J. (1988). *A secure base: Parent-child attachment and healthy human development.* New York, NY: Basic Books.

Broder, J. M. (2009, November 2). Gore's dual role: Advocate and investor. *The New York Times.* Retrieved April 3, 2015, from http://www.nytimes.com.

Cosmides, L., & Tooby, J. (2000). Evolutionary psychology and the emotions. In M. Lewis & J. M. Haviland-Jones (Eds.), *Handbook of emotions* (2nd ed., pp. 91–115). New York, NY: Guilford.

de Jager, P. (1993, September 6). Doomsday. *Computer World.* Retrieved April 3, 2015, from http://search.proquest.com.ezproxylocal.library.nova.edu/docview/215988690? accountid=6579

DeVito, D. (Producer), & Soderbergh, S. (Director). (2000). *Erin Brockovich* [Motion picture]. USA: Santa Ventura Studios.

Dunlap, R. E., & McCright, A. M. (2011). Organized climate change denial. In J. S. Dryzek, R. B. Norgaard, & D. Schlosberg (Eds.), *The Oxford handbook of climate change and society* (pp. 144–160). New York, NY: Oxford University Press.

Ekman, P. (1992). An argument for basic emotions. *Cognition and Emotion, 6*(3/4), 169–200.

Engster, J. (Presenter), & Campbell, F. (Guest). (2014, June 2). Public service commissioner Foster Campbell [Radio broadcast]. In K. Gallagher (Producer), *The Jim Engster show.* Baton Rouge, LA: WRKF 89.3.

Excerpt: Our choice. (2009, November 3). *ABC News.* Retrieved April 3, 2015, from http://www.abcnews.go.com.

Feister, J. B., & Zimmerman, J. (n.d.). The official road to sainthood. *American Catholic.* Retrieved April 3, 2015, from https://www.americancatholic.org/features/teresa/ Sainthood.asp

Garrison Institute. (2012). *Comprehensive Report on the 2012 Climate, Mind and Behavior Initiative.* Retrieved April 3, 2015, from https://www.garrisoninstitute.org

Garrison Institute. (2013a). *2013 Climate, Mind and Behavior Symposium: Synthesis Report: The human dimensions of resilient and sustainable cities.* Retrieved April 3, 2015, from https://www.garrisoninstitute.org/climate-and-behavior/transformational-ecology -reports

Garrison Institute. (2013b). *2013 Climate, Mind and Behavior Symposium: Synthesis Report: Variation and diversity in sustainability and climate work.* Retrieved April 3, 2015, from https://www.garrisoninstitute.org/climate-and-behavior/transformational-ecology -reports

Genghis Kahn biography. (n.d.). *Biography.com.* Retrieved April 3, 2015, from http:// www.biography.com/people/genghis-khan-9308634

Gowdy, J., Bell, R. G., Krall, L., & Walton, M. (2011). *Garrison Institute Report. The social brain and the diffusion of pro-social behavior: Background paper for the Garrison Institute Climate, Mind and Behavior program.* Garrison, NY: Garrison Institute.

Gowdy, J. M. (2007). *Behavioral economics and climate change policy* (Report No. 0701). Troy, NY: Rensselaer Polytechnic University.

Gruen, E. S. (2014). Pompeii. In *Public Libraries*. Retrieved April 3, 2015, from http://www.worldbookonline.com.novacat.nova.edu/pl/referencecenter/printarticle?id=ar438760

Gumuchian, M. (2013, December 17). "Heavy" death toll as thousands flee south Sudan violence, U.N. says. *CNN*. Retrieved April 3, 2015, from http://www.cnn.com

Guralnik, D. B. (Ed.). (1984). *Webster's new world dictionary of the American language*. New York, NY: Simon & Schuster.

Hamilton, J. R. (2012). *Development of emotional processing norms in children and adolescents for the Comprehensive Affect Testing System (CATS)* (Unpublished doctoral dissertation). Pacific Graduate School of Psychology, Palo Alto University, Palo Alto, CA.

Heifetz, R. A., & Laurie, D. L. (2001). The work of leadership. *Harvard Business Review*, 79(11), 130–141.

Howell, J., Crosier, B., & Shepperd, J. (2014). Does lacking threat-management resources increase information avoidance? A multi-sample, multimethod investigation. *Journal of Research in Personality*, 50, 102–109.

Jidenma, N. (2014, January 24). How Africa's mobile revolution is disrupting the continent. *CNN*. Retrieved April 3, 2015, from http://www.cnn.com

Johnson, B. (2011, June 25). Santorum: "There's no such thing as global warming." *Grist*. Retrieved April 3, 2015, from https://grist.org/climate-change/2011-06/24-rick-santorum-glenn-beck-global-warming-skeptic-hoax/

Kelman, A. (2007). Boundary issues: Clarifying New Orleans's murky edges. *Journal of American History*, 94, 695–703. Retrieved March 20, 2014, from http://www.journalofamericanhistory.org/projects/katrina/Kelman.html

Kenya's mobile telephones vital for the poor. (2012, November 10). *The Economist*. Retrieved April 3, 2015, from http://www.economist.com

Kunzelman, M., & McConnaughey, J. (2014, September 5). BP could face fines up to $18B. *The Advocate*, pp. 1A, 5A.

Lee, M. (2014, February 17). Kerry mocks those who deny climate change. *The Advocate*, p. 3A.

Leiserowitz, A., Maibach, E., Roser-Renouf, C., Feinberg, G., & Howe, P. (2013). *Global warming's six Americas in September 2012*. New Haven, CT: Yale Project on Climate Change Communication, Yale University and George Mason University. Retrieved April 3, 2015, from http://environment.yale.edu/climate/publications/Six-Americas-September-2012

Lopez, S. J., Snyder, C. R., Magyar-Moe, J., Edwards, L. M., Pedrotti, J. T., Janowski, K., ... Pressgrove, C. (2004). Strategies for accentuating hope. In P. A. Linley & S. Joseph (Eds.), *Positive psychology in practice* (pp. 388–404). Hoboken, NJ: John Wiley & Sons.

Marlow, A.W., & Boylan, C. (Writers), & Woods, K. (Director). (2012, January 16). Episode 12 [Television series episode]. In A. W. Marlow, *Castle*. New York, NY: ABC Studios.

Maslow, A. H. (1943). A theory of human motivation. *Psychological Review*, 50, 370–396.

Moser, S. C., & Dilling, L. (2011). Communicating climate change: Closing the science-action gap. In J. S. Dryzek, R. B. Norgaard, & D. Schlosberg (Eds.), *The Oxford handbook of climate change and society* (pp. 161–174). New York, NY: Oxford University Press.

Mother Teresa—biographical. (2013). *The Nobel Foundation.* Retrieved April 3, 2015, from http://www.nobelprize.org

Myers, D. (2007). *Psychology* (8th ed.). New York, NY: Worth Publishers.

Napoleon biography. (n.d.). *Biography.com.* Retrieved April 3, 2015, from http://www.biography.com/people/napoleon-9420291

Nemeth, D. F. (2012). Our planet earth: Understanding the big picture. In D. G. Nemeth, R. B. Hamilton, & J. Kuriansky (Eds.), *Living in an environmentally traumatized world: Healing ourselves and our planet* (pp. 57–75). Santa Barbara, CA: ABC-CLIO/Praeger.

Nemeth, D. G., Ray, K. P., & Schexnayder, M. M. (2003). *Helping your angry child.* Oakland, CA: New Harbinger Publications.

Nemeth, D. G., & Whittington, L. T. (2012). Our robust people: Resilience in the face of environmental trauma. In D. G. Nemeth, R. B. Hamilton, & J. Kuriansky (Eds.), *Living in an environmentally traumatized world: Healing ourselves and our planet* (pp. 113–140). Santa Barbara, CA: ABC-CLIO/Praeger.

Nguyen, N. (2010, August 29). Vietnamese Americans, the BP spill, and the lessons of Katrina. *New America Media.* Retrieved April 3, 2015, from http://www.newamericamedia.org

Norgaard, K. M. (2011). Climate denial: Emotion, psychology, culture, and political economy. In J. S. Dryzek, R. B. Norgaard, & D. Schlosberg (Eds.), *The Oxford handbook of climate change and society* (pp. 399–413). New York, NY: Oxford University Press.

Obama, B. (2014, January 28). *President Barack Obama's State of the Union Address.* The White House, Office of the Press Secretary, Washington, DC. Retrieved April 3, 2015, from http://www.whitehouse.gov

Pace, G. (2005, September 7). Mexico sends first-ever aid north. *CBS News.* Retrieved April 3, 2015, from http://www.cbsnews.com

Romig, R. (2011, March 4). Africa's cell-phone revolution. *The New Yorker.* Retrieved April 3, 2015, from http://www.newyorker.com

Rowson, J. (2011, November). Transforming behavior change: Beyond nudge and neuromania. *RSA Projects.* Retrieved April 3, 2015, from https://thersa.org

Rubinkam, M., & Todt, R. (2014, February 15). Scores of trucks, cars crash on Pa. Turnpike. *The Advocate,* p. 2A.

Rudoren, J. (2013, May 8). A lost generation: Young Syrian refugees struggle to survive. *The New York Times.* Retrieved April 3, 2015, from http://www.nytimes.com

Russell, G. (2014, February 16). Nagin's early mistakes foreshadowed future falsehoods. *The Advocate,* pp. 1A, 6A.

Russell, G., & Simmerman, J. (2014, July 10). 10 years: Judge settles on lenient sentence for ex-N.O. mayor in corruption case. *The Advocate,* pp. 1A, 5A.

Scruton, R. (2012). *How to think seriously about the planet.* New York, NY: Oxford University Press.

Senate Historical Office. (n.d.). Albert Arnold Gore, Jr., 45th vice president: 1993–2001. In *Senate History.* Washington, DC: Author. Retrieved April 3, 2015, from http://www.senate.gov/artandhistory/history/resources/pdf/Gore,_Albert.pdf

Snyder, C. R., Train, T., Schroeder, L. L., Pulvers, K. M., Adams, V., & Lamb, L. (2000, Summer). Teaching the hope recipe: Setting goals, finding pathways to those goals, and getting motivated. *Reaching Today's Youth, 4*(4), 46–50.

Sosa, I. (2008, September 11). Cuba's Katrina. *The Washington Post*. Retrieved April 3, 2015, from http://www.washingtonpost.com

Walker, J., & Heffner, F. (2010, Summer). Resilience as a critical factor in the workplace. The *New Worker*.

Wallace-Hadrill, A. (2011). Pompeii: Portents of disaster. *BBC History*. Retrieved April 3, 2015, from http://www.bbc.co.uk

Winerman, L. (2014). Climate change communication heats up. *Monitor on Psychology*, 45(6), 30–35.

Wolman, B. (1989). *Dictionary of behavioral science* (2nd ed.). San Diego, CA: Academic Press.

Y2K: Social Implications. (1998, October). Panel including D. G. Nemeth, R. Landes (Boston, MA), P. Neumann, T. D. Oleson (Framingham, MA), & J. Feiler (Philmont, NY). Conducted by the Boston University Center for Millennial Studies, Boston, MA.

Zabecki, D. T. (2014). Blitzkrieg: World War II. In *World at war: Understanding conflict and society*. Retrieved March 21, 2014, from http://worldatwar.abc-clio.com/

Zolli, A. (2012, November 2). Learning to bounce back. *The New York Times*. Retrieved April 3, 2015, from http://www.nytimes.com

10

The Effects of Pollution and Population on the Environment

Martin Milton

This chapter briefly considers three concepts. The first is the phenomenon of pollution; the second is a reflection on the wider field of ecopsychology and how it might help us enhance our understandings of pollution; and finally, some thought is given to the notion of a psychotherapy-ecopsychology alliance and ways in which this may be useful—both in the consulting room and more widely.

POLLUTION

Pollution has become ubiquitous; it is all around us. We find it in our seas, and it is not just in relation to the Piper Alpha disaster, the *Exxon Valdez*, or other huge, headline-grabbing catastrophes, either. It seems to be that we use it as a limitless dumping ground for plastics, chemicals, and even ships' containers (Darraik, 2002). And then we suffer, as we have to swim in it, surf in it, and at times may be disgusted by the stink of it. It affects us individually, and it literally poisons and strangles many of the nonhuman creatures that exist in the world (Darraik, 2002).

We are experiencing enormous amounts of airborne pollution as well, and again, it appears that humanity assumes that our atmosphere has a limitless capacity to absorb our waste (Schwartz, 1993). It is not just the industrial catastrophes like Bhopal that are to blame, either; our cars, factories, and farms contribute daily. We inhale it daily, we choke on it, and, for an ever-increasing number of urbanites, we become asthmatic in it (Woodcock & Peat, 2007).

Even where significant local resources are available to cope with the effects of pollution, it remains a difficult phenomenon to contain. I work in one of London's beautiful Royal Parks, and despite all of the dedicated care the park gets, the lake still suffers to cope with the litter and other pollutants that get willfully thrown into this urban beauty spot. This is not unique, of course, as you see this in New York's Central Park, Lake Anosy in Central Antananarivo, and most other cities in the world.

In order to consider pollution as a phenomenon, it is helpful to consider our human psycho-geographical history.

HUMAN POPULATION

It is well known that we are in a massive period of human population growth. It is suggested that in 500 BC, there were only 100 million people (Diamond, 1992). This is a relatively small number, especially when we consider that this population was spaced out all over the globe, with most living in small groups. Because of this, most had small and localized environmental impacts. We are in a different period in time, though, and predictions suggest that there will be 8.5 *billion* people by 2025, and 9 billion by 2050 (United Nations, 1991; see also Chapter 1 in this volume [Nemeth & Hamilton, 2015]). This is an enormous number, and the *rate* of growth is also increasing. Therefore, the human population is no longer sparsely spread, but we live in an increasing number of densely compacted areas.

Another way of considering this is to look at more recent history. It is estimated that in 1955, 20% of the human population lived in cities, with the rest in more suburban, rural, and remote contexts (Lederbogen et al., 2011). This pattern has also changed, and it is estimated that by 2015, more than 50% of the population will be living in cities. This isn't just an issue for human aesthetics and our own well-being, either. Larger urban cities have enormous appetites for power and other natural resources and emit a great deal of pollution and other wastes. Urban dwellers carry an inordinately high carbon/environmental footprint (United Nations, 1991).

As well as the impact of our population growth on the planet, these differences have effects on human psychology, too. In small, remote communities, people tend to know others in their community, have contact with the soil, raise domestic animals, and are surrounded by trees, birds, and other animals. This sight and grasp of one's living community fits with our psychology (de Waal, 2006; Dunbar, 2003).

City living is different; we (literally) bump into thousands of strangers on our weekly commutes, we don't know any of these people, and we may go long periods of time without seeing trees, plants, or nonhuman animals. This requires a different, more guarded—and more stressful—style of engagement with our (primarily) human and technological environment (Lederbogen et al., 2011). The natural calming rhythms of nature are lost, as is our awareness of how to relieve stress. We rely on distraction, technology, and foods that rely on many more fats and sugars then our bodies need. De Waal (2006) suggests that this current disease and distress is related to our psychological evolution when he notes that "we are stuck with a human psychology shaped by millions of years of life in small communities so we need to structure the world in such a way that it is recognizable to this psychology" (p. 7).

BACK TO POLLUTION

How do we understand pollution? One view is that pollution is simply an inevitable side effect of an ever-increasing human population—and this is, of course, a topic that few people want to take on. Rather than honestly facing up to the issues that this rise has on us and on other species, it seems that our national (and global) discourse is to assume, argue, and chivvy ourselves on with a hope that our intellect will allow us to find a technological manner to sort out the mess without changing our appetites or practices.

There are other perspectives, too. Pollution may simply be a sign of apathy, or alternatively, it may be a bit like the mess that occurs in our homes when we are stressed and distressed, with little energy for self-care. In this way it may be useful to think of it as a collective symbol of increasing stress.

It is also important to note that pollution patterns vary in relation to economic power, and this leads us to questions as to power and willful neglect of the Other where the wealthy communities pass their pollution on to those less able to contest it—the "Not In My Back Yard" (NIMBY) phenomenon. This allows the powerful to continue to pollute without any actual lived experience of it. Here I am thinking of the West's demand for hardwoods. That means logging and burning happen half a world away; the West gets beautiful furniture, while the forested countries suffer from extended periods of air pollution (not to mention habitat destruction and species extinction).

Other ecopsychologists are suggesting that as well as these issues, pollution and other environmentally damaging behaviors are signs of psychological distress and despair, symbols of widespread individual and cultural depression, or of a collective PTSD. This brings us on to the work of ecopsychology.

ECOPSYCHOLOGY

As is evidenced by this collection, ecopsychology is an approach to theory and practice and is born out of a wide range of intellectual, theoretical, and philosophical fields, including deep ecology, feminism, and shamanism, on the one hand; and it has links with environmental psychology, conservation psychology, climate science, and analytical psychology on the other (Roszak, 1995). As readers will have seen in the earlier sections, ecopsychology focuses on the relationship between humanity, the environment, and nature. This is not undertaken in the way of much human-centered science, which tends to be unidirectional, simply looking at how factor X affects people. The ecopsychological stance is more holistic—including how we affect the world, how we are affected by it, and how there are loops of influence. So it has an interest in both the ecodynamics and eco-kinetics (see Chapter 1 in this volume [Nemeth & Hamilton, 2015]).

Amongst its areas of contribution, ecopsychology offers insights into the ways in which a disconnect from nature is bad for humanity, (Louv, 2006). This has been researched at cultural levels and also at the level of individual distress. In this body of work there are links to such psychological difficulties as eating problems, depression, grief and a sense of loss, and trauma (Adams, 2006; Corbett & Milton, 2011; Eko, 2012; Randall, 2009; Rust, 2005, 2008).

Ecopsychology also helps us consider the notion of healthy transformative relationships and highlights the psychological benefits experienced when we are more engaged with the natural world (Gatersleben, 2008; Louv, 2006; MacGregor, 2013).

PSYCHOTHERAPY

In the United Kingdom, psychotherapy is a distinct profession as well as one activity that psychologists undertake. In relation to environmental concerns, psychotherapy and psychology are professions with distinct and somewhat uncomfortable positions. On the one hand, they are highly attuned to the idio-syncrasies of the individual, while on the other hand, they have an oversight of large-scale human patterns and development. Neither perspective will suffice if one wants to understand or intervene with people and their socioculturally con-structed distress and ecologically damaging behaviors. So psychotherapists and psychologists are required to constantly look beyond the general by paying atten-tion to the meanings of our specific forms of distress and behavior.

Many models of practice have, at their core, a phenomenological and rela-tional stance. This helps us engage as fully as possible with our clients' communi-cations and together to generate understandings of what ails them. We do this with individuals, couples, families, and groups. This skill is valuable and allows us to potentially offer a useful contribution to the ecological domain.

However, psychotherapy and psychology—of all perspectives—often limit themselves to the human-human aspect of life and can be found guilty of over-looking our wider relational processes. Indeed, back in 1972, Searles noted that the professions relegated the world to being a mere backdrop. This is unfortu-nate, as this need not be the case; an alliance between ecopsychology and psychotherapeutic thinking and practice has a number of contributions to make to theory, practice, policy, and even leadership (Nemeth, 2014).

Firstly, this alliance helps enrich our psychological understandings—both in the consulting room and beyond. In terms of client work: "[I]n addition to the traditional question psychotherapists might ask clients at assessment, e.g. 'Tell me about your Mom and Dad' we might also ask 'Tell me about your relationship to the natural world.' It's not a decision of whether to ask about the familial or the ecological, both can be engaged with. At its basis, an ecopsychological awareness is simply an invitation to broaden our thinking" (Milton, 2010, p. 300). We might therefore think of this first contribution of an alliance being a broader awareness of relationships to the natural world that we can incorporate into all our work.

A second contribution might be that psychotherapists actually, physically, take their practice outside. This may simply be traditional therapy as is, but outside in nature to offer a more implicit engagement with nature and its benefits (Jordan, 2014).

Another contribution swings the balance a little more and is more modest about traditional psychotherapeutic theory and practice. It respects the powerful and unique interventions such as vision quests, horticultural therapy, and other nature-based interventions; where appropriate, it offers additional psychotherapeutic thinking (Wise, 2015).

Much of this may not tackle ecological issues such as pollution or climate change directly, but by simply attending to the same issues that traditional, indoor psychotherapy might offer, the place of nature allows people to benefit from nature and may also allow a more holistic experience with nature. This fosters a more engaged, caring, and conscious relationship with nature and the environment through an enriched ecological self (Higley, 2009; Jordan, 2012).

With greater insight into these areas, psychologists and psychotherapists may find that they are both more informed about the issues that we are facing—climate change, pollution, species extinction, habitat destruction, and the like—and more creative and assertive in their ability to contribute to the discussions that *have* to be multidisciplinary. These issues are too complex to be understood in isolation by any single profession, practice, or theoretical perspective. It is important that psychotherapists consider this as they have a unique contribution to make. If psychotherapists abstain from these discussions, if they do not voice the subjective, relational, and psychological aspects, who else will?

ACKNOWLEDGMENT

I am indebted to Dr. Markus Bidell, Regent's University Fulbright Scholar, for the title of this chapter.

REFERENCES

Adams, W. W. (2006). The Ivory-Billed Woodpecker, ecopsychology, and the crisis of extinction: On annihilating and nurturing other beings, relationships and ourselves. *The Humanistic Psychologist, 34*(2), 111–133.

Corbett, L., & Milton, M. (2011). Ecopsychology: A perspective on trauma. *European Journal of Ecopsychology, 2,* 28–48.

Darraik, J. G. B. (2002). The pollution of the marine environment by plastic debris: A review, *Marine Pollution Bulletin, 44*(9), 842–852.

de Waal, F. (2006). *Primates and philosophers: How morality evolved*. Princeton, NJ: Princeton University Press.

Diamond, J. (1992). *The rise and fall of the third chimpanzee: How our animal heritage affects the way we live*. London, UK: Vintage.

Dunbar, R. (2003). The social brain: Mind, language and society in evolutionary perspective. *Annual Review of Anthropology, 32,* 163–181.

Eko, M. (2012). *Depressed individuals' relationship with nature: An interpretative phenomenological analysis account* (Unpublished doctoral study). University of Surrey, Surrey, UK.

Gatersleben, B. (2008). Humans and nature: 10 useful findings from environmental psychology research. *Counselling Psychology Review, 23*(2): 24–34.

Higley, N. (2009). *Connectedness to nature explored: An IPA analysis of people's experiences of their ecological self* (Unpublished doctoral study). University of Surrey, Surrey, UK.

Jordan, M. (2012). Did Lacan go camping? Psychotherapy in search of an ecological self. In M. J. Rust and N. Totton (Eds.), *Vital signs: Psychological responses to the ecological crisis*. London, UK: Karnac.

Jordan, M. (2014). *Nature and therapy: Understanding counselling and psychotherapy in outdoor spaces*. Hove, UK: Routledge.

Lederbogen, F., Kirsch, P., Haddad, L., Streit, F., Tost, H., Schuch, P., . . . Meyer-Lindenberg, A. (2011). City living and urban upbringing affect neural social stress processing in humans, *Nature, 474*(7352): 498–501.

Louv, R. (2006). *Last child in the woods: Saving our children from nature deficit disorder*. Chapel Hill, NC: Algonquin Books.

MacGregor, C. (2013). *An existential formulation of transformative experiences in nature* (Unpublished DPsych thesis). New School of Psychotherapy and Counselling & Middlesex University, London.

Milton, M. (2010). Coming home to roost: Counselling psychology and the natural world. In M. Milton (Ed.), *Therapy and beyond: Counselling psychology contributions to therapeutic and social issues*. Chichester, UK: Wiley-Blackwell.

Nemeth, D. G. (2014, August 25–29). *The changing role of the psychotherapist during times of environmental trauma: From listener to leader*. Keynote paper given to the 7th World Congress for Psychotherapy, Durban, South Africa.

Nemeth, D. G., & Hamilton, R. B. (2015). Introduction. In D. G. Nemeth & R. B. Hamilton (Eds.), *Ecopsychology: Advances from the intersection of psychology and environmental protection*, Volume 1. Santa Barbara, CA: ABC-CLIO/Praeger.

Randall, R. (2009). Loss and climate change: The cost of parallel narratives. *Ecopsychology, 1*(3): 118–129. doi:10.1089/eco.20090034

Roszak, T. (1995). Where psyche meets Gaia. In T. Roszak, M. E. Gomes, & A. D. Kanner (Eds.), *Ecopsychology: Restoring the earth, healing the mind*. San Francisco, CA: Sierra Club Books.

Rust, M. J. (2005, October). Psychotherapy for a change: From inertia to inspiration for action. *Schumacher Lecture*.

Rust, M. J. (2008). Nature hunger: Eating problems and consuming the earth. *Counselling Psychology Review, 23*(2): 70–78.

Schwartz, J. (1993). Particulate air pollution and chronic respiratory disease, *Environmental Research*, 62(1), 7–13.

Searles, H. (1972). Unconscious processes in relation to the environmental crisis. *The Psychoanalytic Review*, 59(3), 361–374.

United Nations. (1991). *Consequences of rapid population growth in developing countries*. New York, NY: Taylor and Francis.

Wise, J. (2015). *Digging for victory: Horticultural therapy with veterans for post-traumatic growth*. London, UK: Karnac Books.

Woodcock, A. J., & Peat, J. K. (2007) *Evidence for the increase in asthma worldwide*, Ciba Foundation Symposium 206: The rising trends in asthma. Retrieved April 25, 2014, from http://onlinelibrary.wiley.com/doi/10.1002/9780470515334.ch8/summary. doi:10.1002/9780470515334.ch8

11

Using Psychology to Advance Environmental Conservation

Florian G. Kaiser

After more than four decades of psychological research on sustainability, environmental protection, and climate-change mitigation and adaptation, there are many lessons that have already been learned. One major lesson is that changing behavior by promoting desirable behavior, and discouraging undesirable behavior, is key. Another lesson is that psychology must work with other disciplines to shape the context of behavior to expand returns in terms of reduced carbon-dioxide emissions, energy savings, and other actual environmental gains (Stern, 2000, 2011). However, even though we have learned quite a bit about the psychological mechanisms pertinent in environmental conservation (Swim et al., 2010), many challenges still remain.

Collections of scholarly articles on the psychological aspects of environmental conservation have been published (Vlek & Steg, 2007; Zelezny & Schultz, 2000). These collections focus on the psychological mechanisms behind—and thus, the constituents of—ecological behavior, or on searches for possible and effective psychological behavior-change measures. This chapter summarizes four works of experts in the field of environmental psychology that focus on three cutting-edge decisions that hold the potential to help environmental psychological science to advance as a more cumulative enterprise: (1) the choice of the ultimate behavioral target; (2) the selection of behavior change measures, and (3) the development of strategies so that sound evidence from environmental psychological science will contribute to effectively solving environmental-conservation-related problems.

The perspectives reported in this chapter aim to answer the following questions: (1) What is the behavioral target or objective when dealing with environmental conservation-related issues? (2) Based on what rationale do we select behavior change measures when dealing with real but unique cases? And (3) what can be done to foster the use of scientifically generated behavior change strategies in a society? The first two cutting-edge bodies of work I describe in this chapter, namely by Thøgersen (2014) and by Otto, Kaiser, and Arnold (2014), address distinct behavioral targets. The third, by Schultz (2014), provides guidance about how to select behavior change measures. The fourth area of work, by Ernst and Wenzel (2014), asks what environmental psychology can do to better foster its knowledge in societies at large. The endeavors of these experts' work summarized below focus on psychology's contributions to environmental conservation, and also on its challenges—the things we should actually know more about.

The first two works recognize people's lifestyles as the target for behavior change efforts in environmental conservation research. Whereas the focus of Thøgersen (2014) is on the ecologically harmful—i.e., the unsustainable consumption patterns of individuals and households—Otto et al. (2014) focus on people's ecological lifestyle, what they do for environmental conservation in general. Based on a conceptual notion proposed by Kaiser, Byrka, and Hartig (2010), Otto et al. argue that people's generic motivation to protect the environment is reflected in their lifestyles—in all the behaviors a person engages in, day in and day out.

CUTTING-EDGE WORK #1: ON THE BASIC CAUSES OF UNSUSTAINABLE CONSUMPTION OF INDIVIDUALS

The first cutting-edge work I report on is by John Thøgersen, professor of economic psychology, coordinator of the Marketing and Sustainability Research Group at Aarhus University in Denmark, and chairman of the steering committee of the global Virtual Community on Sustainability and Consumption. Thøgersen (2014) specifically recognizes consumption patterns—the obviously unsustainable lifestyles of individuals and households—as the behavioral counterpart of the obvious and harmful overall environmental impact of people. The performances that manifest in this consumption pattern of individuals are necessarily quite numerous and rather heterogeneous. As a consequence, and in convergence with other scholars (Stern, 2011), Thøgersen argues that behavioral research should focus primarily on individuals' activities that have extensive negative environmental impacts. Like the behaviors that reflect people's unsustainable lifestyles, the reported driving forces behind them are rather plentiful. Thøgersen provides a novel grouping and structure of what he finds to be the most important drivers of individuals' unsustainable performances. They consist of human needs and values, habits and norms, and personal limitations and structural circumstances. However, as the environmentally harmful side-effects of such behavior are mostly unintended, Thøgersen finds that structural changes (e.g., in the socio-technical context, in the availability of products, and in the consumption norms) rather than psychological changes (based on informational and on educational measures) are by and large more effective when societies wish to transform unsustainable courses of action into more sustainable ones.

CUTTING-EDGE WORK #2: ON THE PSYCHOLOGICAL ORIGINS OF REBOUND AND OF INDIVIDUAL SUSTAINABILITY

The second area of work that I consider cutting edge addresses the target for behavior change efforts in environmental conservation research. In this work, Siegmar Otto, Oliver Arnold, and I—colleagues at the Department of Personality and Social Psychology at Otto-von-Guericke University in Germany—analyzed World Bank data of the per capita energy consumption of certain selected societies. Reporting on this research, Otto et al. (2014) conclude that the prime climate change-mitigating strategy—which predominantly entails disseminating more efficient technologies (e.g., cars, light bulbs, and refrigerators)—has so far not once resulted in a recognizable drop in the per capita energy consumption of societies. The politically instigated efficiency gains seem either to have failed to materialize or to have been completely offset by an increase in the energy demands of individuals. Looking at the psychological origins of this rebound phenomenon, the researchers explain why they believe that promoting individual ecological behaviors that have the most impact in terms of energy efficiency by means of extrinsic, monetary, or social enticements must ultimately fail to overcome rebound. Alternatively, the researchers argue, there is a need to promote people's propensity to forgo commodities, convenience, and other personal benefits and, thus, to encourage people to adopt generally more frugal ways of life. People can do so, for instance, by taking the stairs instead of elevators, by refraining from car use as much as possible, and by reusing instead of replacing things. The researchers identify individual behavior that holds comparatively more costs than benefits than a behavioral alternative as "irrational," and the appropriateness of this attribute might not be readily apparent. I would therefore like to take a moment to clarify the authors' chosen descriptor term (of "irrational behavior").

According to Otto et al. (2014), a behavior is irrational only in relative terms, and for individual actors only. It shows in a person's inclination to forgo benefits by choosing the less beneficial of two behavioral alternatives. From a societal point of view and for humankind in the long term, such "irrational" behaviors of individuals can nevertheless be rational. In other words, ecological behavior is neither unreasonable nor insensible—or irrational in an absolute sense. Finally, the researchers argue that only when people adopt lifestyles that are much more irrational on an individual level as outlined above and, thus, are considerably more intrinsically motivated to act ecologically in general and to allow their respective societies to become much more supportive of the ecological behavioral alternatives of individuals, can rebound eventually be avoided, thus allowing the overall energy consumption of societies to begin to drop.

A Comparison of the Contributions of Thøgersen and of Otto et al.

Despite a similar focus on people's lifestyles and their overall consumption patterns of the two suggestions outlined by Thøgersen and of Otto et al., the differences in their implications for behavior change are striking. Otto et al.'s suggestion leads to using people's generic motivation to protect the environment, and with that identifies an entire behavioral class (i.e., conservation-relevant ecological behaviors) as the ultimate target in environmental psychology. In contrast, Thøgersen's suggestion leads to promoting the more ecological alternative—based on what is generally known about driving forces and psychological and structural barriers of unsustainable behavior (see also Gifford, 2011)—for each single environmentally harmful behavior separately. Thus, Otto et al. recognize human motivation and, thus, psychology to be central; whereas Thøgersen identifies predominantly nonpsychological factors as key to more sustainable lifestyles of individuals.

CUTTING-EDGE WORK #3: A GUIDE ON HOW TO CHOOSE BEHAVIOR CHANGE MEASURES

Although behavior change measures have to be implemented, there is—apart from testing their effectiveness (Osbaldiston & Schott, 2012)—surprisingly little guidance in environmental psychology about how to implement behavior-change measures: what measures, under what boundary conditions, with what types of behavior, and with what persons. Wesley Schultz (2014) from the Department of Psychology at the California State University, San Marcos, provides such implementation rules with regard to what measures work with what behavior, for whom, and under what circumstances. Derived from Community-Based Social Marketing (CBSM; see McKenzie-Mohr, Lee, Schultz, & Kotler, 2012), Schultz brings forth a theoretical framework consisting of two factors, which he argues are critical when making decisions about appropriate behavior change measures: (1) a person's level of motivation (apparent in the accumulated benefits) and (2) the difficulty level of behavior (apparent in its barriers). In other words, he suggests that the decision about the right behavior change measure is a function of people's level of motivation and the difficulty of the behavior to be promoted. For each of four permutations of two motivation levels (high/low) and two difficulty levels (high/low), the author provides prototypical examples of real interventions as evidence for the proposed implementation rules.

CUTTING-EDGE WORK #4: FOSTERING ENVIRONMENTAL PSYCHOLOGICALLY GENERATED BEHAVIOR CHANGE KNOWLEDGE IN SOCIETY

The fourth cutting-edge work is by Andreas Ernst and Urs Wenzel from the Center for Environmental Systems Research at the University of Kassel in Germany. Ernst and Wenzel (2014) explore the barriers that prevent environmental psychological knowledge from becoming effective at solving environmental conservation-related problems. Hence, they ask what we in environmental psychology can do better, and additionally, what we can do to better promote our scientifically generated knowledge. They argue that, in general, four goals must be met: (1) proliferating dependable behavior change knowledge, i.e., doing what an empirical science is supposed to do; (2) developing behavior change strategies, by combining (environmental) psychological know-how with knowledge from inter- and transdisciplinary sources, that in turn are meant to be superior when tackling real-world challenges, such as climate-change mitigation; (3) spreading the word in society at large about the new effective behavior change strategies and influencing the political agenda so that the real-world problem in question receives a higher priority; and (4) converting effective behavior change strategies into governance, i.e., implementing fully functional policy instruments. Whereas the first two tasks reside in the scientific domain, as they deal with the creation of knowledge, the last two tasks deal with what one could call dissemination as they are about raising awareness of the problem and fostering the implementation of scientifically generated strategies in societies.

CONCLUSION

These four contributions provide unique and remarkable insights to the field of environmental psychology. This optimism is shared by Tommy Gärling, professor emeritus of psychology in the School of Business, Economics and Law at the University of Gothenburg in Sweden, and one of the most distinguished scholars in environmental psychology of our time, who similarly appreciates these contributions to the field. He (Gärling, 2014) notes that the focus of contemporary environmental psychology has moved to changing people and their behavior to preserve the human environment rather than changing the environment in which people act. Changing people's environmentally harmful behavior is, however, only justified if such behavior alterations do not offset the conservation goals as rebound effects or harm people in other ways.

In summary, surely, these perspectives have the potential to advance research about environmental conservation in new directions and into yet unmapped territory.

ACKNOWLEDGMENT

This chapter was originally an editorial for a Special Section on Environmental Conservation published in the *European Psychologist* journal. Several edits have been made to accommodate a chapter in the current volume. Reprinted with permission from: Kaiser, F. G. (2014). Using Cutting-Edge Psychology to Advance Environmental Conservation. *European Psychologist* 2014; Vol. 19(2): 81–83. doi:10.1027/1016-9040/a000180 © 2014 Hogrefe Publishing (www. hogrefe.com). All rights reserved.

REFERENCES

Ernst, A., & Wenzel, U. (2014). Bringing environmental psychology into action: Four steps from science to policy. *European Psychologist, 19*, 118–126. doi:10.1027/1016-9040/a000174

Gärling, T. (2014). Past and present environmental psychology. *European Psychologist, 19*, 127–131. doi:10.1027/1016-9040/a000184

Gifford, R. (2011). The dragons of inaction: Psychological barriers that limit climate change mitigation and adaptation. *American Psychologist, 66*, 290–302.

Kaiser, F. G., Byrka, K., & Hartig, T. (2010). Reviving Campbell's paradigm for attitude research. *Personality and Social Psychology Review, 14*, 351–367.

McKenzie-Mohr, D., Lee, N. R., Schultz, P. W., & Kotler, P. (2012). *Social marketing to protect the environment: What works.* Thousand Oaks, CA: Sage.

Osbaldiston, R., & Schott, J. P. (2012). Environmental sustainability and behavioral science: Meta-analysis of pro-environmental behavior experiments. *Environment and Behavior, 44*, 257–299.

Otto, S., Kaiser, F. G., & Arnold, O. (2014). The critical challenge of climate change for psychology: Preventing rebound and promoting more individual irrationality. *European Psychologist, 19*, 96–109. doi:10.1027/1016-9040/a000182

Schultz, P. W. (2014). Strategies for promoting pro-environmental behavior: Lots of tools but few instructions. *European Psychologist, 19*, 107–117. doi:10.1027/1016-9040/a000163

Stern, P. C. (2000). Psychology and the science of human-environment interactions. *American Psychologist, 55*, 523–530.

Stern, P. C. (2011). Contributions of psychology to limiting climate change. *American Psychologist, 66*, 303–314.

Swim, J. K., Stern, P. C., Doherty, T. J., Clayton, S., Reser, J. P., Weber, E. U., & Howard, G. S. (Eds.). (2010). Psychology and global climate change [Special issue]. *American Psychologist, 66*(4).

Thøgersen, J. (2014). Unsustainable consumption: Basic causes and implications for policy. *European Psychologist, 19*, 84–95. doi:10.1027/1016-9040/a000176

Vlek, C., & Steg, L. (Eds.). (2007). Human behavior and environmental sustainability [Special issue]. *Journal of Social Issues, 63*(1).

Zelezny, L. C., & Schultz, P. W. (Eds.). (2000). Promoting environmentalism [Special issue]. *Journal of Social Issues, 56*(3).

12

Managing the Future: Reconciling Differences and Perceiving Truth

Robert B. Hamilton

Our universe began with a bang about 13.8 billion years ago (Hazen, 2012, chap. 1) that occurred at a single point; it has been expanding and changing ever since. The composition of the universe as we now know it is explained well by Hazen (2012) and others.

FORMATION AND EVOLUTION OF EARTH

Our solar system, with the sun as a central star surrounded by Earth and the other planets, was formed about 4.5 billion years ago and has been changing ever since. It is the source of almost all of our available energy and physical needs.

Earth formed from material associated with the evolution of our sun. It has slowly evolved, from a formless, lifeless concentration of space debris through a number of steps that led to the eventual differentiation into land, water, and air inhabited by a diversity of highly evolved plants and animals (BBC, n.d.; Hazen, 2012).

Evolution of Life

Acellular or unicellular life evolved from nonliving precursors about 2 billion years ago; multicellular forms did not appear until about 1 billion years later. A rapid expansion and diversification of living forms began about 550 million years ago. Some began to resemble forms we now know. Many forms evolved and became extinct as is shown in the fossil record (see "History of Life on Earth," n.d.) as physical environments have been slowly changing. At each stage, extant forms were often replaced by newer ones that had a competitive advantage in the constantly changing environments. Mammals did not appear until about 200 million years ago, and humans about 200,000 years ago.

Darwin and Evolution

Because the physical environment was constantly changing, living forms had to change, too, or be replaced by more competitive ones. The history of the earth is characterized by change facilitated through energy use. Once life evolved, the living forms contributed to change themselves by acting on the environment to acquire their energy and material needs and produce waste. Reproduction is an important characteristic of life because the mortality of the living needs to be replaced by the birth of their offspring. Exact duplication during reproduction produces identical offspring and no variation. If the environment changes and organisms do not, survival decreases, and the species is on the way to extinction. This is especially true where various forms are competing for the same resources, even partially.

Survival of a species in a changing environment thus is facilitated by a species changing in compatible ways to continually succeed in the competition for resources and survival. Changes between generations were made possible by the development of sexual reproduction, where progeny receive genetic information from nonidentical parents. The resulting progeny are very similar to the parents, but not identical. Furthermore, each one might be slightly different. As time passed and environments changed, some of the progeny were more suited for them than others. Their chances for survival as individuals and species increased, or at least did not decrease. The terms "survival of the fittest" and "natural selection" are often used to explain this process as described by Darwin (1859).

When I attended graduate school in the 1960s, we knew that sexual reproduction produced variation in offspring but not how. Through the work of Gregor Mendel, who discovered single-character inheritance, and others (Bowler, 1989), we could predict the characteristics of many traits of offspring if we knew the characteristics in their parents. Although Mendel's results were limited, they showed that characteristics of both parents were involved and thus foreshadowed the discovery of the importance of double-stranded DNA (deoxyribonucleic acid) in our inheritance, where we inherit DNA strands from the nucleus or mitochondria of reproductive cells of each parent (Watson, 1980) and mitochondria from the mother (Sykes, 2003).

The amount that we now know about the role of DNA in cellular metabolism and inheritance is an indication of how rapidly our knowledge of the world is changing. We now can map the DNA of individuals precisely, and DNA is used extensively in criminal investigations and trials (DNA Forensics, n.d.) to establish the presence of a suspect's DNA. We can insert DNA fragments (genes) that code for proteins with desired characteristics from one organism into the chromosomes of another to produce GMO (Genetically Modified Organisms) with desired traits. This is controversial to some, although we have been genetically modifying organisms by selective breeding for years without protest. We have cloned animals, and could probably clone ourselves (American Medical Association, n. d.)—and might, if that were to be considered ethical.

Energy Flow in Natural Systems

All life requires energy. In living systems, most energy comes from the sun directly or indirectly. Green plants, with the pigment chlorophyll, are able to convert solar energy into energy-rich compounds that power various metabolic pathways and enable life through the activities of living cells.

The quantity of available solar energy varies geographically. It varies, by season, and by time of day as well as cloud cover. Even the energy output from the sun is not a constant and is affected by conditions on the sun. There is a basic 11-year cycle in output caused by sunspots. Other variations that affect output are not as well understood (Hathaway, 2010). The effect of solar output on weather and tree growth in some regions is so direct that it has been used extensively to determine precise age of archeological objects made of wood (Nash, 1999) because it indirectly affects tree-ring size.

There is competition among plants for solar energy, and many species have growth patterns to maximize the amount of sun hitting their leaves, where photosynthesis usually occurs. Some plants are specialized for lower light intensities and are found in the shade in plant communities. Vegetation is often denser at edges because more light is available there. Openings in forests are also greener because of increased light availability. Stratified habitats, with vegetation in separate strata, are more productive and diverse than nonstratified ones. Because plants provide energy, dense habitats are more productive than less dense ones.

Animals cannot produce their energy directly from the sun and must obtain it indirectly by eating plants or their parts (herbivores), or even more indirectly by eating other animals (carnivores), or both (omnivores). Other species acquire their energy by consuming dead plants or animals or their parts. Because only plants can produce energy, they are the basis of food chains and food webs.

Energy is lost with each transfer in a food chain or food web. That is why there is less energy in every step as energy passes down a food chain or food web. Because of efficiency considerations, there cannot be many steps in these food chains or webs, because available energy is insufficient to support many links. The last link in a food chain is often called the "top carnivore," or sometimes a "keystone predator," because it greatly influences the availability and abundance of other large animals. These are often large, ferocious animal species. Colinvaux (1978) explains this well in his book, *Why Big Fierce Animals Are Rare: An Ecologist's Perspective*.

The amount of energy produced (output) is the energy available times the efficiency, which is usually about 10%. That amount is reduced with every link in the food chain. The most energy is available to the first stage (primary production), and some is lost with each transformation. We could easily feed more vegetarians than meat eaters because there is more energy available at the producer level than the other ones.

Vegetation often grows in strata, with the amount of green vegetation differing in each stratum. Grassland can be considered to have one stratum, while a temperate forest often has three: (1) ground cover, (2) midstory, and (3) canopy. A tropical rainforest has even more because of the extensive presence of vines and other vegetation that occupies intervening areas. More stratified systems utilize energy more efficiently and thus often contain more biomass. Stratification allows more solar energy to be captured as individual species become specialized to capture energy in unique places and in unique ways.

Species sometimes have positive interaction with other residents (symbiosis, mutualism, cooperation, or proto-cooperation) to increase their survival (Martin & Schwab, 2012). It takes a long evolutionary time for these relationships to evolve; when present, they increase diversity and usually make a system more stable.

MacArthur and MacArthur (1961) discovered that bird species diversity (BSD) is related to foliage height diversity (FHD). When FHD is decreased, so is the diversity of birds. They found that in temperate forests, three strata were sufficient to describe BSD. We are supporting increased numbers of humans by harvesting forests with high FHD (measure of vegetation quantity in vertical strata) and replacing them with row-crop agriculture, which usually only has one strata and low FHD. The crops are also treated with pesticides, which reduces food for birds, and agricultural fields are very large with relatively little edge to attract birds. BSD is very low there. Even when we manage forests for wood production, we usually manage it to focus growth into one generation of trees, all of the same ages and thus with reduced FHD. Thus, we are reducing bird species diversity and endangering many species, at least locally. Birds are the group most studied, but from energy considerations alone, the same relationship should exist with all other groups. This relationship with stratification is probably a primary reason for the extraordinary diversity of tropical forests, with vegetation almost continuous from the roots through the canopy. Unfortunately, tropical rain forests are rapidly being harvested and replaced by much simpler systems. Even when forests are managed for timber, they are harvested as soon as tree growth slows and bird and other group diversity is not yet maximized.

Environments and Habitats

The term "environment" refers to the conditions where organisms exist. It describes the conditions that are present and relevant to organisms. We evolved in distinct environments; these are called "habitats" for each particular group of potentially interbreeding organisms that we call "species." A habitat is the precise description of where a species lives. It provides resources and conditions necessary for a species' survival. Our survival, historically and currently, depends on them. The proper physical environment is also essential for survival.

We are all familiar with the earth as it is now, and most of us have seen it change in noticeable ways during our lifetimes. To me, the changes seem to be occurring more quickly now than when I was younger. Because of natural laws, change is inevitable, but many of the changes that are occurring now are human-caused and are perceived to profit those making the changes and not all others. Many changes have unintended consequences that differ from the original goal and may even be inconsistent with the planned change's intent. We must understand as well as possible the relationships among all environmental components to make responsible modifications without unintended consequences. We should especially focus on the effects of the modifications at other locations (spatial considerations) and at later times (temporal considerations).

Habitat Differences

Plants and animals are not distributed randomly in the biosphere. They appear in associations familiar to us all: deserts, forests, grasslands, prairie, tundra, ponds, streams, etc. These groupings are caused by aggregations of species with similar habitat requirements, and thus similar specializations for environmental conditions associated with that habitat (water shortage in a desert, for example.) Several habitat classifications have been developed (Biomes of the World, n.d.).

Places vary by many characteristics that are related to their location. Energy availability is related to the solar radiation received, which is related to a location's latitude and the season. Water availability is often critical; we name some habitats by referencing water or lack of it: dessert, tropical rain forest, and cloud forest are examples. Water availability is influenced by climate, which is influenced by geographical features and their relationships to each other.

The plants and animals living in a habitat are specialized for it. In dry climates, plants are specialized to retain moistures; cactuses, euphorbs, and other succulents are typical examples. (They also are a good example of convergent evolution, where unrelated groups develop similar specializations to cope with similar environmental problems—in this case, low water availability.) In general, dessert plants require little water; however, tundra has little rainfall, too, but evaporation is low there because of its latitude, and tundra is wet. Many of its species are migratory or hibernate because winter conditions provide little protection and daylight. Vegetation is a major feature of a habitat because plants are the basis of food chains and provide the energy needed for the environment's other living components. As water availability increases, habitats change from desserts to chaparral and scrub, then to savannahs and grasslands. Forests occur in wetter areas, but they too range from dry ones to cloud forests or rain forests that may be tropical or temperate. Swamps and bottomland hardwood forests are wet, as are marshes. Marshes are differentiated by salinity. Each habitat has its own distinctive flora and fauna, which is influenced greatly by the vegetation, the base of the food chain, and past evolutionary history. Climate conditions and energy availability may be similar in different parts of the world, and their flora and fauna may have similar characteristics (convergent evolution). The grasslands of America had immense herds of buffalo, while similar habitats in Africa have enormous herds of large herbivores, too; but they are more diverse because of the differences in evolutionary history.

Water is basically fresh when it falls as rain. It picks up nutrients as it moves through our environments and eventually evaporates and falls again. This movement is described as a hydrological cycle (Hubbart, 2010) and is essential to life on earth. Water eventually flows to our oceans, which are salty. Differences in saltiness are called salinity and are very important to living things and profoundly affect habitats (wiseGEEK, n.d.).

Succession

The environments in most places have been rather stable and persistent (e.g., desserts, tundra, tropical forest, grasslands, ocean surface), as long as there have been no dramatic climatic changes or disturbances. These stable habitats are called climax and usually contain the maximum biomass and biodiversity for particular conditions. If a habitat, a forest for example, is clear cut or otherwise destroyed, bare ground or other nonforest habitat is left. It will take years for the forest to return to climax, even if it is not cut again. This pattern of replacement is called succession. In succession, the vegetation will slowly change through a series of steps until climax is reached. This is true of all habitats, but the details differ by habitat. Climax characteristics will be determined by the local conditions, which are static or only change very slowly; the exact species affected will be determined by the preexisting ones. Slight differences in slope or soil or other conditions affect species composition of climax slightly. If a forest is cut, it may take 100 years or more to return to a forest essentially the same as the original (the climax). A highly structured forest like a rain forest or a previously unharvested virgin forest may take much longer. The succession stages that are passed through are predictable and ephemeral in any habitat type. Connell and Slatyer (1977) summarized several theories about succession and factors affecting it.

Unfortunately, most forests that are cut or otherwise destroyed will not return to the climax stage. The stage they reach is determined by when the next disruption occurs. Forests are managed by applying specific disruptions like fire, thinning, or harvest (complete or partial) at specific times. Pine is a successional stage in many southern U.S. forests. Pines are fast growing and occur naturally (they can be planted or encouraged by the tree-harvest method used to harvest the original forest). Even-aged pine forests can be attained by identical starting times and discouraging hardwood competition by fire as the forest is progressing toward its original mixed composition climax. The managed pine forest is a sub-climax and would usually be replaced by hardwoods without natural or management intervention.

Some removed forests may not return to forest at all; the land may be used for agriculture or grazing or other purposes instead. We need to provide resources for a still-growing human population, and a climax forest cannot produce nearly the quantity of resources on a continuous basis for humans as modern agriculture can. It can produce a one-time harvest of timber that cannot be replicated for many years. The diversity lost by clearing a forest may never be replaced, even if a forest is eventually regrown. Undisturbed climax forests and other habitats can support small tribes of native humans, but the density and absolute numbers of individuals are very low. In rain forests, and even in virgin forests elsewhere, the climax forest is the most-diverse stage and is relatively stable: other climax habitats are stable also. The diversity of birds and other fauna is highest at climax (Hamilton, Barrow, & Ouchley, 2005) and perhaps will never be achieved again until climax can be attained. Even then, potential inhabitants will no longer be available to colonize the canopy as we manage the land to maximize tree growth rates for profitable harvest or use the land for agriculture. I have studied birds in old-growth hardwood forests that were somewhat similar to virgin forests, but the largest trees had not grown back yet and the forest was now being managed to remove selected trees once they were large and their growth had slowed. Much of the forest had been entirely cut and replaced with fields used for agriculture, and the landscape is different than the original one. Areas still in forest were being actively managed. Much of the original cutting was subsidized by federal grants to promote agriculture.

These are the kind of changes that we are making to support our growing population and economy. In one place where I have done research, many of the local people were hired for the clearing of areas in the vast forest, but regretted it later. Some, when reminiscing about the former forests, actually cried in regret (personal observation).

As succession in previously harvested areas occurs, biomass is created and stored in the growing trees (standing crop). Carbon is sequestered and removed from the atmosphere in the process. Unfortunately, the trees and other biomass eventually stop growing and they no longer sequester. So sequestering carbon in a growing forest is only effective for the growth of one tree generation. To continue the process, the trees must be removed and new ones planted. Using the removed trees will probably release their carbon dioxide eventually. Of course, new forested habitats can be produced for a time; if they are properly located, they can help achieve conservation objectives of increasing block size, creating corridors, or providing specific habitats that had been previously lost.

Climax habitats are more stable than the ephemeral successional stages that ultimately produce them. Many occupants are adapted to them and dependent on them. When they are harvested, these specialized species lose their habitat and are often not flexible enough to use other habitats or are not competitive enough to survive in them for long. They tend to be somewhat sedentary and not able to find similar habitat to what was lost. Climax habitats often become endangered and are difficult to manage because of the time required to regenerate them. Meanwhile, human numbers are still increasing as are demands for energy and other resources.

Habitats of many species are eliminated when the old growth is harvested and the constituent species become rare or extinct. Some species succeed by moving from one place with suitable habitat patches to another. Their habitats are primarily early-successional stages that are eventually replaced by old growth with its more-competitive inhabitants. They disperse then to other disturbed habitats like edges and tree-fall gaps. Many of these early-successional species' existence are not threatened by environmental changes and their habitats are often created by them; they are benefiting from them because edges are increasing and block sizes are decreasing. The residents of the old-growth and other climax habitats are the ones in trouble. This trend of threatened climax species is occurring throughout the biosphere at all levels.

All habitats are affected by human actions; species are extinct or threatened in many of them. Reports on their status and means of detecting it are readily available on the Internet from many sources. State of the Birds (2014) provides a good overview.

Grassland habitats in the United States have been mostly converted to agriculture and some species have become extinct, endangered, or threatened in them. As I am writing this, there are many articles in the popular press concerning the status of the Greater Prairie Chicken (*Tympanuchus_cupido*) and the Lesser Prairie Chicken (*Tympanuchus pallidicinctus*) that are becoming more endangered because of habitat loss. To me, grassland and cropland are superficially similar, but differ in their seasonality and disturbance. Their landscapes are not greatly different. There are many features of habitats that affect survival.

Ecosystem Concept

The ecosystem concept is a holistic way to evaluate habitats and environments. It can be applied anywhere, and can be simple or complex. In essence, the system to be studied is treated as if it were isolated; it is put in a box, so to speak, and studied as an isolated unit. To determine what is in the box, the inputs to the box and the outputs from the box must be known. This works best when the inputs and outputs can be accurately determined. A "balanced aquarium" is a useful example because the inputs and outputs can be accurately determined. If properly done, an aquarium can persist indefinitely as long as a source of energy is provided. Energy input is necessary because living things require energy, and some energy is lost continuously when it is used in all of the reactions within the box. In a balanced aquarium, sunlight can be the source of energy. As long as there are photosynthesizing organisms present that can be the basis of food chains, energy will be available to the components of the system. Energy and nutrients flow throughout the system to provide the required resources of the components of the system. The plants produce energy that is the basis of the food web in the aquarium. Particular species are not required. Nutrients are used in the food web and eventually recycled by decomposers in the aquarium. The relationships within the isolated area can be evaluated by tracing flows within the system. Energy is often what is evaluated because it is fundamental, but any nutrient or item of interest like nitrogen, the essential element in proteins, can be examined. Inputs and outputs of the system must be analyzed, too, in order to understand how the complete system works. What is in the box at any time is equal to what was in the box at a previous time plus what has entered minus what has left. For a system to remain stable, what leaves it must be replaced—nutrients, for example.

Any area can be analyzed by the ecosystem approach. The area of concern is conceptually isolated (put in a box). Inputs and outputs must be evaluated, so this approach works best in isolated areas where inputs and outputs can be evaluated relatively easily. It is easier to evaluate inputs and outputs of an island than a similarly sized portion of a larger area.

This concept is useful in understanding the input needs for agriculture, aquaculture, and other systems that are periodically harvested.

Using the ecosystem approach is useful for studying the earth's biosphere. If we consider it a system, we must account for the system inputs and outputs. Solar energy is the most important input and we can focus on the factors that affect the transfer of net solar energy to the biosphere; some solar energy is reflected back into space. Greenhouse gases affect this flow and thus could affect our temperature. All relevant inputs should be examined to understand the ecosystem. In theory, all factors that are measured should explain the flow. If not, other factors are important. This should ensure that the evaluation is holistic and no factor is overlooked. We cannot affect the solar output, but factors affecting the input or output of solar energy on earth and how they affect us are important and must be evaluated. It is thus important in understanding climate change. Other outside factors like meteors or solar flares are occasionally important. Meteors can have catastrophic effects (PBS, n.d.). Solar flares can interfere with electronic devices and thus have devastating effects on systems that are regulated or controlled electronically. This was not relevant, until the modern electronic age.

What is happening in the box can be evaluated. If particular geographic areas are studied (put in a box), inputs and outputs must be evaluated and understood in order to understand the entire ecosystem.

Limiting Factors

Each species requires a variety of resources for optimal growth and survival. Each habitat has a combination of resources available, but their distribution and abundance may change in time and space. When a particular required resource becomes scarce or difficult to obtain, species survival may be impacted. This has been called Liebig's Law of the Minimum and means that a needed resource in the shortest supply will limit growth. This law was first applied to plant growth but applies to animal growth as well. Thus, populations of animals and plants will be limited by the resource(s) in the shortest supply. Because all species differ in their resource requirements and means to acquire them, environments have specific resources that affect survival of constituent species unequally.

Nutrients

Animals and plants must obtain all of the nutrients they require in their habitats. Plants require sunlight, carbon dioxide, and water for photosynthesis and other minerals for their metabolism. Both plants and animals require high-energy carbon molecules and oxygen and various other elements for their metabolism and survival. Green plants use photosynthesis to synthesize the high-energy compounds; animals get them from consuming plants, directly or indirectly. Specific minerals and other needs may be absent or rare. These requirements become parts of cells, tissues, and organs and are essential for cellular metabolism. They are recycled through ecosystems, but they are removed when biomass is removed from the system and must be replaced to maintain production if the mineral is a limiting factor.

Many of the nutrients for terrestrial animals are available in the soil and are harvested by plants and then cycled through the system (soil to plants to animals to decomposers, and back to the soil). Water is often scarce on land, so we irrigate. This problem is acute in many areas with reduced rainfall. Oxygen can be scarce or almost absent in water, and aeration is often used in managed aquaculture situations like catfish farming. Nutrients in water can cause oxygen depletion and result in fish kills and dead zones. The molecules required for photosynthesis are readily available, as is sunlight in most places. Sunlight is captured by leaves, and many plants have specializations to maximize sunlight exposure to them. Soils vary greatly in the availability of nitrogen, potassium, and phosphorous, as well as other nutrients they need in less abundance. If quantities of any of these are lower than optimal, productivity can be decreased. Nitrogen, essential in proteins, is often the most critical mineral (Lamb, Fernandez, & Kaiser, 2014); its availability can be improved by cultural practices like rotating crops and planting legumes. Often we use fertilizer, both chemical and organic, to improve the availability of essential nutrients. Many soils that were regularly fertilized by periodic flooding of nutrient-laden water are now deprived of this resource by levees; they have more predictable growing seasons but need the use of artificial fertilizers to produce a bountiful crop. Managing the fertilizers to keep excess from draining back into the water and overfertilizing downstream areas has become a problem and results in problems like dead zones where the fertilized waters concentrate (Achenbach, 2008).

In aquatic habitats, the necessary nutrients are dissolved in the water and in the organisms present. They are recycled in the same way as on land. Availability of particular nutrients is affected by acidity, as they are on land.

Resource Location

Resources are not evenly distributed throughout the environment like they often are when we manage them. They can be clumped together so that finding the clump makes it easy to find all of the individuals in the clump. This situation makes it easy to locate resources once a clump is found, but may make the clump more difficult to find since they are farther apart. Pests can decimate a clump rather easily once it is found. Often managed crops and trees are more susceptible when they are grown together for management convenience and thus attract more pests. This can be devastating without suitable pest management. Resources can be found regularly distributed as they are with many crops. Some resources can be randomly distributed and difficult to locate. These relationships hold at all spatial scales from microscopic to global.

Competition

Any extant species has survived by adapting to the conditions of its habitats to acquire enough resources to meet its needs. Because resources are finite, species that require particular resources need to acquire them in competition with others. The strongest competition is between members of the same species because their resource needs are almost identical. Because they have almost identical anatomical and behavioral specializations to acquire their needs, some have provisions to reduce intersexual competition. The young usually require different resources from those of their parents, and competition with parents thus is reduced. Any resource can become limiting when its availability is insufficient to support those utilizing it. Sometimes a species is characterized by its resource requirements. It is said to have a niche. The niche is the functional position of a species in an environment (Peterson et al., 2011). Cattle are functional grazers in grasslands, for example.

Species can survive and obtain their needs with two basically different strategies. They can acquire the easiest for them to obtain of all available resources and shift from one to another as availability changes. These are generalists. The other strategy is to be a specialist by acquiring a particular resource that it is adept at getting, like the Acorn Woodpecker, Melanerpes formicivorus, or a sapsucker, whose names indicate their specialties. Specialists are better at acquiring the food they are specialized for than generalists, but have fewer alternatives if the specialized food becomes scarce. I am more familiar with birds than other vertebrates. Most bird species' specializations can be inferred by particulars in the shape of the bill and of the legs and feet, which aid them in their acquisition of resources and survival. Most of us recognize sparrows and finches with their thick, seed-cracking beak and recognize ducks from their webbed feet and flattened bill. Behaviors are also specialized. Flycatchers fly from their perches to catch flying insects. Swifts and swallows catch flying insects in flight.

My PhD research (Hamilton, 1975) was done on two closely related bird species, the American Avocet, Recurvirostra americana, and the Black-necked Stilt, Himantopus Mexicanus, in salt-evaporation ponds in San Francisco Bay. Their diet was superabundant there. Food was not a problem for them in that habitat. Both are large shorebirds that feed in shallow water. Avocets have unique bills that curve upward, and stilts have legs that are uniquely long. Competition with other shorebirds is minimal: stilts feed in deeper water and avocets often scrape their bills along the top of the mud. Competition between the sexes was minimized and very subtle for each species. The degree of curvature of avocet bills differed between the sexes. The frequency and types of feeding movements differed between the sexes in a direction that could be attributed to bill-shape differences. In stilts, the bills are straight and did not differ between the sexes, but the leg length was significantly different between them. Males had longer legs. When feeding, males fed in deeper water, but the feeding behaviors were the same. Avocets did not differ in the feeding depth and their legs were the same length. In this habitat, the feeding behavior was different between sexes for both species, although food was superabundant and competition would be minimal.

In addition, the avocets and stilts nested in loose colonies together and fed in loose flocks. I also observed them in a fresh-water marsh where food was not obvious or super abundant. Here the species were territorial and did not form colonies. They adjusted their social system to the conditions.

I could give more details, but the point is that each species had many characteristics that enabled them to compete and survive in the environments they occupy and often share. They are equipped to acquire specific food types, located in specific places or acquired in specific ways, and minimize competition.

With habitats changing, species need to be flexible so they can acquire their resources from a rapidly changing resource base.

Natural selection obviously protected the competitive ability of both of these species and facilitated their survival. Each species has its own story that can be discerned by careful examination. Successful competitors survive; nonsuccessful ones do not.

Both of these species are effective at feeding in the situations I described. They are especially competitive at salt-evaporation ponds and other highly saline habitats inhabited by enormous quantities of brine shrimp, *Artemia salina*.

Population Growth and Carrying Capacity

Populations are potentially interbreeding individuals occupying specific ranges. Species are all potentially interbreeding individuals of the same type. Population ranges of similar appearing forms often do not have overlapping ranges, and interbreeding can only be inferred from their characteristic attributes. Evolution of separated populations leads to the formation of new species (Kimball's Biology Pages, n.d.). This is how new lineages have been formed in the evolutionary past.

Each species or population has a birth rate (fecundity) and a death rate (mortality). The population growth rate is the birth rate minus the death rate. Populations grow when growth rate is positive and decline when it is negative. Adult mortality is replaced by juvenile survival. When environments change, fecundity and mortality may change, and species may prosper or decline; they may become extinct.

Harvesting by humans is justified because an excess of young is almost always produced, and frequently there is a large excess. Hunting or fishing mortality replaces natural mortality to a great extent. If populations are monitored, harvesting regulations can be set that allow for population stability.

For any species, the environment has enough resources to support a certain number of individuals of each species occupying it. This number is called the "carrying capacity." As the environment changes, so does the carrying capacity. Extinction can occur if a population exceeds its carrying capacity for long.

In changing environments, carrying capacity can change. This can lead to cycles in numbers, as described in Chapter 2 in this volume (Nemeth, 2015) for Brown Lemmings. Cycles are especially common in predator/prey interactions (Hoagstrom, 2014) like the brown lemming, *Lemmus trimucronatus*, and its predators as well as its predation on its food.

Habitats and Landscapes

Except for places inhabited by hunter-gatherer societies like those still extant in the Amazon (see Murrietta, 2015), many environments were quite different in the past than they are today. They were essentially climax habitats or slightly modified habitats that extended throughout the area with appropriate climate and other environmental factors. They varied slightly with topography and soil conditions. The only openings were caused by rare fires or storms. Small openings were created by tree falls and lightning strikes. Species diversity would have been high because of the time available to evolve relationships to enhance survival and the large, contiguous habitat blocks. Edges would have been minimal. The types of species favored would have been good competitors and subject to extinction when humans began to fragment the environment.

Island Biogeography Theory

With respect to islands of habitats, numbers of occupying species vary with size of the habitat and its distance from other islands of the same habitat (MacArthur & Wilson, 1963). Basically, the number of species on an island increases with the size of the island and its closeness to the mainland. If immigration rates can be determined as in an archipelago where distances from the mainland vary and extinction rates can be determined relative to island size, expected species on the island can be determined (Island Biogeography, n.d.).

Ice ages are examples of what happens during times of climate changes. Alternating heating and cooling resulted in ice-sheet formations and movement. In the last ice age in North America, ice sheets came south almost to the Gulf Coast. Habitats moved in corresponding ways. Plant and animal species that survived did so by moving with their habitats and thus were not affected much as a species by the changing temperatures as they move with the changing habitats. During the ice ages, the time scale of the climatic changes was long enough to allow the movements of habitats and accompanying flora and fauna. Other environmental changes like volcanic explosions, tornados, and tsunamis occur much more rapidly and are associated with catastrophic changes of flora and fauna.

Extinction

When living species evolved, they were adapted to the environment of that time. Individual species had to change in compatible ways with their environments. When they did so, they survived, but the species slowly changed and eventually became noticeably different from their ancestors. Other species are part of the environment and competition with newer forms often resulted in extinctions.

Major Extinction Periods

Despite the slowly changing species attributes through evolution, there have been periods of relatively sudden environmental changes that resulted in simultaneous increases in extinction rates—sometimes of major groups like dinosaurs. Survival is not necessarily predictable in a rapidly changing world.

Extinctions have occurred since life evolved, but high rates of environmental change have increased extinctions greatly five times in our history. This is so noticeable that they have been called the "big 5." About 450 million years ago, after the evolution of terrestrial plants, about 60% of genera became extinct. The second occurred about 100 million years later and made it easier for the development of forests that eventually produced extensive coal deposits under the right conditions. About 250 million years ago, at least 80% of aquatic genera disappeared. Around 200 million years ago, about half of marine invertebrates and 80% of terrestrial quadrupeds disappeared. The fifth extinction (Cook, 2010) occurred about 65 million years ago and caused the shifting of earth dominance to mammals from reptiles (Leakey & Lewin, 1995; Cook, 2010). In all of these the previous dominant forms were replaced because the changed environment favored other, newly evolved forms.

HUMAN EFFECTS

The relationships between humans and their environment was initially the same as for all other animals, but because of the unique characteristics we acquired, we now are able to modify our environments in unprecedented ways.

The Past

When humans, *Homo sapiens*, evolved about 200,000 years ago, the earth's habitats were like they are now in preserved locations like national parks, but were not fragmented or modified like they are today. Some of the differences today are due to what would be expected in 200,000 years of the earth's changing without humans, but most are due to changes we have made.

Humans evolved in the savannahs of southern Africa from chimpanzee-like forms that evolved into our early hominid ancestors. There were several lineages of human-like species, but ours prevailed (Diamond, 2006). Specific characteristics like upright stance, hairlessness, and development of our brain all facilitated future evolution that led to our success.

Like our ancestors, we originally were hunter-gatherers, who lived in small family-oriented groups. We were similar to our ancestors in how we related and interacted with our environment, but we evolved into a more flexible species that has unprecedented control over its environment. Once humans learned how to use fires, domesticate animals and plants, and make tools and machines, they modified habitats for their own benefit.

We eventually spread out and occupied a variety of habitats. Because different groups had different evolutionary histories (McCulloch, 2010), descendants developed unique cultures that were optimal for survival in their particular habitats. Even though the world is quite different now, these cultural and related religious factions persist today. It took a long time, but eventually some early humans discovered ways to manipulate their environments with fire and tools of various kinds. With this, we became free of the environmental constraints that other species have and became more social and lived in bands and larger groups. Once we became organized into bands, the bands have continuously evolved. It is here that group cohesion became a prominent selective force; altruism evolved and was usually associated with religion. Intergroup aggressiveness also was prominent in protecting the group. The evolution has been both cultural and genetic (Wade, 2014; Wilson, 2012).

These groups were no longer hunter-gatherers, but not all humans have traveled this path; some are still hunter-gatherers, and now some societies have incompatible views of our relationship with the environment. We are now cutting down rain forests still occupied by tribes who need them for their existence.

Humans have been continuously colonizing and exploring the earth since their origin. Various groups have prospered for a while and declined. We do not need to discuss that in detail, but the process is instructional.

Jared Diamond (2011) has studied a number of societies that collapsed and proposed five factors that seemed to cause the collapses: (1) Environmental damage—the most common he encountered was deforestation. (2) Climate change—natural climatic variation could be devastating for societies that were not prepared for it. This occurred when a colony was newly established in an area and had no realization of natural climatic variation. The colonizers sometimes did not prepare, and environmental damages in the changed climate were fatal. (3) Hostile neighbors—for example, the Western Roman Empire finally collapsed from barbarian invasions around AD 476. This occurred after it had been weakened by environmental factors. (4) Decreased support by friendly neighbors—this usually occurred when the neighbors were weakened by environmental and other factors. And (5) inappropriate response to the other factors—this was usually caused by local political, economic, or social factors. Diamond examined a number of examples for each factor. Each one was instructive.

We began as a species, much like any other. Fortunate circumstance and a set of characteristics have combined to give us unprecedented control of our environments. We must use them well. We have a growing population and a world where traditional resources are becoming scarcer and the consequences of our recent actions are still undetermined for both the near and long term.

The Present

We all have a perception of the present. Our perceptions are not the same. We live in different cities, states, and countries. We come from different cultures with different histories and religions. Some of us still live in tribes, existing like our ancestors, and acquiring our resources in the natural environment we cherish. Others may be crowded into cities with no contact with natural environments; the mostly barren of natural habitat, cities, are their habitat (Chiesura, 2003). Subsistence may come with no acquiring of food except in grocery stores, markets, or restaurants. The cities exist without our fully understanding the consequences of living there. Individual wealth varies from almost none to much more than necessary for a comfortable life; some eke out a living dumpster diving, and others manipulate currencies and run vast corporations. Some can make their own decisions, and others have the decisions made for them by dictators or politicians who are supposed to look out for them. We are all different, yet we share the same legacy.

Cultural and religious differences cause most of our world's conflicts (war—humanities' curse—and tribalism [Wilson, 2012]) when people come into contact with people of other cultures in an increasingly shrinking world. At the same time, we are becoming more globalized because of the increasing interdependence of countries throughout the world. With globalization, more and more disparate cultures come into contact and interact. Although our economies are becoming more global, the cultures from which they sprang have not changed much. With respect to the environment, many present cultures seem incompatible almost with their own cultural past, and they certainly are incompatible with some of the other cultures they now encounter. We seem more capable of changing our environments than our cultures and religions (see Wade, 2014; Wilson, 2012).

Environments

The environments we evolved in no longer exist in many places. We evolved in natural systems, and many of us appreciate them instinctively; but we would have difficulty surviving in them now, even if we did not have to compete with others for the resources there. Even though we might not be able to survive without much help in our natural environments, we still like to visit them. Although we have aversions to snakes and spiders, we like little cuddly creatures and natural habitats. We have emotional attachments to plants, animals, and nature (Kellert, 1997; Wilson, 1984).

I was raised in the city, but, for some reason, chose a career that involved close contact with nature. As an adult, I was introduced to hunting. The idea of killing animals was somewhat abhorrent to me at first, but I did it. I heard somewhere that "a person does not hunt to kill," a person kills to hunt. That is how I now feel; hunting seems natural. Although I no longer do it to avoid leaving wounded game, it was second nature to me, even though I did not start until I was 35 years old. I did have prior experience with bird watching, and trapped small mammals as an undergraduate and also as a graduate student. I collected some specimens on a museum collecting trip to Peru in 1967. On this trip I moved out of a tent and slept on the ground under a mist net, where I removed captured bats. I was at ease in unfamiliar natural environments, so I think I somehow maintained an ancestral relationship to natural habitats. To be fair, the other graduate students on the trip did not seem as comfortable. One, a herpetologist, was afraid to venture out at night even though geckos, which interested him especially, were only active then. He would go if I accompanied him.

Many of our recreational activities involve interacting with nature in many ways. Our present emphasis on organic foods, hormone-free meat, or free-range chickens indicates a preference for natural systems over the ones we have developed to provide food more efficiently for the masses.

When America was discovered by Columbus, many habitats had not been greatly affected by the indigenous natives. Europe and Asia had already been greatly changed, and people were very comfortable there and had a history of living in human-modified habitats. When the new colonizers arrived on the East Coast, they began to clear the forests and convert the lands to farms, small at first, as they spread westward. Old-growth forests were cut and, if replanted or allowed to regenerate, were often managed as commercial forests. We were recreating Europe even though the land was occupied by indigenous American Indians with their own way of life; the cultures were different. The colonizers conquered them and managed the land like they would in Europe (see Chapter 8 [Bursill, 2015] for Australia). The grasslands were replaced primarily with farms once they were reached by the westward-expanding colonists. As human densities increased, the original habitat was increasingly harvested and modified until most of the original habitats were greatly reduced in size or had disappeared. As the habitats are harvested and changed, the remaining patches get smaller and smaller. Smaller patches do not contain as much diversity as large patches, and species may be lost (see MacArthur & Wilson, 1963). Rate of habitat loss may have been somewhat slowed now, but the loss is continually occurring and almost complete for some habitat like forests in many areas. In the Pacific Northwest, the final harvesting has become controversial because of a conflict over a threatened species, *Strix occidentalis caurina*, the Northern Spotted Owl, an indicator species for old-growth forest. Andre and Velasquez (1991) discuss the ethical aspects of the controversy. Although their paper is old, the ethical issues and controversy still persist and have not yet been settled in either the judicial courts or the court of public opinion. There are similar controversies elsewhere as our efforts to convert natural habitats continue in order to support our growing numbers and society's failure to solve the ethical questions mentioned here and elsewhere.

Recent Environmental Changes

The world is changing rapidly now, and we all are experiencing it from our human perspective. We acquired special characteristics as we evolved that enabled us to control our environments and its constituents to a much greater extent than other life forms control theirs. Moreover, the changes we have made have facilitated other changes until we now have the ability to modify our environments almost completely.

Many of the modifications we have made are affecting not only us, but other life as well. The environments in which we evolved are disappearing and changing in ways that may ultimately be destructive in both the short- and long-term and in both the physical and psychological sense. For example, honey bees, an essential pollinator for many crops, have been rapidly disappearing in the United States and elsewhere. Since 2004, bee colonies have been dying at rate of over 30% a year. These bees are pollinators of 70% of the world's food-crop species. Their continuing decline could be devastating. Environmental change is undoubtedly the general cause, and although specific reasons have not been fully established, pesticides or diseases may be involved (Pan North America, n.d.).

As plants and animals become extinct, they are no longer available for exploitation. If they have characteristics that would be valuable to humans, they are no longer available. Many compounds present in plants and animals have medical and pharmacological properties that are useful to humans, and others are being discovered regularly. Others have potential to be developed into food, fiber, or biomass plants. There is a rush to preserve these potentially valuable resources before they become extinct. As biodiversity decreases, opportunities to utilize useful characteristics of our flora and fauna lessen. In addition, the habitat changes themselves create new habitats that could best be utilized by some yet to be discovered or created form that utilizes genotypes not currently being used. A holistic discussion of the advantages of maintaining and encouraging biodiversity is given in the web pages of the Rainforest Conservation Fund (http://www .rainforestconservation.org), and shows many ways it would be prudent to preserve biodiversity in tropical rain forests where biodiversity is historically high. Preservation in all habitats is desirable. Coral reefs are also rich in diversity but are endangered by habitat changes including pH changes caused by increases in carbon dioxide diffusing into our oceans (Lenz, 2014; Veron, 2008).

Biologists and ecologists can evaluate the changes we make with respect to their effects on abundance and survival of not only us, but other animals and plants as well as nonliving environmental components. We can also evaluate landscapes and how, because of our actions, the various habitats used by animals and plants are changing in size, location, connectivity, and composition. All of these changes affect the survival of some of the living components of our environments and thus the diversity of living things. As changes accumulate, our environments become more and more differentiated from earlier ones, where we and the local flora and fauna survived and thrived. Many of the changes we have made are impossible or extremely unlikely in natural systems and would not occur naturally. The rate of environmental change is much faster now than historically, and compensatory evolutionary change is highly unlikely because of lack of time. Species have always become endangered and extinct as their environments changed. Diversity often decreases as climax habitats change, shrink, and become rarer from our actions. Generally, when natural environments become less diverse, they become less stable and are less likely to persist (Hooper et al., 2005; Vitousek, Mooney, Lubchenco, & Melillo, 1997). That is certainly not a good thing for the plants and animals that share our planet with us, especially those specialized forms that utilized and evolved in the climax stages, which are becoming increasingly rare and other unique habitats. We cannot be sure of the long-term survival of newly created habitats from a physical or psychological perspective because of the lack of a past history, but they have characteristics of size, stratification, isolation, etc., that we have found affects diversity and survival of component species in negative ways. Stability can probably only be maintained by a continuous input of energy, which is somewhat self-defeating, because the energy input itself causes changes. Studies, comparing the old habitats with newly created ones, can help us evaluate these impacts. Human-induced habitat changes occur much more rapidly than ones without our intervention, and the evolutionary changes in our biota cannot keep up with the environmental changes. Additional changes can be expected to endanger or cause extinction of many forms. Perhaps human inventiveness can clone and save some of them; some may even be brought back from extinction (Switek, 2013). Doing so would be a fantastic scientific achievement, but only academic if survival is restricted to zoos and game farms. Bringing back the habitats where these species could succeed would be even more impressive.

A loss of genetic diversity can be devastating. This is one of the reasons we are seeking to find and preserve wild strains of plant species that are important commercial crops or potential crops. A case of the consequence of loss of genetic diversity occurred in 1970, when about 85% of U.S. cornfields were planted with hybrid corn that had the same gene to avoid interbreeding. A new fungus variety developed at that time that attacked corn with that particular gene. Corn loss was as high as 50% and economic damage was approximately $1 billion. Fortunately, the seed industry was able to remove that gene from the seed corn in one generation by growing new seed during our winter in South America. Devastating losses of such an important crop were thus limited in time. The loss of the crop is a good example of the consequences of loss of genetic diversity (APS, n.d.).

Another example is the potato blight in Ireland, starting around 1845. Potatoes were the main crop in Ireland, and the country depended on it. The potato crop was all cloned from a single variety. A fungal disease developed that was devastating to that variety in moister soil and caused complete crop losses (Understanding Evolution, n.d.). A treatment was not found for several years. The tragedy resulted in a famine with many deaths. Secondarily, it led to an exodus of many Irish people, many of them to the United States. In this example there was a lack of crop diversity that led to the tragedy (Johnston, n.d.).

The examples above are typical unintended consequences. Genetic diversity was decreased to increase yield and convenience, but its lack caused unanticipated difficulties and tragedy.

Norman Borlaug succeeded in greatly increasing yields of wheat by breeding and developing new varieties and growing them with the appropriate amount of fertilizer. He was able to almost triple yields and is credited with saving millions of lives. He won the Nobel Peace Prize for his achievement, which is now called the Green Revolution (Miller, 2012). With modern agriculture as developed in the "green revolution" (Jain, 2010), agriculture is focused on maximizing food production, and competing species are eliminated as much as possible. Essentially, the agricultural aspects of the habitat are maximized, and the competing organisms are minimized. The irony is that the habitat and management are changed to maximize yield, but the changes themselves can cause new problems (Schneider, 2014). Placement and sizes of fields could be managed to maximize the landscape potential of the nonagricultural habitats and minimize the damage to the total landscape (for a landscape ecology overview, see Dramstad, Olson, & Forman, 1986).

Another improvement in food production is the development of aquaculture, which is the production of beneficial plants and animals in aquatic environments (NOAA Fisheries, *Aquaculture in the United* States, n.d.; NOAA Fisheries, *What Is Aquaculture?* n.d.). Although there has been aquaculture for at least 4,000 years, it was only important to a few cultures until recently. It is rapidly expanding now and is becoming increasingly important as a food source, greatly supplementing quantities of otherwise overharvested aquatic species. Hatcheries are an important element as we increasingly manage native fish like salmon (Brown, 2010). Organic wastes can be a problem as can be the obtaining of commercial quantities of "seed" to grow. An increasing trend is growing fish in cages in the ocean or other large water bodies (see Beveridge, 2004).

In addition to the changes we have deliberately made, other changes occur naturally at various rates; some of them are traumatic. In our book (Nemeth, et al., 2012), we described traumatic events that accompany violent (sudden) changes in environments. The changes can affect millions of humans and often have both short- and long-term effects physically and psychologically. These are discussed extensively in Volume 2.

But violent changes are relatively rare. Most environmental changes are constantly occurring and are common and persistent. Natural changes occur slowly and are often pernicious as well as unnoticed. But many other changes are occurring rapidly in order to provide for the needs of an increasing population with a corresponding need for resources and energy. We cut forests and plow fields. Harvesting of trees changes landscapes by decreasing habitat size if the forest were clear-cut, or by reducing the density of trees if other harvesting approaches were used. We change nutrient availability by removing the harvested trees.

We import nutrients (fertilizers) to replace the lost nutrients when necessary. We till the soil. We employ pesticides, many of which are not discriminatory, to reduce animal and plant pests. We irrigate to control water availability. We certainly are affecting change.

And the changes mentioned above are only local ones. We must transport our harvests elsewhere. That requires transportation vehicles and an energy supply, and an infrastructure to facilitate it as well as packaging that must be manufactured, used, and discarded. Much of the packaging is not reusable. The debris still exists and affects some places. Changes in landscape and pesticide usage have long-term effects. Thus our management to supply materials that are essential to providing resources has long-term effects on habitats as well as long-term spatial effects along the supply chain, as well as immediate effects. These all need to be examined when making management decisions. Thus, every day, our world becomes less like that in which we evolved. Most of the changes are made by humans to benefit humans. The decisions are not typically holistic. Relevant temporal and spatial scales are usually ignored in our decision making. We know that many of these changes are very detrimental to plants and animals previously inhabiting the managed areas, and sometimes the areas themselves. We historically have been dependent on some of these plants and animals. Can we survive without them now? What are our psychological perceptions about the changing areas? Do we need these environments to survive in the long term? Do we need them for our happiness?

Endangered Species

Because of habitat loss and other changes, many species are becoming rare and threatened with extinction. In the United States, this has resulted in the passage of the Endangered Species Act (ESA) in 1973 (U.S. Fish & Wildlife Service, n.d.). It provides critical resources for species we formally designate as endangered or threatened. Once a species or subspecies is threatened, its critical habitat is determined and is protected. Conflicts with those who want to use some of the critical habitats are inevitable and frequent.

There are similar lists throughout the world. The most thorough is the International Union for the Conservation of Nature (IUCN) Red List. Founded 50 years ago, the IUCN tries to evaluate the status of every species or subspecies throughout the world. It has several categories of status such as "threatened with extinction" and has a searchable database (IUCN, n.d.). The Red List for 2012 assessed 63,387 species and found 3,947 species critically endangered throughout the world. At threat are 41% of amphibian species, 33% of reef-building corals, 30% of conifers, 25% of mammals, and 13% of birds (IUCN, 2012).

Ever since humans undertook agriculture and began seriously modifying our environments, there have been consequences to us, to wildlife, and to other environmental components. The ESA is an attempt to ensure that our actions are not detrimental to wildlife forms formally designated as threatened or endangered. I see two problems that are interrelated. The ESA considers "species," not habitats specifically; but every "species" has a critical habitat. Although we are endangering species, habitats are being endangered more, and they contain many species. Habitats could contain many endangered forms, and an endangered-habitat designation should protect them all—even those whose status is undetermined or perhaps not even discovered yet. The second problem is that the endangered forms, as defined by the act, do not have to be a species; they just need to be recognizable forms. I believe with proper study, almost any habitat would contain some form(s) that can be argued to be endangered, even though a closely related form or several might be common elsewhere, even nearby. Endangerment designations of a locally rare form is a powerful tool that is used now to oppose almost any proposed habitat alteration. Court hearings can be expensive and seemingly everlasting. Although I fully support critical habitat preservation, the present system does not address that directly. It also makes almost all habitat change decisions under the ESA more controversial and expensive than need be, and causes loss of public support. Decisions (many in court after much litigation) are very slow and expensive. They are not made holistically as they should. But that is the way it is.

Soon after the Endangered Species Act was passed, an important case came up that was eventually settled in the U.S. Supreme Court. It dealt with a tiny fish, the snail darter, *Percina tanasi*, and the construction of the Tellico Dam. The dam affected critical habitat of the snail darter, and the controversy continued until the Supreme Court decided the dam could not be finished. It was after the case was settled that populations of similar snail darters were found to exist elsewhere. This case and its issues are clearly described in HubPages (n.d.).

In December 2008, the U.S. Interior Department ordered 150 billion gallons of water to be diverted from California's Central Valley, prime supplier of agricultural products, to provide water for the critical habitat of the Delta smelt, *Hypomesus transpacificus*, a tiny fish, as required by the ESA (Cohen, 2009). The water diversion along with an ongoing drought, which caused the increased water needs for the smelt, cost the area farmers from $1 billion to $3 billion. This water shortage is continuing, and the Central Valley farmers are now fighting with Indian tribes, fishermen, and environmentalists over 25,000 acre-feet of water from Northern California's Trinity Lake, who want it to protect salmon from diseases associated with low water levels in the rivers (Carlton, 2014). Apparently, regulations conflict and are not clear; it will be decided in courts eventually. These conflicts over declining resources and uncertain priorities are inevitable and increase as resources become scarcer. Water rights agreements and some laws are becoming out of date because of changes engendered by environments responding to increased human demands.

The Convention for International Trade in Endangered Species of Wild Fauna and Flora (CITES) is a voluntary international agreement to regulate international trade of threatened flora and fauna or their parts, like elephant ivory or rhinoceros horn. In 1975, the Unites States signed this agreement; 180 nations have now signed. Trade in endangered forms and habitat threaten many species, and CITES is a valuable tool for protecting endangered species (CITES, n.d.).

The Sixth Extinction

Earlier we discussed before the Big Five extinction events that predated the arrival of humans. We now have changed the environment enough to cause another extinction wave. Leakey and Lewin (1995), in their book *The Sixth Extinction*, say "It's the next annihilation of vast numbers of species. It is happening now, and we, the human race, are its cause." They do not exaggerate; we are mostly the cause. They state that we are losing roughly 50,000 species a year. The average extinction rate has been calculated by many, but is much less than that. Myers (1989) examined the estimates of some scientists and stated that they estimated losses of about 1,000 to 2,000 species per year. Leakey and Lewin (1995) further estimated 50% of the earth's species would be gone in the next 100 years. In the Big Five extinctions, the dominant forms became extinct and were replaced by others in the greatly changed environments. In this extinction, the environment has changed greatly. We do not know about the dominant species, humans, *Homo sapiens*, yet.

There is no question that we are losing many species now. Technically, it is difficult to determine the rates, but they are considerable, and much of our biodiversity is being lost. This literature is available and easy to find. Much of it, however, is from people with a viewpoint or an agenda. Those who are skeptical do not dispute that extinction rates are high now; they mostly claim they are exaggerated. I have found little discussion of whether the loss of species is justified in order to provide more resources for humans. That decision probably depends on the culture of those involved in making it and the relationships to the environment of people of that culture.

Kolbert (2014) accepts that there is a problem but focuses on learning from particular examples of threatened or endangered species. That is the focus now. We accept that species are becoming extinct, and we try to find solutions for particular cases. Restoring past landscapes as much as possible is often involved. There are many causes that contribute and a few solutions, and most of them are openly opposed by some interest group or another—often in the courts.

Habitat Loss

As we convert more and more of our land to human use, it is changed, and the species that could use it change. Environment usually is changed so much that it is no longer useful for species of concern; if not destroyed completely, it becomes fragmented and isolated—both of which reduce diversity.

Most of the above-cited information about current extinctions was published in the last part of the past century. A new study follows worldwide trends from 1970 to 2010 of vertebrate numbers that have declined 52% (Plumer, 2014). This is not an extinction number, but rather a total population size estimate for mammals (minus humans), birds, reptiles, amphibians, and fish. Basically, we are replacing other vertebrates with people.

Exploitation

Once humans encounter animals, we exploit them through hunting and eating them or using their body parts in other ways. If we do not exterminate them completely, we may reduce their numbers sufficiently to cause their demise (Leakey and Lewin, 1995). Our ability to decimate animal numbers is impressive. We succeeded in exterminating the Passenger Pigeon, *Ectopistes migratorius*, probably the most abundant bird on earth during its prime. Their numbers were almost unbelievable, but they are now extinct. Their story is shared in Wildbirds (n.d.). There are similar stories for terrestrial and aquatic species that are often exploited to extinction. Regulating harvest has saved many of these species, but oceanic forms are often particularly endangered because of lack of ownership. The problem is explained by Hardin (1968). Many game species have been hunted to extinction, but, once hunting was regulated, many are now managed on a sustainable basis. Many fish too have been extirpated, but many fisheries are in international waters and are difficult to regulate there because of the "Tragedy of the Commons" (Hardin, 1968).

Introduction of Exotic Species

Leakey and Lewin (1995) gave many examples of extinctions brought about through the introduction of new species to an area. This has almost decimated the unique birds of Hawaii. Unique birds on many isolated islands have been destroyed when rats found their way to the islands. Many specialized and isolated species are destroyed or out-competed by exotic intruders.

Carbon Dioxide Effects

Rapid increase of carbon dioxide in the atmosphere is affecting ocean acidification (Harvey, 2013) and ultimately ocean inhabitants as the pH changed. Carbon dioxide concentration changes occurred such that Veron (2008) believes they were related to the extinctions of oceanic forms, at least of corals. He speculates that the rate of concentration changes is responsible and may cause new extinctions, even if there are no problems on the surface. If global warming occurs, increased fragmentation now will make moving to better habitat much more difficult than in the past. The rate of temperature change would be important to affect the time available for moving to avoid inappropriate habitats. Moving to more suitable habitats would be difficult, with higher human densities and associated infrastructure as well as land ownership problems in a changing habitat that requires relocation. Increased temperatures and carbon dioxide concentrations could be beneficial in some places, and habitat changes would be slow enough for adapting to the new conditions.

Energy

Biomass from plant and animal material from the past has been fossilized. It is now harvested as coal, peat, oil, or gas and utilized to produce energy or for raw materials to produce plastic and other materials. Despite the fact that CO_2 is produced when life is utilizing energy, it was declared a pollutant by Environmental Protection Agency (EPA) administrator Leisa P. Jackson when she signed an Endangerment Finding on December 7, 2009, that allowed the EPA to manage it and five other gases under the Clean Air Act of 1963 without prior congressional approval. Since then, CO_2 emission standards have become increasingly stringent, especially against coal-using power plants. The authority of the EPA to make these changes has been very controversial since its inception (Johnson, 2009). Forbes (McMahon, 2012) among others was critical, while the EPA (*Overview*, n.d.) defended its decision.

Fossil fuel supplies are aggregated (clumped), and current demand gives some regions political leverage and greatly affects world politics. Some alternative fuels, like biomass and ethanol production from crops, use more land and thus decrease land available for conservation purposes. As elsewhere, holistic considerations are often ignored, or political ones like crony capitalism prevail. The effects of decisions on available land are not discussed often, but I believe we must maximize available land for use in habitats for natural undisturbed or minimally disturbed systems in order to preserve as much diversity as possible for adaptation opportunities in rapidly changing environments.

Furthermore, economic progress is now expected and is associated with exponential growth in our economy. Much of this growth is related to energy usage and continued energy and material demands are expected. Continuous exponential growth is impossible, but no one seems to worry about that.

Malthus and Population Growth

In 1798, Thomas Malthus predicted that the human population would be limited by lack of food, because our numbers increase exponentially and our food increases arithmetically. Today, there are about 7.2 billion people; the number is still rising and is expected to reach 9 billion by 2050. Even then, the numbers are expected to increase further after that. The world's population in 1800 was about 1 billion people, and we are still here.

Malthus was very wrong. Why? His assumptions were reasonable. Even though Malthus has been somewhat discredited, Ehrlich (1968) and many others have agreed with him and made similar claims. In every case, the human food supply had an unexpected increase because of changes in production methods and efficiency made possible by some revolutionary event like the Industrial Revolution or the Green Revolution. A key has been the energy augmentation that we provide in tilling, planting, fertilizing, pest management, harvesting, and distribution; in effect we are converting energy to food. Basically, Malthus asserted that the earth has a carrying capacity. I stated earlier in this chapter that the carrying capacity can change if the environment changes, and we have caused many environmental changes. Simon (1994) refuted Malthus by arguing that an expanding human population is a resource, and food too can increase exponentially. That seems to be true in the short term, but it seems extremely unlikely in the long term. Can we invent new fixes forever? The cost of more people is more environmental change. Is that a tradeoff we want to make forever? Not me! It is not possible, and is made more difficult with increasing energy usage, no matter the source. But I do not decide. We all do or should. The tradeoffs must be explicitly stated and understood.

Even though the danger always seems distant, delay makes the consequences worse with time. We are doomed if we cannot make a decision for the long term. Politicians and others who are concerned with the short term will suffer just as surely as our progeny. We must know the tradeoffs for our growing population.

Even with no growth, there are problems with increased population. Pollution may increase, and the cost of cleaning it up may cause further environmental changes. Finite resources, like water, necessary for life, are used in proportion to our numbers. Our present population may be utilizing some resources at unsustainable rates. The energy required for us must also increase. Even though it can be replenished, there is a cost in human and material resources to do so.

Earth's Carrying Capacity

Carrying capacity depends on the environment. Population numbers given above are based on people count and extrapolation of birth and death rates over time. The environment was not directly involved, but does affect birth and death rates. Many, for different reasons, think we have exceeded long-term carrying capacity already (Climate Progress, 2011). Pimentel and Wilson (2004) are especially concerned with the long-term food supply, and Dailey and Ehrlich (1992) discuss the tradeoffs that must be made to provide sufficient resources at various population levels.

Although there is much information easily findable, most is published or sponsored by organizations with particular agendas and tends not to be holistic enough to provide a complete picture. Basically, the carrying capacity depends on how we want to live. If we want to live like hunter-gatherers, as some still do in the Amazon Basin and elsewhere; we have an enormous surplus of people now. The more drastic habitat alterations are, the more food and other resources we can provide the burgeoning population; but our legacy is being destroyed. Many more people could be provided for, but the environment might become almost unrecognizable because of the required changes. Based on demographic trends, our numbers will increase for many years. Pollution, disease, resource scarcity, climate change, etc., could become much worse. We need to focus on the type of environment that we want, and we want to manage it to attain it. Until we know what we want, we cannot determine an optimum carrying capacity. To even support our present numbers will require more environmental changes. Increased demands for social justice and continued economic growth will have their costs. Do we want to change our environments more, or even discuss it? We must have a goal.

Sustainability

Sustainability is the ability to continue an activity indefinitely. When energy is involved, some will be lost, and it must be replaced. Therefore, most activities are not truly sustainable. There is a cost to provide the energy necessary to maintain apparent sustainability. Those profiting from the activity should pay the costs. Scruton (2012, chap. 5) discusses this thoroughly. Too often, those profiting from the activities (the internalities) do not pay the ancillary costs (the externalities) like repairing environmental damages and constructing infrastructure. Those conducting the activity are subsidized by others (society in general, or by specific individuals and groups). Sustainability has become a buzzword, but practically, it is impossible—no matter the popularity! If those profiting, paid the externalities, they would be motivated to minimize them as much as possible, and the damages would be minimized. If they did not pay for the externalities and damages were noticeable, the government would eventually try to reduce them by regulation. Paying bribes and practicing crony capitalism through campaign contributions, etc., might be cheaper than paying the externalities, and damages might not be minimized. Societies should not allow this to keep damage minimal. If an activity continues indefinitely, albeit with a cost, many would call that sustainable. Because energy is required and that is a cost, nothing is really sustainable. It is a hoax. We should advocate responsibility. Those who do the damage should pay for it. Costs for externalities can be included in pricing and justice is done.

To analyze cost of an item or process, all costs to obtain and ship materials as well as costs to deal with wastes, etc., need to be included. We must be more holistic. That way society is not responsible for individual damages. Cleanup costs would be included in product price. Those with the most efficient operations would have cheaper prices and thus a competitive advantage.

For environmental sustainability, Herman Daly in 1990 published these guidelines (Victor, 2013):

1. For renewable sources, the rate of harvest shall not exceed the rate of regeneration,
2. For pollution, the rate of waste generation shall not exceed the assimilative capacity of the environment, and
3. For nonrenewable resources, depletion should require the comparable development of renewable substitutes.

These definitions ignore the energy needed to accomplish the goals. From society's perspective, externalities should not be allowed, and the internalities should be paid by the doer. To be truly sustainable locally, an activity must be sustainable at all levels of organization and at all components of spatial and temporal scales. The view must be holistic. In general, sustainable practices are only sustainable at limited temporal and spatial scales (Scruton, 2012; Thwink, n.d.).

Future Choices

As time passes, we are facilitating environmental changes that are incompatible with our original heritage. Many of these are made to feed and provide for our expanding numbers and increase, worldwide, what we call our "standard of living." It is time to examine our priorities. Do we want to ignore our past and live in a world that focuses on us, or do we want to honor our heritage and reduce the changes we are making to it? We have the power to go either way. Do we have the knowledge and wisdom to make the right choices?

Natural selection assured our survival in our ancestral habitats. Are our current attitudes and perceptions part of our genetic makeup, or are they entirely influenced by our current environments? In other words, do we need our ancestral environments for our psyche? Recent work (Wade, 2014; Wilson, 2012) indicates there are genetic components to our social behavior and culture. If so, can we justify our current practices of deliberate change in order to support an ever-growing population? The two are incompatible, at least in a rapidly-change world.

The world's economy is now global. Most of us are becoming globalized and use a variety of resources from around the world. But people are not homogeneous. Regions are inhabited by specific cultures and religions that are no longer appropriate in a global society. Hopefully, these cultures can adapt to our changing, globalized world in an appropriate way, or we must find a way to maintain our regional differences in a globalized society.

Human success is due to our possession of several traits that facilitate more environmental manipulation than by other species. Our brain is more advanced than the brains of other species and allows for the accumulation, storage, transmission, and understanding of information in hitherto impossible ways. Information available is constantly increasing and can be disseminated rather easily. Even that ability is increasing rapidly as libraries are being augmented or replaced by almost instantaneous searches for information on the Internet and in the "cloud." Customized daily summaries of recent news by category can be provided to anyone with access to the Internet.

The changes we have made to our legacy are our new legacy and our responsibility. We have the power to make more changes and we will need to do so. Will they be the best ones for us and the biosphere? How do we know? How do we decide?

Other Challenges

There have been many other recent changes that could affect our future greatly. Here are some of them. Are we taking them into account?

Nuclear Energy and Weapons

Since the development of the atomic bomb, nuclear energy has become a part of our lives. Potential devastation from the bombs is so frightening that we passed the Nuclear Nonproliferation Treaty in 1970 to lessen the likelihood of future nuclear bomb use (U.S. Department of State, n.d.). Although 189 states have signed, proliferation has not been completely prevented, and there is continued development of nuclear capabilities and newer weapons by some countries. This is still a threat, and apparently an increasing one.

Atomic energy has been developed for peaceful uses as a power source and some other uses. Nuclear power does not produce carbon dioxide and is economical, but it does produce harmful isotopes that produce dangerous radiation. It can be isolated and stored, but there have been major leaks that are public health risks, There have been major accidents at Chernobyl and Fukushima that are discouraging future use without better planning to obtain a site free of environmental risks and a reliable way to safely contain and store wastes. The wastes could be managed and stored safely, but transportation to storage sites would be a problem, and people, so far, are not inclined to accept a nearby storage site.

Electronic and Digital Age

With the invention of the transistor in 1947, the electronic and digital age began (The People History, n.d.). It has evolved from a curiosity to something most of us seemingly cannot live without. I wrote my dissertation on a typewriter in the 1960s, and I am writing this with a word processor. I do not need to go to the library to look things up, but when I did in the past, it was much more difficult than it is now. We are becoming more and more attached to our mobile phones and handheld computers for our everyday tasks as well as our social interactions and entertainment. I wonder what would happen if we did not have them tomorrow. Are the changes occurring in the social media good or bad? It seems we are forgetting what is important, or at least what I think is important. We are forgetting our heritage and changing our culture. Many do not even know now where our food and other necessities come from and the true costs of obtaining them.

Electronics are used for much more than phones and handheld computers. They control many, if not most, of our machines and our information, and the proportion is increasing. What would happen if they stopped working? They could. A properly placed nuclear explosion with an electromagnetic pulse device (Carafano, Spring, & Weitz, 2011) could destroy most digital devices in range, and the range could be quite large. Most of us and industry could not survive for long if our digital devices and all they control stopped working unless we lived on a farm. Even then desperate people might steal what they need or even kill for it. We have become dependent on technology. Is it wise to depend on a device that can be destroyed by people wishing us harm? Solar flares can disrupt electronic devices, too, but only for a brief time.

Computers are becoming smaller and are almost essential to many of us now. When they are connected to the outside, they are subject to viruses and other malignant software. Hackers can break into supposedly secure systems and steal information from supposedly secure databases and can take over control of devices that computers control. Depending on the devices, like power grids, this too can be devastating. Again, we have separated ourselves from natural systems so much that we can hardly survive without the new technologies. This worries me. With so many people depending on their electronic devices working as intended, what happens if they no longer function as intended?

Another aspect of modern electronics that worries me is the dependency many have acquired on them and how it affects human behavior. Rapid communication is not always good. It looks like computer use has outpaced cultural restraints sometimes. There needs to be a way to put its use into perspective.

Warfare and Terrorism

There have often been wars when cultures clashed. With globalization, and increasing human numbers, clashes might increase. With rapid technological advances, understanding of physical principles and needs for new materials for emerging technologies, disputes over availabilities of new essential agreements may increase and be similar to the conflicts we have had over oil supplies from some regions.

Terrorism is the result of a clash of cultures and related differences in religion. It is facilitated by new technologies and increased communications. Terrorists now recruit on social media. It is extremely worrisome that gruesome acts like beheadings or burnings, publicized in the media, attract recruits.

Resource Availability Decline

Most resources we have on earth are finite. There is only so much available for use. As our numbers increase, resources we use become scarce. They can be recycled, but energy will be required, and we should try to minimize energy use. We often can find substitutes for a particular substance, however. In theory, some substances could become limiting. This must be the case for copper, because people are stealing it so often. The more people there are, the more that is needed. Innovation creates demand for new resources that may be difficult to meet because of resource shortages.

Water

Most of the earth's water is salty, but the need is for fresh water, much of which is frozen or otherwise available in the soil or underground. (Global Change, n.d.). The distribution of fresh water and people do not correspond, so there are management issues as water use is determined. Some cities, like Los Angeles, California, are dependent on imported water as are many other users. As our numbers increase, demands will increase, but supply will decrease because of increased pollution (Woodford, 2014) and use. There are often conflicts about water use, as already reported for the California Central Valley. Desalinization is an energy-expensive operation and not feasible in some places because of costs (Kranhold, 2008).

Packaging Pollution

Floating marine debris is becoming an increasing problem, and 80% comes from urban runoff (Clean Water Action, n.d.). This is more than an eyesore; it is almost indestructible and accumulates in the system. Scruton (2012) believes this is brought about by the abandonment of local markets selling local products with minimum management, for imported goods that must be packaged for long-distance markets. He advocates the return to local markets.

Evasive and Exotic Species Problems

As the world shrinks and our environments change, some species find their way to nonnative habitats. Their numbers often increase enough to change the local ecology and cause problems of many sorts. Some of them are deliberately introduced as game species; the Ring-necked Pheasant, *Phasianus colchicus*, a game species, is a good example, and is considered a success by many. Many people believe there is no problem with doing this and often will release a pet, exotic or otherwise, into the wild when they no longer want them. Several good examples include the water hyacinth, which was introduced into the United States as an ornamental but is now the most conspicuous plant is some southern U.S. waterways. These water hyacinths can form almost impenetrable mats and clog waterways as well as outcompete local plants and replace them. (National Wildlife Federation, n.d.). The mats can be so thick that I have observed ground-foraging birds feeding on them. On the other hand, their biomass could possibly be used for fertilizer or other purposes (Bolorunduro, n.d.). Numerous pests are transported to new habitats where they may become excellent examples of unintended consequences. The European Starling (*Sturnus vulgaris*) in America and the kudzu vine (*Pueria montana*) are prime examples. Our habitats are becoming less diverse, and transportation is increasing so exotic species will undoubtedly increase. Many may become major problems like pythons in Florida (Dorcas and Willson, 2011).

Rates of Change

In planning for the future, we understand the importance of humans in shaping the world now and in the past, and the importance of our decision-making in planning and management of the future. Groups from different cultures and evolutionary backgrounds have different perceptions and philosophies about the environment. We all do not necessarily agree on future problems, future opportunities, and appropriate goals for all or any particular group(s).

In our book *Living in an Environmentally Traumatized World: Healing Ourselves and Our Planet* (Nemeth et al., 2012), we emphasized the impacts of traumatic environmental changes on us and ways to deal with them. These changes are perceived as traumatic to us because the rate of change is too fast for us to avoid or too powerful for our infrastructures to handle. Nevertheless, the changes are inevitable because of physical laws that we cannot override.

A meteor strike, an extremely sudden and rare occurrence, is said to be the cause of the extinction of dinosaurs (Alvarez, Alvarez, Asaro, & Michel, 1980; Vellekoop et al., 2014). On the other hand, sea-level rise and falls associated with the formation and melting of glaciers could elicit a slow response similar to that which occurred in the ice ages if environments were not fragmented; there would be no impediments to slow habitat movement in response to slow environmental changes. Original ice-age responses could not have happened in the fragmented environments of the present. Perhaps habitats could move now, if there were time to reduce fragmentation and impediments along any suitable path, in response to an impending emergency. There would be many problems regarding ownership, responsibilities, and rights.

Time scales of environmental change, therefore, are important in determining the effects of change. Habitat conditions are also important.

Future Population Goals

There are many views about how many people the earth can support. Those who have attempted to do this have produced a large range of predictions. Most of them vary because the assumptions vary, primarily in the nature of the earth they are defining as our environment. Is it devoid of any living thing but humans, etc.? These days, we don't explicitly attempt to determine our carrying capacity; instead, we define our ecological footprint or the effect we as individuals and groups have on the environment. This focuses on our energy usage but could include all relevant factors. Because of our focus on global warming and carbon dioxide, we often measure our carbon footprint. Comparing carbon footprints is a way to measure the effect of our activities on the environment, at least with respect to carbon. This is important when energy is obtained from carbon compounds. Carbon will always be important because it is the key to living systems. Almost all carbon we are using now was produced in living systems in the past and sequestered. We could sequester some our excess now by regrowing some of the habitats we have destroyed, but the original diversity will have been lost. Coal power plants are now attempting to capture their carbon emissions and sequester them (Van Loon, 2014). Other sequestering could be attempted by growing algae or other fast-growing plants and burying them securely. It could perhaps be recovered later, if needed.

With this focus and concern, many propose a carbon tax to pay for the presumed cost of our energy usage (Carbon Tax Center, n.d.). This is an objective way to reduce the use of carbon by taxing it. Others propose to decrease carbon emissions by developing cap-and-trade legislation that caps the use but allows users to innovate to comply with the emissions cap (EPA, *Cap and Trade*, n.d.). Perhaps we should generate a discussion of the ways various societies live and their impacts on the environment. The key is really energy sources. How happy are the members of these societies, and what are the values we should have in our relationship with our environment? And with others? Is happiness correlated with energy use? Ecopsychologists should investigate this thoroughly, especially in terms of levels of organizations and temporal and spatial scales. We must be holistic in our approach.

CO_2 increases are due to all of us who expect an increased standard of living, at least as long as burning carbon-based fuel is an important energy source. Reducing our numbers and our energy demand is another obvious solution. Coal and other carbon-based fuel producers are supplying a demand. The demand is not their responsibility. Increasing energy demand is the problem, if there is a problem. If we want to meet demand, we must evaluate all energy sources to find the one(s) with the least problems. Reducing demand is a less-damaging solution, but it depends on the choices made by users to actively encourage reduced amounts of environmental changes and require less energy use in their own lives.

White's Law

It is important here to remember White's Law: that "culture evolves as the amount of energy harnessed per capita per year is increased or as the efficiency of the instrumental means of putting the energy to work is increased." In other words, the more energy that is used, the more a culture is developed (White, 1959). We have a dilemma here. It takes energy to develop a culture, but increased use of energy causes environmental problems. We saw the same thing in the discussion of the dispute between Ehrlich (1968) and Simon (1994) about our future (Sabin, 2013). Here, too, energy can be found through innovation to remove constraints on human population size. We as a culture supposedly advance. The more we advance, the more energy we use, and the more we endanger the environment. Our "progress" is our problem. We need to decide if we should continue to grow and endanger the environment more, or if we should constrain our growth or even reverse it for the good of the planet and all its living forms.

Hydrocarbons and Climate Change

Our concerns about climate change are centered on greenhouse gases, primarily carbon dioxide and methane that are produced when burning fossil fuels and other carbohydrates to produce energy (Karl & Trenberth, 2003). Greenhouse gases absorb radiant energy from the sun and reduce the amount reflected back into space. They thus warm the surface by trapping the heat in the atmosphere like a greenhouse roof does in the greenhouse. Ever since greenhouse gases began accumulating in the air, our atmosphere has been getting warmer. The correlation is not absolute, and the degree of warming varies; recently the temperature has not risen as much as the model used originally predicted. Some even say that a small rise is beneficial because it would increase plant growth (Ridley, 2013). The question now is whether the carbon dioxide released when burning organic fuels to obtain energy is causing global warming or climate change. The debate on this has been heated and lengthy. The issues are complicated. The best explanation I have seen is by Warren Meyer (2012) and is easily understood. Zalasiewicz and Williams (2012) describe climate change and its causes throughout the earth's history.

If equity of standard of living in the world were a goal, many would opt to increase energy use to provide for the needs of those who are behind and who have not used much energy in the past. Thus, there is pressure to increase energy use in the future for our current world population. Doing so could cause additional environmental problems. In addition, many countries have increased their debt to take care of immediate problems. This will require additional energy.

We have stated that there is a finite amount of material on earth (resources). As long as humans do not greatly reduce our growth rate, we will eventually require more resources than are available. This could be true even if all resources were converted to the production of human food. The earth would consist primarily of people and their food. Other problems such as dealing with human wastes would have probably doomed us long before this, and I doubt if such a world as described by this scenario would be acceptable to many. Even now, there are major food problems in much of the world, and many people are starving or are in poverty. In theory, there is enough food for all, but distributing it is costly and is not a high-enough priority for those who could supply the food.

We could alter our eating habits by shifting our diet to lower on the food chain. As our numbers increase, the problem worsens. Foley (2014), in a thoughtful series about the world's food supply, suggests just that. He also stated that eliminating beef would eliminate the methane they produce. It is much more powerful greenhouse gas than carbon dioxide. Shifting our diets would greatly reduce the energy needed to feed us, but we evolved as omnivores and a dietary meat is usual in many cultures.

About Global Warming and Truth Seeking

It is pertinent to point out that alarms of this kind are a recurring feature of human societies, and that there is a good reason for this. For alarms turn problems into emergencies, and so bring the ordinary politics of compromise to a sudden stop.

—Jared Diamond

Increasing levels of carbon dioxide is a concern that we all must deal with in a logical, unemotional manner. Most of what we hear in the media is agenda-driven propaganda (Patrick, 2011) on all sides. We must find the truth through all the deception. We need objective leadership that truly represents the people. Decisions need to be altruistic, not selfish. It will be difficult to find leaders with those motives with our present governments, but it must be done. It is the responsibility of each of us to do our part and insist on altruistic leadership and become informed so that our perceptions are not affected by spin, propaganda, and appeals to our emotions. Our biosphere and all of its component parts are at stake.

REFERENCES

Achenbach, J. (2008, August 15). "Dead zones" appear in waters worldwide: New study estimates more than 400. *The Washington Post*.

Alvarez, L. W., Alvarez, W., Asaro, F., & Michel, H. V. (1980). Extraterrestrial cause for the Cretaceous–Tertiary extinction. *Science, 208*(4448), 1095–1108. doi:10.1126/science.208.4448.1095

American Medical Association. (n.d.). Human cloning. Retrieved September 24, 2014, from http://www.ama-assn.org/ama/pub/physician-resources/medical-science/genetics-molecular-medicine/related-policy-topics/stem-cell-research/human-cloning.page

Andre, C., & Velasquez, M. (1991, Spring). Ethics and the Spotted Owl controversy. Santa Clara University. *Markkula Center for Applied Ethics: Issues in Ethics, 4*(1). Retrieved October 8, 2014, from http://www.scu.edu/ethics/publications/iie/v4n1/

APS. (n.d.). *Historical perspectives of plant diseases*. Retrieved September 21, 2014, from http://www.apsnet.org/edcenter/K-12/TeachersGuide/PlantBiotechnology/Pages/History.aspx

BBC. (n.d.). *Nature: Prehistoric life*. Retrieved September 18, 2014, from http://www.bbc.co.uk/nature/history_of_the_earth#timeline

Beveridge, M. (2004). *Cage aquaculture*. Hoboken, NJ: Wiley-Blackwell.

Biomes of the World. (n.d.). *Introduction to biomes*. Retrieved October 5, 2014, from https://php.radford.edu/~swoodwar/biomes/

Bolorunduro, P. L. (n.d.). *Water hyacinth inundation: Nuisance or nugget*. Retrieved October 15, 2014, from http://aquaticcommons.org/945/1/WH_111-121.pdf

Bowler, P. J. (1989). *The Mendelian revolution: The emergence of hereditarian concepts in modern science and society*. Baltimore, MD: Johns Hopkins University Press.

Brown, B. (2010). *Mountain in the clouds*. Seattle, WA: University of Washington Press.

Bursill, L. W. (2015). Transforming our intentions from extermination to integration: Lessons from Australia's Aboriginal people. In D. G. Nemeth & R. B. Hamilton (Eds.), *Ecopsychology: Advances from the Intersection of psychology and environmental protection*, Volume 1 (pp. 167–191). Santa Barbara, CA: ABC-CLIO.

Carafano, J. J., Spring, B., & Weitz, R. (2011, August 15). *Before the lights go out: A survey of EMP preparedness reveals significant shortfalls*. The Heritage Foundation. Retrieved October 10, 2011, from http://www.heritage.org/research/reports/2011/08/before-the-lights-go-out-a-survey-of-emp-preparedness-reveals-significant-shortfalls

Carbon Tax Center. (n.d.). Pricing carbon efficiently and equitably. Retrieved September 22, 2014, from http://www.carbontax.org/

Carlton, J. (2014, August 27). Drought-stricken California farmers fight release of water for fish. *Wall Street Journal*. Retrieved October 15, 2014, from http://online.wsj.com/articles/drought-stricken-california-farmers-fight-release-of-water-for-fish-1409182836

Carson, R. (1962). *Silent spring*. Boston, MA: Houghton Mifflin.

Chiesura, A. (2003). The role of urban parks for the sustainable city. *Landscape and Urban Planning, 68*, 129–138. Retrieved October 12, 2014, from http://carmelacanzonieri.com/library/6123/Chiesura-RoleUrbanParksSustainableCity.pdf

CITES. (n.d.). *CITES at work*. Retrieved October 9, 2014, from http://www.cites.org/eng

Clean Water Action. (n.d.). *The problem of marine plastic pollution*. Retrieved October 10, 2014, from http://www.cleanwater.org/feature/problem-of-marine-plastic-pollution

Climate Progress. (2011, October 15). We're beyond Earth's carrying capacity now. Will accelerating climate change turn the population boom into a bust? Retrieved

October 7, 2014, from http://thinkprogress.org/climate/2011/10/15/343264/beyond-earths-carrying-capacity-climate-change-population-boom-bust/

Cohen, B. (2009, August 31). Tiny fish threatens to turn California's Central Valley into dust bowl. CFACT. Retrieved October 8, 2014, from http://www.cfact.org/2009/08/31/tiny-fish-threatens-to-turn-californias-central-valley-into-dust-bowl/

Colinvaux, P. A. (1978). Why big fierce animals are rare: An ecologist's perspective. Princeton, NJ: Princeton University Press.

Connell, J. H., & Slatyer, R. O. (1977). Mechanisms of succession in natural communities and their role in community stability and organization. The American Naturalist, 111 (982): 1119–1144.

Cook, J. (2010, April 15). Earth's five mass extinction events. Skeptical Science. Retrieved October 6, 2014, from http://www.skepticalscience.com/Earths-five-mass-extinction-events.html

Dailey, G. C., & Ehrlich, P. R. (1992, November). Population, sustainability, and Earth's carrying capacity: A framework for estimating population sizes and lifestyles that could be sustained without undermining future generations. From Bioscience. Retrieved October 7, 2014, from http://www.dieoff.org/page112.htm

Darwin, C. (1859). On the origin of species by means of natural selection, or the preservation of favoured races in the struggle for life. London, UK: John Murray.

Diamond, J. (2006). The third chimpanzee: The evolution and future of the human animal. New York, NY: Harper Perennial.

Diamond, J. (2011). Collapse: How societies choose to fail or succeed. London, UK: Penguin Books Limited.

DNA Forensics. (n.d.). DNA fingerprinting. Retrieved 5 October 5, 2014, from http://dnaforensics.com/DNAFingerprinting.aspx

Dorcas, M. E., and J. D. Willson. (2011). Invasive pythons in the United States: ecology of an introduced predator. Athens, GA: University of Georgia Press.

Dramstad, W. E., Olson, J. D., & Forman, R. T. T. (1996). Landscape ecology principles: Principles in landscape architecture and land-use planning. Washington, DC: Island Press.

Ehrlich, P. R. (1968). The population bomb. New York, NY: Ballantine Books.

FAO. (n.d.). History of aquaculture. Retrieved October 9, 2014, from http://www.fao.org/docrep/field/009/ag158e/AG158E02.htm

Foley, J. (2014). Where will we find enough food for 9 billion: A five-step plan to feed the world. National Geographic, 225(3), 26–57.

Global Change. (n.d.) Human appropriation of the world's fresh water supply. Retrieved October 10, 2014, from http://www.globalchange.umich.edu/globalchange2/current/lectures/freshwater_supply/freshwater.html#solutions

Hamilton, R. B. (1975). Comparative behavior of the American Avocet and the Black-necked Stilt (Recurvirostridae). Ornithological Monographs No. 17. The American Ornithological Union. Lawrence, KS: Allen Press.

Hamilton, R., Barrow, W., Jr., & Ouchley, K. (2005). Old-growth bottomland hardwood forests as bird habitat, implications for contemporary forest management. In L. H. Fredrickson, S. L. King, & R. M. Kaminski (Eds.), Ecology and management of bottomland hardwood systems: The state of our understanding. Gaylord Memorial Laboratory Special Publication No. 10, Puxico. Columbia, MO: University of Missouri.

Hardin, G. (1968). The tragedy of the common. Science, 162(3859), 1243–1248.

Harvey, F. (2013, October 3). Rate of ocean acidification due to carbon emissions is at highest for 300m years. *The Guardian*. Retrieved October 6, 2014, from http://www.theguardian.com/environment/2013/oct/03/ocean-acidification-carbon-dioxide-emissions-levels

Hathaway, D. H. (2010). The solar cycle. *Living Reviews in Solar Physics, 7.* Retrieved September 6, 2014, from http://www.livingreviews.org/lrsp-2010-1

Hazen, R. M. (2012). *The story of Earth: The first 4.5 billion years from stardust to living planet.* London, UK: Penguin Books.

History of life on Earth. (n.d.). In BBC's *Nature: Prehistoric life*. Retrieved July 15, 2014, from http://www.bbc.co.uk/nature/history_of_the_earth#timeline

Hoagstrom, C. (2014, July 8). Predator and prey: Predator-prey cycles. In *Encyclopedia of Earth*. Retrieved April 3, 2015, from http://www.eoearth.org/view/article/155342/

Hooper, D. U., Chapin, F. S., Ewel, J. J., Hector, A., Inchausti, P., Lavorel, S., . . . Wardle, D. A. (2005). Effects of biodiversity on ecosystem functioning: A consensus of current knowledge. *Ecological Monographs, 75*(3) (Abstract only). doi:10.1890/04-0922. Retrieved January 18, 2014, from http://www.esajournals.org/doi/abs/10.1890/04-0922

Horton, J. L. (2003). *Truth, fact and perception: A constant PR challenge.* Retrieved September 20, 2014, from http://www.online-pr.com/Holding/Truth,FactsandPerceptions.pdf

Hubbart, J. A. (2010, March 6). Hydrologic cycle. In *Encyclopedia of Earth*. Retrieved October 4, 2014, from http://www.eoearth.org/view/article/153627/

HubPages. (n.d.). *The story of Tellico Dam and the Snail Darter.* Retrieved October 9, 2014, from http://bgpappa.hubpages.com/hub/The-Story-Of-The-Snail-Darter

Island Biogeography. (n.d.). *Overview.* Retrieved October 6, 2014, from http://www.islandbiogeography.org/index.html

IUCN. (n.d.). *The IUCN Red List of Threatened Species.* Retrieved October 9, 2012, from http://www.iucnredlist.org/about

IUCN. (2012). *IUCN released Red List of Threatened Species for Year 2012.* Released June 21, 2012. Retrieved October 9, 2014, from http://www.jagranjosh.com/current-affairs/iucn-released-red-list-of-threatened-species-for-year-2012-1340268385-1

Jain, H. K. (2010). *Green revolution: History, impact, and future.* Houston, TX: Studium Press.

Johnson, K. (2009, April 18). How carbon dioxide became a "pollutant." *Wall Street Journal*. Retrieved October 4, 2009, from http://online.wsj.com/articles/SB124001537515830975

Johnston, W. (n.d.). *The Famine 1: Potato blight.* Retrieved September 22, 2014, from http://www.wesleyjohnston.com/users/ireland/past/famine/blight.html

Karl, T. R., & Trenberth, K. E. (2003). Modern global climate change. *Science, 302* (5651), 1719–1723.

Kellert, S. R. (1997). *Kinship to mastery: Biophilia in human evolution and development.* Washington, DC: Island Press/Shearwater Books.

Kimball's Biology Pages. (n.d.). *Speciation: What is a species?* Retrieved October 5, 2014, from http://users.rcn.com/jkimball.ma.ultranet/BiologyPages/S/Speciation.html

Kolbert, E. (2014). *The sixth extinction: An unnatural history.* New York, NY: Henry Holt and Company.

Kranhold, K. (2008). Water, water everywhere. *Wall Street Journal*. Retrieved September 20, 2014, from http://online.wsj.com/news/articles/SB120053698876396483?mod=googlenews_wsj&mg=reno64-wsj&url=http%3A%2F%2Fonline.wsj.com%2Farticle%2FSB120053698876396483.html%3Fmod%3Dgooglenews_wsj

Lamb, J. A., Fernandez, F. G., & Kaiser, D. E. (2014). Nutrient management: Understanding nitrogen in soils. *University of Minnesota Extension*. Retrieved October 5, 2014, from http://www.extension.umn.edu/agriculture/nutrient-management/nitrogen/understanding-nitrogen-in-soils/

Leakey, R., & Lewin, R. (1995). *The sixth extinction*. New York, NY: Doubleday. Retrieved October 4, 2014, from http://www.mysterium.com/sixthextinction.html

Lenz, E. A. (2014). *An ecological and physiological assessment of coral reef responses to past and projected disturbances* (MSc thesis). California State University, Northridge, CA. Abstract retrieved October 4, 2014, from http://news-oceanacidification-icc.org/2014/10/01/an-ecological-and-physiological-assessment-of-tropical-coral-reef-responses-to-past-and-projected-disturbances/

MacArthur, R. H., & MacArthur, J. W. (1961). On bird species diversity. *Ecology, 42*, 594–598.

MacArthur, R. H., & Wilson, E. O. (1963). *The theory of island biogeography*. Princeton NJ: Princeton University Press.

Martin, B. D., & Schwab, E. (2012). Symbiosis: "Living together in chaos." *Studies in the History of Biology, 4*(4), 7–25.

McCulloch, R. (2010). *The races of humanity*. Retrieved September 21, 2014, from http://www.racialcompact.com/racesofhumanity.html

McMahon, J. (2012). EPA chief resigns: Declared carbon dioxide a pollutant. *Forbes Tech.* Retrieved October 3, 2014, from http://www.forbes.com/sites/jeffmcmahon/2012/12/27/epa-administrator-resigns-declared-carbon-dioxide-a-pollutant/

Meyer, W. (2012, February 9). Understanding the global warming debate. *Forbes.* Retrieved October 10, 2014, from http://www.forbes.com/sites/warrenmeyer/2012/02/09/understanding-the-global-warming-debate/

Miller, H. (2012, January 18). Norman Borlaug: The genius behind the Green Revolution. *Forbes.* Retrieved September 20, 2014, from http://www.forbes.com/sites/henrymiller/2012/01/18/norman-borlaug-the-genius-behind-the-green-revolution/

Murrietta, M. (2015). The Pachamama Alliance: Linking environmental sustainability, social justice, and spiritual fulfillment through changing the dream. In D. G. Nemeth & J. Kuriansky (Eds.), *Ecopsychology: Advances from the Intersection of psychology and environmental protection*, Volume 2 (pp. 233–241). Santa Barbara, CA: ABC-CLIO.

Myers, N. (1989). Extinction rates past and present. *BioScience, 39*(1): 39–41. Retrieved April 3, 2015, from http://www.jstor.org/stable/1310807

Nash, S. E. (1999). *Time, trees, and prehistory: Tree-ring dating and the development of North American archeology 1914–1915*. Salt Lake City: University of Utah Press.

National Wildlife Federation. (n.d.). *Invasive species*. Retrieved October 10, 2014, from http://www.nwf.org/Wildlife/Threats-to-Wildlife/Invasive-Species.aspx

Nemeth, D. G. (2015). From chaos to community: The federal response—an account of Lieutenant General Russel Honoré's leadership during Hurricane Katrina. In D. G. Nemeth & J. Kuriansky (Eds.), *Ecopsychology: Advances from the Intersection of psychology and environmental protection*, Volume 2 (pp. 5–13). Santa Barbara, CA: ABC-CLIO.

Nemeth, D. G., Hamilton, R. B., & Kuriansky, J. (2012). *Living in an environmentally traumatized world: Healing ourselves and our planet*. Santa Barbara, CA: ABC-CLIO/Praeger.

NOAA Fisheries. (n.d.). *Aquaculture in the United States*. Retrieved October 8, 2014, from http://www.nmfs.noaa.gov/aquaculture/aquaculture_in_us.html

NOAA Fisheries. (n.d.). *What is aquaculture?* Retrieved October 8, 2014, from http://www.nmfs.noaa.gov/aquaculture/what_is_aquaculture.html

PAN North America. (n.d.). *Pesticide and pollinator decline*. Retrieved September 20, 2014, from http://www.panna.org/current-campaigns/bees?gclid=CJWRh6KD8MACFeRj7AodvEYA3w

Patrick, B. A. (2011). *The ten commandments of propaganda*. Palmyra, MI: Goatpower Publishing.

PBS. (n.d.). *What killed the dinosaurs?* Retrieved September 20, 2014, from http://www.pbs.org/wgbh/evolution/extinction/dinosaurs/asteroid.html

The People History. (n.d.). *Electronics: The digital revolution*. Retrieved October 10, 2014, from http://www.thepeoplehistory.com/electronics.html.

Peterson, A. T., Soberón, J., Pearson, R. G., Anderson, R. P., Martínez-Meyer, E., Nakamura, M., & Araújo, M. B. (2011). Species-environment relationships. In *Ecological Niches and Geographic Distributions (MPB-49)* (p. 82). Princeton, NJ: Princeton University Press. (See also Chapter 2, Concepts of niches, pp. 7*ff*.)

Pimentel, D., & Wilson, A. (2004, September–October). World population, agriculture, and malnutrition. *World Watch, 22–25*. Retrieved October 7, 2014, from http://www.worldwatch.org/system/files/EP175D.pdf

Plumer, B. (2014, September 30). Study: We've wiped out half of the world's wildlife since 1970. *Vox*. Retrieved October 6, 2014, from http://www.vox.com/2014/9/30/6870749/the-world-has-lost-half-its-wildlife-since-1970-wwf-says

Ridley, M. (2013, September 20). A reprieve from Climate Doom. *Wall Street Journal*.

Sabin, P. (2013). *The bet: Paul Ehrlich, Julian Simon, and our gamble over Earth's future*. New Haven, CT: Yale University Press.

Schneider, J. (2014). The (metaphorical) bet: Paul Ehrlich versus Norman Borlaug. *Library of Economics and Liberty*. Retrieved September 19, 2014, from http://econlog.econlib.org/archives/2014/04/paul_ehrlich_ve.html

Scruton, R. (2012). *How to think seriously about the planet: The case for an environmental conservatism*. New York: Oxford University Press.

Simon, J. L. (1994). More people, greater wealth, more resources, healthier environment. *Economic Affairs, 14*(3), 22–29.

State of the Birds. (2014). *The state of the birds 2014: United States of America*. Retrieved October 5, 2014, from http://www.stateofthebirds.org/2014%20SotB_FINAL_low-res.pdf

Switek, B. (2013, March 10). How to resurrect lost species: Genetic experiments could bring back extinct animals. *National Geographic News*. Retrieved October 4, 2014, from http://news.nationalgeographic.com/news/2013/13/130310-extinct-species-cloning-deextinction-genetics-science/

Sykes, B. (2003, September 10). Mitochondrial DNA and human history. *The Human Genome*. Wellcome Trust. Retrieved March 10, 2014, from http://genome.wellcome.ac.uk/doc_WTD020876.html

Thwink. (n.d.). *Environmental sustainability*. Retrieved October 7, 2014, from http://www.thwink.org/sustain/glossary/EnvironmentalSustainability.htm

Understanding Evolution. (n.d.). *Monoculture and the Irish Potato Famine: cases of missing genetic variation*. Retrieved March 11, 2015, from http://evolution.berkeley.edu/evolibrary/article/agriculture_02

U.S. Department of State. (n.d.). *Nuclear Nonproliferation Treaty*. Retrieved October 10, 2014, from http://www.state.gov/t/isn/npt/index.htm

U.S. Environmental Protection Agency (EPA). (n.d.). *Cap and trade*. Retrieved September 22, 2014, from http://www.epa.gov/captrade/

U.S. Environmental Protection Agency (EPA). (n.d.). *Overview of greenhouse gases: Carbon dioxide emissions*. Retrieved October 4, 2014, from http://www.epa.gov/climatechange/ghgemissions/gases/co2.html

U.S. Fish & Wildlife Service. (n.d.). *Endangered Species Act of 1973*. Retrieved October 8, 2014, from http://www.fws.gov/endangered/esa-library/pdf/ESAall.pdf

Van Loon, J. (2014, October 1). Canada to start first carbon-capture coal power plant. *Bloomberg*. Retrieved October 11, 2011, from http://www.bloomberg.com/news/2014-10-01/canada-to-start-first-carbon-capture-coal-power-plant.html

Vellekoop, J., Sluijs, A., Smit, J., Schouten, S., Weijers, J. W. H., Damsté, J. S. S., & Brinkhuis, H. (2014, May). Rapid short-term cooling following the Chicxulub impact at the Cretaceous-Paleocene boundary. *Proceedings of the National Academy of Sciences, 111*(21), 7537–7541. doi:10.1073/pnas.1319253111. PMID 24821785.

Veron, J. E. N. (2008). Mass extinctions and ocean acidification: Biological constraints on geological dilemmas. *Coral Reefs, 27*(3), 459–472. Abstract retrieved on October 6, 2014, from http://adsabs.harvard.edu/abs/2008CorRe..27..459V

Victor, P. (2013). Herman Daly Festschrift: Herman Daly and the steady state economy. In *Encyclopedia of Earth*. Retrieved from http://eoearth.org/view/article/153483/

Vitousek, P. M., Mooney, H. A., Lubchenco, J., & Melillo, J. M. (1997). Human domination of Earth's ecosystems. *Science, 277*, 494–499.

Wade, N. (2014). *A troublesome inheritance: Genes, race and human history*. New York: Penguin Press.

Watson, J. D. (1980). *The double helix: A personal account of the discovery of the structure of DNA* (Norton Critical Ed.). New York: W. W. Norton & Company.

White, L. (1959). *The evolution of culture: The development of civilization to the fall of Rome*. New York: McGraw-Hill.

Wildbirds. (n.d.). *The extinction of the American Passenger Pigeon: The true story*. Retrieved October 6, 2014, from http://www.wildbirds.org/apidesay.htm

Wilson, E. O. (1984). *Biophilia*. Cambridge, MA: Harvard University Press.

Wilson, E. O. (2012). *The social conquest of earth*. New York: Liveright Publishing Corporation.

Wilson, E. O., & Hass, R. (2014). *The poetic species: A conversation with Edward O. Wilson and Robert Hass*. New York: Bellevue Literary Press.

wiseGEEK. (n.d.). *What is salinity?* Retrieved October 4, 2014, from http://www.wisegeek.org/what-is-salinity.htm

Woodford, C. (2014). Water pollution: An introduction. *ExplainThatStuff!* Updated May 24, 2014. Retrieved October 10, 2014, from http://www.explainthatstuff.com/waterpollution.html

Zalasiewicz, J., & Williams, M. (2012). *The Goldilocks planet: The four billion year story of Earth's climate*. New York: Oxford University Press.

About the Editors

ROBERT B. HAMILTON (VOLUME 1 EDITOR), PhD, is a retired Associate Professor from the School of Natural Resources, formerly the School of Forestry, Wildlife, and Fisheries, at Louisiana State University, where he served until his retirement. As a teenager, he became interested in the outdoors and the environment although he has never lived in the countryside.

He graduated high school in 1954 and started college in engineering. Although interested in mathematics and science, after several years his outdoor interests prevailed, and he changed his major to zoology. After graduation, he served for three years as an officer in the U.S. Navy and "saw the world." Afterwards, he attended the University of California at Berkeley to get his PhD. While there, he had opportunities to see more of the world while participating in research in Alaska on lemmings, and going on a museum-collecting trip to the wilds of Peru. His research in San Francisco Bay was a comparison of the ecology and behavior of two closely related birds, the American Avocet and the Black-necked Stilt. His approach was much more holistic than most current research because it combined aspects of anatomy, behavior, and ecology to explain how each of these closely related species could minimize completion in relatively simple habitats. He was able to see patterns and relationships not normally discerned. The holistic nature of his research led to his dissertation being published as written by the American Ornithologists' Union as a monograph.

He started his professional life on the faculty of a small regional university in Louisiana where he taught introductory biology and most natural history courses. This further increased his holistic background. After several years, he joined the faculty at LSU in 1972. At LSU he taught wildlife courses and developed a research program that primarily was centered on breeding success of bottomland hardwood forest birds in various managed habitats. He had numerous research contracts and supervised many master's and PhD students. Venturing into wildlife management was an opportunity to see new relationships and become even-more holistic.

He had an opportunity early in his career to participate in a NSF postdoctoral workshop on using linear computer modeling to analyze biological systems. This broadened his already broad interests in birds and wildlife to include ecosystem considerations. An indication of his holistic approach is that he is the only person who has served as president of both the Louisiana Chapter of the Wildlife Society and president of the Louisiana Ornithological Society.

Dr. Hamilton has always considered himself more of a philosopher than an ornithologist or wildlife manager. He has always been a holistic thinker and has spent many years analyzing wildlife management in a broad sense. Many of its problems seemed to him to be due to a too-narrow vision. After retiring, he started paying attention to national issues and decided that special interests were narrower than desirable and sometimes pushed their narrow views to the detriment of the holistic picture and the national interests. Our leaders seem more concerned with reelection than their constituents. Public discourse is becoming almost completely propaganda, and should be viewed skeptically. His holistic views are difficult to fit into a limited space, but he hopes he has approached that in these books.

JUDY KURIANSKY (VOLUME 2 EDITOR), PhD, is a world-renowned clinical psychologist with extensive experience working with individuals, families, groups, and communities in varied settings and cultures, as well as leading trainings and workshops worldwide. On the faculty of Columbia University Teachers College and a visiting professor at Peking University Health Science Center in Beijing, China, she was a senior research scientist at the New York State Psychiatric Institute and the Maudsley Hospital in London. She is an expert in relationships and in trauma, and the range of her expertise is evident in her book topics, from international relations and the environment (*Beyond Bullets and Bombs: Grassroots Peacebuilding between Israelis and Palestinians* and *Living in an Environmentally Traumatized World: Healing Ourselves and Our Planet*) to personal relationships (*The Complete Idiot's Guide to a Healthy Relationship, 31 Things to Raise a Child's Self Esteem,* and *Sex Education: Past, Present and Future*), and in her many publications and features on disaster recovery, women's empowerment, well-being, HIV/AIDS education, human rights, cinematherapy, schizophrenia and depression, and supervision in psychotherapy. Her book series for Praeger are "Practical and Applied Psychology" and "Sex, Love, and Psychology." Her many projects include the Global Kids Connect Project in China and Japan, and the Girls Empowerment Programme and the Post-Ebola Children's Workshop in Africa. Also a musician, her Stand Up for Peace Project presents symposia and concerts with original music. She serves on the boards of U.S. Doctors for Africa, Voices of Africa Mothers, the World Psychiatric Association Disaster Psychiatry Section, and the Library of American Broadcasting, and is a member of the Women's Foreign Policy Group. A fellow of the American Psychological

Association, she cofounded the Media Division and is the Public Policy liaison for the International Division.

At the United Nations, she is chair of the Psychology Coalition of NGOs accredited at the UN and the main NGO representative of the International Association of Applied Psychology (IAAP) and the World Council of Psychotherapy. The organizer of many events at UN commissions, she was a panelist at the UN International Day of Happiness and a respondent at the UN Interactive Dialogue of the General Assembly on Harmony with Nature. In partnership with the Ambassador of Palau to the UN, Dr. Caleb Otto, she has also led the successful advocacy to include "mental health and well-being" in the Sustainable Development Goals, as well as other advocacy about psychosocial support and disaster recovery.

Dr. Kuriansky has hosted many conferences, including the U.S.-Africa Business Summit, the U.S. Doctors for Africa Health Summit, and several awards ceremonies honoring First Ladies of Africa. Her many awards include the "Lifetime Achievement in Global Peace and Tolerance" from Friends of the UN, the Award for Distinguished Professional Contributions from IAAP, the "First International Outreach Award" from American Women in Radio and TV, and several humanitarian awards. An award-winning journalist who has hosted top-rated radio call-in advice shows and *Money and Emotions* on CNBC, and who has been a television feature news reporter for WABC-TV, WCBS-TV, and others, she comments on news for media worldwide, including CNN and CCTV in China. Her many articles and columns have been published in professional journals, and mainstream media, including the *Singapore Straits Times*, *South China Morning Post*, *Chicago Tribune WomenNews*, *Newsday*, the *New York Daily News*, *Family Circle*, and *Hanako Magazine* in Japan, and her opinion editorials are posted on *ABCNews.com*, *FoxNews.com*, and the *Huffington Post*. She has produced many educational documentary films, including *Youth Mental Health: Youth and UN Ambassadors Speak Out* and *Progress of the First Ladies of African in Achieving the Millennium Development Goals*.

A graduate of Smith College, Dr. Kuriansky earned a master's degree from Boston University and her PhD in clinical psychology from New York University and studied at the University of Geneva. Her website is http://www.DrJudy.com.

DARLYNE G. NEMETH (SET EDITOR), PhD, MP, MPAP, CGP, an accomplished clinical, medical, and neuropsychologist, has a broad-spectrum practice at the Neuropsychology Center of Louisiana (NCLA) in Baton Rouge, Louisiana. She also was director of neuropsychology at Sage Rehabilitation Hospital Outpatient Services. Dr. Nemeth was among the first medical psychologists in Louisiana to obtain prescriptive authority. She is a fellow of the American Psychological Association (APA) and serves as Louisiana's delegate to the

APA Council of Representatives. Dr. Nemeth has served as the World Council of Psychotherapy's (WCP) United Nations (UN) nongovernmental organization (NGO) delegate and vice president for the U.S. chapter. She is now WCP's co-secretary general.

As an expert in group dynamics, Dr. Nemeth has been nationally and internationally recognized for her Hurricane Anniversary Wellness Workshops, which were offered to the victims/survivors of Hurricanes Katrina and Rita in the summer of 2006. Anniversary Wellness Workshop Training Programs were also conducted in China at the 2008 WCP Meeting and in Australia at the 2011 WCP Meeting. In August, 2014, Dr. Nemeth gave the Keynote Address on Psychological Leadership in the Event of Environmental Trauma at the WCP Meeting in Durban, South Africa.

Dr. Nemeth obtained a bachelor's degree from Indiana University in music and radio/television broadcasting, a master's degree from Oklahoma State University in higher education/student personnel, a second master's degree and a doctoral degree from Louisiana State University in clinical psychology, and a postdoctoral master's degree from the California School of Professional Psychology in clinical psychopharmacology. Dr. Nemeth is active in the practice of clinical, medical, and neuropsychology, and psychopharmacological management. She has written chapters on the history of psychotherapy in the United States, anger management for children, and pediatric medical psychopharmacology.

In March, 2003, she was the lead author on a book titled, *Helping Your Angry Child*. Dr. Nemeth served as the lead editor for the 2012 book, *Living in an Environmentally Traumatized World: Healing Ourselves and Our Planet*, published by ABC-CLIO/Praeger. In 2012, she was also the lead author on an anniversary wellness workshop article that was published in the *International Journal of Group Psychotherapy* (*IJGP*). Dr. Nemeth published an article in 2013 in *Ecopsychology* on preparing individuals and communities for hurricane anniversary reactions. She has developed a Hope Therapy Group Program for brain-injured adults and was the lead author on an article about this process (published in *IJGP* in January 2015).

Besides being in active clinical practice at NCLA, Dr. Nemeth also serves as an externship adviser for future psychologists on placement from their respective universities. She is currently serving in a leadership role on the Executive Committee of the Louisiana Psychological Association. She is a member of the American Group Psychotherapy Association, where she has obtained recognition as a Certified Group Psychotherapist (CGP). Dr. Nemeth has served as a member and past Vice Chair of the Louisiana State Board of Examiners of Psychologists.

Her website is http://www.louisiananeuropsych.com.

About the Contributors

LESLIE WILLIAM (LES) BURSILL, OAM, is a Dharawal (Aboriginal Australian) historian, archaeologist, anthropologist, and publisher, born in Hurstville, New South Wales, on February 4, 1945. His maternal Dharawal forebears hailed from the area between Kangaroo Valley and the coast near Berry and Nowra. Mr. Bursill was made a justice of the peace at Sutherland Court House in 1976. In 1995, he was appointed lecturer in mental health and counseling at the University of Sydney and in 2008, he was appointed adjunct lecturer at Charles Sturt University, Wagga Wagga. His many awards include the Australia Centenary Medal in 2001; the NSW Police Commanders Award for excellence in teaching in 2007; a Premiers Heritage Volunteer Award in 2009; a Certificate of Excellence for Teaching from the Australian College of Educators; and the Order of Australia Medal in that same year.

DOMINIQUE G. HOMBERGER, PhD, is a professor of biological sciences at Louisiana State University. Her broad research interests include comparative anatomy of vertebrates (lampreys, sharks, alligators, mammals, and humans), biomechanics, 3D imaging and animation, evolutionary biology, and the ecology of parrots and cockatoos in their natural environment, as well as the philosophy and history of science. Her other interests encompass social history, psychology, political science, economics, and education, among other subjects, and she sees her specialized research in biology as a part of a broader cultural endeavor.

FLORIAN G. KAISER, PhD, is a Professor of Personality and Social Psychology at the Otto-von-Guericke University in Magdeburg, Germany, since 2008. His research interests include environment protection and environmental education for sustainable development, stress and health, and evidence-based psychological policy support. He received his PhD from the University of Bern, Switzerland, in 1992, and was a postdoctoral research fellow at the University of California, Berkeley, and the University of Trier, Germany; an assistant professor at the Swiss Federal Institute of Technology in Zürich, Switzerland; and associate professor at Eindhoven University of Technology, the Netherlands. He has published more than 60 articles in refereed journals, including the *Journal of Applied Social Psychology* and *Personality and Applied Psychology: An International Review*. He serves on the editorial board of the *Journal of Environmental Psychology* and is a fellow of the American Psychological Association.

SUSAN MELMAN, MA, is a native New Yorker now making her home on Whidbey Island in Puget Sound in the state of Washington. She holds an MA in theater and has worked professionally in theater and with regional theater companies for the past 36 years. She is the recipient of the Outer Critic Circle Award and the Lucille Lortel Award for *Jelly Roll*, the best off-Broadway musical of 1995. She has produced and directed an original New Orleans musical, *Salty Dogs*, for the Edinburgh Jazz Festival. She is the author of two plays, *Blackwater in the Attic* and *Blooms of Orchard Street*, and her poetry was published in *The Louisiana Review*. She currently acts as dramaturge for Whidbey Island Center for the Arts in Langley, Washington.

MARTIN MILTON, DPsych, CPsychol, CSci, AFBPsS, UKCP Reg, SFHEA, is a Professor of Counselling Psychology at Regents University, London. He also runs an independent practice in psychotherapy and supervision. Prof. Milton gained his BA from the University of Natal (Durban), his BA (Hons) from the University of South Africa, his MA (Antioch) from the School of Psychotherapy and Counselling Psychology at Regents College, and his DPsych from City University (London). His research and specialist interests include LGBT psychology, existential psychotherapy, and eco-therapy and the therapeutic aspects of the natural world. In this regard, he has contributed to the Education Committee of the Jane Goodall Institute UK and on Bristol Zoo's Advisory Group on the Social Sciences. Prof. Martin served a term on the editorial Board of the journal *Ecopsychology* and is assistant editor for the *European Journal of Ecopsychology*.

GLORIA ALVERNAZ MULCAHY, PhD, CPsych, comes from the Monterrey Bay area of California, and is of Tsalagi/Aniyunwiya ancestry. She is an academic, psychologist, researcher, mixed media artist, musician, poet, and member of the League of Canadian Poets. She is Professor Emerita, University of Western Ontario, Canada; Academic Research Associate, Centre for Research and Education on Violence Against Women and Children & Adjunct Professor Faculty of Education. She has authored numerous publications and produced several documentary films focusing on indigenous social issues, the environment, and mental health issues. Dr. Mulcahy serves as WCP vice president for the Canadian Chapter and as a WCP NGO representative to the United Nations.

DONALD F. NEMETH, PhD, has worked in the academic, research, and corporate worlds. He taught geology at Citrus College in Azusa, California, and at California State University in Los Angeles, California. His dissertation research, conducted on the North Slope of Alaska, concentrated on land forms near the apex of the Colville River delta. He was a member of the research staff at the Institute for Environmental Studies at Louisiana State University, Baton Rouge, Louisiana, studying salt domes in Northern Louisiana as possible sites for the disposal of nuclear waste. Dr. Nemeth worked as a geologist for Marathon Oil Company in Lafayette, Louisiana, developing offshore oil and gas fields in the Gulf of Mexico. Dr. Nemeth is currently president of Envirosphere Consulting, LLC, in Baton Rouge, Louisiana. His website is http://www.info@envirosphereconsulting.com.

ANDREW S. NESBIT, BS, graduated from Roanoke College in Virginia, earning a bachelor of science degree in psychology and neuroscience and has been accepted at the Vermont Law School where he has received an environmental scholarship to pursue environmental law. Andrew is the son of Scott and Michelle Nesbit, who own and operate a wetlands consulting firm in Baton Rouge, Louisiana. As a high school student employee, Andrew assisted in field operations of the wetland business including data collection, soil and water sampling, vegetation surveys, hydrologic surveys, and field mapping. Born in Baton Rouge in 1991, and a graduate from Louisiana State University Laboratory High School in 2009, Andrew is an avid hiker who has spent summers in the Pisgah National Forest hiking the nearby Appalachian Trail.

SCOTT P. NESBIT, MS, is a consulting wetland ecologist in Baton Rouge, Louisiana. He earned a bachelor of science (horticulture) and a master of science (agronomy–soil microbiology) from Louisiana State University, and has 30 years of experience conducting all phases of wetland ecological field surveys for private landowners and public resource agencies. Since 1997, Mr. Nesbit has been the technical agent responsible for establishing over 25 approved wetland mitigation banks in coastal and noncoastal South Louisiana. Mr. Nesbit has worked extensively within the lower Mississippi River and Atchafalaya River floodplain, and was the project manager for the Louisiana Department of Natural Resources' Coastwide Reference Monitoring System, the largest continuous coastal wetlands monitoring program in the United States.

TRACI W. OLIVIER, MS, is a doctoral candidate at Nova Southeastern University in Fort Lauderdale, Florida, majoring in clinical psychology with a neuropsychology concentration. She will be completing her internship at the Kennedy Krieger Institute at Johns Hopkins University. Olivier completed an elective practicum under the supervision of Dr. Darlyne G. Nemeth at the Neuropsychology Center of Louisiana in Baton Rouge, Louisiana, where she was part of several projects about environmental trauma. Olivier has authored and coauthored several peer-reviewed journal articles, poster presentations, and symposia for state, national, and international conferences.

YASUO ONISHI, PhD, adjunct professor at Washington State University in the Department of Civil and Environmental Engineering and president of Yasuo Onishi Consulting LLC, works extensively on U.S. and international environmental and energy issues and is a pioneer in conducting environmental and risk assessments. He received two awards in 2011 from the U.S. Department of Energy, called "The Secretary's Achievement Award," for his contributions to the response to the 2011 Fukushima nuclear accident and the 2010 Gulf of Mexico oil spill accident. His computer models are the most advanced contaminant transport codes for surface waters to date. He has been the U.S. government coordinator of the Chernobyl nuclear disaster water and soil environments, an environmental adviser to the International Atomic Energy Agency, an adjunct member of the National Council of Radiation Protection and Measurements, and a member of the National Academy of Sciences' oil spill committee, as well as chief scientist of the Pacific Northwest National Laboratory.

Index

United States, 42, 47–48; volcanoes and, 41–44. *See also* Volcanic eruptions

Earth Summit (1992), 163

Ecological behavior, 229

Ecological crisis, 118–19

Ecology, 9

Ecopsychology, 9–10, 221–22; awareness, 223; contributions, 222–23; Hamilton's introduction to, 30–33

Ecosystem: concept of, 240–42; degradation of Spanish Lake subbasin, 77–79; dysfunctional, causes for, 109; Spanish Lake subbasin, 76–77; wetland (*see* Wetland ecosystem)

Eco-vision of Mother Earth, 156–60

Effective communication for survival, 200–201

Elayn Hunt Correctional Facility in St. Gabriel, 84

Electricity: availability and transmission, 24–25; fossil fuels, 21; hydroelectric energy, 21; nuclear energy, 53; solar panels, 20; wind and, 22–23

Electronic and digital age, 262–63

Electronic changes, effects of recent, 8

Elephants: background, 141–42; communication, 143; conflict over land use, 145; feelings, 142; ivory tusks, 147; Nemeth's experiences on, 145–48; poaching, 144–45; reproduction and birth, 142–43; symbols, 143–44; trunk, multipurpose organ, 142

Elephant Whispers conservancy, 141, 145–46

Ellet, Charles, 204–5, 208

Endangered species, 254–56

Endangered Species Act (ESA), 30, 254–55

Endangerment designations, 254

Energiewende (Germany), 21

Energy, 19, 258; availability and transmission, 24–26; chemical, 20–21; cost evaluation, 25; fission, 23; flow in natural systems, 235–36; fossil fuels, 21; fusion, 24; geothermal, 22; Gulf of Mexico BP oil spill, 54–55; hydroelectric, 21; importance of, 1; nuclear, 52–54; oxidation, 20; past changes, 17–18; perspectives of change, 16–17; present and future changes, 18; reduction, 20; satisfying needs, 52–55; solar, 19–20; wind and current, 22–23

Environment, perceptions of: challenges and conclusions, 210–13; communication begets resolution, 203–4; effective communication for survival, 200–201; influence of feelings and needs, 194–95; nonevent, 197–98; power of greed, 207–8; power of truth, 206–7; price of illusions, 204–6; prosocial behavior and inspired leadership, 209–10; resilience and preparation, 196–97; resistance versus credibility, 201–3; seeking solutions, 195–96; six-stage recovery process from disaster, 196; social brain, logic, emotions, and perception, 208–9; when it becomes personal, 199–200

Environment, understanding: atmosphere, 49–51; background, 37–39; consequences of warmer earth and man's effort to prevent change, 51–56; disasters, 39; earthquakes, 44–49; humanity's early ancestors, 56; restless earth, 39–41; volcanoes and earthquakes, 41–44

Environmental changes, 1–2; capacity for, 92–94; climate change, 8–9; effects of recent electronic changes, 8; importance of considering concept of, 16–18; mudslide effects, 30; rates of change, 5–7, 265–66; recent, 7–9, 250–54; significance of DNA in inheritance and biology, 8; time scales of, 266

Environmental conservation, 228

Environmental conservation, cutting-edge work: fostering environmental psychologically generated behavior change knowledge in society, 231; guide on choosing behavior change measures, 230–31; psychological origins of rebound/individual sustainability, 229–30; unsustainable consumption of individuals, causes, 228–29

Environmental crisis: confusion, denial, wishful thinking, and paralysis regarding, 102–5; warnings, 102

Environmental perspectives: background, 4–5; concept of political correctness, 12; ecopsychology, 9–10; green, as symbol for environmental conservation, 21; holistic approach, 12–16; importance of considering concept of change, 16–18; people agendas, 11; precise nature of, 27; rates of change, 5–9; resources, 18–30; seeking truth, 10–12